The Bribery Syndrome:

How Multinational Corporations Collude with Dictators to Raid Africa's Natural Resources

Joe Khamisi

Published by Jodey Book Publishers, USA

jodeybookpublishers@mail.com

Printed in the USA

Also by Joe Khamisi

The Politics of Betrayal: Diary of a Kenyan Legislator (2011)

Dash Before Dusk: A Slave Descendant's Journey in Freedom (2014)

The Wretched Africans: A Study of Rabai and Freretown Slave Settlements (2016)

Kenya, Looters and Grabbers, 54 Years of Corruption and Plunder by the Elite, 1963–2017 (2018)

Dedicated to Mother Africa

Table of Contents

INTRODUCTION

The widespread perception is that Africa is corrupt, Africans are corrupt, and that you cannot do business in Africa without bribery. But these statements are sweeping generalizations – it's a bit like saying every Englishman cannot dance. – Kevin Korgba

Over the years, discerning scholars and researchers exploring the subject of corruption and bribery in Africa have concentrated overwhelmingly on the demand side rather than the supply side of graft. More books, articles, and speeches have been written about the African traffic policeman who demands a few dollars to clear a passage, and the African despot who exuberantly plunders a country's resources, than the multinational corporation (MNC) that collects billions of dollars in profits through corruption, bribery, and fraud.

Reference is made to "African corruption," but hardly to "European corruption" or "American corruption"—which begs the question, why? Just as corruption and bribery are widespread in Africa, they are also prevalent in Europe, the Americas, Asia, and the Arab world, and they manifest themselves in all sectors: oil and gas, mining, pharmaceuticals, defense, aviation, hospitality, infrastructure, and others. The only difference is the degree of malfeasance.

While Africa's 54 countries lose $50 billion[1] yearly to corruption, the European Union's (EU) 28 countries part with between $200 billion to $1 trillion every year.[2] The voracity in both the public and private sectors has reached a point of threatening the democratic integrity and national security of EU member states and even EU unity itself.[3] In the recent past, newspapers across Europe have increasingly carried stories about corruption in the EU member nations involving not only individuals but senior government officials, politicians, political parties, and multinational companies. In 2018, the Global Economic Crime Survey by PricewaterhouseCoopers (PwC) showed 23 percent of United Kingdom (UK) companies reported experiencing bribery or corruption compared to 6 percent

---

[1] All currency figures are in US dollars unless otherwise noted.
[2] "The Cost of Corruption Across the EU," The Greens/EPA, December 2018.
[3] Heather A. Conley, "Judy Asks: Is the EU Too Lax on Corruption?" *Carnegie Europe*, October 11, 2018.

the previous year, which compares favorably with countries in the Middle East and Latin America. Corruption, bribery, and abuse, referred to by some as "the scourge of Europe,"[4] have also caused political tensions in a number of European countries, among them Italy and the Czech Republic, and in 2018 led to the toppling of Prime Minister Mariano Rajoy's government in Spain.

The European Parliament has also found significant social and political costs in graft, including greater inequality, higher levels of organized crime, and a weaker rule of law. Among the 28 EU countries, Cyprus, Czech Republic, Lithuania, Latvia, Spain,[5] appear at the top of the European corruption tables, while Denmark, New Zealand, Finland, Singapore, Sweden, and Switzerland, tag at the bottom.[6]

In the United States (US), corruption enquiries received at the Office of Government Ethics in the year ending May 2017 increased by more than 5,000 percent compared to the same period in 2012.[7] In addition, graft and greed among America's corporate entities have diminished public trust and confidence vital to a healthy society.[8] The 2018 Transparency International (TI) Corruption Perceptions Index (CPI) showed the United States had plummeted by four points to score 71 out of 100, thus dropping from the top 20 for the first time since 2011.[9] The US Federal Bureau of Investigation (FBI)—the agency charged with detecting and prosecuting domestic crimes—says public corruption poses a "fundamental threat to our national security and way of life."[10]

---

[4] "European Corporations Are More and More Tackling the Scourge of Bribery," *Cambridge Pro-Business*, May 25, 2019.
[5] Thomas Chenel and Ruqayyah Moynihan, "These are the 13 Most Corrupt Countries in Europe," *The Business Insider, France*, February 13, 2019.
[6] Josephine Moulds, "These are the World's Least – and Most – Corrupt Countries," World Economic Forum, article, February 5, 2019.
[7] US Congress, Joint Economic Committee, *The Cost of Corruption to the American Economy*, May 2017.
[8] Judeen Bartos, *Corporate Corruption* (Green Haven Press, 2012), 7.
[9] In the CPI ranking, 0 is highly corrupt while 100 is very clean.
[10] "Public Corruption," FBI, undated.

MNCs, which have their origins in the late 1800s, are defined as global entities headquartered in their home countries but maintaining regional offices and subsidiaries overseas. Some MNCs, like ExxonMobil, Apple Inc., Chevron Corporation, General Motors, and the Swedish Aktiebolaget Svenska Kullagerfabriken (SKF), have assets abroad running into billions of dollars and employing thousands of employees. And, because there are "small" and "mega" conglomerates, experts have created phrases to distinguish the two. In her book, *Secret Empire,* Janet Lowe calls the behemoths of world business "meganationals" because of their global spread, assets, and revenues.[11] The Washington-based Foreign Policy Group refers to companies like ExxonMobil, BlackRock, HSBC, DHL, and Visa as "metanationals," explaining that those corporations have legal domicile in one country, corporate management in another, financial assets in a third, and administrative staff spread over several more. They control trillions of dollars in tax-free money, which is stored in offshore accounts and replenished with money flowing in from markets overseas.[12]

With their enormous investments and power of influence, the MNCs occasionally "play God" and ruthlessly run roughshod over developing countries by dictating legislation and micro-managing policies to favor their operations. They keep African governments "at their beck and call"[13] and call shots as they wish. Many of them keep millions of dollars in slush funds to bribe corrupt officials under the guise of consultancy fees or commissions, and use their sway to exploit natural resources in conflict countries such as the Democratic Republic of Congo (DRC) and South Sudan, albeit with the full cooperation of avaricious leaders. The list of government officials and company executives caught in the web of corporate rot over the years reads like a "who's who" on the world

---

[11] Janet Lowe, *The Secret Empire: How 25 Multinationals Rule the World* (Irwin Professional Pub, 1992), 110–51.

[12] Parag Khanna, "These 25 Companies Are More Powerful than Many Countries," The Foreign Policy (FP) Group, article, March/April 2016.

[13] "Who is More Powerful – States or Corporations?" *The Conversation*, article, July 10, 2018.

stage of graft. It includes presidents, prime ministers, cabinet officials, politicians, top civil servants, chief executives of major companies, and lobbyists. This book seeks to explore corruption, bribery, and kickbacks by MNCs in Africa as well as the plunder and destruction of cultural values and critical African resources such as forests, riverways, and ocean beds (one report says $29 billion per year is stolen from Africa in illegal logging, fishing, and trade in wildlife).[14] The book also looks at the growing tendency by some international companies to fuel conflicts in Africa by illegally supplying arms and covertly providing financial assistance to countries to achieve dominance and influence. At the same time, *The Bribery Syndrome* does not shy away from criticizing ravenous African dictators who collaborate with MNCs to rape the continent. Both the rogue multinationals and the African elites are guilty of gross abuse. I hope this book will provide a new perspective on "African corruption" and expose, in a more explicit way, the hitherto hidden illegal activities of MNCs on the African continent.

---

[14] "How the World Profits from Africa's Wealth," Honest Accounts, article, 2017.

PART ONE

CHAPTER 1

CORRUPTION AND BRIBERY

Do not take bribes, for bribes blind the clear-sighted and upset the pleas of the just. – Exodus 23:8

Oftentimes people confuse corruption with bribery, viewing these terms as synonymous. The global watchdog TI and the United Nations (UN) define corruption as an abuse of entrusted power for private gain. It is usually the elected officials, civil servants, and other influencers who take bribes in exchange for contracts, favors, and influence, while corporate entities, executives, and their agents offer those bribes. That is why corruption—which is inherently more complicated to detect than bribery—is inextricably linked to politics and governance. Partakers of corruption ordinarily connive behind closed doors and exchange payments through convoluted channels to avoid detection.

Conversely, bribery identified as "permitted grease payments,"[15] or an act of accepting an item of value in exchange for specific treatment or influence, is a "narrower, more direct, less subtle"[16] form of illicit dealing. For example, an applicant who wants quick service at the Department of Immigration may surreptitiously pass a bribe to an official through the palm of a hand or slip a brown envelope into his jacket pocket to receive special treatment. A judge may secretively receive a bribe to render a one-sided ruling, or a policeman may choose not to write a speeding ticket in exchange for "something small." In all instances, money is paid secretly, and no receipts are given to avoid exposure and a paper trail.

In cases where MNCs must pay huge amounts of money to government officials for contracts, a briber may choose to use an agent, a bank, or an offshore company to channel the illicit payoff to the principal. Many approaches are used to deliver bribe money: for example, by bank transfers directly to overseas accounts, or, by couriers who physically deliver briefcases bulging with money to the residences of receivers.

---

[15] Richard L. Cassin, "*Bribery Abroad: Lessons from the Foreign Corrupt Practices Act,*" Lulu.com, 2008, 58.
[16] Henry N. Pontell and Gilbert Geis, *International Handbook of White-Collar Corporate Crime* (Springer, 2007), 406–411.

There are also other, more eccentric ways of conveying illegal money to bribe-takers. In the notorious "Operation Car Wash" scandal involving a major Brazilian multinational, Odebrecht, in the mid-2000s, bribe cash was at times delivered by *doleiros*—black market dealers, or "mules," who "travelled with shrink-wrapped bricks of banknotes concealed beneath their clothing."[17] Operation Car Wash, which began in Brazil in 2014, revolved around allegations that officials of the state-owned oil and gas company Petrobras were bribed by construction companies in exchange for inflated contracts. More than 80 politicians, including businessmen and a former popular president, Inacio Lula da Silva, known simply as "Lula," were implicated, and some of them jailed, in the massive scandal that went beyond the borders of Brazil.

Kickbacks, on the other hand, are transactions normally negotiated in advance between two parties, unlike in bribery, where one party extorts money from another. For example, instead of a purchasing officer recommending good but cheaper office items, he colludes with another seller to offer more expensive items to include his commission. In most African countries, the average going rate of a kickback is 10 percent of the value of goods, services, or a contract. Where an item or service costs millions of dollars, the return to the handler becomes quite attractive. The word "kickback" is derived from the English common usage to describe the way one kicks a benefit to another in an illegal scheme, and it is meant to get one party to cooperate in an illicit transaction[18] —a *quid pro quo*—or, in the more commonly used phrase, "one hand washing another." Kickbacks can be paid in cash, expensive cars, vacations, real estate, or other forms.

---

[17] Linda Pressly, "The Largest Foreign Bribery Case in History," *BBC*, news, April 22, 2018.

[18] Jose Edgardo Campos and Sanjay Pradhan, *The Many Faces of Corruption: Tracking Vulnerabilities at the Sector Level* (World Bank, 2007).

Experts agree that corruption, bribery, and kickbacks have serious consequences to the economy of a country. They fuel public distrust, weaken democracy, and distort markets, thus driving up costs for companies and consumers.[19] The World Bank (WB) says those three evils can influence a government's choice of firms to supply goods, services, and works, as well as impact the terms of their contracts. They can also influence the allocation of government benefits either to enterprises or individuals, and they can change the outcome of legal processes by inducing the government either to ignore illegal activities or to favor one party over another in court cases or other legal proceedings.[20]

Multinationals and Africa

MNCs were in Africa many years before most countries gained independence in the 1960s—pilfering the continent's massive natural resources and exploiting the indigenous people through unscrupulous labor practices. After independence, MNCs expanded their dominance and took advantage of the imperfections and vulnerabilities of corrupt African leaders to amass enormous profits, which they exported to banking institutions overseas.

A study by the UN Economic Commission for Africa (UNECA) on "Cross-border Corruption in Africa" showed that between 1995 and 2014, 99.5 percent of the cases of bribery on the continent involved non-African firms,[21] mostly global corporations. Professor Robert Neid of Trinity College, Cambridge University, writes in his book, *Public Corruption: The Dark Side of Social Evolution,* that "Rich countries and their agencies [multinationals] … commonly have been and are accomplices in corruption abroad, encouraging

---

[19] Franklin Atadja, "The Effects of Bribery and Corruption on Multinational Corporations," seminar in multicultural management (DDBA-8524), essay, Walden University, October 2013.
[20] "Helping Countries Combat Corruption: The Role of the World Bank - Corruption and Economic Management," The World Bank Group, article, September 1997.
[21] UN Economic Commission on Africa, "African Governance Report IV, Measuring Corruption in Africa: The International Dimension Matters," 69.

it by their actions rather than impeding it."[22] TI noted in its 2007 CPI that "bribe money often stems from multinationals based in the world's richest countries."[23] Even President Muhammadu Buhari of Nigeria—one of the most corrupt countries in the world—lashed out at MNCs during the London Anti-Corruption Summit in 2016, blaming them for promoting corruption and engaging in dirty deals globally. True, the demand side (bribe-takers) are to blame for promoting corruption, but a case can be made that the supply side (bribers) also bears responsibility for the proliferation of the vice. As will be seen in this narrative, some of the biggest global MNCs have been incriminated in multimillion-dollar corruption and bribery lawsuits relating to Africa. Their common defense is that bribing foreign officials is the only way to effectively compete on the world market. That argument may not be entirely true, since there are many foreign companies that trade abroad without having to resort to dirty tricks.

Nevertheless, it is safe to say the private sector is the epitome of graft worldwide and the engine of bad conduct. Other than failing to devise innovative solutions to fight venality, the private sector appears to be an accomplice in the malfeasance largely because of its deafening silence on the matter. That has pushed some executives, like Magda Wierzycka, a billionaire co-founder of the Cape Town–based financial services group Sygnia, to categorically state that the private sector is as corrupt as the public sector. Of all the big scandals in Africa in which billions of dollars were lost, foreign firms were the bribers and the African elites were the takers. It is quite understandable why the private sector is silent on the issue of corruption. It fears losing support from political leaders and missing out on tenders from governments. Therefore, companies cling to the only option available to them: playing along and sharing illegal profits with rapacious officials.

---

[22] Robert Neild, *Public Corruption: The Dark Side of Social Evolution* (Anthem Press, 2002), 209.
[23] Transparency International, "Persistent Corruption in Low-Income Countries Requires Global Action," article, September 25, 2007.

In Africa, there is a phrase, "create-loot-share," which describes connivance in graft between government officials, politicians, and business executives. How it works is that devious individuals lobby for projects and then substantially inflate the cost of contracts to provide a slice of illegal revenue to participants. This cunning form of theft raises the costs of, for instance, construction, making it too expensive for governments to complete projects. In Kenya, for instance, the construction of the 485-kilometer Mombasa-Nairobi Expressway was delayed after it was found officials had inflated costs from $1.8 billion to $3 billion to account for kickbacks. In numerous cases, the World Bank has been forced to withdraw from projects due to corruption and non-compliance of key planning procedures. The aftermath of "create-loot-share" is the presence of "white elephant" projects all over the continent—from dams, to hospitals, to agricultural projects, to infrastructure; some half-completed, and others standing unused as a testimony to official ineptitude and mismanagement by corrupt regimes.

In Africa, inflated contracts from "create-loot-share" schemes run into the trillions of dollars. In Nigeria alone, between 2009 and 2014, a government agency responsible for vetting procurement contracts salvaged $2 billion from fraudulently bloated contracts. And the conspiracy is not confined to physical projects only: in the legal parley are cases where private lawyers hired by the state entered into deals with plaintiffs and judges to share monetary judgments. Cases of judges facing judicial action due to participation in "create-loot-share" deals have been reported in many countries, including South Africa, Nigeria, Kenya, Ghana, Mali, Liberia, Cameroon, and the DRC, where in 2009, 96 judges suspected of corruption were sacked. In the private sector, company executives help cartels to manipulate contract bids and overstate costs to benefit all participants.

The insidious system also exists in the wildlife-rich nations of Tanzania, South Africa, and Kenya, where game rangers, police, customs officials, judges, and poaching cartels work together to annihilate wildlife resources for profit. This enigmatic camaraderie between the public and private sectors is the root cause of a culture of foreign corruption and bribery on the continent.

CHAPTER 2

_____

OLD TO MODERN CORRUPTION

At first glance, MNCs appear to be real developmental partners, but a careful examination of their intrinsic undertones would disclose their devilish savvy in exploitation as they retard African economies, sap resources, leaving the hitherto buoyant natural resource base barren, thereby leading to an anomalous situation that injects underdevelopment [rather] than development. – Tangwe Abraham.

In the 1700, the British East India Company (BEIC) was caught in a series of bribery scandals in India. Founded with a mission to engage in international trade and exploration, the BEIC had its India office in Bengal, then a fast-growing industrial city. Leading the company was Major General Robert Clive, a controversial and fearless Welsh national who was notoriously known for engaging in practices that abused market power and common business tendencies.

His proclivity for bribing Indian Mughals (Viceroys/Nawab) in exchange for duty-free privileges in trade was considered uncouth by both Indian traders and some British aristocrats. In the early 1750s, Clive entered into an agreement with one Mughal to facilitate the movement of British goods through preferential treatment. The agreement was bitterly opposed by local leaders, among them the incoming Mughal, Prince Siraj-ud-Daular. Over time, tensions boiled over between Clive and Prince Siraj, and in June 1757, the Welshman and his troops marched into the small village of Palashi in West Bengal to challenge Prince Siraj's troops. Mathematically, Clive's 3,000 poorly equipped men were no match for the 50,000-man Mughal army, fully armed with canons and supported by war elephants. Afraid he would be overrun with heavy losses to his men, Clive came up with an unconventional idea: why not bribe Mi Jafar, the commander-in-chief of the Nawab forces? Money changed hands, and the viceroy's troops, supported by their French allies, were defeated well before the war started. Siraj was captured and executed.

The Welsh tactician knew after arriving in India in 1744 that giving and accepting bribes was the only way the company could survive. He therefore used money to get what he wanted and accepted bribes from Mughals in the form of rare paintings, carvings, and expensive objects.[24] Through crude business practices, the BEIC expanded its operations beyond Bengal to cover the rest of India,

---

[24] Milton S. Gwirtzman, "Is Bribery Defensible?" *The New York Times*, October 5, 1975.

earning the distinction of being the first known British multinational to use bribery as a tool of political and economic manipulation in the developing world.[25] That new form of crime, involving illicit acts committed by citizens of one country in the territories of others, led to a public discussion in the United Kingdom about corporate responsibility, bribery's toll overseas, and the morality of profit gained by corruption.[26]

Three years after winning the Battle of Palashi, Clive left for home, carrying artifacts worth millions of dollars in a massive pillage that brought to the fore the word "loot," meaning "plunder" in Hindustani. By the eighteenth century, that word was in common use in Great Britain due to an increase in cases of bribery and corruption in the country and in its territories. By then Clive was a wealthy person with millions of British pounds deposited in a bank, a matter which attracted a probe into his fortunes by the British Parliament in 1772.

Soon, corruption became a buzzword in the ruling empire of Great Britain. At one point the BEIC bought off parliamentary opposition with money and donated 50 gold crowns worth (approximately $500,000 today) to the British Crown in return for its continued right to govern Bengal.[27] Subsequently, graft reached the monarchy itself. During the rule of King George, III between January 1760 and 1820, the monarch routinely engaged in political corruption by intervening frequently to manipulate elections[28] and buying and rebuying legislators to maintain loyalty to the court. What Clive did in India was therefore partially similar to what the king of Great Britain and Ireland did during his reign, though in different circumstances.

----

[25] David Montero, *Kickback: Exposing the Global Corporate Bribery Network* (Viking, 2018), 14.
[26] Ibid., 15.
[27] William Dalrymple, "The East India Company: The Original Corporate Raiders," *The Guardian,* March 4, 2015.
[28] Melvin Eugene Page and Penny M. Sonnenberg, *Colonialism: An International, Social, Cultural, and Political Encyclopedia* (ABC-CLIO, 2003), 1, 11–12.

The immoral practices of the BEIC were well-known in the United Kingdom. After returning to Britain in 1785, the man who succeeded Clive as governor of Bengal, Warren Hastings, was in 1788 impeached for looting and corruption. He was accused of paying himself money in excess of his allowances and for other infractions while in India. During the trial before the House of Lords, prosecutors who were members of the House of Commons called Hastings the "enemy of humanity"[29] for corruption and atrocities that took place under his watch in India. They also blasted the BEIC for bribing members of parliament (MPs) and for using money plundered in India to inject itself into British politics. Hastings did survive the impeachment and was acquitted in 1795. Gripped by financial challenges, the BEIC staggered until 1874, when it finally collapsed, closing a historic chapter in the British multinational dominance of India.

Modern-day corruption

The deceitful foreign business habits of the early centuries were not much different from those used today by rogue multinationals. The only difference is that today's corporations apply sophisticated ways of paying bribes to foreign officials and choose even more intricate channels to hide their illicit gains in secret offshore accounts. The ancient bribe-giving of paintings and carvings has been replaced by lavish vacations, expensive vehicles, and lots of cash. Companies like the global retail store Walmart, IT market leader Hewlett-Packard, telecommunications giant Alcatel-Lucent, British pharmaceutical colossus GlaxoSmithKline, US oil field service conglomerate Halliburton, and many others have, at one time or another, been caught bribing foreign public officials in violation of standing laws and regulations, among them the US Foreign Corrupt Practices Act (FCPA), the UK Bribery Act 2010, and the Convention of the Organization for Economic Cooperation and Development (OECD), three of the most consequential anti-

---

[29] Mahesh Shantaram, "Warren Hastins: Impeachment and Estimate," History Discussion, article, undated.

bribery protocols in the world.

After the dramatic resignation of President Richard Nixon on August 9, 1974 over the Watergate debacle, congressional investigators found 400 MNCs, among them blue-chip US enterprises, that had participated in a slew of overseas briberies. The investigations revealed that some US multinationals had paid an estimated $750 million in bribes to overseas officials, including contributions to foreign political parties to secure government contracts. Goodyear Tire and Rubber Company and American Airlines made payments to President Richard Nixon's Committee to Re-elect the President (CRP) and failed to report the payments to authorities. Ashland Oil Company and Gulf Oil Corporation also admitted to the US Senate sub-Committee on Multinational Corporations to having contributed $100,000 each to Nixon's re-election campaign in 1972.

The corrupt activities of the US MNCs led to the enactment of the FCPA in 1977, making it illegal for American enterprises and their subsidiaries to bribe foreign government officials. The FCPA has tough provisions, one of them being a section on "accounting provisions" which requires that a company must maintain record-keeping and internal controls and file reports with the Securities and Exchange Commission (SEC), an independent agency that enforces federal security laws. The FCPA also prohibits US citizens from giving anything of value "to any person while knowing that all or a portion of such money or thing of value will be offered, given, or promised, directly or indirectly, to any foreign official."[30] Heavy fines of up to $100,000 and a maximum of five years in jail per violation can be imposed on officers, directors, stockholders, and agents of companies violating the FCPA's anti-bribery provisions. For infringing on the accounting provisions, corporations and other business entities can be fined up to $25 million, and individuals $5 million and imprisonment for up to 20 years. The FCPA is based on the belief that "corruption is bad for business, and US persons, companies, and those operating within the US financial system,

[30] US Department of Justice, "Foreign Corrupt Practices Act."

should not profit from it."[31] Billions of dollars in kickbacks have been traced since the legislation was enacted, and US and foreign company executives jailed and/or fined following immoral activities across the world.

The US aircraft company McDonnell Douglas Corporation was among the first to be prosecuted under the FCPA in November 1979 for bribing overseas officials. A federal grand jury indicted the St. Louis–based company and four of its executives on allegations of defrauding Pakistan International Airlines of $1.6 million. McDonnell Douglas was charged with concealing payoffs to four Pakistani sales agents in the purchase of a DC-10 and making false statements to the Export-Import Bank, which financed the sale. It was also cited for hiding other payoffs amounting to $6 million to airline personnel and state officials on sales in South Korea, the Philippines, Venezuela, and Zaire.[32] The company pleaded guilty to 11 counts and paid the US government $1.2 million to settle pending civil and criminal proceedings and a further $55,000 in criminal fines. In return, the government dropped criminal charges against the four executives: James S. McDonnell III, son of the company founder; John C. Brizendine, president of the Douglas Aircraft Company, a division of McDonnell Douglas; Charles M. Forsyth, executive vice president of Douglas Aircraft; and Sherman Pruitt Jr., sales manager of Douglas Aircraft.

The chairman of the US Senate sub-Committee on Multinational Corporations, Frank Church, who started investigating US companies in 1975, summed up the whole situation thus: "The bribes and payoffs associated with doing business abroad represent a pattern of crookedness that would make—in terms of

---

[31] "2017 Year-end FCPA Update," Gibson Dunn, report, January 2, 2018.
[32] Jack G. Kaikati and Wayne A. Label, "American Bribery Legislation: An Obstacle to International Marketing," *Journal of Marketing* 44, no. 4 (Autumn 1980): 38–43.

its scope and magnitude—crookedness in politics look like a Sunday school picnic by comparison."[33] The amounts paid as bribes to principals through intermediaries, consultants, and brokers were astonishingly high; so were the profits earned by MNCs from successful contracts.

In 2017, the US Department of Justice (DOJ) and the SEC managed to apprehend 14 business entities and yield $1.92 million from fines, penalties, disgorgement, and pre-judgment interests. In 2018, 16 multinational companies paid a staggering $2.89 billion in resolution with the DOJ and SEC to resolve FCPA cases, compared to only $890 million in 2008. Six individuals pleaded guilty in 2018 to FCPA-related criminal charges and were either jailed or fined.

In the United Kingdom, the enactment of the Bribery Act 2010, which became operational in April 2011, affirmed the government's determination to tackle foreign bribery. The Act replaced a patchwork of statutory and common law offenses dating back to 1889 and provided a new strict liability offense for companies and partnerships for failing to prevent bribery.[34] The Act makes the offering, giving, requesting and receiving of bribes an offense carrying up to 10 years imprisonment and an unlimited fine. The law pertains to all UK companies, citizens, and residents, wherever the bribery occurs, and to non-UK nationals or companies if an act or omission forming part of the offense takes place in the United Kingdom. The legislation has a near-universal jurisdiction that allows the prosecution of an individual or company with links to the United Kingdom, regardless of where the crime occurred. If, for example, a parent company in one country appoints an agent in another country, and that agent bribes a foreign official for the benefit of the parent company, then the Act could be used to investigate and prosecute the parent company if one of its

---

[33] David Montero, "The Second Half of Watergate Was Bigger, Worse, and Forgotten by the Public," *Longreads*, November 2018.
[34] "Understanding the UK Bribery Bill," McGuireWoods, commentary, undated.

subsidiaries is located in the United Kingdom. The Bribery Act also saw the highest number of bribery investigations in 2018, numbering between 70 and 75, with officials from the Serious Fraud Office (SFO) saying it was the busiest year that yielded both wins and losses in the fight against bribery worldwide.

On the other hand, the OECD Convention makes it a criminal offense for any person to intentionally offer, promise, or give any undue pecuniary or other advantage—whether directly or through intermediaries—to a foreign public official in order to obtain or retain business or other improper advantage in the conduct of international business. From 1999, when the Convention came into force, until the end of 2017, 184 corporate entities and 560 individuals were criminally sanctioned by the OECD, with some individuals going to jail for up to five years for foreign bribery.

CHAPTER 3

HOW MNCs ARE ROBBING AFRICA

We hear Africans are corrupt, but the question remains, what about international companies which give bribes so as to be favored in investment projects on the continent? They too should be punished. – Charles Ngereza

For a number of years, debate has raged over the role of MNCs, especially in Africa. The WB and other institutions believe MNCs are promoting corruption by bribing African government officials to get profitable contracts and influence policies for their benefit, while non-governmental organizations (NGOs) like Oxfam believe MNCs are taking advantage of poorly structured legislation in Africa to exploit the continent's resources, especially in conflict areas. A case in point is the DRC, where MNCs and their African agents are depleting forest reserves and mineral resources, especially coltan—which is used to produce cell phones and laptops—at an alarming rate. What is happening in that country can only be described as mass looting and a full-blast exploitation of Africa.

And while it is true that some MNCs have robust and visible corporate social responsibility programs and help host countries to sustain development, others are satisfied only with providing low-paying jobs to locals and misusing workers. The "good" multinationals normally establish a well-developed code of conduct. They also strive to achieve some social missions in order to do business ethically, minimize negative environmental impacts, raise public attention on certain issues, raise funds and donations, increase employees' job satisfaction, and more.[35] But there is evidence in this narrative and others showing that MNCs support corrupt governments to become even more corrupt. In the process, greedy African leaders benefit and covetous MNCs, intermediaries, accountants, and lawyers gain, while an increasingly cynical citizenry loses.

Oxfam International's executive director, Winnie Byanyima, (now the Executive Director for the UN Program on HIV/AIDS) blamed MNCs for "hemorrhaging" Africa of billions of dollars every year through the non-payment of taxes.[36] Between 1980 and 2009, an

---

[35] Lok Yiu Chan, "Corporate Social Responsibility of Multinational Corporations," Global Honors Theses, University of Washington Tacoma, Spring 2014.
[36] "Multinational Companies Cheat Africa Out of Billions of Dollars," Oxfam, June 2, 2015.

estimated $1.2 trillion to $1.4 trillion left Africa in illicit financial flows due to trade mispricing and other losses. An illicit financial flow is defined as money obtained illegally and transferred for use elsewhere.[37] In 2018, UNECA said the outflow had reached more than $50 billion a year.

Kenya alone, according to a 2015 report of the Tax Justice Network – Africa (TJN-A), was losing $6.2 billion annually through tax evasion by multinational companies. Additional losses are incurred through exemptions on import duties and value-added tax (VAT) on imported plants, machinery, raw materials and equipment, stamp duties on legal instruments, and import duties on inputs. There is also a huge loss on repatriated dividends by companies manufacturing goods locally for export. The neighboring countries of Uganda, Rwanda, and Tanzania forfeit $370 million, $176 million, and $500 million, respectively, to MNCs every year.[38]

Let's put it another way. In 2015, Africa received $161.6 billion in loans, personal remittances, and aid in the form of grants. During the same period, $203 billion left Africa through repatriated profits by multinationals and illegal money transfers. Substantial amounts of money are also lost when unprocessed agricultural goods are taken out of sub-Saharan Africa for processing abroad, considering that the vast majority of value of goods is earned abroad.[39]

Money is also "stolen" through what is called "profit shifting," a system in which multinationals repatriate profits by moving profits to tax havens in the United Kingdom, Switzerland, and Caribbean islands, among other places, where they pay less in taxes. Byanyima says if such revenue was invested in education and healthcare, societies and economies would further flourish across the continent.

---

[37] Masimba Tafirenyika, "Illicit Financial Flows from Africa: Track It, Stop It, Get It," *Africa Renewal*, December 2013.
[38] John Hilary, "Extracting Minerals, Extracting Wealth," *War on Want*, undated.
[39] "How the World Profits from Africa's Wealth," Honest Accounts, 2017.

Leonce Ndikumana, a professor of economics at the University of Massachusetts Amherst, asserts that "multinational corporations use two techniques to dodge taxes: royalty payments to affiliated trademark holders located outside of Africa, and management fees paid to affiliates and subsidiaries within corporate groups outside the continent."[40] Once the money is transferred overseas, it stays beyond the reach of African governments. An example is SABMiller of South Africa, which for centuries had been producing Castle beer. Its trademark was registered and owned in Rotterdam. Every year, South African Breweries Ltd —one of SABMiller's largest operating companies—paid royalties amounting to millions of dollars to SABMiller BV in the Netherlands.[41] The company was also accused of avoiding paying taxes in Mozambique, Tanzania, and Zambia, thus depriving those countries of colossal amounts of revenue. In 2016, the company was acquired by America's Anheuser-Busch.

Furthermore, some African countries still maintain outdated colonial statutes that are more detrimental than useful to the welfare of their people. Malawi, for example, has a 60-year-old, colonial-era tax treaty with the United Kingdom that makes it easy for UK companies to limit their tax obligations to Malawi. The treaty was negotiated between the British government and the then-UK-appointed governor of Nyasaland when Malawi was still a colony. The treaty regulates how money transfers between the two countries are taxed and also makes it difficult for Malawi to tax British companies operating in the country. Activists led by the anti-poverty NGO Action Aid International have campaigned to have the treaty renegotiated so that the tax money could be channeled toward the country's economic and social needs. That campaign has yet to yield positive results.

---

[40] Leonce Ndikumana, "The Issue of Private Sector Corruption in Africa," *Third World Resurgence*, no. 309 (May 2016): 24–29.
[41] Ibid.

In 2004, Uganda signed an almost-similar tax treaty with the Netherlands exempting companies that are resident in the Netherlands, but operating in Uganda, from paying certain taxes. As a result, Uganda loses millions of dollars in revenue every year. For failing to curb this type of manipulation, some say, "African governments are as guilty as the multinational corporations … in diverting funds that should go towards attempting to improve the quality of life of the continent's hundreds of millions of poor people."[42]

In addition, not in all cases do African countries earn money from the enormous fines and other restitutions ordered by foreign courts for corruption and bribery crimes committed on the continent. Goodyear Tire and Rubber Company subsidiaries in Kenya and Angola, for example, were fined $16 million, and ordered to pay an interest of $2.1 million by the SEC in 2015, for paying $3.2 million in bribes to government officials in those countries in violation of the FCPA. It is not known if any of that money reached the two African countries. In May 2016, the US-based financial services company Och-Ziff Capital Management was fined $414 million by the SEC for greasing the palms of government officials in Niger, Guinea, Chad, Libya, and the DRC, but the penalty money remained overseas even though the crimes occurred in the West African countries. Asked one observer: why not keep the money on the continent to fortify their own anti-corruption campaign?[43]

The manipulation of Africa by MNCs is in sync with what George Rich declared years ago about the domination of the continent by the West: "If you ever intend to have children, and want them to live prosperous lives, you damn well better make sure we control

---

[42] Victor Kgomoeswana, "Africa Still Losing Billions through Illicit Financial Flows by Multinational Corporations Despite Increasing Awareness of the Problem," *The Sunday Independent*, May 21, 2018.
[43] Irumire David Okhumale, "Africa Fighting Corruption on Its Own Turf," *Corporate Compliance Insights*, June 21, 2017.

the African continent."[44] Indeed, the West *does* partially control Africa, and that domination has existed since the land expropriations of the nineteenth century. The early interests of colonial powers in Africa of controlling human and natural resources have now shifted to exerting political influence through aid. Developed countries bombard the continent with aid and loans; they decide how much to pay for Africa's raw materials, choose who rules, and even dictate the system of government and institutions a country must have. This forces the adoption of Western democracy by all means, and resisters are punished. "Buy, rig, or steal, is the name of the game and if that doesn't work, send in the French army and UN "peacekeepers" and rocket the presidential residence and just take over by brute force."[45]

An African problem?

So, is corruption and bribery "an African problem"—an "entrenched part of African political culture, as one scholar opinionates?"[46] Barney Warf, a professor at the University of Kansas, in his paper entitled *Geographies of African Corruption*, says Africa is arguably the most corrupt continent on the planet, and agrees with other scholars that African corruption is pervasive and the world's most severe.[47] That view is widespread in the West, but could that be true?

There are many, even in Africa itself, who believe Africa has failed itself. Early in 2019, a video clip trended on social media showing a Nigerian lady begging on the streets of Canada, with the recorder pummeling her with questions as to why she left her country to

---

[44] John Perkins, *The Secret History of the American Empire: Economic Hit men, Jackals, and the Truth About Global Corruption* (Penguin Group (USA), 2007), 192.

[45] Thomas C. Mountain, "Destroying Africa with Western 'Democracy,'" *Foreign Policy Journal*, article, 1 May 2012.

[46] Barney Warf, "Geographies of African Corruption," *PSU Research Review* 1, no. 1, Emerald Publishing Ltd., 2017.

[47] L. Lawson, "The Politics of Anti-Corruption Reform in Africa," *Journal of Modern African Studies,* 47 (2009): 73–100.

panhandle in a "white man's" country: "Why are you Africans running away from Africa to live with the white man? So, you people in Africa can't manage your country? The questioner, who identified himself as an American, repeated those questions over and over again, and the only response from the visibly embarrassed poor lady, with her hands outstretched for alms, was, "Our government in Nigeria is corrupt. Just spare me 20 dollars, please!"[48] While it is easy to sympathize with the lady, it is not difficult to understand the reasoning behind the questions.

Two days after that clip was published, someone posted a video of a middle-aged woman who identified herself as a Ghanaian. She was traveling in a European city by bus and carrying a green alms bucket, begging for money to build a church "so that Jesus Christ can come and solve our [Africa's] problems." She bellowed, "We have too many problems [in Ghana]. We don't have enough accommodation for children. We have no drinking water; we have no ambulances, so please donate."[49] The sparse crowd only sneered at her, and no one offered any donation.

Beginning with the first generation of pre-independence leaders, such as Kenya's Jomo Kenyatta, Zimbabwe's Robert Mugabe, and Ivory Coast's Felix Houphouet-Boigny, to relatively recent ones like Uganda's Yoweri Museveni and South Africa's Jacob Zuma, African presidents have used their positions of power to loot national resources without caring about citizens and their misery. They have promoted corruption and bribery, fostered impunity, and shown the way for subordinates to follow suit.

That is the reason why African leaders and public officials are derisively painted in the worst possible light, and that is not without justification. African politicians and civil servants are not only perceived to be corrupt; they *are* indeed so. The word *wabenzi*

---

[48] Grace Afua Somuah-Annan, "Video: American Shames Nigerian Woman Begging on the Streets of Canada," Pulse.com, February 2, 2019.

[49] Abu Mubaik, "Joyce Dzidor Mensah Mocks Akufo-Addo's National Cathedral: Sarcastically Begs Foreigners for Donations, Pulse.com, February 17, 2019.

was crafted during President Nyerere's early reign in Tanzania to describe the *nouveau riche* who bought Mercedes-Benz cars as a symbol of wealth amid mounting poverty. An African joke says there are more Mercedes-Benz vehicles in any one African country than there are in Germany, the original manufacturer of the trendy, expensive brand. The spiteful *wabenzi* word is still being used in parts of eastern Africa to describe the corrupt ones. In Lesotho, the deviously corrupt are called *bobolu,* a derogatory word that conjures an image of greed and selfishness. In Kenya, the lowly use the word *buda,* or boss, to describe the halves – as in the phrase "the haves and have-notes" or, those who have grabbed properties belonging to the public. And within the corruption lingo are terminologies such as "tenderpreneurs" and "legislooters," referring to the characters—including MPs—behind illegitimate deals that impoverish the continent.

Blame it on traditions and slavery?

Some writers and researchers have blamed colonialists and European and Arab slavers for introducing graft in Africa. They argue that during slavery, European and Arab slave traders routinely bribed African chiefs with trinkets and guns to get them to mobilize people to raid rival villages for slaves, who were then handed over to the captors for shipment and sale abroad. That argument elicits diverse opinions, with some rubbishing it and others insisting that, "Slavery is corruption: it involved theft, bribery, and exercise of brute force as well as ruses," and that slavery should therefore be seen as one source of the precolonial origins of modern corruption.[50]

Some have pointed a finger at African traditions of spontaneous gift-giving. In Africa, it is common for people to gift those in authority for a job well done or just as a way of saying thank you for a deed. However, such gifts can sometimes be conceived as bribes, especially when accompanied by requests for favors such

---

[50] Patrick Manning, *Slavery and African Life: Occidental, Oriental, and African Slave Trades*, (Cambridge University Press, 1990), 124.

as finding a job for a son of the giver or expecting better school grades from a teacher.

Yet others blame "the politics of the belly"—the inclination to self-aggrandizement—for the proliferation of graft on the continent. And some argue that corruption is prevalent because of a "lack of strong institutional controls."[51] Indeed, many African countries have weak anti-corruption laws—if they exist at all. But even where laws exist, they are not implemented, either because of political reasons or because of fears of unsettling the status quo.

As for colonialism, here is one example which illustrates its role in African corruption. In 1990, the British colonial government approached Baganda chiefs and asked them to sign an agreement demarcating the boundaries between the kingdom of Baganda and the British Uganda protectorate. In the agreement, the British Commissioner, Sir Harry Johnston, tactfully agreed to allocate hundreds of square miles to the Bagandan king, queen mother, queen sister, regents, and chiefs. The Bagandans took that as a show of magnanimity on the part of the white administrator, but the colonialists saw it differently. None of the local leaders resisted the attractive offer and in fact welcomed it with ardor. They signed the agreement joyfully, congratulating themselves on their capacity to negotiate.[52] The fact of the matter is, the Bagandan king and his cohorts had hawked their country willingly in exchange for personal benefits. That was bribery in its crudest form.

Nevertheless, whatever the historic or contemporary reasons for the high levels of corruption presently in Africa, the fact remains: the continent has and continues to be raped of its resources at an astronomical rate by both the insiders (the African elite) and outsiders (the multinationals) to the detriment of future generations.

In one survey, a large number of people in sub-Saharan Africa admitted to paying and receiving bribes in return for material

---

[51] John Mary Waliggo, "Corruption and Bribery - An African Problem?" *Africa Files*, article, March 1, 2007.
[52] Ibid.

possessions. In its report entitled *A People and Corruption: Africa Survey 2015,* TI outlines the extent of "chicanery, skullduggery and subterfuge" that occurred in 2015 in the 28 countries constituting sub-Saharan African. The report surveyed 43,143 people, many of whom complained of their government's failure to meet common expectations in the fight against graft. The report lays out a picture of pervasive misconduct by leaders and citizenry alike throughout the region.

It is safe to say that, over the years, the corruption and bribery industry has evolved into a multibillion-dollar enterprise. The good-natured African tradition of paying small bribes, called *dash* in most of West Africa and *kadzama* among the Mijikenda tribes of Kenya, to chiefs and other people in authority as an appreciation of work done has been replaced by a high-level, well-organized, and elite form of bribery involving exchanges of money by crooked multinationals running into the tens of millions of dollars in return for political influence and lucrative contracts.

While it is appreciated that Western organizations help to open new horizons in developing nations by offering job opportunities to locals, introducing new technologies, and producing high-quality products for local consumption, it can also be argued that these companies perpetuate negative effects on citizenry within the areas where they operate by encouraging graft through the bribery of officials. On the other hand, African leaders have made themselves open for exploitation by mismanaging their regimes and encouraging nepotism, tribalism, politically instigated conflicts, and human rights abuses. How some of those leaders found themselves in power may have something to do with their proclivity for material things. Leaders like Nigeria's Sani Abacha and Sudan's Omar al-Bashir took power through military coups and used oppressive means to retain dominance and amass wealth. Daniel arap Moi of Kenya and Jacob Zuma of South Africa attained and upheld power by manipulating electoral processes through corruption and fraud. All of them governed with an iron fist and used fiat to rob their nations.

Some of the African leaders were hoisted to power with the assistance of multinational firms, deceitful NGOs, and business moguls eyeing to exploit resources. Some of those organizations funded mercenaries and provided financial resources to opposition politicians in the hope of reaping rewards once their surrogates came to power. Foreign governments desirous to impose puppets into leadership positions supplied money, military materiel, and mercenaries to overthrow democratically elected regimes. As late as 2019, France was accused of arming the government of President Abdel Fattah al-Sisi of Egypt against activists fighting for democracy.

Earlier on, in 1993, one French oil executive admitted that his company financed the re-election campaign of Congo-Brazzaville's president Denis Sassou Nguesso, who lost to archrival Pascal Lissouba. Ironically, in 1997, it was Lissouba who told a French court, during a hearing for a corruption case against the French state-controlled oil company Elf Aquitaine, that he too was offered arms by the same company that financed Nguesso. Also, in 2003, Elf Aquitaine (which was acquired by Totalfina in 2000 to form TotalFinaElf and renamed Total SA in 2003), did concede to paying cash bribes to President Omar Bongo amounting to $13 million, as well as to leaders of Cameroon, Congo-Brazzaville, and Angola, among others, to influence the continuation of oil explorations in those countries. Even in 2019, oil companies in Equatorial Guinea continued to manipulate that country's leader, President Teodoro Obiang, and his henchmen and henchwomen to prolong and expand their business interests in the country.

US congresswoman Cynthia McKinney said, during a congressional hearing in Washington, DC on April 16, 2001, that Western nations "have incited rebellion against stable African governments … [and] have even participated in the assassination of duly elected and legitimate African heads of state and replaced them with corrupted and malleable officials."[53] Among the victims of brutish foreign government assassination plots were the Cameroonian anti-colonial opposition leader Felix-Roland Moumie, who was poisoned in 1960; the first prime minister of an independent Congo, Patrice Lumumba, who was brutally murdered in 1961; former president Sylvanus Olympio of Togo, who was killed in 1963; and the founding president of the Mozambican Liberation Front, Eduardo Mondlane, who was killed when a device hidden in a book he was handling exploded in 1969. One report in June 2019, claimed France alone may have been responsible for the assassination of 22 African presidents since 1963.[54]

But there are also those who were forced out of office for corruption and mismanagement of state affairs. Angola's Jose Eduardo dos Santos, Zimbabwe's Robert Mugabe, Gambia's Yahya Jammeh, South Africa's Jacob Zuma, Ghana's Kwame Nkrumah, Burkina Faso's Blaise Compaore, the DRC's Mobutu Sese Seko, Côte d'Ivoire's Felix Houphouet-Boigny, Mauritius's Ameenah Gurib-Fakim, and Algeria's Abdelaziz Bouteflika are only a few of the names of those booted out or unwillingly made to resign under pressure for, among other things, abuse of office.

Western countries have also been accused of instigating the deadly civil war in the eastern part of the DRC—through its proxies Rwanda and Uganda—in order to loot the vast mineral wealth in the region.[55] In the process, the war has caused massive losses of life estimated at more than five million people and the displacement of tens of thousands of villagers since the conflict erupted in 1994. The same type of Western conspiracy caused conflicts in dozens of other African countries, including Somalia, South Sudan, and Libya.

---

[53] Cynthia McKinney, "Covert Action in Africa: A Smoking Gun in Washington DC," House Committee on International Relations, April 16, 2001.
[54] Takudzwa Hillary Chiwanza, "France has Assassinated 22 African Presidents Since 1963, The African Exponent, online news, June 29, 2019.
[55] Fredrick Ngugi, "Western Multinational Corporations Are Profiting from Poor Africans," Face Africa, online news, February 14, 2017.

At the same time, multinational oil companies are also denounced for the destruction of the oil-rich Niger Delta in Nigeria by heavily polluting the environment, compounding the destruction of the wetland and coastal marine ecosystems already in danger from militant groups. But that is not all. Countries, including Switzerland and the United Kingdom, continue to accept illicit money from corrupt African leaders in their financial institutions. London and the British Overseas Territories and Crown Dependencies, such as the British Virgin Islands, the Cayman Islands, and Jersey, are some of the most popular tax havens for those wishing to hide or launder money; so are banks in Switzerland, South Africa, France, Spain, and other foreign lands.

Asked once why he was holding vast amounts of money in offshore accounts, the combatively defiant President Felix Houphouet-Boigny of Ivory Coast said, "I do have assets abroad. But they are not assets belonging to Côte d'Ivoire [Ivory Coast]. What sensible man does not keep his assets in Switzerland, the whole world's bank?" And he added, "I would be crazy to sacrifice my children's future in this crazy country without thinking of their future."[56] That is why it is sometimes difficult to differentiate between personal income and state money under the control of African heads of state. In other African countries, there are secret bank accounts holding public monies controlled individually by the president which are not subject to audit, making it difficult to know whether those monies are used for official or personal undertakings.

Offshore industry

In the 2017 Panama Papers revelations, leaders and officials of seven African countries were implicated in the rogue offshore finance industry in Panama, among them a former Ivory Coast president, a nephew of a former South African president, a son of a former president of Ghana, a widow of a former Guinea dictator, and others. Jacob Zuma's son, Khulubuse Zuma, denied having

---

[56] *La Croix*, Paris, article, March 13, 1990.

an offshore account, as claimed by the Panama-based law firm Mossack Fonseca. "We often point fingers at foreign multinationals that come to make a fortune here in Africa," said Maxime Domegni, a Togo journalist who was involved in "The Plunder Route to Panama," a report produced by a consortium of journalists. "But this investigation shows the extent to which African oligarchs are complicit in plundering the continent."[57]

The enabler?

That Britain has a corruption problem is something that is acknowledged by both the political establishment and the private sector in that country. In fact, the history of the British establishment is, in many ways, a history of corruption.[58] From 1621, when Lord Chancellor Francis Baron, the highest legal officer in the land, was accused of taking bribes from litigants appearing before him, to relatively recent cases of commercial bribery involving some of the country's biggest companies, Britain's place in worldwide corruption is cemented.

The non-partisan NGO Global Witness described the United Kingdom as an "enabler of corruption," (and) ... when asked whether the United Kingdom played a role in facilitating corruption, the executive director of TI, Robert Barrington, blurted out: "Unambiguously, yes."[59] In 2016, a 12-year study of 900 business executives found that bribery had become a way of life for British companies working in emerging nations, and that 85 percent of managers had resorted to bribery. Professor Andrew Kakabadse, who led the study, said the days of brown envelopes were gone

---

[57] Kate Hairsine, "Panama Papers: Africa's Elite are Plundering their Countries," *Deutsche Welle,* October 18, 2017.
[58] David Whyte, *"How Corrupt Britain?"* (Pluto Press, 2015), 24.
[59] UK House of Commons, "Tackling Corruption Overseas," International Development Committee, 4th Report of Session 2016–17, October 11, 2016, 13.

and that bribery had turned into a "highly organized, almost professionalized, business of agents taking 'facilitation fees' to secure deals."[60]

Anti-corruption agitators blame the UK government for allowing the nation's capital, London, to be used for money laundering. Investigative journalist Nicholas Shaxson described the city as the epicenter of secrecy jurisdictions, along with British Commonwealth countries and former Crown colonies like Hong Kong, Mauritius, and Singapore, which are used as hidden conduits for dirty money originating from the rest of the world. By the time the illegal money reaches London, Shaxson said, its origins can no longer be traced, "hidden behind a complex of secretive offshore bank accounts, companies and trusts."[61]

The use of London and its dependences in laundering dirty money is a matter of great concern. Professor Richard Rose of the University of Strathclyde in Glasgow gave, in 2015, the example of the DRC, where the Department for International Development (DFID)—which is responsible for administering overseas assistance—was spending $200 million annually in aid, yet an equivalent of $1.36 billion from mining were lost via British tax havens and London-listed companies. TI estimates 90 billion GBP (about $110 billion) of illicit funds were being cleaned in London every year,[62] a good share of it from theft and drug trafficking. On this, the London *Sunday Times* commented in one of its editorials, "This whiff of scandal is bad news for London's reputation as a financial center."[63]

---

[60] Alan Tovey, "Bribery a Way of Life for Companies Operating in Emerging Markets." *The Telegraph* , October 26, 2016.

[61] Nicholas Shaxson, *Treasure Islands: Tax Havens and the Men Who Stole the World* (Vintage, 2012), 104.

[62] Robert Barrington, "London, the Money-Laundering Capital," *The World Today*, Catham House, publication, April & May 2018.

[63] "London, the Money-Laundering Capital," *The World Today*, Tribute Content Agency, April 13, 2018.

Examples of rapacious African leaders using London as a hiding place for stolen money are many, but one example in particular will suffice. In 2010, Christine Ibori-Ibie, sister of the former Delta State governor James Ibori, was convicted in the United Kingdom for helping her brother steal $101.5 million from the state, which she stashed in UK bank accounts. Ibori-Ibie was found guilty of nine counts of money laundering and mortgage fraud, jailed for five years and ordered to return all the proceeds of her criminal act. Three others—a former Delta State governor, Emmanuel Uduaghan; his deputy Professor Amos Utuama, and David Edevbie, who was Ibori's commissioner of finance—were absent and could not be tried before the London court. In February 2012, James Ibori himself pleaded guilty before a UK court to 10 counts of conspiracy to launder money and to obtain money by deception and fraud and was sentenced to 13 years in prison. He was freed in 2016 after serving part of the sentence.

Another governor of Bayelsa State in the core Niger Delta region allegedly stockpiled an estimated $55 million overseas, bought mansions in the United States, and sent his children to private schools in England. The official established an offshore company in the United Kingdom which he used as a conduit for illegal money destined for banking in Europe. He was impeached in 2005, and part of the loot suspected to have been stolen from the public was recovered and restored to the Bayelsa state. Such cases question the United Kingdom's commitment to tackling corruption overseas. In October 2016, the British House of Commons resolved that any British commitment must go beyond the concern over the cost of corruption to the United Kingdom's economy and extend to countries and citizens around the world who are being held back, and often held in poverty, by corrupt activity.[64]

The United Kingdom has also been blasted by critics for using aid

---

[64] UK House of Commons, "Tackling Corruption Overseas," International Development Committee, 4th Report of Session 2016–17, October 11, 2016, 5.

as a smokescreen to hide the exploitation of Africa.[65] The country offers aid, loans, and investments to sub-Saharan countries but uses its power and influence to ensure that British mining companies dominate Africa's raw materials. One report claims 101 companies listed on the London Stock Exchange (LSE)—most of them British—have mining operations in 37 sub-Saharan countries and control $1 trillion of the continent's most valuable resources, including copper, platinum, diamonds, oil, gas, and coal.[66] This scenario appears to support what Walter Rodney, the Guyanese academic and social justice agitator, said in 1973, that the way Africa helped to develop the West was the same way the West is helping to under-develop Africa through resource manipulation.

---

[65] Chloe Farand, "Black Gold: Mapping London's African Oil Hub," *Desmoguk*, May 14, 2018.
[66] "The New Colonialism: Britain's Scramble for Africa's Energy and Mineral Resources," *War on Want*, article, July 2016.

CHAPTER 4

THE SCRAMBLE FOR OIL

Oil creates an illusion of a completely changed life, life without work, life for free. Oil is a resource that anaesthetizes thought, blurs vision, corrupts. – Ryszard Kapuscinski, Shah of Shahs

If there is one sector in Africa that is most exploited by MNCs and continues to be the cause of foreign-supported armed conflicts between political groups locked in debilitating rivalries, it is oil. The black gold has, and continues to be, at the center of warfare in numerous sub-Saharan African countries where millions of people continue to die needlessly as leaders fight for control of oilfields. And even in countries where mass conflicts have been avoided, the so-called "oil curse" has resulted in mass disenchantment, extreme poverty, terrorism, and rebellion. This is because oil wealth is traditionally concentrated in the hands of a few capricious elites in government and business. To make it worse, MNCs extracting oil in Africa, much like those in power, don't seem interested in the welfare of locals or their environment and tend to listen only to corrupt and insatiably greedy politicians willing to accommodate their interests. This is evident in countries like Equatorial Guinea, Angola, and Nigeria, where ignominious African leaders and their regimes have been "captured" by multinationals.

By threading their way into the African mindset, venal foreign companies have succeeded in exploiting the continent. In the process, they make a lot of money, but when caught by the law, the ramifications are usually severe.

A serious breach of criminal law

Rolls-Royce, established in 1904, is a major manufacturer of luxury cars and world-class power and propulsion systems, but its history of bribery and corruption goes back to the early 1980s, when the company agreed to pay two third-party intermediaries (TPIs) $18.8 million to secure a tender for T800 engines for Thai Airways. Those who received the bribe money were government employees and officials of Thai Airways. TPIs are companies that handle sales, distribution, and maintenance in countries where a firm does not have enough people on the ground. In 2017, the SFO accused the engineering giant of 12 counts of failure to prevent bribery, conspiracy to corrupt, and false accounting. Rolls-Royce did not reveal the names of recipients, even after a formal request was made in February 2017 by Thai president Jarumporn Chotikasathien. Thai Airways eventually secured the tender, and the money paid to the TPIs was referred to as "success fees."

In addition, the SFO identified 12 middlemen the firm had retained to broker lucrative deals in 12 countries: Nigeria, Angola, South Africa, Saudi Arabia, Azerbaijan, Kazakhstan, Brazil, Iraq, Iran, China, India, and Indonesia. A 2016 investigation by the British Broadcasting Corporation (BBC) and *The Guardian* newspaper found Rolls-Royce was using illegal payments to boost its business in those countries. The engine manufacturing giant admitted that between 2000 and 2013, it paid more than $35 million in bribes to officials in those countries to provide confidential information on bids. In Angola, it paid $2.4 million and was awarded three contracts. In Nigeria, it paid unspecified bribes and got two energy infrastructure contracts, though it eventually pulled out of the deal.

Described by a UK court as "a jewel in UK's industrial crown,"[67] Rolls-Royce agreed to pay $671 million to finalize cases with the SFO and $170 million to the DOJ. In Brazil, the company reached an agreement with the prosecutor's office to pay $25 million to authorities after admitting giving a $200,000 bribe to an official of the state-owned Petrobras in a $100 million contract to supply turbine generators.

The judge, Sir Brian Leveson, said in his judgment in May 2017 that Rolls-Royce had participated in the most serious breaches of criminal law in the areas of bribery and corruption. The company apologized for its action, saying in a statement in January 2017 that the uncovered bribery in the past does "not reflect the manner in which Rolls-Royce does business today."[68] Many pundits thought Rolls-Royce was treated leniently for a grievous crime, especially

---

[67] "The Rolls-Royce Case Lands the UK's Serious Fraud Office in the Anti-Corruption Big Leagues," Anti-Corruption & Governance Center, blog, February 24, 2017.
[68] "Rolls-Royce Apologies after 671 Million BP Bribery Settlement," *BBC*, news, January 18, 2017.

after the court in Britain ruled the fine would be paid in installments on an interest-free five-year payment schedule.

"You bribe, we get you"

For the past few decades, global tobacco multinational companies have fought to capture the African and Asian markets to boost declining sales in the West. In some countries, that fight has featured criminal tendencies. The Swiss-based Alliance One International and the Virginia-headquartered Universal Corporation are rated as "smoke" leaders, accounting for 70 percent of the market share in the leaf tobacco industry.[69] Both are global companies relied upon by cigarette manufacturers for quality tobacco leaves. But that is not where their similarities end.

In 2010, the two companies were cited by the DOJ for conspiracy to violate the FCPA by paying bribes to overseas officials and violating the books and records provisions of the FCPA. Their subsidiaries, Alliance One International AG (AOIAG) of Switzerland and Alliance One Tobacco Osh, LLC (AOI-Kyrgyzstan), as well as Universal Leaf Tabacos Ltda of Brazil (Universal Brazil), pleaded guilty before a West Virginia district court to three separate counts of bribing Thai government officials to secure contracts for the sale of tobacco leaves to the state-run Thailand Tobacco Monopoly. AOI-Kyrgyzstan also pleaded guilty to bribing Kyrgyzstan government officials in connection with the purchase of Kyrgyz tobacco.

AOIAG was ordered to pay a criminal fine of $9.45 million and surrender $10 million in profits, while AOI-Kyrgyzstan was fined $4.4 million and asked to return $4.5 million in profits. The parent companies entered into a non-prosecution agreement with the DOJ in which the companies were to retain an independent compliance monitor for a minimum of three years to oversee the implementation of an anti-bribery and anti-corruption compliance

---

[69] "What is Alliance One International's Fundamental Value?" *Forbes*, March 23, 2018.

program and to report periodically to the department.[70]

Alliance One was also singled out for making improper payments in China, Greece, and Indonesia, while Universal was named for bribing officials in Malawi and Mozambique. In Malawi, subsidiaries of Universal Corporation and Alliance One International reportedly operated as a cartel to smuggle low-cost raw tobacco from the neighboring countries of Zambia and Mozambique with the intention of undermining local farmers and the government. In 2006, a fuming President Bingu Mutharika of Malawi asked the transgressing companies to uphold ethical standards or leave, but due to the unrestrained trade powers the two firms commanded in that country, nothing happened.

Another cigarette giant, the $75 billion British multinational cigarette and tobacco manufacturer British American Tobacco (BAT), was accused of manipulating through bribery politicians and officials in Kenya, Uganda, Burundi, Rwanda, and the Comoros Islands, plus one former member of the World Health Organization (WHO), to secure business and frustrate efforts to pass anti-tobacco legislation.

In Uganda, the BBC *Panorama* program reported that BAT recruited a Ugandan MP to "infiltrate, influence, and spy on the cohort of anti-tobacco activists in Uganda in order to minimize legislative/political/regulatory risk for BAT."[71] It was also alleged that BAT, maker of the popular Dunhill brand, was targeting the most fragile, war-torn, and unstable countries in Africa and the Middle East,[72] such as South Sudan, the DRC, Iraq, and Syria, in their campaign to increase sales without caring about the lives of people in those volatile countries.

---

[70] US Department of Justice, "Alliance One International Inc., and Universal Corporation Resolve Related FCPA Matters Involving Bribes Paid to Foreign Government Officials," press release no. 10-903, August 6, 2010.
[71] Richard Bilton, "The Secret Bribes of Big Tobacco," *BBC Panorama*, November 30, 2015.
[72] Sarah Boseley, "Revealed: How British American Tobacco Exploited War Zones to Sell Cigarettes," *The Guardian,* August 18, 2017.

To undermine tobacco control bills in African countries, representatives of WHO's Framework Convention on Tobacco Control (FCTC) from Burundi and Comoros were allegedly paid $3,000 each, and a former representative from Rwanda $20,000, claimed the BBC's *Panorama* program in November 2015. The program also linked a Kenyan trade minister and a justice minister with having received favors of travel and cash. The minister denied the charge, but Martha Karua, leader of the political party National Rainbow Coalition (NARC), said she received the money but didn't know it was meant to be a bribe.

Hundreds of secret documents released by a whistleblower, former BAT employee Paul Hopkins, alleged the company had been bribing officials in East Africa for years. The documents also revealed letters had been sent to the governments of Namibia, Togo, Uganda, Gabon, the DRC, Burkina Faso, and Ethiopia, warning them that by legislating against tobacco company interests, they would be breaching their constitutions and international trade agreements and jeopardizing their economies. The bribery allegations reached the United Kingdom's SFO, which launched an investigation against BAT. In 2017, the company announced its own investigations, saying it took the issue "extremely seriously."[73] The outcome of those investigations is unknown.

The aggressive methods used by tobacco multinationals to promote their products in Africa also involve aggressive spying against rivals and bribing tax and police officers. Whistleblower Hopkins claimed that BAT paid "a shed load of money"[74] to high-ranking Kenya Revenue Authority (KRA) officials to spy on and acquire files of BAT's main rival, Mastermind Tobacco, as well as make tax demands to Mastermind in order to intimidate and ruin the company's reputation. He also claimed BAT set aside $43,000 to bribe five union officials to organize workers to disrupt operations

---

[73] Simon English, "Serious Fraud Office Probe into Tobacco Giant BAT on 'Bribery' Claims," *The Evening Standard,* August 1, 2017.

[74] "US Government Urged to Reject BAT-Reynolds Merger over Bribes to Kenyan Officials," *Money Markets*, February 7, 2017.

at the rival company.

For unexplained reasons, the Office of the Prime Minister in Kenya dragged itself into the bribery allegations when it sent a letter to KRA on May 4, 2010 asking the tax agency to stop freezing Mastermind's bank accounts with respect to tax arrears estimated at billions of Kenyan shillings. The intervention by the prime minister's office into the issue raised suspicion that bribery could have extended beyond the KRA. In its response to the allegations, BAT defended itself by saying it does not tolerate corruption no matter where it takes place.[75]

In South Africa, BAT allegedly paid a security firm to spy on competitors using cameras. A former employee of Forensic Security Services (FSS) swore an affidavit in 2016 confirming the espionage scheme as BAT struggled to control the multimillion-dollar trade in South Africa. BAT South Africa cut ties with the FSS after the allegations emerged. The Cape Town-based AmaBhungane Centre for Investigative Journalism said in a report that the scramble for domination of the tobacco industry in South Africa is "fraught with subterfuge and deception with double and triple agents all employed and deployed to protect massive tobacco profits," adding that many of the operatives were former apartheid-era spies, spooks, and cops.[76]

Oil contracts

The Dutch company SBM Offshore N.V., maker of offshore oil drilling equipment, and its US subsidiary SBM Offshore USA Incorporated is another foreign company caught in a bribery scandal abroad. While the company earned more than $2.8 billion in profits from fraudulent deals, it paid out $240 million in fines to the Dutch government and $342 million to Brazilian authorities in

---

[75] "The Secret Bribes of Big Tobacco Paper Trail," *BBC,* news, November 30, 2015.
[76] Marianne Thamm, "SARS Wars: Massive Data Leak Alleges British American Tobacco SA's Role in Bribery and Corruption," *The Daily Maverick,* August 16, 2016.

2017. SBM Offshore N.V. and SBM Offshore USA Incorporated were indicted in the Southern District of Texas before Judge David Hittner for an offense committed between 1996 and 2012. It involved a conspiracy to remit more than $180 million to third parties in exchange for lucrative oil-services contracts, knowing very well that part of the money was to be used to bribe government officials in Angola, Brazil, Equatorial Guinea, Iraq, and Kazakhstan. SBM Offshore and its US subsidiary pleaded guilty to violating the FCPA.

Anthony "Tony" Mace, a UK citizen and former board member of SBM's US subsidiary, and Robert Zubiate, an American citizen and former sales marketing executive at SBM USA, were sentenced by a Houston court to 36 months and 30 months respectively for paying bribes to officials of state-owned companies: Petrobras in Brazil, Sonangol in Angola, and GEPetrol in Equatorial Guinea. They were also fined $150,000 and $50,000 respectively.

According to the DOJ, Mace maintained a spreadsheet showing payments he authorized to five Equatorial Guinea officials amounting to $16 million, as well as payments to SBM's Brazilian intermediary, deliberately ignoring the fact that the ultimate recipients were Petrobras officials. Zubiate also acknowledged using a third-party sales agent to pay bribes to Petrobras officials. In November 2017, SBM agreed to sign a three-year, $238 million deferred prosecution agreement (DPA) with the United States over its role in the conspiracy, while SBM USA pleaded guilty to one count of conspiracy to violate the FCPA. A DPA is an arrangement in which a prosecutor agrees to offer amnesty on the condition the defendant fulfills certain conditions. In this case, SBM was to put in place an enhanced system of internal controls to address and mitigate corruption and compliance risks, in addition to demoting or sacking employees who were involved in the misconduct.

PART TWO

CHAPTER 5

EAST AFRICA

Corruption should be treated in the same way as treason … it is ridiculous that we are concerned with punishing petty thieves and ridiculing prostitutes who resort to shameful acts out of necessity, while we condone people in high positions who take bribes. – Tanzania's Julius Nyerere, addressing the nation in Dodoma, 1978

KENYA

The economy of Kenya is heavily dependent on MNCs. The total number of MNCs in the country is hard to discern, since more companies are entering the country than leaving. In the 1990s, MNCs in the nation's capital of Nairobi were limited to just over a dozen: BAT, Coca-Cola, British Petroleum, General Electric, General Motors, Citibank, Barclays, Exxon, Shell, IBM, Del Monte, Lonrho, Unilever, and Cadbury Schweppes. By 2018, dozens more had been added on to the list, including the International Finance Corporation (IFC), Visa International, Pepsi, Nestlé, General Electric, PwC, Huawei, Proctor and Gamble, South Africa's First Rand Bank, Google, and dozens of state-owned Chinese companies. Numerous MNCs are listed on the Nairobi Stock Exchange, making East Africa's most cosmopolitan city a leading regional destination for multinational firms. In 2015, *Fortune* magazine named Kenya as one of seven outstanding emerging markets worth investing in globally, and in 2018 it again named Nairobi, along with Casablanca, Dubai, Johannesburg, Lagos, and Cairo, as a city with the highest appeal for foreign companies. In 2016, the cable network CNN ranked Kenya among the top eight emerging markets investors should embrace.[77]

Although Kenya still ranks high as an attractive destination for investors in sub-Saharan Africa, there are firms which choose to skip the country for other destinations. Demand for bribes by public officials, delays in issuing licenses and permits, and huge inflows of cheap merchandise and counterfeits are some of the reasons why foreign investors skip Kenya for other destinations. In one case, Samsung aspired to set up a regional office in Nairobi to cater to eastern Africa. Those plans were abandoned after "a top government official asked for a USD $10 million parting kickback

---

[77] Medrine Nyambura, "KEPSA Offers Solutions to Corruption in Kenya," Hapa Kenya, article, May 19, 2016.

for the license."[78] Samsung moved to Ethiopia. The giant South Korean electronics maker also cancelled plans to build an assembly plant for television sets, laptops, and printers promised in 2014, citing Kenya's unwillingness to offer protection from cheap imports, especially from China. The same reason was given by chocolate maker Cadbury Kenya and battery manufacturer Eveready East Africa before they closed shop in 2014 and left. Similarly, Aliko Dangote, the Nigerian billionaire, planned to extend his vast empire to Kenya in 2018 by purchasing two companies, one for limestone mining and another for cement production, but scrapped the plans on account of rampant corruption. "There are people in that place [Kenya]," Dangote dejectedly told a Nairobi journalist, "who put greed and personal interest ahead of national interest. I didn't think Kenyans would be more corrupt than Nigerians."[79] Dangote did not name the individuals, and the Kenyan government did not react to that damning accusation.

Government officials, from immigration to customs officers and top public servants whose responsibility includes approving major projects, are always ready to cash in on investors willing to pay bribes. Data provided by the Ethics and Anti-Corruption Commission (EACC) in 2018 showed the average bribe for tenders is $2,000, but that amount can go up exponentially depending on the cost of the project.

The growth of the bribery industry in Kenya has boosted a network of secret bank accounts in offshore destinations abroad where recipients of ill-gotten monies hide their loot. In recent years, the number of Kenyans stashing away illicit money in Switzerland, Mauritius, Dubai, the Caribbean, and the Channel Islands, among other places, has risen. Seeing a substantial increase in offshore banking, the Kenyan government announced in 2016 an amnesty that shields account holders from the requirement of declaring the

---

[78] Mfonobong Nsehe, "Corruption and 'Tenderpreneurs' Bring Kenya's Economy to Its Knees," *Forbes*, article, December 1, 2015.
[79] Paul Wanjama, "Aliko Dangote Reveals Why He Aborted Plans of Investing in Kenya," Kenyans.co.ke, article, August 21, 2018.

source of their money or even accounting for previous tax returns. Within three years, 1,600 owners of offshore accounts responded and wired back to the country approximately KSh1 trillion (about $10 billion).[80] In 2018, however, the National Bureau of Economic Research (NBER)—a private American research organization—estimated that $50 billion was still being held by Kenyans in offshore tax havens.

In 2009, Kenya enacted the Proceeds of Crime and Anti-Money Laundering Act (POCAMLA) to target money laundering, tax evasion, terrorist financing, bribery and corruption, theft, fraud, and drug trafficking. The legislation was adopted following alarming reports of money laundering in the banking sector. A former internal auditor of Charter House Bank turned whistleblower, reported that the institution—nicknamed "a money laundering machine"[81]—had evaded taxes and engaged in money laundering to the tune of $1.5 billion. Among the bank's customers were some of the biggest drug kingpins in the country, a number of them on the blacklist of the US government.

In Jersey, a court in 2016 stripped a Jersey-registered company, Windward Trading Limited, of more than $4.5 million in assets after finding it guilty of laundering money for a former Kenyan Cabinet minister and the CEO of the state-run electricity company, between 1999 and 2001. The court ordered the seizure of millions of dollars in Jersey accounts belonging to the two and ordered their extradition to face money laundering, fraud, and misconduct charges. The court heard Windward was a conduit for kickbacks allegedly paid by companies to win Kenya Power tenders. By end of 2019, the two officials were yet to be extradited to the United Kingdom.

---

[80] "Kenyans Wire Back Sh1trn in Offshore Bank Accounts," *Business Daily*, May 21, 2019.

[81] Euphemia Godspower-Akpomiemie and Kalu Ojah, "Money Laundering, Tax Havens, Transparency and Board of Directors of Banks, Munich Personal RePEc Archive, Paper no. 89550, March 27, 2018.

In 2016, the government launched investigations of several multinational companies suspected of tax evasion and money laundering. One of the companies was ZTE Kenya Limited, a subsidiary of the controversy-ridden Chinese technology conglomerate ZTE. For years, the company had defied requests from the KRA to provide documents of financial status and had refused to respond to correspondence that could determine taxes owed. The taxman was demanding $14 million in unpaid taxes over a five-year period. It is unknown whether the KRA ever received the money.

In an unrelated case in August 2016, a director of the state-owned China Aero Technology International Engineering Corporation (AVIC-ENG), affiliated with the government Aviation Industry Corporation of China (AVIC), Huang Hongyou, was charged on several counts of failing to file tax returns. The bank accounts of New X-Tigi Technology Company, a Chinese software manufacturing firm, were frozen following allegations that it was evading taxes and stashing profits in a Hong Kong bank. Another Chinese firm, Housemart Company Limited, had to cough up $22 million in October 2018 to settle a tax matter after its accounts were closed by the KRA. The importer of construction materials and household commodities had earlier gone to court to fight closure after the tax body discovered the company was depositing money in seven other companies in order to reduce its income tax and VAT. Housemart executives denied links with any of the seven named companies.

Early in 2019, dozens of KRA employees were questioned by investigators for assisting traders in using port facilities to evade taxes. The evasion was contributing to the government's failure to meet its tax targets. In 2019, the state had to borrow from overseas facilities to plug a $110 million hole in its $30 billion budget.

In November 2018, the KRA told the local publication the *Daily Nation* that it had recovered $9.3 million over a period of four years from 150 multinationals operating in the country. The cat-and-mouse game between crafty Chinese entities and tax authorities in East Africa had been going on for years. In neighboring Uganda, the tax collector found that out of 148 companies caught evading taxes, 90 were Chinese. The Uganda Revenue Authority (URA) stripped them of their tax clearance certificates (TCCs) issued for the year 2017/2018 and annulled the input tax arising from the fake invoices they had submitted to the URA.

Similarly, in Tanzania, the state-owned China Communications Construction Company Limited (CCCC) had its equipment temporarily detained by the government in early 2018 when it attempted to leave the country without paying millions of dollars in taxes from the construction of the 260-kilometer Dodoma-Iringa road. The government also named two other companies with outstanding taxes: China Henan International Cooperation Group (CHICO) and the China Railway Seventh Group (CRSG), a subsidiary of the giant China Railway Group Limited.

Two other foreigners, Le Van Dai, a Vietnamese national and the head of Halotel Tanzania, and Sherif El Barbary, the Egyptian managing director of the Zanzibar telecoms company Zantel, were in 2018 charged in Dar es Salaam with tax evasion. They were accused of illegally importing communications equipment, circumventing the state's telecommunications traffic monitoring system, and occasioning a loss of $530,000 in levies to the government. Four others—Chinese citizens Lei Cao and Huang Yu Meng of Shunshe Company Limited, and two Tanzanians, Jimmy Mosha and Willy Ndoni of Halotel—also faced charges for using unregistered SIM cards and operating illegally between January 2017 and April 2018. All such cases corroborate widely circulating assertions, especially in the Western media, that some Chinese companies are not only corrupt but also deceptive in the way they conduct business.

In 2019, the US government listed Kenya among global hotspots for money laundering. Washington said the country had insufficient controls on the circulation of ill-gotten money just like Pakistan,

Afghanistan, Azerbaijan, Canada, China, Mexico, Russia, and others. The US Department of State Bureau for International Narcotics and Law Enforcement Affairs said money laundering in Kenya was fueled by domestic and foreign criminal operations that take advantage of Kenya's liberal laws and the vibrancy of the financial sector.

A graft-blighted society?

Some have described Kenya as a "graft-blighted society,"[82] a country so ravaged by graft that many of its citizens have given up hope in their leaders. The TI CPI ranked the country as the 144th least corrupt country out of 175 nations, compared to a record low of 52 in 1996. More than a dozen MNCs and foreign companies have been linked to corruption scandals in Kenya, among them the tire company Goodyear, BAT, Israeli construction group Shikun & Binui, several UK-based firms, the US courier FedEx, and a host of Chinese companies. They all entered the list of shame for collaborating with Kenyan public officials to steal public money.

In 2010, a UK company specializing in security documents including ballot and examination papers, Smith and Ouzman (S&O), was taken to court and convicted in London in December 2015 for bribing officials of the Interim Independent Electoral Commission, now known as the Independent Electoral and Boundaries Commission (IEBC), in regard to the printing of electoral materials, and for compromising officials of the Kenya National Examination Council regarding test papers.

The SFO claimed in court documents that S&O paid $545,091 to IEBC officials through an intermediary to obtain a tender for the materials. Two company executives, Christopher Smith and Nicholas Smith, were convicted in 2014 in what came to be known as the "chickengate" scandal, the code used to describe the commissions. The former was jailed for 18 months, the sentence

---

[82] Michela Wrong, *It's Our Turn to Eat: The Story of a Kenyan Whistle-Blower* (HarperCollins, 2009), 261.

suspended for two years, and the latter was imprisoned for three years. Some top officials of the Kenyan electoral body and Kenya National Examinations Councils who allegedly received bribes from S&O were charged in court, but by 2019—when the two British convicts had already left jail—the case was still pending. The Kenyan suspects denied receiving illegal payments. The failure of the Kenyan government to prosecute its nationals in the scandal is a further demonstration of classic impunity and a show of political unwillingness to fight corruption characterized in all administrations since independence in 1963.

In 2010, S&O was implicated in an almost-similar bribery incident in Mauritania in which $76,182 was paid to an official of the Ministry of the Interior; in Ghana, where $38,403 was illegally paid to agents to bribe officials to win a $903,000 tender for the supply of examination materials; and in Somaliland, where the company allegedly paid $32,000 to an agent, part of which was meant for electoral officials.

At the time the "chickengate" scandal exploded, the WB slapped Macmillan Publishers Ltd with a three-year ban for bribing South Sudanese officials in an unsuccessful bid to secure a book contract. Two years of investigation and a raid at the company offices by the City of London's police led the SFO to charge Macmillan Publishers. Apart from being banned from taking part in WB projects, the company was fined $17.7 million by the SFO. The firm also agreed to audit its operations in Uganda, Rwanda, and Zambia during the period between 2002 and 2009.

Also banned by the WB were two subsidiaries of Oxford University Press for allegedly making illegal payments to government officials in Kenya and Tanzania in exchange for contracts to supply school textbooks between 2007 and 2010. Oxford University Press East Africa Limited and Oxford University Press Tanzania Limited were blacklisted in 2012 and prohibited from bidding for WB-funded projects. The company agreed to pay $500,000 to the WB as part of a negotiated settlement. It also committed to contributing $2.5

million to non-profit educational organizations in sub-Saharan Africa.

The revelations of misconduct were a big blow to the reputation of the two giant British publishing companies that have been associated with Africa for decades. No known action was taken against those involved in any of the three African countries.

Anti-corruption legislation

About three years after assuming office, President Uhuru Kenyatta took a seemingly more positive role against corruption which went far beyond the hitherto empty promises by his administration. He spearheaded the enactment of a tough anti-corruption legislation called the Bribery Act 2016, which provides stiff penalties of fines, jail terms, and blacklisting of individuals and companies that give or receive bribes in exchange for influence or favors. The Act bars company directors found to have violated the Act from serving in any other company for up to a decade, and individuals found guilty of bribing or receiving bribes from a foreign official from contesting elections for public office. The law came into effect on January 13, 2017.

The new legislation, modeled on the United Kingdom's Bribery Act 2010, was widely welcomed by the private sector in Kenya which, for years, had maintained silence on corruption even as public officials were being roasted for participating in graft, especially in illegal procurement practices. For the first time, in 2017, the Kenya Private Sector Alliance (KEPSA) admitted corruption was rife in the private sector and stated the organization had no moral authority to stand up to government when it came to graft. Vimal Shah, the chief executive of a local MNC, Bidco Oil Refineries, agreed: "The private sector often points out the high levels of corruption in government, but we overlook the fact that the vice is alive within the private sector itself."[83] Hundreds of companies and thousands

---

[83] Frankline Sunday, "Private Sector Corruption on the Rise, Endangers Long Term Investment," *The Standard* Digital News, January 28, 2015.

of employees of companies affiliated with KEPSA have signed a code of conduct in line with the UN Global Compact Initiative, which revolves around the key areas of anti-corruption, environmental protection, human rights, and labor standards. The code encourages firms to conduct clean business and demonstrate efforts against bribery and corruption in their operations.

Sebastian Gatimu, a researcher at the Pretoria-based Institute for Security Studies (ISS), said that in every public-sector corruption scandal, there are one or several private-sector companies involved: "It takes crooked, rent-seeking business people, banks and companies—local and foreigners—supported by equally unethical accountants and lawyers to arrange the bribes, to front shady companies and to channel the loot."[84] Navigating Kenya's corrupt bureaucracy presents a gigantic hurdle for businesspeople and investors. One must be prepared to pay kickbacks for everything, from the mundane activity of acquiring a birth certificate or a driver's license to the more complicated process of bidding for tenders and registering property, which require the intervention of lawyers and banks.

There are also kickback payments that are bizarre in nature. In 2014, a cargo ship packed high with containers entered the Kenyan port of Mombasa after a month-long, wavy journey from Stockholm, Sweden. Anxiously awaiting the vessel in the coastal town was Hans-Frederik Dydensborg, president of Global Medical Aid. The organization had collected medical equipment, including scanners, microscopes, and endoscopy and X-ray equipment, among other items, for donation to a rural hospital in Kenya. All along, Dydensborg had been corresponding with a Kenyan who claimed to run a foundation for disadvantaged people and had requested assistance from Dydensborg. However, upon arrival, the person who was supposed to meet the Danish lawyer to clear the goods worth $30,000 was nowhere to be found. Instead, he

---

[84] Caroline Mutoko, "Private Sector Corruption is Dangerous," *The Star* (Kenya), November 16, 2015.

left a message asking Dydensborg to pay a kickback of $20,000 to port customs officers to have the goods released. On checking, the philanthropist discovered the so-called foundation was a briefcase organization owned by a Kenyan MP and that the whole arrangement was a scam. When he returned to Kenya two years later, Dydensborg found the goods had accumulated a tax bill of $70,000 and storage charges amounting to tens of thousands of dollars. Disappointed and feeling betrayed, the Danish citizen abandoned the cargo and flew back home.[85] Such cases of manipulation where foreign entities—especially religious organizations—are tricked into parting with money for diverse purposes have discouraged many philanthropists from helping alleviate poverty and hunger in the country.

Kenya's ports of entry, especially the deep sea-port of Mombasa, are an internationally known conduit for illegal smuggling of contraband ranging from animal products such as elephant tusks to illicit drugs and stolen vehicles from overseas. In May 2019, detectives caught four 20-foot containers of smuggled ethanol in Nairobi declared as imported spaghetti. The ethanol from the United Arab Emirates (UAE) was worth $150,000 and was suspected to have come through the border with Tanzania. Ethanol is a hot commodity in Kenya, used by illegal manufacturers to produce illicit brews which are then sold cheaply to residents of sprawling slum colonies in major towns. One report said the smuggling of the potent chemical is costing Kenya $49 billion a year.[86] Hundreds of Kenyans have died from drinking alcohol made from ethanol, a product produced by the fermentation of agricultural products such as corn and sugarcane. It depresses the central nervous system and leads to death.

---

[85] Daniel Tsuma Nyassy, "Donor Takes Back Sh30M Equipment after Refusing to Give Out Kickbacks," *Daily Nation*, July 9, 2016.
[86] "An Inside Job: Kenya's Struggles to Stop Ethanol Smuggling," *The East Africa Monitor*, April 29, 2019.

Kickbacks are commonly a child of manipulated procurement processes. In 1998, a Kenyan minister failed to adequately respond to accusations made in Parliament that he, his permanent secretary, and a chief supplies officer had received kickbacks to approve a $460,000 drug tender, and that a director of a company contracted to supply drugs to the government medical stores received a share from the controversial deal. For a whole week, Kenya's Parliament discussed the deal with one MP, Orwa Ojodeh, pummeling the minister of health, Jackson Kalweo, for allegedly conspiring with the company in which the permanent secretary and a supplies officer had an interest. Kalweo denied the allegation. In May 1999, Attorney General Amos Wako ordered an investigation into the claims after it emerged that despite payment, the drugs were not supplied. At the end of it, no action was taken against the officials.[87] Since then, the situation has worsened in the health sector, and bribes and kickbacks are distressingly commonplace. Patients pay bribes to access maternal care, to receive surgery and emergency treatment, and even to access mortuary services. In addition, foreign medical facilities are known to bribe doctors to get them to send patients to hospitals abroad. In 2016, the Kenya Ministry of Health lamented about Indian hospitals offering Kenyan medical workers kickbacks of up to $2,000 per patient to get referrals, even in cases where treatment was available locally. The situation got so serious that in 2018 the ministry investigated 880 Kenyan doctors believed to be part of a cartel responsible for sending an estimated 10,000 cancer, kidney, joint replacement, and dental surgery patients to India every year, depriving the country of more than $100 million in revenue annually. The outcome of that investigation was not revealed.

---

[87] John Braithwaite, *Corporate Crime in the Pharmaceutical Industry* (Routledge & Kegan Paul, 1984), 24–26.

At least 70 percent of kickbacks from tenders in Kenya are due to fraudulent procurement methods.[88] Violation of those processes continues to take place despite the existence of the Public Procurement and Disposal Act and a host of Treasury circulars which set out tendering procedures to ensure fair, equitable, transparent, competitive, and cost-effective methods. And examples are many. In 2016, Kenyan officials approved a Chinese company blacklisted by the WB for a $400 million tender to build the Kipevu oil terminal at the Mombasa port. Fifteen companies sent bids, but they were all disqualified in favor of the disgraced CCCC, banned by the WB in 2009 for engaging in "collusive practices" in the Philippines. The ban was to expire in January 2017, but the tendering process in Kenya was started in 2016 when the restriction was still in effect. The state-owned Chinese firm contended that the WB ban related only to roads and bridges, which was not true. The ban was total. The EACC investigated the matter after suspecting graft and found the cost of the terminal had mysteriously gone up from $150 million to $250 million and then to $400 million. Each time the price went up, some greedy officials were earning commissions. The scandal of the Kipevu oil terminal was not unexpected, given the fact that the Kenya Ports Authority (KPA), the implementing agency of the project, has a dubious reputation for corruption. Dozens of top KPA officials have been arrested—and their cases were still pending by the end of 2019—for corrupt activities involving huge amounts of bribes and kickbacks for projects carried out mainly by Chinese contractors at the port.

On May 23, 2014, with much pomp, Uhuru Kenyatta broke ground at Jomo Kenyatta International Airport in Nairobi for the construction of a $65 million terminal to be known as Greenfield. It was an ambitious project, intended to expand the airport and cater to the growing number of arrivals. The ceremony alone cost the Kenyan taxpayers an astounding $750,000, and its itemization

---

[88] Mfonobong Nsehe, "Corruption and 'Tenderpreneurs' Bring Kenya's Economy to its Knees," Forbes, article, December 1, 2015.

was questionable. In addition, a consultant was paid $1.3 million, and a global auditing firm pocketed $70,000 for finding a financier. The tender was issued in 2011 to two Chinese companies, Anhui Construction Engineering Group and AVIC-ENG, which were paid $43 million in advance of the commencement of work. The initial contract was for $654 million, but in 2013 a variation was made which added another $95 million, supposedly to cater to a 16 percent VAT, even though the original figure had taken all taxes into consideration. That raised a red flag. It pointed to something fishy and attracted strident criticisms over the way the whole process had been undertaken. By the end of 2019, the government had not made its position clear on what it wanted to do with the culprits. In advanced jurisdictions, heads would have rolled.

Then followed a public verbal tussle between a top Cabinet official and the management of the Kenya Airports Authority over the implementation of the Greenfield project. The latter wanted the project terminated altogether, claiming it was no longer tenable, while the former insisted it had to proceed to save the government from embarrassment. Several government agencies had warned against the contract before it was awarded, partly because no funds had been allocated by the Treasury. There were also doubts as to whether the project had been approved by the Cabinet, notwithstanding the presence of the president at the ground-breaking ceremony. At the center of those wrangles was a disagreement over kickbacks amounting to tens of thousands of dollars. But the key questions were: was there not a feasibility study to confirm the project's viability before a commitment was made? And why did officials proceed with the processes when they knew there was no money? In 2016 the government cancelled the tender. By the end of 2019, the site was still empty, and the fate of the advance money paid to the Chinese companies remained unknown. The Parliamentary Public Investment Committee, which interrogates the finances of government agencies, said the project "could have been a conspiracy to swindle the public." In 2019, Anhui Construction Engineering Group sent a notice to the government demanding $50 million even though it had not done the work, signaling what could be a protracted fight.

The dam debacle

In 2019, a group of three Kenyan Cabinet ministers and top officials quietly slipped out of the country for Rome, Italy. The reason for their travel was to collect kickbacks from contractors bidding for tenders involving dam construction projects in Kenya. Government investigators suspected the officials could have pocketed up to $40 million in bribes from the contractors in the $660 million deal. The money was reportedly wired to an Italian company in 2017, surreptitiously rerouted to a London bank, and then transferred to a facility in the Kenyan capital of Nairobi, where it was withdrawn by unknown people. The zigzag manner in which the money was conveyed was typical of a money-laundering scheme. Who were the officials who collected the loot in Kenya? Investigators wanted to find out. Suspicion zeroed in on officials of the Ministry of Water and Sanitation and the Ministry of Finance.

This is how the scandal played out. The Italian contracting company, Co-operativa Muratoi e Cementisti, through its Kenyan subsidiary, CMC di Ravenna, was awarded the $660 million tender to construct two dams, Kimwarer and Arror in the Rift Valley, under the supervision of the state corporation, the Kerio Valley Development Authority. The works, nevertheless, were not carried out, and in the midst of investigations into the matter, CMC di Ravenna— which had already received a down payment of $210 million— quietly closed shop and vanished from the sites. Executives of the company denied wrongdoing but offered to cooperate with the Kenya government. Reports of the company's mysterious departure, however, alarmed the director of public prosecutions, Noordin Haji, and the director of criminal investigations (DCI), George Kinoti, and one could feel fits of unrestrained fury coming from the two crime-busters. The two officials then travelled to Italy for further investigations, and soon thereafter, numerous officials including three ministers, former senior government officials, MPs, and executives of over 100 business entities, were summoned by the DCI to record statements. In July 2019, Treasury Cabinet secretary Henry Rotich, his permanent secretary Kamau Thugge, and two dozen other government officials were charged in court with abuse of office and conspiracy to defraud in relation to the scandal. They all pleaded not guilty. The arrests of the two top Treasury officials caused ripples in the financial pond and precipitated a cabinet reshuffle. In September 2019, Kenyatta cancelled the Kimwarer dam altogether and ordered a fresh process on the Arror dam.

Even as money was being stolen by the Italian construction company and investigations were ongoing over previous scams, the Kenyan government in May 2019 allocated another $250 million for dam construction through the notoriously corrupt National Irrigation Board (NIB), a government parastatal. NIB is a den of kickbacks, and dozens of its projects have been cited for procurement irregularities and outright theft and corruption. It has been cited by the auditor general on many occasions for inflating costs, undertaking ghost projects, and cooking financial books with respect to dams and irrigation schemes in which billions of dollars were lost.

In March 2019, Kenya's Parliament had to step in and stop the construction of 24 dams across the country worth $18 billion. It was alleged that officials did not do due diligence and may have received kickbacks to approve them.

The high rate of corruption in the dam sub-sector may be due to the fact that contractors tend to be recycled. CMC di Ravenna, which was under investigation for the Kimwarer and Arror dam scandal, was featured again in yet another dam project: the Lowaat dam in Turkana County. Though it was not selected from among the ten companies which bid for the $190 million project, the fact that it submitted an offer in the first place is itself an illustration of how far cartels can go to secure contracts. The winner of the

Lowaat dam contract, the China International Water and Electric Corporation (CWE), was not clean either. It had been blacklisted by six multilateral development banks (MDBs), including the WB and the African Development Bank (AfDB) in September 2014, for its shady activities in Uganda and Southeast Asia. The tender itself was questionable. The CWE had submitted a bid for $17.9 million, but officials unilaterally increased the amount to $18.5 million, supposedly to take care of kickbacks.

In 2017, a Chinese company was accused of bribing Kenyan politicians to secure a $360 million tender for the first phase of the Thwake multi-purpose dam in the eastern region. Each one of the politicians reportedly received $6,000 from Gezhouba Construction Group Corporation to influence the awarding of the tender. Suspicion of corruption on the deal surfaced as a minister and his principal secretary tore at each other over whether the tender should go to Gezhouba or to another company. Gezhouba and its subsidiaries were blacklisted by the WB and the AfDB for 18 months in 2015 over fraudulent practices in three bank-funded projects in China. The Kenya Ministry of Water and Irrigation, which issued the tender for the dam, had also given the same company a tender to construct the $680 million Northern Water Collector Tunnel in central Kenya.

Soleh Boneh International

The road construction industry is one of the most abused sectors in most developing countries, including Kenya. In 2010, The Kenya Ministry of Roads awarded a $140 million tender to Israeli's Housing & Construction Holding Company, known as Shikun & Binui (S&B), the parent company of Soleh Boneh International Ltd, for the construction of the Mau Summit-Kericho-Kisumu highway. The road, stretching a distance of 56 kilometers, was funded by the WB. Also, on the spot was a section of the Nairobi/Mombasa road, another WB project, which consumed $4.8 million.

As it turned out, according to Israeli officials, both contracts were issued to the company under murky circumstances, stoking embers of suspicion that S&B had bribed Kenyan government officials to obtain the tender. By early 2018, three years after work began, only 30 kilometers of the Mau Summit-Kericho-Kisumu road had been completed. On February 20, 2018, Israeli investigators, with support of the Kenya Police, raided the company offices in Israel and Kenya and arrested several company executives on allegations of being behind the bribes amounting to millions of shekels (the Israeli currency). The investigators confiscated bank records and documents.

A former accountant with S&B in Nairobi, Shai Skaf, said in court documents that the firm kept two books: one showing the real financial activities of the company and the other indicating amounts of bribes paid to public officials in East Africa. "When in Africa, be African," Skaf was allegedly told by his boss when he showed concern. "They all give and take bribes. Why do you think profitability here runs at 40 percent, and in Nigeria 65 percent, and in Israel 4 percent?"[89] Skaf claimed he was beaten by unknown people in Kenya in August 2016, and fled to Israel the following day.

In April 2019, Israeli police said they had gathered enough evidence to charge the accused company executives with bribery of a foreign public servant, misrepresentation of corporate documents, conspiracy, disruption of legal proceedings, money laundering, and misreporting to authorities, which were committed between 2008 and 2016.

As is normally the case when top Kenyan government officials are linked to big corruption scandals, the bribe recipients in the Israel connection were not named. No known investigation was conducted by the Kenyan authorities on the construction scandal, and if it was, the public was not informed. The WB, which also conducted its own investigation, had not released its report by the first quarter of 2019.

---

[89] Shuki Sadeh, "Bribery Scandal at Israeli Construction Giant Blows Cover Off Its Business Practices in Africa," *Haaretz*, March 9, 2018.

Soleh Boneh, which has had a substantial work portfolio in Africa since the 1960s, also stands accused of bribing officials in other African countries. *Haaretz*, an Israeli newspaper, quoted police as saying that eight people, current and former executives of Sole Boneh were involved in—or knew about—the methodical bribery of government officials in several African countries, including Nigeria, to get infrastructure projects. In Israel, the bribing of foreign officials was added to the criminal code in 2008 as part of the country's accession to the OECD and the UN Convention against Corruption. The offense carries a seven-year jail term.

TANZANIA

Even in the quasi-socialist African nation of Tanzania, formerly Tanganyika, middle-class citizens were catapulted to the ranks of millionaires through corruption, especially after the incorruptible founding father Julius Nyerere left office in 1985. Not that there was no corruption during Nyerere's tenure in office, but there was a leadership code that was strictly adhered to and criminal laws that were rigidly implemented, providing stiff jail penalties for graft, including 16 lashes. "If someone takes bribe," said Nyerere during one historic address in the capital of Dodoma, "both the giver and the receiver will swim in hot soup."[90] That warning did not however stop millions of dollars—especially during the last years of Nyerere's presidency—from changing hands in illicit deals in the mining, energy, and infrastructure sectors. The evil practice of corruption and bribery went full speed after Nyerere left and the rather languid Ali Hassan Mwinyi took over, culminating in donors freezing aid to the country in November 1994.

While in office, Nyerere always complained about the *magabacholi*, wealthy foreigners who exploited Tanzanians by sending their money abroad as the *walalahoi,* the ordinary people, suffered. He wished for the creation of Third World MNCs "owned by us and controlled by us to serve our purposes and to remain independent of the great Transnational Corporations which now dominate the world economic scene."[91] Nyerere's wish was partly accomplished. Today, African-owned multinationals— rebaptized African multinational enterprises (MNEs) by Westerners—though not as endowed and as global as their Western counterparts, are gradually making their presence felt globally.

---

[90] "Corruption is a Fracture which Will Disintegrate Tanzania – Nyerere," Jamii Forums, November 20, 2011.
[91] Julius Nyerere, "Unity for a New Order," speech at Arusha, February 12, 1979

The Dangote Group, a Nigerian multinational industrial giant and the largest African-owned conglomerate in sub-Saharan Africa, generating more than $4.5 billion in revenue per year, is already climbing the ladder in cement production, oil refineries, agriculture, and transportation. Its founder, Aliko Dangote, was noted by *Forbes* magazine in 2019 as Africa's richest man, with a net worth of $14 million. He retained that title for eight years in a row.

Orascom Construction Industries, based in Cairo, Egypt, and a family business of the Sawiri family specializing in industrial construction, infrastructure, and fertilizer businesses, is another example of Africa's rise in the international business theater. The company operates in 18 countries in Europe, North America, the Middle East, and Africa, and has an annual revenue of over $4 billion.

Then there are East African multinationals, including the Kenya Commercial Bank, Bidco Oil Refineries, and Britam Holdings. Several South African companies—among them MTN Group Limited, which deals in telecommunications; Gold Fields, in metals and mining products; and Steinhoff International Holdings, in furniture and homeware—have also gone global. The best coffee in New York, Boston, and Washington, DC cafes comes from Rwanda, a small eastern African country, under the brand name Bourbon Coffee. These may be baby steps compared to what the mammoth Western and Asiatic companies have accomplished, but they are nevertheless progressive steps toward a more broad-based future.

In Tanzania, the genesis of public corruption was the mass nationalization of the economy in the 1960s and the shortage of consumer goods that followed. Citizens desperate for survival and government officials anxious to take advantage of the situation saw corruption as an advantageous solution for both. People had to bribe to obtain supplies from cooperative stores. Government officials in those outlets became rich through bribes and kickbacks that streamed in like the waters of the Nile River.

After taking over from Mwinyi in 1995, President Benjamin Mkapa moved quickly to try to dismantle the corruption cartels that had entrenched themselves during Mwinyi's lackluster administration. He appointed a commission to investigate graft chaired by Prime Minister Joseph Warioba. That move led to the resignation in December 1966 of the deputy defense minister, Dr. Juma Ngasongwa, whose name appeared in the damning commission's report. He was subsequently exonerated and returned to the Cabinet. But not much of what was recommended in the corruption report was implemented, and the malfeasance continued.

From March 2012 to 2013, the government sought to raise money through a sovereign bond to fund water, electricity, and infrastructure projects as part of its five-year development plan. The bond was intended to raise $600 million through a placement by the Stanbic Bank of Tanzania (SBT) and the UK-based Standard Plc. SBT, a subsidiary of the Standard Plc, paid $6 million to a "local agent" by the name of Enterprise Growth Market Advisors (EGMA) as fees, which was 1 percent of the money raised for the government. The problem was that there was no competitive bidding. The $6 million was allegedly deposited at SBT in the account of EGMA, an advisory group headed by Harry Kitilya, who also served as the commissioner general of the state-owned Tanzania Revenue Authority.

The account at SBT was emptied within days, raising a red flag with the bank's management, who quickly alerted the SFO to the suspicious transactions. The money was allegedly withdrawn by a top executive of Tanzania's Capital Markets and Security Authority. The SFO, which investigated the matter on the basis that the banks had UK links, claimed the money was a bribe to get Tanzanian officials to favor Stanbic and Standard Bank in the bond deal, which yielded $8.4 million in fees, which the two institutions allegedly shared. Moreover, investigations found that EGMA did not provide any services pertaining to the transaction and therefore did not deserve any payment. The Standard Bank was named for failing to prevent the bribery, contrary to the UK Bribery Act 2010.

In the United States, the SEC in November 2015 charged Standard Bank Plc with failing to disclose EGMA's involvement in the bond offering to investors despite red flags suggesting some of the proceeds were going to EGMA for the purpose of influencing the Tanzanian government's selection of bankers for the transaction. The Standard Bank agreed to settle the SEC's charges by paying a $4.2 million penalty.

In the United Kingdom, on November 30, 2015, High Court judge Brian Leveson approved a DPA and ordered the Standard Bank Plc —which had by then become the ICBC Standard Bank Plc following the acquisition of a 60 percent share by China's ICBC in February 2015—to pay Tanzania $6 million plus interest. It also ordered it to pay $32.6 million for the settlement of the UK investigation and another $4.2 million for related charges. Approximately $7 million went to compensate Tanzania.

That was the first time since the UK Bribery Act 2010 came into force in July 2011 that the DPA arrangement had been used to settle a criminal matter. The DPA was introduced into British law in 2014 and provides that a company charged with wrongdoing may agree to sanctions that could include fines and additional supervision in return for legal proceedings being suspended.[92]

A former chief executive of Stanbic Bank, Bashir Awale, was fired, and the former head of investment banking, Shose Sinare, who introduced EGMA to the transaction, resigned from the bank in 2013. By April 2019, the Tanzanian government was still looking for two Kenyans linked to the transactions for questioning. Efforts to have the Nairobi authorities cooperate to have them extradited to Tanzania had not borne results by mid-2019.

---

[92] Estelle Shirbon, "British Court Approves Landmark Plea Deal over Standard Bank Bribery," Reuters, November 30, 2015.

The matter did not end there. In March 2019, Kitlya and four others were hauled into a Dar es Salaam court, accused of having facilitated the foreign bond issue, thus occasioning a loss of $6 million to the government. Facing the same charges of forgery, uttering false documents, obtaining money by false pretenses, money laundering, and organized crime were former Miss Tanzania Shose Mori Sinare, Stanbic Bank's former chief legal counsel Sioi Graham Solomon, and two Ministry of Finance officials—the Commissioner for Policy Analysis and Debt, Bedason Shallanda, and his assistant Alfred Misana.

Before that, in 2016, the Standard Chartered Bank (SCB) had found itself in a Dar es Salaam court accused of buying more than $100 million in "dirty debt" and using it to demand compensation from the government while knowing the loan had been part of a multimillion-dollar embezzlement scheme. The bank bought the debt from Independent Power Tanzania Limited (IPTL) in 2005, when the power plant project was in dire financial trouble and mired in corruption allegations. IPTL was incorporated in 1994 for purposes of constructing and operating the 100-megawatt diesel-fueled Tegeta power plant in Dar es Salaam.

The VIP Engineering and Marketing company had a 30 percent shareholding in IPTL, while Mechmar Corporation (Malaysia) Berhad—said to have close ties with Malaysian prime minister Mahathir Mohamed—was the majority owner, with 70 percent of shares. In January 2005, Mechmar went into receivership, and SCB (Hong Kong) bought IPTL's debt for $74 million using part of the funds in what was known as the Tegeta Escrow Account (TEA), opened after IPTL went into receivership. However, by the time the process of arbitration was over, more than half of the money in the TEA had already been paid to IPTL's new owner, Pan African Power Solutions (PAP), owned by Harbinder Singh Sethi. The wealthy Asian made his millions in Kenya from graft-ridden construction tenders given to him by President Daniel arap Moi.

In 2016, VIP went to the Supreme Court of New York demanding

$490 million in damages from the SCB Group, Mechmar, the Finnish engineering firm Wartsila Nederland BV, and Wartsila Tanzania Limited, accusing them of fraud, money laundering, corporate waste and oppression, diversion of funds, and conversion of IPTL and VIP property. The SCB denied the allegations, describing them as baseless and adding that the debt was legitimate.

In a related court filing in a Dar es Salaam court, the director of legal affairs in the Ministry of Lands, Housing and Human Settlements Development, Ruzonzibwa Mujunangoma, who was himself facing separate corruption charges, supported the charges against SCB, claiming the bank stole funds and assets from IPTL. Mujunangoma, as well as Theophillo John Bwakea, the principal engineer of the state-owned Rural Energy Agency, were alleged to have received $275,000 and $137,000 respectively from a consultant of VIP and the director of IPTL, James Rugemalira, in 2014, as a reward for favorably handling IPTL affairs as a provisional liquidator of IPTL after it was put under receivership. The money was also for preparing a policy to allow the private sector to produce and sell electricity to the government-owned Tanzania Electric Supply Company (Tanesco), respectively.

It was Rugemalira who was instrumental in pushing the IPTL concept through the state bureaucracy, and during that time, bribes were allegedly paid to senior politicians and government officials, including an attorney general, regulators, judges, lawyers, and bankers, each receiving as much as $1 million. In the end, it was Tanzanian power consumers who bore the direct and indirect costs of the scam through higher electricity costs.[93] Apart from firing a few officials, President Jakata Kikwete did little to punish those who stole from the TEA escrow account, choosing instead to accept resignations and preferring minor prosecutions. One of the

---

[93] Brian Cooksey, "IPTL, Richmond and 'Escrow': The Price of Private Power Procurement in Tanzania," Africa Research Institute, Briefing Note 1702, November 2017.

victims was the minister of lands, Anna Tibajuka, a junior player in the drama, who was sacked. Tibajuka admitted receiving $1 million from Rugemalira but said the money was for the construction of a girls' school and was not corrupt money.

In 2017, Rugemalira and Sethi, owner of PAP, were charged with six counts of economic sabotage, forgery, impersonation, running a criminal syndicate, and obtaining money by false pretense in relation to a loss of $22.1 million, which they allegedly received from the Bank of Tanzania (BOT) as part of the TEA scandal. They pleaded not guilty. Two judges who were ensnared in the matter resigned, while former energy and mining minister William Ngeleja, who was also named in the 2014 Parliamentary report, surrendered the money he received from one of the loot beneficiaries. The case was still ongoing by mid-2019.

Back to Sethi's activities in Kenya and his association with the ruling class. This individual enjoyed unfettered access to President Moi and top officials of his government and the ruling party KANU, and he managed to bag some of the most exorbitantly priced contracts through his firm, Ruaha Concrete Company Limited. Using kickbacks, Sethi built a number of projects, including a nine-kilometer access road for the corrupt Kenya Pipeline Company. The cost of the project rose from approximately $4 million in 1995 to $10 million by the time it was completed in 1998. He was also favored with tenders for numerous other government agencies but ran afoul with the KRA when he failed to pay millions of dollars in taxes.

Chavda and sisal farms

One of the early corruption scandals in Tanzania was that of the Chavda brothers, Vidyadhar G. Chavda and P. G. Chavda, which took place in 1993 during Hassan Mwinyi's presidency. The blustery Vidyadhar, the elder of the two, arrived from India in 1978 and worked for several years as an architect. He then shifted to financial services, where he consummated several deals, some of which were illegal. In 1994, the two brothers and others obtained a $3.5 million loan from the government's Debt Conversion Program (DCP), which Vidyadhar helped to create in an effort to reduce the nation's outstanding debt. The idea was to sell the debt to third parties at a reduced rate. However, the program flopped and ended up costing the government over $100 million. The DCP loan the Chavdas took out was for the rehabilitation of abandoned sisal farms in Tanga, where the Chavdas proposed to create 1,400 jobs and earn $42 million for the exchequer, but instead the money was diverted toward the purchase of unusable machines and spare parts from abroad.

A parliamentary committee in 1994 ruled that the money was embezzled by the Chavdas and two other Asian businessmen, Jeetu Patel and Subbash Patel, who in 2008 were named in a case in which the equivalent of $58 million was withdrawn from the External Payment Arrears account at the BOT and paid to 22 companies.

Top officials, including some from the Office of the President and the Ministry of Home Affairs, were reportedly bribed to cover up the misdeeds. Following incessant criticisms from opposition leaders, the government abruptly shut down the DCP program and deported the Chavdas in February 1995, leaving the taxpayers to absorb the loss. For reasons no one could explain, Vidyadhar—who occupied an undeserved position of privilege—was back in Tanzania within a few months. That is when, for the first time, TI rated Tanzania as one of the most corrupt nations, and the former president Nyerere admitted before the Dar es Salaam Press Club that "Tanzania stinks of corruption." In 2010 the Tanzanian government reopened investigations into the DCP misappropriation scandal, but nothing came out of it.

BAE Systems radar scam

In 1999, after Nyerere's death, the country was hit by yet another scandal, this one much bigger than the Chavda scandal—a shoddy deal pertaining to the purchase of a civil aviation radar system from British Aerospace Engineering (BAE). The acquisition of the $40 million radar system was opposed by both the WB and the International Civil Aviation Organization as unnecessary in a poor country like Tanzania. They also felt the deal was overpriced. British Cabinet Minister Claire Short was also unhappy about the purchase, accusing the arms industry of being "notorious for grubby behavior."

Coincidentally, businessman Sailesh Vithlani, who brokered the sale, was the same person who later, in 2002, acted as the agent for the controversial purchase of a luxury Gulfstream jet for President Benjamin Mkapa. Experts lamented that the $40 million price tag on the aircraft was inflated, alluding to underhanded dealings. When the SFO investigated the deal, it discovered a good portion of the kickbacks paid to Vithlani were used to bribe officials in Mkapa's government. A top Tanzanian official who provided legal advice on the transaction was himself found to have stashed $1 million in an offshore account, leading to suspicion that the money came from BAE. Vithlani reportedly received $12.4 million from the radar deal in commission, which he allegedly deposited in a Swiss bank. It could not be established what commission he received for the jet. Following the controversy, the Asian businessman left Tanzania for fear of prosecution.

In the United Kingdom, BAE agreed in a Southwark Crown court in 2010 to a $42 million plea bargain for failing to keep proper accounting records. Part of the money, $37.6 million, was paid to Tanzania as a "charitable payment" to be used for educational projects and the purchase of textbooks and school supplies. An agreement was signed between the Tanzanian government and the SFO on how the money was to be used. In the United States, BAE paid a fine of $400 million to the DOJ for conspiring to make false statements about an internal program required to comply with anti-bribery laws. The penalties were announced simultaneously in London and Washington. The US fines were with respect to arms deals in Tanzania, Saudi Arabia, the Czech Republic, and Hungary. In early 2010, the DOJ lashed out at BAE for making "hundreds of dollars in payments to third parties despite knowing of a 'high probability' the money would be passed on to influential foreign officials to favor BAE."[94]

While acknowledging owning the offshore account, Attorney General Andrew Chenge brushed off criticisms about the magnitude of the stash, describing it as "small pocket change."[95] He was forced to resign while still pleading his innocence amid mounting pressure from the public. Neither Chenge nor some other officials named in the scandal were convicted, a matter seen by Tanzanians as a direct betrayal of Mkapa's election pledge to stamp out corruption. A government statement denied that any Tanzanian was involved in the radar scandal, and Chenge's US-based lawyer, J. Lewis Madorsky, blamed political and personal motives of the politician's detractors as the reason for the accusations.

Bribery investigations implicating BAE were also conducted in South Africa, Romania, and Qatar.

Land theft?

A controversy erupted in Tanzania in 2016 over a $6.6 million land tender announced by the prime minister's office and the WB to design, supply, install, and commission an integrated land management information system (ILMIS). Seven bids were examined for the WB-funded project, which was also to include indexing of data and migration into the ILMIS database, the design and installation of an ILMIS web application to provide controlled access to stakeholders, and the purchase, deployment, and installation of hardware and equipment. In April 2016, after tender

---

[94] Jackie Bennion, "BAE Will Pay $450 Million to Settle Long Running Bribery Case," *Front Line World*, PBS, February 5, 2010.
[95] "Tanzania: Chenge – I Am Proved Innocent," *The Citizen*, February 13, 2011.

processing was completed, IGN France International JV, which specializes in geographical information and operates largely overseas, was selected to carry out the project. The decision was opposed by one of the bid losers, Israeli's Sivan Designs D. S. Limited, prompting the Public Procurement Appeals Authority (PPAA) to rule the process as irregular.

The Israeli company claimed some officials were bribed to certify that IGN France International JV was qualified to undertake the works based on a similar project it undertook in Benin. However, the WB supported the award to the French company, thus dismissing the claims of bribery. "Unhappily the decision by the World Bank prevails,"[96] said the country director, Bella Bird, in August 2016.

Another notable scandal surrounding a foreign company in Tanzania involved the US-based Richmond Development Company Limited LLC in 2006. After an intense international competition for the contract, the little-known Houston, Texas company, was chosen to supply 100 generators at a cost of $75 million to ease a serious electricity shortage. However, it was soon found that the company, which signed a contract on June 23 with Tanesco, the state electricity company, had neither the professional know-how nor the equipment to undertake the project, which involved the provision of 100 megawatts of power.

A multi-party Parliamentary committee chaired by MP Harrison Mwakyembe reported to the House in February 2008 that Richmond "lacked experience, expertise, and was financially incapacitated."[97] The committee discovered the whole bidding process was allegedly scarred by corruption and gross irregularities and asked the prime minister, who had personally approved the contract in June 2006, to take full responsibility for the loss of taxpayers' money, given that the generators were never supplied and the works had to be passed on to another company, Dubai-based Dowans Holdings,

---

[96] Athuman Mtulya, "Tanzania: World Bank Defends Award of Sh. 14 Billion Tender," *The Citizen*, August 18, 2016.
[97] "Tanzania PM to resign over graft," *BBC*, news, February 7, 2008.

six months later to finish the project. But Tanesco did not want to have anything more to do with the contract and terminated the deal with Dormans, a decision which cost the state-run agency $66 million in compensation following an arbitration decision by the Paris-based International Chamber of Commerce (ICC) Court of Arbitration and an affirmation of the judgment by the Tanzanian High Court in September 2011.

In the meantime, there was a surge of anger and frustration throughout the country as electricity went on and off, ruining perishable goods, stunting the production of goods, and leaving consumers with heavy losses. Citizens were further shocked in January 2017, when the head of the Prevention and Combating of Corruption Bureau, Edward Hosea, closed the investigation and declared no offense had been committed. The scandal nevertheless resulted in the resignation of Prime Minister Edward Lowassa, who was accused by Parliament of having acted inappropriately by approving the deal; the minister for minerals and energy, Nazir Karamagi; and the minister for East African cooperation, Ibrahim Msabaha, who were Richmond's biggest backers in government. A follow-up audit by the Public Procurement Regulatory Authority (PPRA) concluded the procurement process had been "influenced by higher authorities," but gave no names. Nonetheless, it was not difficult to guess who the recipients of bribes and kickbacks were in this unscrupulous skullduggery. An agent of Richmond in Tanzania, Naem Adam Gire, was the only individual prosecuted on charges of misleading Tanesco by allegedly forging and uttering documents showing that Richmond was financially and technically capable of undertaking the project. He was, however, acquitted due to a lack of evidence.

Barrick troubles

If there is one foreign company operating in Africa that has been accused of everything from murder to bribery to illegal money dealings, that company is African Barrick Gold, later known as Acacia, a subsidiary of the Toronto-based Barrick Gold Corporation.

The company received some gut-wrenching slaps from the Tanzanian government and from non-profit NGOs for its activities at the North Mara mine in northern Tanzania. Barrick Gold owns 63.9 percent of Acacia.

In 2014, reports alleged the Canadian gold company had made $400,000 in illegal payments to government officials and consultants to value the land around where the mine was situated. The reports further said that bribe money ranging between $19,000 and $121,000 was paid to a top official of a government task force overseeing land valuation for the company on the understanding that he would give some of it to other officials to compensate for their time. Barrick hit back, saying the payments were legitimate expenses and allowances tied to an agreement with the Tanzanian government and that the company was committed to ethical and transparent business practices in compliance with the law.[98]

A tribunal committee appointed in 2016 to investigate revenue loss from mining reported that Acacia had engaged in a "sophisticated scheme of tax evasion"[99] to escape paying more than $40 million in corporate taxes between 2010 and 2013 while paying dividends of $400 million to its shareholders from profits obtained from the country. In July 2017, the government slapped Acacia with a $40 billion tax bill with another $150 billion in interest and penalties for under-declaring export revenues with respect to its two mines, Bulyanhulu and Buzwagi, over a 17-year span between 2000 and 2017, but Acacia contended it had declared all revenues according to the law. An incensed President John Magufuli felt the company was cheating Tanzania, a country which depends on mining for 3.5 percent of its GDP, and described Acacia's activities as a "kind of exploitation"[100] since it was not even registered in the country.

[98] "Barrick Gold Accused of Money Deals," *The Citizen*, June 21, 2014.
[99] "Tanzania Tax Tribunal Orders Acacia to Pay $41.3 million," Reuters, April 6, 2016.
[100] Yomi Kazeem, "Tanzania Has Hit a British Mining Company with a Fine Worth Two Centuries of Revenue," *Quartz Africa*, July 25, 2017.

And that was not all. In mid-2017, Tanzania claimed the London-listed company had "under-reported the gold and copper levels in its concentrate exports by more than 10 times."[101] In a dramatic response, Magufuli banned exports of unprocessed copper and gold from Acacia mines and fired his mines minister, Sospeter Muhongo, after learning metal shipments by the company had been understated. After months of a stormy relationship between the government and Barrick, the two sides reached an agreement in October 2017 in which the latter was to give Tanzania 50 percent of its mining revenue, a $300 million goodwill gesture, and a 16 percent stake. The state was also to participate in decisions relating to the firm's operations, investment, planning, procurement, and marketing. Barrick's nefarious activity in Tanzania was perhaps one of the best examples of manipulation and exploitation of mining resources in Africa.

However, it was the systematic violence at the mine over the years that caught the world's attention in a big way. Gangs of people constantly raided the site to steal ore. In 2011, a group of 800 (Barrick put the number at 1,500) "criminal intruders"[102] invaded the North Mara mine in one of a series of attacks in which hundreds of people were physically and sexually assaulted and at least 65 killed, allegedly by police or the mine's own security guards, according to two NGOs, Mining Watch Canada and the United Kingdom's Rights and Accountability in Development (RAID). In July 2013, 12 Tanzanians sued Barrick in a British court seeking compensation for the deaths and injuries, and in November 2014 the matter was settled out of court.

The company has also run into other troubles elsewhere, including allegations of killings and gang rapes by its private security personnel in Papua New Guinea, environmental infractions in Chile and the Dominican Republic, claims of corruption and tax

---

[101] John Aglionby and Henry Sanderson, "Acacia Mining Accused of Operating Illegally in Tanzania," *The Financial Times*, June 12, 2017.
[102] Garry White, "African Barrick Mine Raid Leaves Seven Intruders Dead," *The Telegraph*, May 17, 2011.

evasion in Peru, and accusations that Barrick deposited $90,000 in the bank account of a Zambian envoy to Canada to facilitate the hosting of a Zambia–Canada cultural exchange program organized by the government to mark Zambia's independence celebrations. Nevers Mumba, Zambia's High Commissioner in Ottawa, was charged in a Ndola High Court with abuse of authority for receiving the money from Barrick between 2009 and 2010 and failing to convey it to the Zambian government. He was also charged with engaging electrical contractors to carry out work at the embassy without following established procedures. He was found guilty on September 12, 2018 but was discharged on mitigation.

UGANDA

"Letting the Big Fish Swim" is the title of a 63-page bombshell report[103] that blasts the government of Uganda for failing to deal with high-level corruption and for letting sharks glide away with billions of dollars belonging to the public without facing prosecution. The report is the product of a comprehensive observation of Uganda's corruption environment by Human Rights Watch and Yale Law School's Allard K. Lowenstein International Human Rights Clinic. "Scandal after scandal," says Maria Burnett, senior Africa researcher, "the government's patronage politics and lack of political will undermines the fight against corruption in Uganda."[104]

For 27 years of his reign, President Yoweri Museveni, a former bush fighter, has been preaching about his resolve to end corruption, undoubtedly the biggest threat to Uganda's prosperity. Yet every year, there are members of the executive and judiciary branches, as well as Parliament, who find themselves in the jaws of sharks as they face allegations of corruption. Unfortunately, the so-called "big fish" are never prosecuted for large-scale graft.

To be fair, however, graft did not start with Museveni. Both in times of peace and during the long periods of civil war, Uganda was dogged with unbridled corruption. A story is told of a British agent of a printing firm who, during Idi Amin's chaotic rule, went to negotiate a contract to print two million Ugandan shillings in 100-shilling notes. At the close of the talks, the agent asked how he was going to be paid. "Print three million and take one million shillings for yourself,"[105] Amin is said to have replied.

---

[103] "Letting the Big Fish Swim: Failures to Prosecute High Level Corruption in Uganda," Human Rights Watch, report, October 21, 2013.

[104] "Uganda: Free Pass on High-Level Corruption: Large-Scale Graft Deprives Ugandans of Basic Rights," Human Rights Watch, report, October 21, 2013.

[105] Martha Honey and David B. Ottaway, "Idi Amin Squandered the Wealth of Uganda," *The Washington Post*, May 29, 1979.

So, while it is impossible to confirm that conversation from anyone alive, it illustrates the conduct or lack of it of Ugandan leaders: from Milton Obote to Idi Amin, Yusuf Lule, Godfrey Binaisa, and General Tito Okelo to the incumbent, the song of corruption has been sung but not completed. The political and armed upheavals that took place in the country after independence in 1962 gave both civilian and military leaders an opportunity to exploit the country's rich agricultural resources, coffee and tea, and mineral resources such as copper and later oil. During the famous coffee "boom" of 1976–1977, as the political crisis under the pugnacious Idi Amin peaked, some smart Ugandans (and many influential Kenyans) became millionaires as they smuggled huge quantities of coffee across the border with Kenya to sell overseas.

But the biggest financial scandals have taken place under Museveni, at the helm since 1986. There is the case of the China Harbor Engineering Company (CHEC) and the China Civil Engineering Construction Corporation (CCECC) over a multimillion-dollar standard-gauge railway (SGR) project in Uganda. The latter was the first to sign a framework agreement with the Ugandan government in January 2012 worth $1.74 billion. Before the project got underway, CHEC offered $1.25 billion. The discount was sweet music to officials, who changed their minds, cancelling the deal with CCECC in April 2014. In the background, two camps in the Ugandan Ministry of Works wrangled. They exchanged nasty correspondence, with each side fighting to control the works. One newspaper that saw the correspondence said the exchange was dominated by allegations of "blackmail, spying, and stealing of documents."[106] One group wanted the CHEC contract terminated altogether and the project put under the control of the Uganda Railways Corporation (URC), while the other rooted for the Ministry of Works. Corruption was suspected, as the project, intended to link Mombasa with Uganda and Rwanda, was inflated by at least $600 million.

---

[106] Frederic Musisi, "Government Officials Renew Fight over Shs8 Trillion Railway Deal," The Daily Monitor, June 18, 2018.

Incensed by all the infighting, President Museveni called a Cabinet meeting on July 25, 2014 and expressed his deep displeasure at the almost-daily public sparring between the two companies. Things got uglier after CCECC sued the government. An out-of-court settlement was eventually reached, splitting the route: CCECC would take the western route and CHEC the eastern route. By mid-2019, however, the construction work had not begun due to financial and other reasons, and eventually in October, Kampala announced it had suspended the SGR to concentrate on revamping the old meter-gauge railway network built by British colonialists. Like the China Road and Bridge Construction Company (CRBC), CHEC is a subsidiary of the disgraced CCCC, which has a reputation of corrupting officials in many countries. The CCCC has a profile of more than 700 projects in more than 100 countries overseas valued at $100 billion, but its reputation has been tarnished by its tendency to pay bribes and kickbacks.

Altogether, contracts totaling $2.4 billion had been given to Chinese companies in Uganda as of July 2018, among them a security cameras project, a pipeline from Kabale to Hoima in Uganda into Tanzania, and construction of the Karuma and Isimba dams, as well as the construction of phosphate fertilizer, glass, and sulfuric acid factories. Chinese companies are also building numerous roads in Uganda.

In a rare case in 2011, Uganda blocked a $74 million loan from the Import and Export Bank of China (EXIM) meant for a digital immigration project after detecting procurement flaws. Huawei Technologies of China and the Uganda Broadcasting Corporation (UBC) had already signed a memorandum of understanding (MOU) when the opposition leader, Nandala Mafabi, claimed the list of equipment in the tender was completely different from the list in the contract. Moreover, he said, the cost of the project, which should have been no more than $28 million, had been substantially inflated, raising suspicion that corruption may have played a part.

The Chinese ambassador to Tanzania, Lu Youqing, admitted in

July 2014 that Chinese companies were engaged in bribery and ivory trafficking in Africa and lamented it was tarnishing China's image.

Oil exploration

Tullow Oil is an Irish company which has invested heavily in the oil and gas sector in Africa. Among its bragging rights on its website is a line referring to itself as "Africa's leading independent oil company." Tullow operates in more than 20 countries and boasts revenue of more than $1 billion. Since it entered the continent via Senegal in 1986, Tullow has followed an aggressive business policy. In trying to win contracts, however, the company has not always followed the straight path. One of the countries in which the oil giant faced allegations of bribing officials to win favors is Uganda, where the company operated three oil blocks in the oil-rich Lake Albertine Rift.

In 2011, Tullow Uganda Limited was a subject of debate in the Ugandan Parliament when it was accused in documents tabled by legislator Gerald Karuhanga of paying $100 million to "expert" bureaucrats, including three senior officials—a former prime minister, a foreign minister, and a former energy minister—to get concessions for oil fields. One of the three allegedly received $23 million in kickbacks. It was alleged the money was wired to the officials from Tullow's accounts with the Bank of Valetta in Malta. However, Tullow denied the allegation, saying it had evidence that "irrefutably proves that no payments of any sort have been made to the Ugandan government ministers by Tullow."[107] It said the evidence included sworn letters from Maltese and British police certifying that the documents used to support claims of bribery were forged. The three Ugandan officials also denied the allegations. After its own investigation, the Ugandan Parliament also agreed,

---

[107] Jocelyn Edwards, "Tullow Refutes Bribery Accusations in Uganda," Reuters, April 12, 2012.

announcing they had not seen any evidence to buttress claims that the ministers were involved in bribery and corruption.

But that was not the only controversy in which Tullow found itself. In 2013, it was alleged that the company attempted to bribe President Yoweri Museveni with $50 million to avoid paying $313.5 million in capital gains tax (CGT) after Heritage Oil Company uploaded its 50 percent stake to Tullow in a $1.45 billion deal in 2010.[108] That claim of bribery was denied by Kampala, with the government there saying Museveni was "gravely injured" by the report. Tullow eventually apologized to Museveni, describing Heritage's claim as "groundless mudslinging."[109]

Nevertheless, when Heritage refused to pay the CGT, the government pressured Tullow to settle the tax bill ahead of Tullow finalizing a joint venture with France's Total and China's National Offshore Oil Company (CNOOC). The $2.9 billion partnership deal with the two entities was to develop oil fields in the Lake Albert basin on the border with the DRC, believed to hold 2.5 billion barrels of oil.

The deal was inordinately delayed because of the tax wrangles. Eventually, Tullow paid the CGT liability to the URA on the condition that Heritage would reimburse it. Heritage refused to pay Tullow the money, and the matter reached a London court. In a judgment in June 2013, Justice Burton of the High Court ruled in favor of Tullow's indemnity claim and ordered Heritage to pay $313 million to the URA. The court also cleared Tullow of allegations that it had bribed Ugandan officials. In a surprise move in August 2019, Tullow called off the sale to Total and CNOOC citing the tax dispute.

In a related matter, WikiLeaks released a diplomatic cable in 2009 alleging that Italian oil giant Eni had made personal payments to Ugandan officials, including President Museveni, to win exploration

---

[108] "Museveni '$50m Bribe': The Inside Story," *The Observer*, March 17, 2013.
[109] Harriet Dennys, "Tullow Oil Apologizes to Uganda Government over Bribery Allegations," *The Telegraph,* March 22, 2013.

licenses. It was claimed Tullow's Uganda head of external relations, Andy Demetriou, told the US ambassador in Kampala, Jerry P. Lanier, that the inducements were paid to the security minister, who was also the secretary general of the ruling National Resistance Movement (NRM), through a holding company. The leaked cable claimed the allegations could have been connected to the Tullow/Total/CNOOC deal in which Eni failed to secure a place in the partnership. However, Demetriou denied meeting any US official. The squabble between the oil companies was fueled by top Ugandan officials, who were pulling in different directions in a dishonorable fight for bribes and kickbacks. It would be surprising if such high-level jostling took place without the knowledge of Museveni. Amama Mbabazi, who Museveni appointed prime minister in May 2011 despite featuring in the allegations of bribery, denied the accusations.

Uganda has an oil and gas revenue management policy containing a section on transparency promising that "all parties involved in the management of oil and gas revenues shall observe the highest standards of transparency."[110] But the policy, like many others in Uganda, was as useless as the anti-corruption unit formed in December 2018 by Museveni to filter complaints on corruption. Though complaints have been lodged with the unit, no high-level official has been successfully prosecuted for corruption as a result.

Although the Ugandan mining sector is under the Directorate of Geological Survey and Mines (DGSM), there are claims of a "shadow system" controlled by lawyers, MPs, foreign-backed investors, and even a pop star, which exploits Uganda's mineral wealth. Moreover, the DGSM itself is riddled with corruption. It allows poorly qualified companies to win licenses based on their connections at the expense of well-qualified and conscientious companies.[111] Also to blame is President Museveni, who often influences the awarding of exploration permits against laid-out

---

[110] "The National Oil and Gas Policy for Uganda," Ministry of Energy and Mineral Development, February 2008.
[111] "Uganda: Undermined," Global Witness, report, June 5, 2017.

regulations.

In 2016, for example, Justice Irene Mulyagonja, the inspector general of government who is charged with eliminating corruption and abuse of authority, lamented that an exploration license given by DGSM to Uganda Hui Neng, an affiliate of Guangzhou Dongsong Energy, a Chinese fertilizer manufacturer, was tainted with fraud and wanted the contract cancelled. Instead of reprimanding the DGSM and rebuking the firm, Museveni scolded the inspector general and allowed the company, which was short of financial capital, to proceed. The company could not, due also to a litany of demands from locals demanding compensation for land they claimed had been stolen from them to build the $600 million phosphate mine. It was not until the end of 2018 that the plant, located in the Sukulu hills on the outskirts of Tororo on the Uganda/Kenya border, began operations, apparently after a lot of money had changed hands.

In June 2017, an embarrassed President Museveni cancelled a $175 million Chinese copper mining venture following allegations that top government officials in the ministries of finance, energy, and the attorney general's office, as well as a former minister, had pocketed a $1 million bribe to influence the deal. The Uganda-registered Tibet Hima Mining Company Limited (THMCOL), a subsidiary of Tibet Automobile of China, allegedly won the 25-year contract in 2013 to extract five million tons of copper at Kilembe in the western region. However, Museveni said THMCOL was not competent to undertake the massive project and that it won the bid through fraudulent means. What Museveni did not say was that he was not brought up to speed when sweeteners were shared, hence his lamentations. The concession agreement was eventually terminated at the end of 2017 following the recommendations of a commission of inquiry in what was seen as an example of catastrophic mismanagement of the mining sector. However, Hima went to court, claiming it had already sunk $33 million into the concession, which was to run up to 2038. The court ruled the company had acted too late, since the state had already assumed ownership of the mines.

Seized on arrival

In April 2008, a Ugandan presidential advisor, Ananias Tumukunde, flew to Britain for medical attention. Unbeknownst to him, a trap had been laid out for his arrest by the Overseas Anti-Corruption Unit (OACU). The presidential advisor on science and technology landed at Heathrow Airport and was promptly seized and handcuffed by Scotland Yard detectives on allegations of bribery. He had $130,000 in cash.

Tumukunde was a wanted person for receiving $103,000 in bribe money from a British firm, CBRN Team Limited, for a contract with a Ugandan firm for the supply of security equipment and training during the Commonwealth Heads of Government meeting in Kampala in November 2017. After signing the $271,000 contract, the Ugandan demanded $107,000 from the company to meet local tax payments. The company agreed and made five payments to Tumukunde and a Ugandan army officer between June 2007 and February 2008, which violated the UK Bribery Act 2002.

When information reached British authorities that Tumukunde was to arrive in London, they laid a trap. He was charged before a Southwark Crown Court on September 22, 2008 for money laundering. He was sentenced to 12 months in prison and deported after his sentence. During investigations, $68,000 found in two UK bank accounts belonging to Tumukunde and the military officer was confiscated and returned to Uganda. The army officer was not charged. Also charged was Niels Tobiasen, managing director of the Wiltshire-based CBRN. He pleaded not guilty to paying bribes and was convicted and imprisoned for five months.

GMO Bill bribes

The fierce debate inside the Ugandan Parliament on whether the country should adopt biotechnology in the country's agricultural sector was fueled not only by a desire to alleviate poverty but by promises of kickbacks by MNCs scrambling to sell their products. MPs had two options: to pass the national biotechnology and biosafety bill known as the GMO Bill and open the gates for an international seed company operating in Uganda to conduct crop research and other companies to market their products, or reject the bill altogether and miss out on the freebies.

The bill was initially introduced in 2012 with the full support of the Ugandan government, but politics and greed held up debate until 2017. President Museveni wanted the legislation to pass urgently so that the country could immediately apply modern biotechnology through research to increase food production of genetically modified organisms (GMOs) to feed its millions of starving people. But opponents said the technique would not be safe and would benefit large-scale farmers while hurting smallholders. "This bill is meant to enslave Ugandans to the multinationals; it is also politically suicidal,"[112] said one MP. But the shock came in July 2017 when several MPs admitted in Parliament to having received bribes from a multinational firm to pass the bill. A company, which they did not name, gave each MP $100 to attend briefing meetings meant to influence them to support the bill. There were also reports of politicians and journalists being showered with fully expense-paid trips to Brazil, which had embraced GMOs. Few countries in Africa use the new technology. South Africa allows the cultivation of corn and soybeans, while Egypt and Sudan cultivate GMO cotton using the system. Altogether, 14 African countries, among them Kenya, Uganda, Tanzania, Ethiopia, Malawi, Mozambique, Burkina Faso, Cameroon, Ghana, Ethiopia, and Swaziland, use the new-tech cotton seeds.

The Ugandan minister of state for planning was blasted by civil society organizations, including NGOs Caritas Uganda and Action Aid Uganda, for colluding with US seed manufacturer Monsanto to push the enactment of the GMO bill. Allegations were made that

---

[112] Sadab Kitatta Kaaya, "MPs Claim They Were Bribed over GMO Bill," *The Observer*, July 5, 2017.

the minister was bribed. Because of its controversial nature, the bill was temporarily shelved, but it was subsequently sent back to Parliament in 2018 and passed.

Monsanto is a global seed manufacturer and the biggest biotech multinational operating in East Africa. Its most popular weed killer, until it was banned in most countries, was DDT. In addition to killing weeds, the chemical also killed fish and caused tumors in animals. Lake Nakuru in Kenya was the home of many flamingos, but spillage of DDT residues into the water by companies operating on the fringes of the lake resulted in tens of thousands of the birds dying, virtually killing the tourism business in the area.

When questioned as to why they use such dangerous agricultural chemicals in developing countries, multinationals say all they are doing is "helping to feed a hungry world."[113]

DDT was outlawed in many countries after the Stockholm Convention of 2001 on Persistent Organic Pollutants, which confirmed it was dangerous to humans and plants. The convention is a global treaty to protect human health and the environment from chemicals.

The biggest blow to Monsanto, now owned by the German agrochemicals and drugs conglomerate Bayer, was in 2018 when a California jury awarded Dewayne Johnson, a school groundskeeper, $289 million in punitive and compensatory damages after concluding that Roundup, another popular Monsanto product, caused his cancer. It was the first among thousands of pending cases in the United States against the company over the use of the weed killer. In March 2019, another US resident, Edwin Hardeman, contracted non-Hodgkin's lymphoma after allegedly using Roundup for 26 years. A six-member jury in San Francisco ruled that Roundup's key ingredient, glyphosate, was a "substantial factor" in Hardeman's cancer. And in the same state of California, Monsanto was ordered by a court in May 2019 to pay more than

---

[113] Russell Mokhiber, *Corporate Crime and Violence: Big Business Power and the Abuse of the Public Trust* (Sierra Club Books, 1988), 187.

$2 billion in damages to a couple, Alva and Alberta Pilliods, which claimed Roundup caused their cancer. While American victims of the killer weed choose to go to court to get justice, no court case against Monsanto has been reported in Africa, where its products are widely used, and tens of thousands of people may have died or are enduring terminal diseases.

Monsanto works with pro-GMO organizations, such as the Howard Buffett Foundation and the Bill and Melinda Gates Foundation, to research, experiment, and sell its products on the continent.

In Uganda, the company's main concentration is on maize, a popular foodstuff, where Monsanto sells Roundup and other glyphosate brands. Special precautions, especially in the dosage, are required in using Roundup, but it is not clear whether farmers in Africa are cautioned sufficiently to avoid the dangers of contamination. Monsanto's potato brand Bt was considered toxic enough for major American fast food restaurants like McDonald's and Burger King and firms like Pringles and McCain to withdraw it in the mid-2000s. European food distributors, among them Unilever, Heinz, and Nestlé, agreed to ensure that their products do not contain biotech ingredients.[114]

Cotton

In Kenya, a campaign to introduce Bacillus thuringiensis (Bt) cotton, one of Monsanto's creations, has been met with tremendous opposition from groups of farmers who believe the product is a danger to human life and the environment. Tests in France showed Bt failed to integrate naturally into the environment and stayed in water and the environment for decades before biodegrading. The introduction of the variety in Kenya, therefore, was hurting Kenyans and benefiting the multinational. This is another way in which international companies put profits ahead of human life and the environment.

---

[114] Marie-Monique Robin, *The World According to Monsanto: Pollution, Corruption, and the Control of Our Food Supply, an Investigation into the World's Most Controversial Company* (The New Press, 2010), 321.

In other African countries where Bt has been introduced, such as South Africa, Mali, and Burkina Faso, the reaction of farmers has been mixed. In Burkina Faso, the GMO cotton seed was introduced with much fanfare in 2008 and became popular among small-scale farmers, but while it proved capable of resisting bugs, its quality dropped, forcing farmers to abandon it in 2016. Once Africa's largest producer of cotton, Burkina Faso is now fourth on the continent behind Benin, Mali, and Côte d'Ivoire. Apart from attracting a host of pests, the product is also said to be relatively expensive compared to other varieties. In Mali, farmers totally rejected the GMO technology, while in South Africa, GMO crops have been almost completely integrated into the country's food culture.

In the cotton-growing regions of India, Bt is called "the seed of suicide." It is the ingredient villagers use to kill themselves when faced with mounting debts borne out of failed crops. Opponents of Bt in India claim the seeds are not only expensive to buy, but contain a form of technology "in which seed produced by a crop will not grow – crops will not produce viable offspring seeds or will produce viable seeds with specific genes switched off."[115] Thus, when crops fail farmers are left with loan debts to pay, and some opt to kill themselves. Monsanto entered India in 1949 and has been promoting its products heavily in the media. Bt was advanced as the panacea to reduce or eliminate the need to spray for bollworms,[116] but farmers, especially smallholders who make up the majority of Indian cotton farmers, disagree.

---

[115] Vandana Shiva, "The Seeds of Suicide: How Monsanto Destroys Farming," Global Research, article, October 21, 2018.
[116] Marie-Monique Robin, *The World According to Monsanto,* (New Press, 2010), 295.

PART THREE

CHAPTER 6

NORTH AFRICA

Corruption in Egypt is giant, amorphous, and finally ungraspable.
– John R. Bradley

EGYPT

Lockheed and Egypt

When caught in a case of misconduct, most multinationals would come out to vigorously defend their integrity. That is what Lockheed Aeronautical Systems Company, a division of Lockheed Corporation, did when busted in a bribery scandal involving the purchase of three C-130H Hercules cargo aircraft in Egypt in 1989 to be financed by US loans under the Foreign Military Financing (FMF) program. Although Lockheed had agreed that no commissions would be paid, in line with Egyptian laws and FMF requirements, the aircraft maker undertook the payment of a commission of $1.8 million, representing $600,000 for each plane, to Egyptian legislator Leila I. Takla, who had been the firm's consultant since 1980. Takla did assist Lockheed to secure the contract by using her influence as a legislator. When the commission payment was discovered, Takla and her husband requested that the $1.8 million be scrapped and replaced with a $1 million "termination payment" to avoid any further queries. But the matter had gone too far.

"We would strongly defend ourselves," Lockheed said when the scandal blew out, but soon, under heated pressure, the company chose to settle the matter after its own internal probe "found that regrettable mistakes in judgement were made by a few employees in the marketing organization in the late-1980s."[117] Eventually, Lockheed admitted making illegal payments of $1 million and a monthly retainer totaling $129,000. In April 1989, Egypt and Lockheed entered into an agreement worth $79 million, but the agreement was reduced by $1.8 million in line with a clause which prohibits the payment of commissions. The MP was then owed $1.8 million. But that arrangement leaked, and Lockheed cancelled the deal. After renegotiation, however, the Egyptian politician was paid $1 million as a termination fee.

---

[117] James F. Peltz, "Lockheed Agrees to Pay Record Fine," *The Los Angeles Times*, January 28, 1995.

The DOJ filed a case against Lockheed and two other employees for violating FCPA provisions. In 1994, a US district judge in Atlanta, Georgia, Marvin H. Shoob, imposed a criminal fine of $21.8 million and a civil settlement of $3 million against Lockheed for bribing foreign officials and falsifying documents to hide the true nature of the payments. Allen R. Love, director of Middle East and North Africa sales at Lockheed Aeronautical, pleaded guilty to a charge of aiding and abetting Lockheed in making the payment. He was fined $20,000 and given three years of probation. Suleiman A. Nassar, a regional vice president for Lockheed International, pleaded guilty and was sentenced to 18 months in prison. Takla was not prosecuted in either the United States or Egypt.

In another defense-related case, the former president of aerospace and defense firm ACL Technologies Inc. (ACL), Thomas Wurzel, was hauled to court in 2009 for authorizing illicit payments to an Egyptian-based agent while knowing part of the money would go to Egyptian Air Force (EAF) officials to influence a contract for the construction of a military aircraft depot for F-16 combat aircraft in Cairo. As a result of those actions, United Industrial Corporation (UIC) and ACL won the contract with gross revenues of $5.3 million and $267,000 respectively, according to the DOJ.

A District of Columbia court was told that between 2001 and 2002, Wurzel approved three payments to the Egyptian agent—a retired EAF general—ostensibly for labor contracting work for equipment and materials and for marketing services, knowing well that a portion of the money would go to EAF officials. Wurzel was also accused of authorizing his officials to create false invoices to conceal a $100,000 "advance payment" to the agent in 2002 for "equipment and materials," and another payment of $50,000 for "marketing services." Because there was insufficient evidence to charge him with actual bribery, Wurzel was cited for violating the FCPA's books and records provisions, and internal control provisions. He neither denied nor admitted the charges but was ordered to pay a $35,000 civil penalty for authorizing payments to an agent. In addition, UIC paid $267,571 in disgorgement and $70,108 in pre-judgment interest for violating the anti-bribery and books and records provisions of the FCPA, and it was barred from violating FCPA violations in the future.

Sanitation mess

In 1994, a project funded by the US Agency for International Development (USAID) found itself entangled in a corruption scandal in Egypt. Metcalf & Eddy International (M&E), a Delaware-based environmental engineering company, was offered two contracts: one in 1994 for $10 million to provide architectural and engineering support to projects managed by the state-owned Alexandria General Organization for Sanitary Drainage (AGOSD), and the second in 1995, a $25 million contract to provide services in support of the maintenance of wastewater treatment facilities. The facilities were in Alexandria, Egypt's second-largest city, and the contracts were for cleaning the polluted beaches along the Mediterranean coast, resulting from the incessant dumping of raw sewage into the sea by city authorities. M&E was also to improve two existing sewerage systems, increase pump capacity, enlarge the sludge dewatering and disposal facilities, and build additional support facilities.

The flow of raw waste into the sea was blamed for numerous diseases in the area, including intestinal problems, skin rashes, and eye infections. The project was to be funded by USAID and managed by local agencies, but its completion was inordinately delayed as costs rose, prompting Egypt's Parliament to demand a probe. M&E executives blamed Egyptian contractors, saying they were not qualified to carry out a project of that magnitude.

Although the chairman of AGOSD did not participate in the evaluation and scoring of bidders in the selection process, it was alleged he used his position to influence the results. In 1999, the DOJ filed a civil complaint before a Massachusetts district court stating M&E had treated the chairman of AGOSD and his family to two trips to the United States and Europe, complete with a hefty cash per diem, in exchange for awarding the two contracts to M&E amounting to $36 million, thus violating the FCPA. It was alleged the trips were "to induce the official (Chairman) to use his influence to effect and influence an act of the Government of Egypt."[118] The chairman of the state-run AGOSD, his wife, and his two children made an all-expenses-paid visit to Boston, Chicago, Disneyland, and Washington, DC on the first trip in October 1994. While in the United States on the sponsored trip, the chairman reportedly signed an order on behalf of AGOSD recommending M&E for the Phase One project. The company eventually got the contract.

M&E then paid for another trip for them to Paris, Boston, and San Diego in August 1996, at a time when the contract was under consideration. Again, M&E got the contract, and the Phase Two contract was extended by USAID for an additional six months. In both cases, the Chairman received 150 percent of the estimated per diem expenses in a lump sum before leaving Egypt.

The DOJ told the court the perks were things of value that benefited the chairman. In a civil settlement between the DOJ and M&E, the company agreed—without admitting to or denying the allegations—to pay a fine of $400,000 and the costs of the investigations to the US government, amounting to $50,000 for violating FCPA provisions. No criminal charges were filed against M&E, and the Egyptian government did not follow up on the matter.

---

[118] "The First Travel and Entertainment Enforcement Action," FCPA Professor, analysis, June 16, 2014.

ALGERIA

For 20 years, until April 2019 when he was forced out by mass protests, the oil-rich North African country of Algeria was in the firm hands of President Abdelaziz Bouteflika, assisted by a cohort of trusted allies. However, during the last six years of his rule, Bouteflika was hardly seen in public—a recluse struggling to fight off health issues resulting from a stroke. Although he had on several occasions admitted his country was bleeding from corruption, bribery, and nepotism, "ills that have festered in the body of our society, and become crippling parasites,"[119] Bouteflika failed to stop the drain, especially within his own government, including the military. The drain expanded after he fell sick, as allies and businessmen went on a spree of looting which eventually led to his regime's collapse.

Algeria was born out of a protracted revolutionary war between the Algerian National Liberation Front and France, its colonizer. The war ended in 1962, but it was not until two years later that the country bordering the Mediterranean coastline became independent. A number of leaders ruled the country before Bouteflika came to power in April 1999, and along the way were corruption scandals, some local and others with international ramifications.

There was what the media called the "scandal of the century" in 2002, in which an Algerian billionaire, Rafik Khalifa, was engaged in fraudulent activities through his $1 billion empire, the El Khalifa Group, which included a bank and an airline. In 2007, he was convicted in absentia and sentenced to life for stealing millions of dollars from his own bank to fund a luxurious lifestyle, including buying a $36 million villa in Cannes, apartments in Paris, and a corporate jet. He also financed the French football team, Olympique de Marseille. The Khalifa Bank, which had existed since the 1990s, collapsed in 2003, sinking with it between $1.5 billion

---

[119] Ahmed Marwane, "Fighting Corruption in Algeria: Turning Words into Action," The Washington Institute, Fikra Forum, analysis, December 12, 2018.

and $5 billion of clients' money. After the theft was discovered, Khalifa, who for years was the darling of elites in government and the corporate sector, fled to Britain, where he was arrested and spent three years in jail before being extradited to Algeria in 2013 and sentenced to 18 years in prison.

Another notorious case was the East-West Highway scandal. In 2006, Bouteflika commissioned the infrastructure project that was to cut across the country from the border with Tunisia in the east to the Moroccan border in the west. The six-lane highway, stretching 1,216 kilometers, was one of Bouteflika's signature undertakings. Seven foreign companies belonging to a consortium from Japan and China got the tenders to construct what was originally a $6 billion highway. Instead, the cost ballooned to $17 billion due to corruption and kickbacks. Senior officials in the Ministry of Public Works and some security agencies were found to have engaged in extortion and influence-peddling and received money estimated at up to $5 billion from the contractors to award the tenders. European banks were also said to have been complicit in the scheme. Bouteflika fulminated and ordered the arrest and prosecution of 14 people for money laundering and embezzlement of public funds. They were given long prison terms. Seven firms—Japanese Consortium (COJAAL), Pizarroti, China Rail Construction Corporation (CRCC)/CITIC, Isolux Corsan, Coba, SMI, and Caraventa—were also prosecuted for their part in the scandal and were each ordered to pay approximately $55,000 in fines.

Gas explodes

Another high-profile corruption scandal in Algeria involved the state hydrocarbons firm Sonatrach, which in 2009 awarded no-bid, single-source contracts to an Algerian/German electronics control systems company, Funkwerk Plettac, and Italy's Saipem Contracting Algeria. The contract was for the supply of gas turbines to the Amenas gas project—one of the largest wet gas projects in

Algeria—close to the border with Libya. A 2004 set of regulations allowed the direct awarding of contracts only in exceptional circumstances, such as when a tender is needed for quick processing for the national interest. It was not determined whether that was the case in this process. Algeria is the largest natural gas producer and the third-largest oil producer in Africa, which has attracted large multinationals such as the United Kingdom's BP, France's Total, Norway's Statoil (now renamed Equinor), and Spain's Repsol.

In March 2015, what some media described as one of Algeria's most notorious corruption scandals opened in a packed courthouse in Algiers. The case attracted a lot of attention because some of those on the docket had close ties to President Bouteflika. Moreover, the president and some of his top officials regularly used Sonatrach as an automatic teller machine to finance their political goals.

Fifteen people, including Saipem and Funwerk, were charged with a raft of offenses, including embezzlement, money laundering, corruption, and bribery, in return for awarding tenders to foreign companies. The court jailed eight people, including Sonatrach CEO Mohamed Meziane, who was sentenced to five years' probation, and his upstream vice president Belkacem Boumediene, who got five years in prison on charges of embezzling public funds and money laundering. Saipem and Funwerk were fined $37,000 and $47,000 respectively.

The Justice Ministry announced in 2017 that more than 3,000 cases of corruption had been recorded since 2013, but many of them implicated ordinary Algerians and not the top officials in the government and the military. Things began to change in the last few years of Bouteflika's regime, and after his ouster, the new leaders began a sweep of people suspected to engage in corruption in what was called "Clean Hands" campaign. Several individuals—including a former energy minister, officials of the Industry Ministries, and the head of Cevital, Algeria's biggest private company, Issad Rebrab—were questioned by police. One of the first top officials to be detained was former prime minister Ahmed Ouyahia, a close ally of Bouteflika for many years. The government made it clear that it would revisit old cases and prosecute those found to have squandered public money.

THE REPUBLIC OF SUDAN

Among African countries that have experienced extreme violence, few can beat Sudan on the length of conflict and pauperization of its people. Located between eight countries and abutting the Red Sea in the northeast, Sudan sits on millions of barrels of oil, yet 40 percent of its people live in extreme poverty. Its large population is subjected to political, religious, and economic marginalization, and sections of the country live in constant fear of militia attacks and bombardments from government brigades.

After gaining independence from the United Kingdom and Egypt in 1956, Sudan experienced one military coup after another until Omar al-Bashir, a military officer, led his own revolt against Prime Minister Sadiq al-Mahdi on June 30, 1989. He ruled the country for 30 years until his waterloo came early in April 2019, and he was overthrown by the army after weeks of street protests against his rule. Throughout his administration, al-Bashir was surrounded by a small group of loyalists and sycophants who misadvised him on the stern action he took against his opponents, particularly in the conflict areas of Darfur, South Kordofan, and Blue Nile. That small clique of loyalists shared with al-Bashir the massive revenues from the oil sector without caring about the welfare of millions of starving citizens in the sprawling country.

For decades after independence, Sudan was unknown in the international trading platform. Things changed in 1997 when the United States slapped trade sanctions against the country for harboring terrorists wanted in the United States for criminal offenses, among them Osama bin Laden of the notorious al-Qaeda group. Al-Bashir allowed the terror organization to establish at least three training camps in North Sudan for rebels from six countries and used Sudan's patronage to run a weapons-shipment network.[120] As a result, American financial institutions stopped dealing with Sudan, and the country became "an economy run

---

[120] Nick Kochan, *The Washing Machine: Money, Crime & Terror in the Offshore System* (Gerald Duckworth & Co. Ltd., 2006), 72.

on cash," which in turn created a fertile ground for corruption and money laundering.[121] Under growing pressure, al-Bashir expelled bin Laden in 1996, and the al-Qaeda leader took refuge in Afghanistan. The US economic sanctions against Sudan ended in 2017.

There are those who argue that by isolating Sudan through sanctions, the international community unintentionally insulated the country from international discourse, forcing the country to adopt socialist policies that ended in the confiscation of private businesses and the curtailment of competition. That may well be true because Sudan never quite recovered from that isolation. Until the 1990s, when it started exporting oil, Sudan's economic mainstay revolved around agriculture and livestock. The black gold—which emerged about the same time the sanctions were imposed—did not only bring fame to the semi-nomadic country, but fueled rivalry and created an elite group that amassed immense wealth through corruption and the looting of oil revenue of Africa's largest country.

In the gold sector, graft is characterized by bureaucratic and political corruption, which includes the embezzlement of public company gold revenue, tax exemptions and holidays, cronyism, nepotism and patronage in the granting of trade licenses, and concessions.[122] Smuggling is also a big problem for the country. UN estimates put gold smuggled from Sudan to the UAE between 2010 and 2014 at $4.5 billion. In May 2019, detectives seized 241 kilograms of gold from a plane that landed in Khartoum from the Nile River State, said to belong to a Moroccan export company. The final destination of the gold was not revealed, but officials believed it was being smuggled out of the country.

Even al-Bashir's predecessors had a bloat of corruption and human

[121] Matthieu Favas, "Sudan's Big Business Is Lobbying the Trump Administration to Help Attract Foreign Dollars," Quartz Africa, news, March 19, 2018.
[122] "The Politics of Mining and Trading in Gold in Sudan: Challenges of Corruption and Lack of Transparency, Sudan Transparency Initiative," Sudan Democracy First Group, report, undated.

rights abuses on their shoulders. Gaafar al Numeiri, who ruled the country for 15 years from 1969 to 1985, when he was overthrown in a military coup by his former close friend and appointee, General Abdel Rahman Mohammed Hassan Swareddahab, was both a dictator and an incorrigible looter. Large numbers of political opponents and civilians were killed during his reign.

The Enough Project, a Washington-based non-profit organization agitating for human rights, says that throughout his reign, President Omar al-Bashir oversaw the entrenchment of systemic looting, widespread impunity, political repression, and state violence so that he and his inner circle could maintain absolute authority and continue looting the state.[123] It was "a violent kleptocracy," said the group.

The Human Rights Watch report in 2015 cited killings, mass rapes, beatings, and looting by government-supported militias called the Rapid Support Forces (RSF) and called for its disbandment. Al-Bashir, however, denied that his government was involved in genocide. Ironically, as Sudanese militias were engaged in atrocities in the south, South Sudan armed groups were committing similar cruelty against their own people in the south: raping girls as young as 12 years old and abducting and killing innocent civilians. Areas around the major onshore oilfields in Melut and Muglad basins, the Upper Nile, Unity State, and Western Kordofan, south of the country, were the battleground between government forces and the opposition South Sudan People's Liberation Army (SPLA).

That same year, the Khartoum government hauled two South Sudanese missionaries to court on a criminal charge that carried the death penalty for remarks criticizing a corruption scandal in a church and complaining about the treatment of Christians in the country. Yad Michael and Peter Yen were visiting Khartoum when they publicly lambasted the government for corruptly selling land and property belonging to the Khartoum Bahri Evangelical Church.

---

[123] "Sudan's Deep State: How Insiders Violently Privatized Sudan's Wealth, and How to Respond," The Enough Project, article, April 2017.

They were lucky to be charged with breach of peace and managing a criminal or terrorist organization than the more serious charge of "spying," which would have sent them to the gallows. They were freed six months later in light of the fact they had already served their sentences based on the new charges.

Sudan, a predominantly Moslem country which adheres to Islamic *sharia* law, does not tolerate Christianity, and many incidences of arrests, torture, and killings of non-Moslems have been reported. In times of famine, it was common for the government to block food supplies from reaching the needy in the south.

In 2011, al-Bashir made a high-profile visit to China for talks with officials of a country that had for years insulated Sudan from the US sanctions. The 2009 warrant of arrest from the International Criminal Court at the Hague against al-Bashir, on charges of committing crimes against humanity, made the Sudanese leader almost a pariah on the world stage. Al-Bashir avoided arrest by restricting his travels only to friendly countries and to the AU headquarters in Addis Ababa. The African body and member nations refused to cooperate to have him arrested. But in China, he enjoyed red-carpet treatment, and his talks with President Hu Jintao underscored a desire for Sudan to continue with the oil flow into China which for years had stood at about 7 percent of Beijing's oil requirements. Although China supported Khartoum materially and financially, it also aided Juba in the Sudanese conflict.

Al-Bashir's partial isolation appeared to embolden him to carry out even more atrocious attacks against the south and to increase the suppression of the opposition and the media. In October 2012, when the editor-in-chief of the independent daily *Al-Tayar* published a story linking al-Bashir to corruption, he was arrested, convicted, and fined $1,400 or six months in jail; the reporter who wrote the story accusing al-Bashir and his family of being inextricably linked to corruption, Mohamed Zine El Abidine, was given a three-year suspended sentence. Al-Bashir always blamed criminal cartels instead of his own government for involvement in corruption, money laundering, and smuggling.

In March 2018, US Congressmen Jim McGovern, a Democrat, and Randy Hultgren, a Republican, co-chairs of the bipartisan Tom Lantos Human Rights Commission, wrote to President Donald Trump asking him to make Sudan under al-Bashir accountable for corruption and human rights abuses and "to create strong incentives for the democratic reforms necessary to end the suffering and oppression there."[124]

What was disheartening was that al-Bashir's Sudan was backed in its virulent actions by MNCs hungry for the country's natural resources, including gold reserves. Multinationals usually exploit countries in conflict and under despotic regimes. Like its neighbors South Sudan, the DRC, the Republic of Congo, Equatorial Guinea, Zimbabwe, and Angola, Khartoum fits the bill.

Thus, oil companies like Canada's Araki Energy Corporation, Malaysia's Petronas Oil Corporation, China's National Petroleum Corporation, and at least half a dozen other major players made money out of Sudan while secretly aiding one or both sides in the succession conflict that ended with the independence of South Sudan on July 9, 2011. Other oil companies, like Chevron, could not withstand the hostilities after some of their executives were killed or kidnapped during the first conflict from 1955 and 1972, and they either temporarily shut down operations or closed shop altogether. Even after the second conflict ended in 2005, life did not improve for the marginalized, mostly African populations of Darfur and Kordofan, as well as those inhabiting the Red Sea Hills

---

[124] Jim McGovern, "Bipartisan Group of 57 Lawmakers Call on Trump to Hold Sudan Accountable for Corruption, Human Rights Abuses," press release, March 28, 2018.

and the Blue Nile. Just as multinationals exploited the country through heavily tilted oil contracts, so did the government of Sudan exploit its own people through marginalization.

In 2017, TI's annual review, which uses business and government sources for its rankings, ranked Sudan among the most corrupt nations in the world along with Somalia, South Sudan, North Korea, and Syria. And despite the fact that Sudan signed the UN Anti-corruption Convention in 2005 and the African Union Convention on Preventing and Combating Corruption, and it has the Illegal Wealth Act, which prohibits money laundering and the smuggling of commodities, Sudan has taken few serious steps to combat bribery and corruption either in the public or the private sector. To help the country contain corruption and improve transparency, the WB in 2017 gave Sudan $5 million toward fiscal reforms.

Early in 2018, al-Bashir surprised even his most virulent critics when he ordered the arrest of 16 prominent businessmen and bankers, a director of the state petroleum company, and three officers of the National Intelligence Security Services (NISS) on charges of embezzlement and theft of public funds. The amounts involved were not revealed, and the case did not proceed. There were reports in May 2018 that some Cabinet ministers were in the pockets of at least 200 major companies and regularly received bribes to influence contracts for family members, political allies, or business associates of the president. Because the laws prohibiting officials from engaging in businesses are opaque, officials establish companies and use them to siphon public money through the illegal allocation of tenders. Much of the illicit revenue is banked abroad, notably in Malaysia. Some $16 billion is suspected to be invested abroad, one report says.[125] Without public disclosure regulations, Sudanese government officials engage in corrupt practices with impunity, knowing all too well there is no law in the country that provides a criminal penalty for official corruption.

---

[125] Khalil Charles, "Can Sudan's President Win His War on Corruption?" *The Middle East Monitor*, May 8, 2018.

THE REPUBLIC OF SOUTH SUDAN

Africa and the world were extremely excited when South Sudan gained full sovereignty and became the Republic of Sudan in 2011, six years after a comprehensive peace agreement was signed with Sudan, ending years of armed conflict. It was a joyous moment for the newest independent African nation, landlocked between Ethiopia, Kenya, the DRC, and the Central African Republic.

Sadly, the jovial but no-nonsense John Garang de Mabior, leader of Sudan People's Liberation Army (SPLA), the first vice president of Sudan after the signing of the Comprehensive Peace Agreement in Naivasha, Kenya, on January 9, 2005, was not present to witness the occasion. As he flew home from consulting the Ugandan president, Yoweri Museveni, in Uganda at the end of July 2005, his chartered helicopter crashed in the Zulia mountains, about 18 kilometers from the Ugandan border, and the charismatic bush fighter was killed.

On Independence Day, July 9, 2011, his long-time deputy, Salva Kiir Mayardit, was sworn in as president. To the majority of the 12 million Sudanese people, independence meant long-term peace and stability. But that was not to be. In 2013, a power struggle erupted in the capital of Juba, leading to a full-fledged cutthroat and bloody armed conflict between the national army and anti-government forces. Fighting was heavier around the lucrative oil fields in Unity State, forcing the oil fields operator there, Greater Pioneer Operating Company, to shut down and evacuate the area. Oil fields in the Upper Nile region, which also saw heavy fighting, underwent frequent closures.

The deployment of UN peacekeepers and the use of Ugandan forces on the side of the government did not yield tangible results, as the Chinese and Europeans continued to supply arms to both sides in the conflict, ignoring an EU arms embargo. The arms were often channeled through the Kenyan port of Mombasa into Uganda and finally into South Sudan.

The Swiss Graduate Institute of International and Development Studies in 2010 talked of Kenya's involvement in arms trafficking into South Sudan after satellite imagery showed tanks, which had arrived through the port of Mombasa, parked at the Sudanese army headquarters. The names of Egypt and Uganda also surfaced on UN lists among the major suppliers of arms to Juba. What all this meant was that Kenya, Uganda, and Egypt, among others, were complicit in the arms imports and were therefore fueling the conflict.

While the US sanctions against Sudan were ongoing, a few companies tried to puncture the embargo. One of them, a private security contractor, Blackwater Worldwide, attempted for two years to acquire a lucrative contract to sell defense equipment to South Sudan, ostensibly to defend Christians from Moslem/Arab military dictatorship but also to exploit the oil and mineral reserves in the region. Blackwater and its owner, Erik Prince, were in the bull's eye of a US federal investigation into allegations of sanctions violations, illegal exports, and bribery in contravention of US export control regulations, according to McClatchy, a news outlet. Although the military contractor was not criminally charged for selling satellite phones in 2005 and committing to deliver security services in 2006, it agreed before a US district court in New Bern, North Carolina in 2012 to pay a fine of up to $7.5 million in settlement of 17 criminal counts for violating trade sanctions against Sudan by selling arms and owning illegal weapons. The company, which changed ownership and became Academi LLC, also agreed to meet audit requirements and comply with export controls to avoid prosecution.

In the meantime, as fighting continued, MNCs flowed into South Sudan to take advantage of the government's vulnerability by signing cheap contracts with President Kiir for oil exploration in areas previously affected by the civil war. However, more than half a dozen companies that had operated in Sudan before South Sudan became independent either disagreed on terms or shied away from engaging with the new nation due to conflicts and corruption.

Whatever oil revenue came in, Kiir, who likes to wear a Texan "ten-gallon hat," and his associates, especially those from his home state of Warrap, siphoned it off and invested it either in expensive real estate in neighboring countries or shipped it to offshore accounts for safe keeping. South Sudan is the seventh-biggest oil producer in Africa after Nigeria, Libya, Algeria, Angola, Egypt, and Equatorial Guinea,[126] and it derives 98 percent of its revenue from oil. But with price fluctuations and the unending civil conflict, South Sudan has had to turn to the IMF and foreign financial institutions such as the Qatar National Bank to balance its military-eschewed budget.

The biggest public scandal in South Sudan was the grain saga in 2008, called the Dura Saga project, a food security program meant to provide grain in preparation for a projected famine in 2008. The government paid 290 companies $1 million to supply grain, but no food was delivered. Some of the companies were barely a week old when they were contracted, meaning they were specifically formed to exploit the public, and almost all did not sign any contract with the government. Authorities launched a criminal investigation to prosecute those involved, but soon the investigation fizzled out and no one was prosecuted.

In 2012, the South Sudanese government announced $4 billion had mysteriously disappeared from the Treasury. A seemingly furious Kiir wrote to 75 unnamed former and sitting government officials asking them to return the money. In 2013, he sacked two ministers for corruption, Finance Minister Kosti Manibe and Cabinet Affairs Minister Deng Alor, accusing them of transferring $8 million from the public coffers to private accounts. Observers

---

[126] David Morse, "How Oil Drives the Genocide in Darfur," *The Sudan Tribune*, August 18, 2005.

felt at the time that the move was not so much a genuine effort to stamp out graft but an attempt to push out his opponents from the government.

Casco Petroleum Overseas Limited, which provided inland freight transport in Kenya, the DRC, Uganda, and South Sudan, admitted in 2015 to paying regular kickbacks to customs officials and police to allow the transit of goods into Juba. It also admitted to tax evasion in South Sudan. Casco is an offshore company registered in the British Virgin Islands and owned by the Anatol Stati family—one of the richest in Moldova, a former Soviet republic.

In 2017, the South Sudan Parliamentary Committee on Finance and Economic Planning said in a report that it was shocked when it discovered that "revenues accruing from oil were not deposited into the Bank of South Sudan…. The bank literary has no reserves …. It is empty," said an MP who wanted to remain anonymous. "Whatever was there before the war has been depleted."[127] What the committee didn't say was that South Sudan had become a kleptocracy, with leaders embracing self-aggrandizement and individualism and engaging in a grotesque abuse of power. The state-owned Nile Petroleum Corporation (NILEPET), which oversees oil exploration, production, and marketing, reports directly to Kiir, and it is generally known that top officials of the organization collude to ensure oil revenue is directed to Kiir's and his allies' personal accounts. Some of the money is used to fuel the ongoing conflict against Kiir's archenemy Riak Machar.

Money laundering and currency speculation are also rampant within the higher ranks of government and the military in South Sudan. Foreign exchange rates on the black market are often influenced by the elite and fluctuate upward rapidly. They could double, triple, or even quadruple within a short period of time, or tumble down the cliff like goslings, turning currency holders into millionaires or paupers in the blink of an eye.

---

[127] "S. Sudan Does Not Keep Oil Revenues in Central Bank," *The Sudan Tribune*, August 31, 2017.

In 2016, a Kenyan banking institution partly owned by the Kenyan government was suspected of laundering millions of dollars belonging to senior Sudanese government officials. The revelation was exposed in a two-year investigation by the US-based The Sentry, which named top army commanders as offenders. In a 13-page report, the organization, co-founded by Hollywood actor George Clooney and activist John Prendergast, also claimed that a total of $3.03 million moved through the US-dollar personal account of an army lieutenant general at a leading Kenyan bank between January 2012 and early 2016, when he was the army's deputy chief of staff for logistics. It claimed the officer "transferred or withdrew nearly $1.2 million and moved 'significant assets' overseas via correspondent account at the bank and other regional leaders" during the four years of The Sentry's study. Some of the money came from a Chinese engineering firm supplying mine explosives. Another army general received $367,000 in transfers to his personal account at the same bank between February and December 2014.

The Sentry's investigation report revealing massive illegal payments to government and military officials by the state oil company NILEPET shocked the world. A total of $80 million, representing 84 transactions, was recorded in documents of the state-owned company as having been paid to politicians, military officials, government agencies, and companies owned by politicians and their families. The payments, six of which were to an airline company partly owned by the First Lady, Mary Ayen Mayardit, were noted as security expenses. The illegal transfer of the money further exposed Kiir's administration as a notoriously corrupt regime in a country where 80 percent of the country's population of 12.5 million lives on $1 a day.

Finance and Economic Planning Minister David Deng Athorbei had to fight off allegations published by The Indian Ocean Newsletter (ION), in 2016, that he and his son, Apar Athorbei, were using several bank accounts at another Kenyan bank to launder money. Some of the accounts were in the names of companies they controlled. The report alleged that $200,000 in bribes was regularly deposited in those accounts by a British company which prints money for South Sudan. The minister vigorously denied the allegations and threatened to sue the ION, but the claims were considered so serious that the SFO offered to investigate the Bank of England's banknote printer after it won a contract to print 500 million Sudanese pounds in 2015. The conclusions of that investigation were not clear. No one was prosecuted by Kiir's government for violating currency laws. The SFO raided two offices of De La Rue International Limited, a money-printing company in London.

Without legislation to bar conflicts of interest in South Sudan, the field is open for government officials to run private companies and then use those companies to bid on government tenders. Nothing prevents a minister, for example, from forming a company which then bids for a government contract.

A 28-year old chubby-faced Sudanese man, Lawrence Lual Malong, who claims that God made him rich, posted a video on social media in 2018 of himself "swimming" in a tub full of US dollars. When he visited Uganda later that year, he was arrested and detained by the security authority there and charged with fraud for allegedly obtaining $1.9 million from an Ethiopian businessman claiming he could sell him gold. The case was ongoing in April 2019.

Although bribery in the South Sudanese oil industry is hidden in multinational bureaucracy, it nevertheless exists. In 2011, an Israeli businessman was briefly detained for attempting to bribe the Sudanese minister of petroleum and mining, Dhieu Dau. The businessman's lawyer, Kiir Choi, denied the bribery allegation, and the accused was released from the northern division police station without charge.

The internal strife inside South Sudan is hurting the country's economy. Global Witness estimates that between 2011 and 2016,

$8 billion of oil revenue was lost to conflicts and corruption in the country. So far, absolute peace has eluded the country, and both Kiir and his opponent Riak Machar have chosen to take hardline positions for reasons of greed over mineral revenues. Reconciliation efforts by political and religious leaders have hit a snag many times over, leaving the country to slide further down the cliff of destruction.

Khartoum has not been helping either. Over the years, it has been stealing South Sudanese oil, sabotaging that country's economy. South Sudan accuses Khartoum of having stolen approximately six million barrels of its oil worth $600 million as the product made its way via a pipeline through Sudanese territory to Port Sudan for onward shipment to markets overseas. For using the services of its northern neighbor, the South is also paying for transit, transportation, processing, and marine terminal usage fees. However, Juba expects the transit problem to cease once the 2,000-kilometer, $24.5 billion Lamu-Southern Sudan-Ethiopia Transport Corridor (LAPSSET) pipeline project from the Kenyan port of Lamu to South Sudan is completed. The second channel, expected to ease transportation through LAPSSET to avoid Khartoum taxes, will take the South Sudanese oil by pipeline through Ethiopia to Djibouti, a distance of about 1,000 kilometers. South Sudan and Djibouti signed an agreement on the project in 2013 but work on it is yet to start.

Meanwhile, Nigeria's Oranto Petroleum—owned by Nigerian billionaires and politicians led by Prince Arthur Eze—announced in 2017 that it was committing $500 million toward what it called a comprehensive exploration campaign on a 25,150-square kilometer area in South Sudan. Oranto and a sister company, Atlas Petroleum International, are part of the Atlas Oranto Group, which operates 20 oil and gas acreages in Equatorial Guinea, Ghana, Liberia, Namibia, Nigeria, Benin, Côte d'Ivoire, Sao Tome and Principe, Senegal, and Guinea.

The deal, like so many other oil deals in Africa, was not entirely favorable to South Sudan. The government's NILEPET, which oversees oil operations, was apportioned only 10 percent of the shares, while Oranto kept 90 percent, meaning the Nigerian company is to export most of the revenue, leaving the people of South Sudan with a pittance. Like in many oil-producing countries in Africa, South Sudan rarely floats international bids for concessions, but even when it does, the company favored by the leadership and willing to pay a bribe is the only one assured to win.

Global Witness reported in March 2018 how the state-owned NILEPET was being directly controlled by Kiir and his inner circle and how it was being used to funnel millions in oil revenue to pay security officers and ethnic militias without caring about oversight and accountability. Michael Gibb, campaign leader for conflict resources at Global Witness, said the government oil corporation was serving "the interests of a narrow cabal and was being used to prolong the brutal conflict." It has "been captured by predatory elites,"[128] the NGO said.

In 2017, US authorities sanctioned close associates of President Kiir for allegedly profiting from corruption. General Malek Reuben Riak Rengu, the army's deputy chief of staff in charge of military procurement; Michael Makuei Lueth, the information minister; and Paul Malong Awan, the former chief of staff of the SPLA, were barred from visiting the United States. Any assets they had in the United States were blocked, and American citizens were prohibited from engaging with them. The three were believed to use American banks to hide their corruption proceeds.

Another South Sudanese cited by the United States is Benjamin Bol Mel, Kiir's former principal financial advisor and head of ABM Thai-South Sudan Construction Company Limited (ABMC), which

---

[128] "South Sudan's Leadership Uses State-Owned Oil Company NILEPET to Funnel Millions into Brutal Security Services and Ethnic Militia," Global Witness, report, March 6, 2018.

received millions of dollars in road contracts in Juba and other parts of the country in a single-source scheme that smelled of corruption. Mel is one of several officials and businesspeople, among them the former president of Gambia Yahya Jammeh, who were sanctioned by the United States for human rights abuses and corruption in December 2017. American companies and individuals were prohibited from having any commercial or financial transaction with Mel.

A 2018 report by the London-based Conflict Armament Research Organization named Great Britain, Israel, Austria, and Romania as some of the countries fueling the civil war in South Sudan by supplying military jets, surveillance aircraft, and ammunition. Israel is known to have given arms and surveillance equipment worth millions of dollars using the former head of the Israeli Army's directorate, Major General Israel Ziv, as a middleman. The US government sanctioned him in 2018. However, it found no evidence suggesting governments in those countries directly knew about the arms transfers.

Ziv is a retired major general who reportedly sold $150 million worth of arms, including rifles, grenade launchers, and shoulder-fired rockets, to South Sudan using an agricultural company as a cover. The US Treasury Department said the Israeli owner of a security firm, Global CST, also planned to organize attacks by mercenaries on South Sudanese oil fields and infrastructure in order to create a problem that only his organization could solve. Also censured was Oba William Olawo, a Sudanese businessman accused of trading in arms and armaments to South Sudan who, in 2017, reportedly fueled intra-clan ethnic violence that led to thousands of civilians being killed.

There is a bleak hope that the UN embargo, imposed in July 2018 over arms sales to South Sudan, would bear fruit in the near future. A researcher for the London-based Conflict Armament Research Organization, Justine Fleischner, said in 2018 that although China stopped shipping arms to Sudan in 2014, what had already been shipped was capable of sustaining the conflict for years.

In the meantime, several peace agreements, signed under the auspices of the Intergovernmental Authority on Development and the AU since 2015, have failed to shut down the atrocities between warring South Sudanese sides. By the end of 2019, people were still being killed in the country, the UN arms embargo notwithstanding, while tens of thousands of people have fled to neighboring countries.

In June 2018, the United States said it was looking into the accounts of President Kiir, his perennial opponent Riek Machar, and other senior government officials to see if they had profited from the civil war and laundered their loot through Kenyan banks or other foreign financial institutions. Present and former Sudanese leaders and military officers own vast real estate properties in Kenya and Uganda, and the US-based Enough Project has asked the two countries to seize those properties, but Kenya, whose leadership has extensive business interests in South Sudan, has refused to take punitive action against the corrupt Sudanese leaders.

At the independence of South Sudan, Americans were sympathetic to the situation in the country and poured in millions of dollars in aid. This situation was no longer the same in 2018. When a senior Sudanese government official, Taban Deng Gai, went to Washington, DC in October of that year to ask for money to fund the peace deal, he was mocked and derided in a closed-door meeting. Former US government officials and humanitarian organization executives who had previously worked in South Sudan accused the Juba government of squandering American aid money and frustrating peace efforts, rubbishing Deng's defense of the state's commitment to peace "with a mixture of gasps, muffled laughter, and eye rolls by those in attendance."[129]

In the meantime, South Sudan, which maintains 3.5 billion barrels of oil reserves, resumed production in 2018 after a protracted

---

[129] Robbie Gramer, "Remember South Sudan? Washington Would Prefer Not To," FP News, October 4, 2018.

suspension of production due to civil war at the profitable Unity State oilfields. The oilfields were expected to increase oil output from 130,000 to 350,000 barrels per day—the same level as at independence—bringing in a revenue of $5 billion in the next few years.[130]

In September 2018, South Sudan extended its Exploration and Production Sharing Agreements (ESPA) with the dominants of the oil industry in the country, namely the CNPC, Malaysia's Petronas, India's Oil and Natural Gas Corporation, and the national entity NILEPET, for another six years, reviving hopes of better times ahead. Details of those agreements, as usual, were not revealed. However, hopes for future prospects dimmed in mid-2010 when China's CNPC, India's ONGC and Malaysia's Petronas, threatened to exit Sudan due to the country's failure to pay oil bills amounting to $500 million for oil extracted from their joint blocks.

Oil is not the only national asset causing conflict in South Sudan. There is also a scramble for the rare teak wood, which is in great demand in Asian countries such as India, Vietnam, and Thailand. The timber, which takes over 50 years to mature, is grown largely in the Yei River region controlled by the South Sudan People's Liberation Movement in Opposition (SPLM-IO) under Machar and is a significant foreign exchange earner. Like in the oil industry, concessions for lumbering have been issued through questionable deals, suggesting money could be changing hands.

---

[130] Sam Mednick, "Oil-Rich South Sudan to Resume Production in War-Hit Region," AP, News, August 30, 2018.

PART FOUR

CHAPTER 7

WEST AFRICA

Scandals are numerous, ministers grow rich, their wives doll themselves up, the members of parliament feather their nests and there is not a soul down to the simple policeman or the customs officer who does not join in the great procession of corruption. – Franz Fanon on West Africa, 1961

EQUATORIAL GUINEA

The coming to power in a military coup by Teodoro Obiang Nguema Mbasogo in 1979 also ushered in a boundless surge of kleptocracy that propelled one of Africa's largest oil producers into a poverty-ridden nation in which three-quarters of the population of one million live in abject poverty.

While his psychotic predecessor, Francisco Macias Nguema, declared himself the country's "unique miracle"[131] and was known for engaging in cannibalism and collecting human skulls,[132] he was also a dictator and murderer who ordered the killing of half of his Cabinet and hundreds, if not thousands, of citizens who opposed his policies during his reign between 1968 and 1979. Upon assuming power, Obiang ordered the arrest, trial, and execution of Nguema at the infamous Playa Negra (Black Beach) prison and then began a long stint of authoritarian rule. Soon he was to become one of the world's most crooked leaders, who turned corruption "into an art form"[133] and violated every rule in the human rights book.

An Equatoguinean radio program called Bidze-Nduan (Bury the Fire) described Obiang as "like God in heaven" and "in permanent contact with the Almighty. He can decide to kill without anyone calling him to account and without going to hell because it is God himself, with whom he is in permanent contact, who gives him this strength."[134] However, his wrinkled face carrying the weight of gold-rimmed glasses and a head with a layer of thick, dyed black hair do not give any inkling he could be anyone other than a clan member of the Akoakam-Esaugui, which he was. He has a brutish facial expression and a mean disposition befitting the title "the

---

[131] Michael Peel, "The Big African Oil Grab," *The New Statesman,* America, April 10, 2008.
[132] Ian Birrell, "The Strange and Evil World of Equatorial Guinea," *The Observer*, 22, October 2011.
[133] "How Equatorial Guinea Turned Corruption into an Art Form," Human Rights Watch, report, June 15, 2017.
[134] "Equatorial Guinea's 'God,'" *BBC*, news, July 26, 2003.

torturer-in-chief,"[135] which he earned from opponents for his brutality.

Controlled by a relatively small clique of "about 200 people, including the president, his many children and parents"[136] called the Nguema/Mongomo group, Equatorial Guinea has one of the highest per capita GDPs in the world at $32,000, but it ranks 135th out of 188 countries in the UN Human Development Index due to poor delivery of health, education, and other basic necessities. Equatorial Guinea is a good example of the so-called "resource curse," where a country with ample natural resources fails to provide for its people. His dream, as Obiang told the King and Queen of Spain during a visit to the capital of Malabo in 1979, of making Equatorial Guinea the "Switzerland of Africa" turned out to be a pipe dream.

The causes of the country's woes are bribery and corruption. Between 2005 and 2017, the WorldData.info Development of Corruption Index ranked Equatorial Guinea at 83 against Africa's average of 67.9 and the worldwide level of 56.9. Scholar Geoffrey Wood said corruption in Equatorial Guinea is so entrenched "it can be classified as a criminal state,"[137] even though in 2004 the country was said to have the fastest-growing economy in the world.[138] A large proportion of its population lives in abject poverty, while a small percentage in leadership and the military enjoy a life some citizens of Switzerland would be envious of.

[135] Neal Baker, "Meet the World's Most Terrifying Man," *The Sun,* September 10, 2016.
[136] "Equatorial Guinea – Corruption," GlobalSecurity.org, commentary, undated.
[137] Ken Silverstein, "Teodoro's World," Foreign Policy, feature, February 21, 2011.
[138] Jon Lunn, "Equatorial Guinea: A Quick Outlook," House of Commons Library, International Affairs and Defense section, June 24, 2011.

In addition, President Obiang is shamelessly nepotistic to the point of being a subject of mirth. One of Obiang's five wives was the minister of health and social action; one of his sons, Teodoro Nguema Obiang Mangue, commonly known as "Teodorin," was the minister of forestry and then vice president; another, Gabriel Mbaga Obiang, was minister of mines, industry and energy; and yet another, Ruslan Obiang, headed the Sports Ministry.

While President Obiang tries to maintain a façade of secrecy about his wealth, his family members, particularly Teodorin, are flashy with their affluence. Teodorin's extravagance was evident in the mansions he owned in Europe and the United States, the top-of-the-line vehicles he drove, and the expensive suits and accessories he wore. His assets in Switzerland worth $13 million were auctioned in mid-2019. Many described him as a spoiled child living high on taxpayers' money.

President Obiang and his family own almost everything in Equatorial Guinea, from shares in major oil companies to hotels, restaurants, and construction projects. They travel in private jets with bodyguards in tow and carry large amounts of money for shopping in trendy world capitals. The country, says John Bennett, a former US ambassador to Equatorial Guinea, is "the world's finest example of a country privatized by a kleptomaniac without a scintilla of social consciousness."[139]

There are numerous allies-turned-foes who have spilled the beans about illegal activities executed by the Obiang family. Upon being jailed for nine years for trafficking 14 kilos of heroin in Madrid in 1997, a former information minister, Santos Pascal Bikomo, wrote an open letter in which he described how the president, his son Teodorin, and the president's brother Armengol distributed drugs

---

[139] Leif Wenar, *Blood Oil: Tyrants, Violence, and the Rules That Run the World* (Oxford University Press, 2016), 255.

in Europe using shipments of tropical timber, diplomatic bags, and even Obiang's baggage during state trips.[140] None of those claims were verified, but the fact that they were made by a man who was close to the ruling hierarchy show how deeply involved Obiang's family was in illegal activities to amass wealth. The reason Teodorin was appointed as the top manager of all forests in the country was give him a chance to "eat" from the lucrative timber industry. The country is a large supplier of timber to China and European countries.

In 2017, a French court convicted Teodorin in absentia for embezzling $175 million from Equatorial Guinea to fund his lavish lifestyle in Europe. He was given a three-year suspended sentence and fined $35 million. In the United States, he agreed to forfeit $30 million after reaching a settlement on money-laundering accusations pertaining to a $30 million mansion in Malibu, California and a $38.5 million private jet suspected to have been bought using corrupt money.

But that was not the only time the young millionaire with boyish intensity found himself in trouble. In September 2018, Brazilian officials, while checking Teodorin's plane after landing at an airport near São Paulo in the southeast with his entourage, found a suitcase full of money on the plane—$1.4 million in total—and bags filled with diamond-studded watches estimated at $15 million. Officials seized the goods, since they were not covered by diplomatic immunity.[141] Brazilian laws do not allow people to bring into the country more than $2,400. The money was suspected to be part of the loot the Obiangs were stealing from public coffers.

The former Spanish colony is the fourth-largest oil-producing nation in sub-Saharan Africa, behind Angola, Nigeria, and Sudan,

---

[140] Adam Roberts, *The Wonga Coup: Guns, Thugs, and a Ruthless Determination to Create Mayhem in an Oil-Rich Corner of Africa* (Public Affairs, 2006), 45.
[141] Tom Rogan, "Celebrate Brazil's Ambush of a Corrupt Delegation from Equatorial Guinea," *The Washington Examiner*, September 17, 2018.

and earns billions of dollars from oil every year. ExxonMobil Corporation was the first company to explore oil in the country in 1995 and was followed by Amerada Hess, Marathon Oil Corporation, and others, creating a boom for the ruling elite who entered into joint ventures with the foreign firms.

In 1996, one giant US company entered into a joint venture with Socio Abayak, a company owned by Obiang, and leased land and buildings from Abayak which are managed by Obiang's wife, Constancia Mangue Nsue.

Another oil company paid Obiang $2 million for two pieces of land on Bioko island, an area known for its hydrocarbon deposits. The agent negotiating the sale was Abayak. And because there are no conflict-of-interest laws in the country, Obiang family members and government officials operate with impunity, running private companies and bidding for state tenders. Teodorin said once that it was not uncommon, nor against the law, for a Cabinet minister to end up with a chunk of the "contract price in his bank account."[142]

MNCs always trampled on each other to reach the ear of the callous African dictator in the hope of reaping great returns from Equatorial Guinea. To get there, they use money, and lots of it, to grease the palm of the first family. One oil company reportedly paid $385,000 into the personal account of Obiang's wife, Constancia. Others contributed as much as $275,000 each for what was called "student funds." In total, more than $4 million was paid by oil companies to support over a hundred students abroad, "most of whom were the children or relatives of wealthy or powerful officials."[143] ExxonMobil was also accused of "keeping failed states failing."[144] Paul Wolfowitz, a former WB director, said the company was "aiding corruption to assure its profits helped cripple Equatorial

---

[142] Sarah Saadoun, "Ill-Gotten Goods: Equatorial Guinea is a Case Study in Self-Dealing," Human Rights Watch, report, July 20, 2017.
[143] Adam Roberts, *The Wonga Coup: Guns, Thugs and Ruthless Determination to Create Mayhem in an Oil-Rich Corner of Africa* (Public Affairs, 2006), 228.
[144] M. Ibrahim, P. Wolfowitz, B. Cardin, and R. Offenheiser, "Who Else Is to Blame?" Forbes Policy, 2010.

Guinea."[145] Another US company paid up to $50,000 yearly to send Teodorin to Pepperdine University in Malibu, California. The companies either denied the allegations or refused to comment when queried by Human Rights Watch.

A 2004 US Senate report investigating money laundering in the US banking industry found that in addition to paying for scholarships, oil companies also hired companies associated with Obiang and rented property from government officials and their relatives, moves that raised what the report said, were concerns related to corruption and profiteering. Out of 28 properties leased by one of the companies in the country, for example, 18 belonged to Obiang family members and people connected to the family.

The Senate report also named the United States' Riggs Bank for handling the proceeds of corruption estimated at $700 million in 60 accounts and a dozen certificates of deposit belonging to Obiang family members and government officials. For handling stolen money, Riggs was fined $25 million by US authorities. It was reported that, on occasion, Equatorial embassy staff arrived at Riggs Bank carrying suitcases full of cash for deposit, money believed to be from the sale of oil.[146] However, the government claimed the money was part of the national assets and not the property of individuals. In addition to Riggs Bank, the US-affiliated HSBC Luxembourg also held proceeds belonging to Obiang, his family, and officials. The Madrid branch of Banco Santander Central Hispano reportedly received more than $26.5 million from the government's oil account at Riggs Bank in Washington, DC for the account of Kalunga Company, believed to be partially owned

---

[145] Naman K. Shah, "Corporate Philanthropy and Conflicts of Interest in Public Health: ExxonMobil, Equatorial Guinea, and Malaria." *Journal of Public Health Policy,* 34, no. 1 (January 2013), 121-136.
[146] US Senate Permanent Sub-Committee on Investigations, "Money Laundering and Foreign Corruption: Enforcement and Effectiveness of the Patriotic Act: A Case Study Involving Riggs Bank," July 15, 2004.

by the young Teodorin, between June and December 2000,[147] according to a report submitted to the US Senate by Banko Santander in the United States. The Riggs accounts had three authorized signatories: Obiang himself, his son Gabriel, and his nephew, Melchor Esono Edjo, the secretary of state for treasury and budget. Two signatories were needed for withdrawals, and one of them had to be Obiang's.[148]

Riggs was further found to have helped Obiang open an overseas shell firm, Otongo S.A., incorporated in the Bahamas. He also allowed wire transfers of $35 million from the Washington, DC accounts to two unknown companies with accounts in bank secrecy jurisdictions and $1 million to another bank controlled by the African dictator.

Several US oil companies paid illegally obtained money not only to Obiang's accounts but to the accounts of other senior Equatorial Guineans at Riggs Bank. The Senate report said the bank paid little or no attention to its anti-money-laundering obligations, turned a blind eye to evidence suggesting the bank was handling the proceeds of foreign corruption, and allowed numerous suspicious transactions to take place without notifying law enforcement. Riggs was eventually sold to a rival in 2004.

Interestingly, Obiang was a frequent visitor to the United States and was received with the pomp and dignity normally accorded to heads of state, even though for years US officials had looked upon the country as a laughingstock.[149] During a visit to the State Department in 2006, Secretary of State Condoleezza Rice described Obiang as a "good friend"[150] of the United States, and

[147] Hugh O'Shaughnessy and Paul Lashmar, "HSBC and Santander Slammed in Senate Money-Laundering Report," The Independent, September 5, 2004.
[148] Stephane Mayoux, "E. Guinea Warning after Bank Probe," BBC, July 21, 2004.
[149] Ken Silverstein, The Secret World of Oil (Verso, 2014), 63.
[150] "Remarks with Equatorial Guinean President Teodoro Obiang Nguema Mbasogo before the Meeting," US Department of State, January 20, 2001.

she never mentioned the state of absolute corruption in Equatorial Guinea, even though she insisted on the need to expand democratic space and respect for human rights. American officials occasionally visited Malabo as well and pledged support to the corrupt African leader, perhaps to protect US oil interests there.

President Obiang owns properties in Paris, Madrid, and Las Palmas—as well as a $2.6 million residence in Potomac, Maryland, in the United States—many of which were subject to investigations by host countries to find out whether they were bought with public funds. A 107-page Human Rights Watch report, titled *Well Oiled: Oil and Human Rights in Equatorial Guinea,* said Obiang used the oil boom to entrench and enrich himself at the expense of the people. "Obiang controls the oil, the government, and the country," said Arvind Ganesan, director of the business and human rights program at Human Rights Watch.[151]

Moreover, doing business in Equatorial Guinea can be both profitable and dangerous. In 2013, the Spanish government warned investors to be careful when dealing with the Obiang clan, saying any dispute could lead to detention and even death. That was evident in the case of Valencia-based businessman Robert Cubria. He sold several warehouses to Genoveva Andeme Obiang, one of the president's daughters, who was also the co-director of the Senegal-based Central Bank of West Africa (BEAC). When the deal collapsed, his passport was confiscated, and he was forced to take refuge in the Spanish Embassy for two months. Before he was allowed to leave the country, he had to pay a "gift" of $57,000 in building materials.[152] The Equatorial Guinean government also habitually framed recalcitrant investors with false rape charges, convicted them, and jailed them at the infamous Black Beach prison for months on end before letting them go, minus their assets.

---

[151] Jad Mouawad, "Oil Corruption in Equatorial Guinea," *The New York Times*, July 9, 2009.

[152] Jose Maria Irujo, "The High Price of Doing Business in Equatorial Guinea," *El Pais*, April 3, 2013.

The Obiangs have full control of oil resources. Oil contracts in Equatorial Guinea are open only to the president and his small elite of insiders, since oil Is considered a "state secret." However, Obiang's Equatorial Guinea is not the only country that kept its oil contracts under seal. Kenya, for example, had brushed off demands from civil society organizations for contract disclosure on oil discoveries by Tullow Oil in 2017, despite an earlier promise by President Uhuru Kenyatta that the documents would be made public. That left the local Turkana people in the dark as to what their rights were or whether they had any. Conversely, in February 2018, Ghana opened a registry of all contracts, licenses, and permits signed with multinational oil companies, a move hailed as a positive first on a continent where transparency and accountability are gravely lacking.

By keeping oil transactions as a "state secret"[153] in Equatorial Guinea, Obiang and his relatives are able to stash huge amounts of money extracted from multinational oil companies in offshore accounts without expecting questions from anyone. Ministers and senior government officials also benefit from government tenders, which they inflate to reap the highest illegal monetary yields. The monies they steal end in banks or offshore accounts overseas. Instead of using the oil revenue to improve the standards of the largely disadvantaged population in a place where electricity is unreliable, water is scarce, the infrastructure is abysmal, and diseases such as malaria are endemic, the government spends it on corruption-prone infrastructure projects to make more money.

The state builds "white elephant" projects, which rise majestically skyward in the capital of Malabo like kites in distress, and constructs hundreds of kilometers of roads to nowhere, not to speak of "empty 5-star hotels."[154] The only people who live lavishly are the oil executives, who reside in specially insulated compounds in the

---

[153] "Equatorial Guinea's Leaders Accused of Pilfering Oil Revenues," *VOA*, news, October 30, 2009.
[154] "How Equatorial Guinea Turned Corruption into an Art Form," Human Rights Watch, analysis, June 15, 2017.

city that stand out as "a securitized monument to escalating petro-inequality and the failure of the state to invest in its newfound wealth in public services."[155]

Obiang's corruption complex extends beyond the borders of his country. In 2015, the Russian family of Vladimir Kokorev, his wife Julia, and his eldest son Igor were arrested in Panama and charged with laundering $30 million on behalf of President Obiang. The Spanish Money Laundering Prevention Unit had been monitoring the Kokorevs since 2003. As the net was closing in following allegations that Kokorev had laundered $26.5 million smuggled from Equatorial Guinea into Spanish real estate, the family fled their home in Madrid, only to be arrested in Panama. They were repatriated back to Madrid. The money, which came out of a New York account of GEPetrol, Equatorial Guinea's state oil company, was traced to an account held by the Kokorevs in Las Palmas. Kokorev and his family were released in 2017 after spending more than two years in preventive prison in Las Palmas.

Kokorev together with Vladimir Stefanov, a Lithuanian businessman who ran a fleet of cargo ships linked to Obiang; and two Ukrainians, Vladimir Yevdokimov, a former member of the Ukraine security services, and Roman Chelnokov, Equatorial Guinea's honorary consul in Ukraine, reportedly worked as a cartel in a string of deals meant to exploit Equatorial Guinean riches. The foreigners denied any links to the Obiang family and said whatever evidence Spain had against them was manipulated.

---

[155] Hannah C. Appel, "Walls and White Elephants: Oil Extraction, Responsibility, and Infrastructural Violence in Equatorial Guinea," *Ethnography* 13, no. 4, special issue on infrastructural violence (December 2012): 439–465.

CHAD

In the west African nation of Chad, all contracts beyond $10 million must be approved by the president and the minister of economy and finance. But procurement officials circumvent this requirement by splitting large contracts into small units and distributing them to top government officials, cronies, and businesspeople with high connections to the executive, notwithstanding the fact that public officials are barred from engaging in commercial activities.

Chad's president, Idriss Deby, who has ruled the country since 1990, is among Africa's longest-serving leaders and has admitted more than once that many of the richest Chadians have amassed large fortunes from corruption and the embezzlement of public money. His vocal condemnation of corruption and bribery have not yielded much, given the fact that his own family members are involved in plundering the country's main oil resources. Thus, riches from oil are concentrated among a few, despite persistent WB demands that oil revenue be put in a trustee account to cater to development in the landlocked country of 15 million people. The WB demands were put across to Chadian officials during negotiations to fund the Chad–Cameroon Oil Pipeline.

The 1070-kilometer pipeline, which was completed in 2003, transports crude oil from southwestern Chad through tropical forests inhabited by the Bakola pygmy people to a floating facility 11 kilometers off the Cameroonian coast, near Kribi city. However, the experiment suggested by the multilateral organizations, to have oil money deposited in a special account, failed and no positive impact on the livelihood of the people has been seen. Houses even in the capital of Ndjamena lack toilets; electricity and water are scarce, educational and health facilities are poor, and unemployment is high, thus breeding crime among dejected youths. The frustration of the WB was expressed in a statement in 2008, which lamented that Chad had failed to follow through on the 2001 agreement, as well as on another one in 2006 to the effect that oil money be allocated to eradicate poverty and improve education, health, infrastructure, rural development, and governance.[156] Instead, Chad continued to use the money derived from its dozens of oilfields for other purposes, including buying arms to fight militia groups. The country has been plagued by insurgency since the late 1960s, following tensions between the Arab-Muslims in the north and the Christians in the south of the country. A substantial amount of money was also directed at building unnecessary infrastructure projects "which are susceptible to corruption."[157] After much prodding from global organizations, Chad agreed to repay the money to the International Development Association (IDA), which is part of the WB, and to the International Bank for Reconstruction and Development (IBRD). That payment process was completed in September 2008.

New hope for Chadians

One of the biggest oil producers in the former French colony was ExxonMobil which entered the country in 1996 to explore oil in the Doba basin of southern Chad. Due to a poor road infrastructure between Doba and the capital N'Djamena, ExxonMobil acquired its own fleet of planes and built airstrips, to make it easier for company staff to travel between the two points. The entry of the American-based oil giant brought hope to the people of Moundou town in Doba whose life was punctuated by poverty and lack of essential services including electricity. The exploration of oil was therefore "seen as manna from heaven."[158] But their hope was only partly realized. The lucky Chadians were employed at the ExxonMobil plant, but the majority of people remained jobless. Nearby slum settlements such as the Satan Village and Moudadoigne mushroomed and expanded. Locals lived in darkness at night and

---

[156] "World Bank Statement on Chad-Cameroon pipeline," press release no. 2009/073/AFR, September 9, 2008.

[157] Annalisa M. Leibold, "Aligning Incentives for Development: The World Bank and the Chad-Cameroon Oil Pipeline," *Yale Journal of International Law* 36, no. 167 (2011): 177.

[158] Yorbana, Seign-goura. "Representations of oil in Chad: A blessing or a curse? In: *African Spectrum*, 52, no. 1, (2017): 65-83.

water was scarce. Conversely, ExxonMobil's expansive facility at Kome was all lit-up, thanks to a 120-megawatt generating plant that produced "six times as much electricity as the entire Republic of Chad."[159] But more concerning was the fact that the ExxonMobil facility also attracted girls who abandoned school to work as prostitutes. Local farmers who were paid large amounts of compensation for their land by the oil firm abandoned fields and spent their money on prostitutes. The rate of AIDS infection dramatically increased.[160] Neither the government in N'Djamena nor the oil company saw nothing wrong with the rapidly changing landscape at Kome and did nothing to improve living conditions.

In the meantime, China had entered the market and had bought exploration rights to a large oil zone. For nine years, Chad supported Taiwan but in 2006 it established relations with Beijing which built large infrastructure projects including highways and a new international airport in exchange for Chadian oil. Other companies such as Esso Chad, a consortium of US and Malaysian firms, the China National Petroleum Corporation (CNPC), the Anglo-Swiss's Glencore, and the Canadian Caracal Energy, followed, though China remained Chad's biggest foreign investor and one of its biggest creditors. But China's presence in Chad has also been controversial. In 2014, CNPC was fined $1.2 billion by authorities there for dumping spilled crude oil into open ditches which was a violation of local environmental standards.

Diplomatic cover

In a case believed to be the first of its kind, the SFO in 2018 recovered $6.2 million from two Chadian diplomats who had accepted bribes from a Canadian firm, Caracal Energy Incorporated, formerly known as Griffiths Energy International Incorporated. The SFO

---

[159] "When ExxonMobil Came to Chad," Slate, article, April 5, 2007.
[160] Ibid.

was involved because it was a UK broker who worked on the takeover of Griffiths, and the corrupt proceeds were deposited in the Royal Bank of Scotland, which was within its jurisdiction.

Griffiths had sold shares to a nominee of the diplomats for about $1 million using a front company called "Chad Oil," which was set up less than a week before the deal was negotiated. The diplomats used the company to buy discounted shares, which they then sold to others at a much higher price for profit. In exchange for the deeply discounted shares, the diplomats helped Griffiths win exclusive oil development rights in Chad. Griffiths self-reported the illicit transaction. After a three-day trial, the UK's High Court ruled in favor of the SFO and ordered that Griffiths be fined $10.35 million and that the money be handed over to the DFID to invest in projects that would benefit the poorest people in Chad.

Griffiths had been involved in another case in 2013 involving Chadian diplomats. He admitted to bribing Chad's former ambassador to the United States and Canada, Mahamoud Adam Bechir, his wife, and Youssouf Hamid Takane, Chad's deputy chief of mission in the United States. In 2015, the High Court approved a DOJ request for the seizure of assets held by the three amounting to $34 million.

Bechir, who introduced Griffiths to opportunities in Chad in 2008, was transferred from the United States to South Africa, where he was sacked as the top diplomat.

GABON

Omar Bongo was among the longest-serving African presidents. He ruled a country with a population of less than two million people for 41 years and died in 2009, leaving behind a country in financial ruins despite its rich natural resources including oil, gold, manganese, and wood. A debonair man with a penchant for expensive French suits, fully furnished planes and boats, and luxury villas in Europe, Bongo was a French-speaking African with fine tastes who was besotted with the French culture.

He was also unashamedly corrupt, with several big multinational companies feeding his appetite for acquisitiveness with cash kickbacks and gifts in exchange for public tenders. Observers have thrown a spate of derogatory descriptions at Bongo: "an obscure thug ... on the payroll of the French secret service,"[161] "a tiny natty man, very black,"[162] "one of the greediest ... the only postcolonial African Head of State to take his country's riches as a personal reward for the burdens of office,"[163] and an African ruler "who has made the country the world's biggest per capita consumer of champagne."[164]

Nevertheless, the man who wore lifts in his shoes to pump up his height was a consequential darling of France which saw nothing wrong in his pompous and materialistic behavior. He courted the French and consorted with oil companies, unwittingly giving them an immense power of influence. The French-owned oil company Elf Aquitaine, for example, was "a veritable state within a state" in Gabon and reportedly paid Omar Bongo approximately $57 million

---

[161] Alain Lallemand, "Making a Killing: The Field Marshal," US Center for Public Integrity, article, November 15, 2002.
[162] "Our New Best Friend – Who Needs Saudi Arabia When You've Got Sao Tome," *The New Yorker,* October 7, 2002.
[163] Alex Perry, "Gabon Faces Bongo's Disastrous Legacy," *Time*, June 10, 2009.
[164] Tom Burgis, *The Looting Machine: Warlords, Oligarchs, Corporations, Smugglers, and the Theft of Africa's Wealth* (Public Affairs, 2015), 139.

every year to maintain its presence in the country.[165] And for the millions of dollars France pumped into the personal accounts of the president, Gabon responded by allowing Paris to use it as a base for military and espionage activities in the region.[166] After Elf's entry in the 1960s, more than half a dozen other giant oil companies followed: Italy's Agip, South Africa's Energy Africa Gabon, the United Kingdom's British Petroleum and Tullow Oil, and America's Shell Oil, Amerada Hess, ExxonMobil, Amoco, Occidental Petroleum, and Marathon Oil.

Bongo was also a lavish show-off and a consummate philanderer. One writer narrates how, during the oil boom of the 1970s, he spent half of the country's budget building hotels and purchasing armored Cadillacs to impress visiting heads of state during the Organization of African Unity (OAU), now African Union (AU), summit in Libreville in 1977.[167] It was also reported how an Italian fashion designer supplied Bongo with prostitutes, and how, during an international beauty contest in Libreville, the president "took a shine to Miss Peru, who found herself ushered into the presidential bedroom." [168] The terrified young woman bolted.

A US Senate subcommittee report said Bongo accumulated huge sums of money and used the American banking system for illicit transfers. Between 1985 and 1999, the Gabon leader opened several accounts at the Citibank Private Bank and used it to deposit, invest, and transfer over $130 million, believed to be the proceeds of corruption from French oil companies. The bank also helped Bongo establish a shell corporation in the Bahamas called Tendin Investments, another in Paris called Leontine Limited, and

---

[165] Leif Wenar, *Blood Oil: Tyrants, Violence, and the Rules that Run the World* (Oxford University Press, 2016), 127.

[166] Jon Henley, "Gigantic Sleaze Scandal Winds Up as Former Elf Oil Chiefs Are Jailed," *The Guardian,* November 12, 2003.

[167] Nicholas Shaxson, *Poisoned Wells: The Dirty Politics of African Oil* (Palgrave, 2007), 81.

[168] "Omar Bongo," *The Telegraph*, June 8, 2009.

yet another one in New York under the name "OS."[169] The bank also allegedly gave Bongo millions of dollars in loans. During the first three decades of his long rule, Bongo's wealth was ignominiously estimated to be $200 million.[170]

However, like most despots, Bongo was "an embezzler on a grand scale" and an expert at hiding the money trail. He would use his Citibank accounts in Paris, New York, Switzerland, Bahrain, Jersey, London, and Luxembourg under discreet names such as Tendin Investments, Leontine, and OS to confuse even his own closest associates. Bongo accounts were protected with cunning code names, suggesting at one time the use of phrases like "New York USA" and "Fort Knox Securities."[171] Some of the illicit money banked abroad was plowed back into the country to bribe supporters to ensure his re-election.

In the early 2000s, Bongo decided he wanted to acquire arms for his personal protection and hired a Washington, DC–based lobbyist, Jeffrey Birrell, to find out how Gabon could purchase six US-built C-130 aircraft, three US-built armored vehicles, and three unarmored vehicles from the government of Saudi Arabia. The Senate report said $18 million in suspect funds were wire-transferred from Gabon to US bank accounts allegedly maintained by Birrell in the name "The Grace Group LLC," a corporation formed by him and his wife. The lobbyist received the funds primarily from Bongo and an entity called Ayira. Birrell then allegedly transferred $9.2 million of the Ayira funds to an account in Malta bearing the name of the Gabonese president. Between 2005 and 2007, the report claimed, millions of dollars in suspect funds flowed in and out of the United States through the lobbyist's accounts for the purchases of various units.

---

[169] US Senate Permanent Subcommittee on Investigations, "Keeping Foreign Corruption Out of the United States, February 4, 2010, 108
[170] US Senate Permanent Subcommittee on Investigations, "Report on President Omar Bongo. Private Banking and Money Laundering: A Case Study of Opportunities and Vulnerabilities," November 9, 1999.
[171] Nick Kochan, *The Washing Machine: Money, Crime & Terror in the Offshore System* (Gerald Duckworth & Co. Ltd., 2006), 172-13.

While the sale of the vehicles was completed toward the end of 2005, that of the aircraft took much longer to process, as the US government pondered how to comply with the requirements of the US Arms Exports Control Act. The C-130 was on the US munitions list, so it was subject to export controls. Even with non-delivery, Birrell still demanded a compensation of $850,000 from the Gabon government for his efforts on the transaction plus $253,000 in expenses. Birrell did not disclose to the Senate subcommittee how much he received.[172]

In the meantime, a holding company run by Bongo family members, Delta Synergie, listed as a "cargo and freight" company but with interests in a wide array of sectors such as textiles, media, insurance, banking, and aviation, sent a formal request to the US State Department for permission to "re-export" the C-130 aircraft from Saudi Arabia to Gabon for commercial use. That application was rejected. With the support of Saudi Arabia, Gabon and Birrell wrote dozens of appeals to the US government and used multiple channels to secure clearance from the State Department. It was almost a year, until July 2006, that a final approval was given by the US Congress for the purchase of the aircraft.

In March 2007, three non-profit anti-corruption organizations— Sherpa, a French law association; Survie, a French NGO; and the Federation of the Congolese Diaspora (FCD)—filed a complaint with the French public prosecutor alleging that the ruling families of Gabon, Equatorial Guinea, Angola, Burkina Faso, and Congo owned millions of dollars' worth of properties in France "that could not be the fruits of their official salaries … but would have likely required the use of stolen public assets."[173] The complaint was eventually rejected by the appeals courts.

---

[172] US Senate Permanent Subcommittee on Investigations, "Keeping Foreign Corruption Out of the United States,", February 4, 2010, 120.
[173] A legal memorandum prepared by Sherpa and Transparency International, French Court of Appeals, June 2009.

During his tenure, Bongo displayed to the WB and the International Monetary Fund (IMF) a determination to end corruption in his country, but in reality, he was a collaborator. The Gabon Commission to Combat Illicit Enrichment (CNLCEI), which he established in 2004 to identify and root out corruption, was nothing but an "all bark and no bite" body that never prosecuted anyone in the top echelons of the government; and Gabon's membership in the UN Convention against Corruption was more cosmetic than serious.

In 2010, a year after Bongo died and his son Ali Bongo took over the presidency, French judges launched another investigation to determine whether the estimated 33 properties worth millions of dollars owned by Bongo and his family in France came from money illegally obtained in Gabon. That investigation, which also included families of the presidents of the four other countries named above, was terminated in 2017 without any action being taken against anyone.

In 2015, France arrested Ali's chief of staff, Maixent Accrombessi, during a visit to Paris on allegations he received bribes from Marck, a French maker of military uniforms, in exchange for a business contract. Ali bitterly condemned the arrest and called it a humiliation. From all perspectives, Ali had his own unique habits in addition to those he inherited from his father. He lacked his father's charm but loved the good life. The scandalous activities of the French oil company Elf, which had started during Omar Bongo's tenure, continued after Ali took over. The Elf scandal was described as "probably the biggest political and corporate sleaze scandal to hit a western democracy since the second world war."[174] Thirty-seven people, including former Elf chairman Loik Le Floch-Prigent, and a former director, Alfred Sirven, were given jail terms totaling 60 years and fined an estimated $39 million by a French court in November 2003 for paying massive amounts of bribes designated as "royalties" to African leaders.

---

[174] Jon Henley, "Gigantic Sleaze Scandal Winds Up as Former Elf Oil Chiefs Jailed," The Guardian, November 12, 2003.

The latest corruption scandal that got the vice president and the forestry minister fired was in May 2019, when 300 containers of the expensive *kevazingo* timber, popular for making furniture in Asia, mysteriously vanished from the port of Owendo outside the capital of Libreville days before they were to be exported. The containers with false labels were found in warehouses owned by Chinese firms. The value of the timber was estimated by officials at $250 million. Although 200 containers were quickly recovered, an infuriated and embarrassed President Bongo dismissed Vice President Pierre Claver Maganga and Minister Guy Bertrand Mapangou, saying they had to take responsibility for the fiasco. The Chinese owners of the warehouses were arrested. There has been increased smuggling of the precious wood in recent years from the Congo Basin of Gabon through the ports for export, especially to China, where it fetches up to $2,000 per cubic meter. The wood is treated as "sacred" and its exploitation was banned by the government in March 2018. But Chinese loggers working with corrupt officials, villages, and illegal sawmills continue to deplete Gabon's forests.

A "fixer" fixed

A joint venture consisting of Och-Ziff Capital Management Group LLC, a New York–based hedge fund management company and an entity incorporated in the Turks and Caicos Islands, got into trouble when one of its employees, a France/Gabon national, Samuel Mebiame, was seized for bribing high-level government officials to earn business opportunities and mining rights for the joint venture in Chad and Niger. The joint partner was not named, but reports mentioned a holding company founded by a South African businessman.

Mebiame, the son of a former prime minister of Gabon, Leone Mebiame, who ruled between 1975 and 1990, was described by the DOJ as a "fixer" who also made illegal payments to public officials in Guinea to gain advantage for the joint venture there.

The bribes paid in Niger amounted to $3 million, remitted either directly or through intermediaries, including lawyers. In Niger, Chad, and Guinea, payments were sometimes made in the form of luxury cars and high-class travel, including private rental of an Airbus jet. In return, Mebiame obtained concessions for uranium and mining rights.

Those activities landed Mebiame and Och-Ziff in a US court in September 2016 for violating the FCPA's provisions, including anti-bribery, books and records, and accounting control provisions, in Chad, Niger, Libya, and the DRC. The company subsidiary, OZ Africa Management GP LLC (OZ Africa), also pleaded guilty to a count of criminal information related to large-scale bribe payments in the DRC.[175]

Och-Ziff agreed to pay $412 million, and the CEO Daniel Och $2.2 million, for violating the FCPA. Mebiame, who earned commissions amounting to $3.5 million through 2012, admitted to charges of corruption before US federal court judge Nicholas Garaufis in Brooklyn, New York, and was jailed for two years.

[175] US Department of Justice "Gabonese National Pleads Guilty to Foreign Bribery Scheme," press release no. 16-1445, December 9, 2016.

GHANA

Ghana was the first sub-Saharan African country to gain independence in 1957. A new constitution in 1960 transforming the country from a dominion headed by the Queen of England to a republic led by a former liberation fighter achieved what Marcus Garvey—Kwame Nkrumah's friend of many years and an advocate of black emancipation—called "African redemption from colonialism."[176]

With dozens of other colonized lands also eyeing the big prize from the British, Spanish, French, and Portuguese imperialists, Ghana's coming-of-age was hailed around the world as the beginning of Africa's liberation. For nine years, Nkrumah—*Osagefyo*, "a Warrior Chief Who Defeated the Enemy and Saved the Nation" in the Akan language—ruled the West African country with vigor and sometimes highhandedness. He angered some who accused him of dictatorship, "megalomania," "narcissism," and "despotism," especially when he erected a monument to honor himself [177] and built a motorway in his name, but Nkrumah was dearly respected by many African leaders, especially those he met in Europe, like Kamuzu Banda of Malawi, Jomo Kenyatta of Kenya, Julius Nyerere of Tanzania, and Kenneth Kaunda of Zambia, as well as a majority of the Ghanaian people.

However, despite being revered as a redeemer, Nkrumah was criticized for letting corruption thrive. Ministers and officials of state corporations routinely demanded 10 percent as kickback when signing contracts. Also, Nkrumah occasionally awarded multimillion-dollar contracts to foreigners without consulting line ministers, raising questions of integrity. The country's ruling party, the Convention People's Party (CPP), existed through corruption, with one report claiming 90 percent of its income came from

---

[176] Robert Vinson, "Marcus Garvey's Africa," Africa is a Country, newsletter, undated.
[177] St. Clair Drake, "Nkrumah the Real Tragedy," CIA, press release no. 200/03/4, June 5, 1972.

illegal means.[178] Tawia Adamafio, the former CPP secretary general, lashed out at the galloping graft in the country, saying in his memoirs that Ghana under Nkrumah had become "a howling monster threatening to wreck the whole nation."[179]

One example of suspicion of graft came when the German government guaranteed a $12 million contract for a German firm to improve the capital city of Accra's water and sewage system. When the WHO and the UN Special Fund commissioned a study on the project, they found that the cost, which should have been $8 million, had been substantially buttressed.[180] That fiasco put the president in an awkward position to defend the discrepancy.

Nkrumah nationalized companies and expanded colonial controls on imports, capital transfers, minimum wages, and rents, among others, and prohibited diamond mining corporations from exporting the gem except through the Ghana Diamond Marketing Board, established in 1963 to market diamonds. Many times, the reputation of the board came under scrutiny. The main producer of diamonds was the state-run Ghana Consolidated Diamonds, while the Precious Minerals Marketing Corporation purchased minerals from small producers. Nkrumah was blamed for establishing too many state enterprises in a short period of time, many of which were operating at a loss due to mismanagement and corruption.

The controls caused shortages of commodities and raised demand, which in turn fueled bribery and corruption allegations. Ministers and their wives acquired goods at controlled prices from government stores and sold them on the black market, thus reaping huge profits and causing the birth of the word *kalabule,* or profiteering, among Ghanaians.[181]

---

[178] Herbert H. Werlin, "The Roots of Corruption – The Ghanaian Enquiry," *The Journal of Modern African Studies* 10, no. 2 (July 1972): 247–266.
[179] Tawia Adamafio, *By Nkrumah's Side* (Westcoast Publishing House, 1982), 9.
[180] "The Fall of Nkrumah and the Corruption He Supervised," Ghana Web, online news, November 10, 2010.
[181] George B. N. Ayittey, *Africa Betrayed* (St. Martin's Press, 1992), 166.

If that was not enough, Nkrumah set up his own personal dictatorship, instituting a personality cult that reached grotesque proportions. Every day, the mainly government press extolled his intellectual brilliance, his foresight, and his integrity. He assumed the grand titles and created an official ideology, calling it Nkrumaism.[182]

Meanwhile, Nkrumah's Cabinet ministers were inexorably pushing through multimillion-dollar contracts with foreign corporations for a 10 percent fee. His anti-corruption policy had failed, and so had his socialist experiment. The country was reeling from rampant unemployment, increased foreign debt, poverty, and a government that was stifling opposition and violating basic human rights. At dawn on February 24, 1966, while Nkrumah was away attending a peace meeting in Hanoi, the Democratic Republic of North Vietnam, as a guest of President Ho Chi Minh, he was overthrown by the combined force of the military and police.

In 1970—four years after Nkrumah's overthrow—the government of Edward Akufo-Addo formed the Presidential Commission on Bribery and Corruption under the chairmanship of Justice P. D. Anin, who was given the mandate to probe the prevalence and methods of bribery and to determine whether there were factors in society contributing to the ills. "Do we draw a line between the 'customary drink' under our traditional practices, and bribery and corruption of public officers and others holding positions of trust?"[183] Anin asked at the inaugural meeting, suggesting that finding an answer to that question would help eradicate graft.

When the commission's report was finally released, a number of recommendations were made on how to deal with the menace within the public sector to discourage civil servants from the taking of bribes. The most interesting paragraphs in the report cited a

---

[182] Martin Meredith, *The Fortunes of Africa: A 5000-year History of Wealth, Greed, and Endeavor* (Public Affairs, 2014), 597.

[183] "Final Report of the Commission of Enquiry on Bribery and Corruption," vii, Ghana Publishing Corp., 1975, 1-161.

hypothetical example of a politician, a military official, and a bureaucrat, who cannot afford to live a life of lavishness. What does one do in this situation? He "resorts to dishonest means and manners ... and either goes to steal, takes bribes, or corrupts, to achieve his aim. He refuses to cut his court according to his cloth. He cannot discipline himself, and as a result, falls victim to bribery and corruption,"[184] the report answered. But like many such commissions before, including one established by Nkrumah himself in the late 1950s, nothing came out of it.

While the higher echelons of society concentrated on big contracts from which they reaped millions of dollars in kickbacks, mainly from mining companies, lower-ranked public servants went for *dash* in exchange for services in government offices.

By the mid-1980s, the gold and diamond sectors were still reeling from massive corruption initiated during Nkrumah's rule. Seventy percent of Ghanaian diamonds were being smuggled out of the country by gluttonous cartels, occasioning billions of dollars in losses to the state. Also contributing to the loss was the ban on small-scale mining in 2017 by President Nana Akufo-Addo, which was meant to curb illegal mining and reduce environmental degradation by *galamsey*, small-scale miners. Mining companies such as Newmont Ghana Limited, a subsidiary of the US-based Newmont Mining Corporation, supported the ban on small miners, which meant higher profits for the foreign companies.

In 2016, Newport, which operates in Australia, Indonesia, the United States, Peru, and Suriname, apart from Ghana, had to respond to corruption allegations of its own involving the bribing of foreign officials. It announced it was working with the SEC and the DOJ on ways to comply with the provisions of the FCPA, though it did not specify where the alleged misbehavior had occurred.

---

184   Final Report of the Commission of Inquiry on Bribery and Corruption, Republic of Ghana, 1975, 4.

Reports in 2018 showed that diamond production in Ghana had tumbled immensely, from 2.8 million ounces in 2015 to only 200,000. Also on a downward spiral was gold, which in 2016 produced 4.1 million ounces. In general, mining contributes close to 40 percent of the country's total exports, 90 percent of which are gold exports. However, a 2019 Bank of Ghana report said of all the gold exported, Ghana gets only 1.7 percent of the revenue, with the remaining 98.3 percent being gobbled up by MNCs. For example, between 1990 and 2002, the country produced gold worth $5.2 billion but earned only $87.3 million in corporate income taxes and royalty payments. In 2017, the country's gold revenue was $3.52 billion, up from $3.25 billion in 2016, according to the Ghana Chamber of Mines. About 98.3 percent of that revenue was retained by MNCs. Such shocking statistics support the case that MNCs are not in Africa to help Africa but to exploit the continent of everything it has.

In Ghana, corruption does not exist only in the mining sector. In 2012, Huawei, a Chinese telecommunications company, was accused of making illegal campaign contributions to the ruling National Democratic Congress (NDC) in the hope of getting a $43 million tax exemption. A rival political party, the Alliance for Accountable Governance (AFAG), showed invoices and other documents as evidence that Huawei paid huge amounts of money for campaign material for NDC. AFAG also claimed the Chinese firm was awarded what it called "the juiciest contracts to be doled out by the government," worth $150 million, to build an e-government platform. Both the government and Huawei denied the allegations.

Corruption: Not letting up

The seed of corruption planted by the founding father of Ghana contaminated all the administrations that followed. Nkrumah's overthrow in 1966 was followed by years of military and civilian chaos featuring a motley of civilians and uniformed people: Lieutenant General Joseph Ankrah, Brigadier Akwasi Afrifa, Ni

Amaa Ollennu, Edward Akufo-Addo, General Kutu Acheampong, Lieutenant General Fred Akuffo, Flight Lieutenant Jerry Rawlings, Hilla Limann, John Kufuor, John Atta Mills, John Mahama, and Nana Akufo-Addo, most of whom were corrupt.

The chaos saw former president Acheampong executed by a firing squad for allegedly squandering public money after Flight Lieutenant Jerry Rawlings staged a coup against General Fred Akuffo in July 1979. Almost two decades later, Rawlings was himself accused of receiving a $5 million bribe from Nigerian dictator Sani Abacha for undisclosed purposes, and for selling a state-owned property, Nsawam Cannery, to his wife, Nana Konadu Agyemang, for a song. Konadu was charged in court with six counts relating to the divestiture of the cannery, but that case flopped. Rawlings, who was nicknamed "junior Jesus," did not deny receiving "blood money" from dictator Abacha, but said it was $2 million and not $5 million, and that he used it "for the welfare of Ghanaians."

That is the fallacy of African leaders. They preach water but drink wine. They forget election promises and engage in the same malfeasance they condemned so vigorously during campaigns. Rawlings, according to the independent online news bulletin, GhanaWeb, talked probity and accountability but practiced corruption. If the Abacha/Rawlings bribery event had taken place during the military upheavals proceeding Nkrumah's overthrow, it's most likely the flight lieutenant would have been executed, as happened to Acheampong, and perhaps the execution would have taken place at the same notorious army firing range 6.4 kilometers from the capital of Accra. However, by the time he took power, things had changed, as the country was gradually moving toward democracy.

At his inauguration in January 2017, Nana Akufo-Addo, like several of his predecessors, announced renewed measures to fight corruption, and as a show of that commitment, he suspended four High Court judges found to have used their office to influence the outcome of court cases. The question remains: will Akufo-

Addo succeed where all his predecessors failed?

Kinross Gold Corporation

The SEC in 2018 punished the Canadian gold mining company Kinross Gold Corporation for paying Ghanaian and Mauritanian vendors and consultants huge amounts of money, some of which ended in the hands of government officials as bribes to intervene in the acquisition of gold mines.

The company, which has mining interests in the United States, Brazil, Russia, Chile, Ghana, and Mauritania, acquired the Tasiast gold mine in northwestern Mauritania and the Chirano gold mines in northwestern Ghana between 2010 and 2014 from Canada's Red Back Mining Incorporated for $7.1 billion. However, it failed to address the compliance and internal control issues. And even after discovering that accounting controls and disbursement for goods and services at the two mines were inadequate, the company failed to take action to remedy the situation.

The SEC found that Kinross did not verify payments made in cash to politically connected vendors and consultants and did not record them in its books. In one case, it paid a Ghanaian consultant $1,000 for a work visa for a company staff member, part of which went to a government official who facilitated the transaction.

Also in 2014, the company awarded a $50.1 million logistics contract to a French company, Schenker, linked to a Mauritanian company, Maurilog, owned by Mohamed Yahya, a former Mauritanian general commissioner of private investments and a close ally of Mauritanian president Mohamed Ould Abdel Aziz, without following its own bidding and tendering procedures. Kinross also failed to conduct due diligence when hiring a politically connected consultant to facilitate contacts with high-level Mauritanian government officials and paid vendors and consultants without ensuring the payments were consistent with policies prohibiting improper payments. In addition, the company's bid was not even the lowest.

As part of the settlement, Kinross, one of the world's biggest gold producers, did not admit or deny wrongdoing. In March 2018, it reached a settlement with the SEC to pay a civil penalty of $950,000, to cease and desist violating the provisions of the FCPA, and to report the status of its anti-corruption compliance procedures and internal controls within a year.[185]

A top SEC official blasted Kinross for repeatedly failing to put in place anti-corruption compliance programs and adequate accounting controls.

A donation or a bribe?

A bribery scandal surrounding a Norwegian company, Scancem International ANS, owners of the cement producer Ghacem, brought to light the vulnerability of the Scandinavian nation to bribery and corruption in Africa. Investigations launched in 2017 by the Ghanaian auditor general revealed that between 2002 and 2004, the company bribed Ghanaian officials to the tune of $22 million to win favors.

A Norwegian publication, *Dagens Naeringsliv Magasinet,* in its 21/22 April 2007 edition, claimed a former top official in the erstwhile Ghanaian NDC government received more than $4 million in bribes from Scancem "with the purpose of consolidating the then Norwegian-owned firm's hold on the local cement industry."[186]

Austin Garmey, a former deputy minister of employment in the NDC government of Jerry Rawlings, reportedly admitted taking $240,000 from Scancem on behalf of the party ahead of the 2000 general elections, but he said it was a donation to the party and not a bribe. The publication also named a former president and his wife, along with a presidential staffer, as some of the beneficiaries of illegal payments from the company between 1993 and 1998. Jerry Rawlings, a former president of Ghana, denied the bribery

---

[185] US SEC, "Case Information: In the Matter of Kinross Gold Corporation, " Stanford School of Law, Foreign Corrupt Practices Act Clearing House, March 2018.
[186] "Norwegian Multinational 419er Scams Ghana Big Time," Africa Resource, August 18, 2007.

allegations.

Two Ghanaian journalists—Gabby Asare Otchere-Darko, managing editor of *Statesman*, and Kweku Baako Junior, managing editor of the *Crusading Guide*—travelled to Norway to investigate the scandal and implicated Ghana's former ambassador to Norway, who once worked for Ghacem, as among those who were allegedly bribed with an estimated sum of $209 million.

In Norway, a district court was told how Scancem participated in extensive corruption and bribery in Ghana, and how Tor Egil Kjelsaas, the man who managed Scancem operations in Ghana, Togo, and Nigeria, was the one in charge of the scheme. The court was hearing a case in which Kjelsaas was charged with embezzling $4 million, given to him by the company to bribe top Ghanaian government officials, which he allegedly deposited in an account in Luxembourg. Between 1993 and 1998, $2.5 million had gone through that account and another $1.7 million through a bank in Geneva, Switzerland. Kjelsaas claimed the Luxembourg account belonged to prominent Ghanaian politicians. Investigators could not determine who owned the second account, though they suspected it belonged to a wife of a former president. The bribe money was paid directly either in cash in Ghana, banked in the officials' accounts in Luxembourg or Switzerland, or shipped to Ghana and handed over to the recipients in envelopes. Kjelsaas refused to cooperate and did not attend the court proceedings due to health problems. In September 2006, district court judge Trine Standal found Kjelsaas not guilty and awarded him costs in the case.

Mabey & Johnson

There were stunning revelations in a London court in 2009 that a British bridge-building company, Mabey & Johnson (M&J), paid "a wide-ranging series of bribes"[187] to foreign government officials

---

[187] David Leigh and Rob Evans, "British Firm Mabey and Johnson Convicted of Bribing Foreign Politicians," *The Guardian*, September 25, 2009.

around the world to win contracts. The dramatic admission before a Southwark Crown Court in London sent shivers in Ghana, Angola, Mozambique, Madagascar, Bangladesh, and Jamaica, where some public officials were under investigation for bribery.

The Reading-based company, owned by some of the richest families in Britain, confessed to having paid $1.2 million to politicians and officials through agents in those countries between 1993 and 2001 to secure export orders worth $90 million. The agents were paid between 5 percent and 15 percent in commission, part of which was diverted to government officials. Five recipients, who were from Ghana, served in the government of John Atta Mills; two were from Madagascar, one from Jamaica, two from Angola, and one each from Mozambique and Bangladesh.

What made the scandal worse was that some of the projects it built corruptly overseas, such as bridges in Ghana and one in Ethiopia, were defective, and the firm had to rebuild them at additional costs. M&J has built bridges in more than 100 countries.

The names of the bribed individuals were revealed in court in September 2009. In Ghana, they included a former roads minister who received approximately $70,000; his deputy, $13,000; a works minister, $32,000; the chairman of an inter-city transport corporation, $32,000; and a health minister, $20,000. The case was prosecuted by the SFO, since many of the company's contracts were paid for by British taxpayers through the United Kingdom's Export Credit Guarantee Department. The court ruled that the M&J executives "viewed themselves as infallible, exempt from established mores, invincible, and were unremorseful for their actions."[188]

In another case at the same court, M&J's sales director, David Mabey, was jailed for eight months for making $420,000 in illegal payments to the Iraqi government of Saddam Hussein in the UN's oil-

---

[188] David Saprong, Jana Sajdakova, and Kweku Adams, "The Mabey and Johnson Bribery Scandal: A Case of Executive Hubris," *Thunderbird International Business Review*, 61, no. 2, March/April, 2019: 387-396.

for-food program. The program, established in 1995, allowed Iraq, then under global sanctions imposed after the first Gulf War, to sell its oil in exchange for food and drugs for its desperate population. The managing director, Charles Forsyth, was sentenced to 21 months; Richard Gledhill, turned prosecution witness, was given an eight-month sentence suspended for two years. M&J was also fined a record $8.4 million. Part of the money, $833,000, was paid to Ghana as compensation. M&J vehemently denied approving bribes to overseas officials, though other questionable contractual dealings had occurred in the past in the Philippines, Papua New Guinea, Panama, and the Dominican Republic.

BENIN

Among the countries the FCPA focused on in 2004 was Benin, the tiny West African nation. In October 1998, the state-owned telecommunications company Afronetwork entered into a joint venture with Titan Corporation (Titan), a corporation headquartered in San Diego, California and a global military and intelligence contractor.

During a meeting between Afronetwork and Titan the following month, the former introduced someone to Titan it identified as a "business advisor" of the Marxist-Leninist Benin President Mathieu Kerekou. Titan subsequently hired the unidentified "advisor" to assist the company in its development of a telecommunications project in exchange for 5 percent of the value of all equipment installed in Benin.

In the process, Titan earned close to $100 million from the contract, and as per agreement, paid the "advisor" $2.3 million, which it wired to an offshore account in Monaco on the French Riviera. Some of the money, according to officials of the SEC, was used in Kerekou's re-election campaign in 2001, including for buying campaign merchandise such as T-shirts and posters. He won the election. According to some reports, Titan also gave Kerekou's wife $1,850 for earrings. In its books, however, Titan recorded the payments as "consulting services."

The DOJ and SEC got wind of the transactions and took the company to court for violating FCPA provisions, falsifying company books, and aiding in the filing of a false tax return. On March 1, 2005, Titan pleaded guilty to the three felony counts and was ordered to pay a $13 million criminal fine by Judge Robert T. Benitez in a San Diego court. The company was also asked to pay $12.62 million in disgorgement, along with $2.86 million in pre-judgment interest. The head of Titan Africa Incorporated, Steven Lynwood, pleaded guilty to paying bribes to a foreign official and falsifying tax returns. On June 23, 2006, he was sentenced to six months' imprisonment, three years' supervised release, and a fine of $5,000. Titan ceased operations in Benin in 2002. No one was convicted in Benin for participating in the illegal deal.

GUINEA

Guinea (not to be confused with Equatorial Guinea and the multiple Guineas in French territories) is undoubtedly a popular destination for the wealthy. As the French billionaire Vincent Bollore was making fortunes in port management in the capital city of Conakry, Beny Steinmetz, an Israeli French national, was scooping up immense revenues from the mining of iron ore in Guinea's remote Simandou mountain range.

Steinmetz's BSG Resources company (BSGR) knew just how to do it: recruit as an associate the second most influential person in the country, Mamadie Toure, the fourth wife of President Lansana Conte. At the time, Toure's brother was the vice president of BSGR Guinea, so the circle of collusion was complete. With the two people pulling strings at the top, opportunities were wide open for the company to enjoy preferential treatment with the full knowledge of the big man at the presidential palace.

Originally, it was an Anglo-Australian mining company, Rio Tinto, which acquired exploration rights at Simandou—rated as one of the world's biggest pits of untapped ore deposits—in 1997, but those rights were suspended in 2008 by President Conte and handed over to BSGR for an estimated $500 million. In one of the contracts allegedly signed by BSGR and Pentler Holdings Limited—a British Virgin Islands–registered offshore company with shares in BSGR mining interests in Guinea—a signature believed to be that of Conte confirmed receipt of $2.4 million channeled through US banks by Frederic Cilins, a BSGR agent in Guinea. Cilins was a frequent visitor to Conakry and always brought expensive gifts such as MP3 players and mobile phones for top officials.[189]

---

[189] Bastian Obermayer and Frederik Obermaier, *The Panama Papers: Breaking the Story of How the Rich and Powerful Hide Their Money* (One World Book, 2016), 204.

However, a BSGR spokesperson contended that the signature was "forged" and the allegations "entirely baseless,"[190] and blamed Hungarian fellow billionaire George Soros for trying to upend him from two mines in Guinea. However, a report presented to a Paris court in March 2018 by Riley, Welch, LaPorte & Associates Forensic Laboratories Incorporated, a global forensic firm, showed there was "no evidence to indicate any of the disputed documents were fraudulently produced."[191]

Not too long after acquiring mining rights at Simandou in 2012, BSGR sold 50 percent of its holdings to a Rio de Janeiro–based Brazilian company, Vale, for a staggering $2.5 billion in a sale described as "the corruption deal of the century."[192] BSGR denied corruption had played a part in the transaction. Alpha Conde, who had taken over as president of Guinea in 2010 from acting president Sekouba Konate, claimed owners of the Simandou rights had acquired the rights fraudulently and asked them to compensate the government. Rio Tinto responded by paying $711 million. BSGR refused to comply and was booted out of Guinea in 2014.

A report of a joint investigative exercise involving the United States, Switzerland, Israel, and Guinea alleged that Steinmetz had given President Conte and his wife $30 million in bribes to get metal mining licenses for activities which generated $5 million in profits between 2006 and 2012. Mamadie later turned FBI informer and secretly taped Cilins during conversations at the Jacksonville airport, Florida. According to the FBI, Cilins urged Mamadie to destroy evidence which showed the Simandou rights were won after Guinean government officials had received millions of dollars

[190] "New Evidence Ties BSGR to Company Behind Guinea Mine Bribery," Global Witness, report, August 15, 2013, 1–2.

[191] Robin Pagnamenta, "Steinmetz Bribery Contracts Not Forged, Expert Says," *The Times*, April 17, 2018.

[192] Bastian Obermayer and Frederik Obermaier, *The Panama Papers: Breaking the Story of How the Rich and Powerful Hide Their Money* (A Oneworld Book, 2016), 202–203.

in hand-backers. In August 2017, billionaire Steinmetz and four other suspects, including Tal Silberstein, a former advisor to the Austrian Chancellor, were arrested for questioning by police in Jerusalem on suspicion of money laundering, fraudulent filing of corporate documents, fraud and corporate breach of trust, obstruction of justice, and bribery. They were held on house arrest and released. Cilins, a French national, pleaded guilty in a New York court in July 2014 to a charge of obstructing federal grand jury investigations and was sentenced to two years in jail, after which he was deported to France in early 2015.

During their husband's tenure, Toure's four wives were implicated in a number of bribery scandals involving millions of dollars, some of which were revealed in the Panama Papers, a collection of 11.5 million secret files about holders of offshore accounts compiled by the International Consortium of Investigative Journalists (ICIJ).

But Alpha Conde's regime was not itself as white as cotton. Corruption that was pervasive in previous regimes persisted right under his nose. In November 2016, Rio Tinto, the Anglo-Australian mining giant, admitted paying $10.5 million to the president's French advisor, banker Francois de Combret, for rights to Simandou iron ore. Leaked emails from 2011 showed that three senior executives of the company—CEO Tom Albanese, head of iron ore Sam Walsh, and the former executive in charge of Simandou, Alan Davis, discussed the payment to Combret in light of his "very unique and irreplaceable services and closeness to the President" of Guinea.[193] Guinea's mines minister, Abdoulaye Magassouba, said the government was not aware de Combret was working for Rio Tinto at the time, which was hard to believe in a country where intelligence-gathering was a top government priority. Following the scandal, the WB, which had a small stake in Simandou, withdrew from the project, and Rio Tinto terminated the

---

[193] Neil Hume, "Rio Tinto CEO: Decision to Tell Regulators About $10.5m Payment Not Taken Lightly," *The Financial Times*, November 14, 2016.

contracts of Alan Davis as well as that of the legal and regulatory affairs group executive, Debra Valentine.

In a dramatic new development in 2019, BSGR and the Guinean government agreed to restore the former's rights to Simandou in a settlement brokered by French president Nicolas Sarkozy. That ended seven years of wrangles over corruption allegations against the Israeli billionaire Steinmetz. The agreement called for the withdrawal by the government of allegations that Steinmetz and BSGR paid bribes to Guinean public officials to obtain mining rights.

Ex-Guinean minister caught

Was it a loan or a bribe? This is what a jury had to decide in the trial of a former Guinean minister for mines and geology, Mahmoud Thiam, who was facing a money-laundering charge in a New York court in 2017. "It was a loan," Thiam lamented in a video interview in a grim room at the FBI's New York offices in December 2016. "… [It was only] a verbal understanding. No interest rates [were paid]. Nothing,"[194] he said without blinking an eye.

Thiam, a dual Guinea/US citizen and former banker, was making his case in a post-arrest interview over allegations that $8.5 million he received from a Chinese conglomerate was more than a gift. Thiam was arrested at his luxurious apartment on Manhattan's Upper East Side and was formally charged in December 2016. Before that, he had occupied key positions in the US financial sector: he worked for 14 years with Merrill Lynch and UBS Investment Bank in the United States before returning home in 2009 to take up the ministerial portfolio.

It was while working with the Conakry government that he allegedly received the money from China International Fund and China Sonangol International—a joint venture with the government—

---

[194] Richard Vanderford, "Alleged Bribe Was a Loan, Ex-Guinea Mines Minister Tells FBI in Interview Played for Jury," M-Lex Market Insight, April 27, 2017.

between 2009 and 2011 in exchange for exclusive mining rights for iron, gold, diamond, and bauxite deposits. He then laundered the money into the United States. The money was initially deposited in a Hong Kong bank account, from which Thiam transferred $3.9 million to the United States and purchased a $3.75 million estate in Duchess County, New York.

According to US investigators, Thiam concealed the payments by falsely claiming to banks in Hong Kong and the United States that he was employed as a consultant and that the money was income he had earned from the sale of land before becoming a minister. That explanation was disputed in court, since Thiam was a government official in Guinea, and as a dual citizen his conduct was a violation of FCPA regulations.

The jury agreed, and US district judge Denise L. Cote of the Manhattan Federal Court sentenced the former minister to seven years in prison in August 2017, followed by three years of supervised release, for one count of involvement in a transaction involving a property with a criminal source and one count of money laundering. "Mahmoud Thiam engaged in a corrupt scheme to benefit himself at the expense of the people of Guinea," said the acting assistant attorney general, Kenneth A. Blanco. "Today's sentence sends a strong message to corrupt individuals like Thiam that if they attempt to use the US financial system to hide their bribe money they will be investigated, held accountable and punished."[195]

---

[195] US Department of Justice, "Former Guinean Minister of Mines Sentenced to Seven Years in Prison for Receiving and Laundering $8.5m in Bribes from China International Fund and China Sonangol," press release no. 17-939, August 25, 2017.

LIBERIA

Ellen Johnson Sirleaf came into the presidency in 2005 with a declaration of zero tolerance on graft, a promise to end "an imperial style of presidency,"[196] and a determination to return the onetime slave colony to the glory that prevailed before the military coup that propelled an army master sergeant, Samuel Doe, to the highest office in 1980.

Both Doe and Charles Taylor, who preceded Sirleaf, were accused of stealing billions of dollars from government coffers in schemes that benefited themselves and their cronies and of spearheading 14 years of civil war that left more than a quarter of a million people dead. Relatively young and boisterous, the two were not the kind of role models to steer the country toward prosperity. Doe, who ruled between 1986 and 1990, was a man of unparalleled ruthlessness, a brutal savage who annihilated his opponents, among them former President William R. Tolbert, Junior. In 1990 he was overthrown, and in turn tortured and executed by rebel leader Prince Johnson, an ex-ally of Charles Taylor.

Taylor, on the other hand, was a flamboyant warlord and a war criminal now serving a 50-year prison term in the British city of Durham after conviction in 2012 by the International Criminal Court for aiding and abetting the commission of war crimes. After becoming president—his term stretched from 1997 to 2003—Taylor, brimming with brash bravado, became a darling of the United States, running a modern-day pirate state where he seemed to be in business with every type of international criminal syndicate on the planet.[197]

A large part of the money Doe and Taylor stole from the exchequer came from the rich iron ore project at Mount Nimba along the Liberian border with Guinea. Major mining multinationals like the

---

[196] "Ellen Johnson Sirleaf: Toward African Leadership," *The Globalist*, October 10, 2011.
[197] Nick Kochan, *The Washing Machine: Money, Crime & Terror in the Offshore System* (Gerald Duckworth & Co. Ltd., 2005), 42.

French Bureau de Recherches Geologiques et Minieres, Japan's Sumitomo Corporation, and the United Kingdom's African Mining Consortium Limited had camped there, earning Taylor millions of dollars in royalties every month. Revenues also came from timber and rubber plantation kickbacks.

When she was sworn into office on January 16, 2006, Sirleaf—the first elected female head of state in Africa—called corruption "public enemy number one,"[198] and in Parliament in 2015, she described it as "a vampire of development." All that turned out to be pure rhetoric. Not too long after that, she appointed her three sons to senior government positions. One of them, stepson Fombah Sirleaf, headed the National Security Agency, and another, Robert Sirleaf, managed the key National Oil Company of Liberia (NOCAL) until 2013, when he resigned. Under Robert, the organization was dogged by corruption and mismanagement, and it eventually collapsed in 2015. Another son, Charles Sirleaf, was the deputy governor of the Central Bank of Sierra Leone but was suspended through his mother's instructions in 2012 for failing to declare his assets. The appointment of her children to state positions dented President Sirleaf's reputation and raised doubts about her commitment to fight corruption and nepotism in the public sector.

In 2010, Fombah found himself at the center of an investigation by the US Drug Enforcement Administration (DEA) when it was revealed that a group of traffickers planned to bribe him with $100 million to allow a consignment of cocaine to pass through the country. A campaign called Operation Relentless, jointly run by US and Liberian officials, did not directly link Fombah to the criminal act, but a Russian citizen who was allegedly part of the group, Konstantin Yaroshenko, was arrested in Monrovia by security agents sent by Fombah.

---

[198] Tamasin Ford, "Ellen Johnson Sirleaf: The Legacy of Africa's First Elected Female President," *BBC*, news, January 22, 2018.

In a bombshell report titled *The Deceivers* in 2016, the NGO Global Witness named Fombah and other senior Liberian government officials as recipients of kickbacks amounting to $950,000 from a UK-based mining company and a well-connected Liberian lawyer. The bribes were paid for the officials to influence a change in the law to enable the mining company to secure one of Liberia's last large mining assets, the Wologizi iron ore concession in northern Liberia.

Part of Fombah's benefits, it was alleged, was a $7,598 hunting trip to South Africa paid for by the company. There was no evidence, however, to suggest that Fombah returned the favor. Also benefiting from the largesse were a speaker of the House of Representatives, who received $75,000; a chairman of the National Investment Committee (NIC) and a minister, each getting $50,000; a chairman of the Public Procurement and Concessions Commission, who got $10,000; and two other people identified only as "bigboy01" and "bigboy02."[199] All payments were referred to as "consulting fees."

The Liberian lawyer who was also a prominent figure in Sirleaf's Unity Party allegedly received $200,000 as a "political contribution" in April 2010. The mining company denied the allegations, saying it conducted its business "in a responsible and ethical manner." In 2016, Sirleaf's government launched a presidential task force headed by the minister of state without portfolio, J. Fonati Koffa, to delve into the matter, and the United Kingdom offered to cooperate. Lawyer Varney Sherman, Parliamentary Speaker Alex Tyler, and the deputy minister of lands, mines and energy, Ernest C. B. Jones, were arrested in May 2016 and charged with misusing their positions to amend the public procurement and concession law to favor Sable. Two months later, a Liberian grand jury indicted Andrew Groves, the chief executive of Sable, and Tolbert of the NIC. However, in July 2019, they were all set free due to lack of "convincing evidence."

---

[199] "Liberia: Triple Trouble," *All-Africa.com*, news, August 15, 2016.

In the meantime, Sable conducted an internal investigation and found no evidence implicating the company in dubious dealings. There was also no independent evidence that Sable benefited from the deal.

By then, the reputation of Sable/DMC had been tarnished following allegations that it had bribed a senior Liberian minister to acquire the Western Cluster iron ore concession in 2008.[200] Sable was disqualified from the bid, despite having paid over $1 million in bribes to Liberian officials. The company was eventually cleared, but the 25-year lease for the iron ore deal, worth $1.6 billion, was instead given to an Israeli company, Elenilto Minerals and Mining, in January 2011 amid controversy over its ability to carry out the work. Within six months, however, Elenilto had resold its contract, pocketing a cool $123.5 million without doing any work in Liberia.[201]

Liberia was not the only country where Sable engaged in shady deals. In Guinea, Sable allegedly helped President Alpha Conde with logistics during the election campaign in 2010, and allegedly bribed Alpha Mohammed, Conde's son, to secure mining rights for Mount Nimba iron ore deposits. Two years later, the company was awarded the rights.

Sirleaf's government was also accused of entering into illegal contracts with 20 of Liberia's largest companies in logging, Agri-industrial enterprises, and mining between 2006 and 2011, raising complaints from locals about the deprivation of their lands and the dangers of environmental degradation. During one visit to an affected village, Sirleaf scolded the locals: "You are trying to undermine your own government. You can't do that. If you do so all the foreign investors coming to Liberia will close their businesses and leave, then Liberia will go back to the old days."[202] You can see where Sirleaf's priority was: to please the foreigners and damn

---

[200] "Sable Rich Seam of Bribes," *Africa Confidential*, news, October 31, 2018.
[201] Thomas Kaydor, Jr., *Liberian Democracy: A Critique of the Principle of Checks and Balances* (AuthorHouse, 2014).
[202] Silas Kpanan'ayoung Siakor and Rachael S. Knight, "A Nobel Laureate's Problem at Home," *New York Times*, January 20, 2012.

the locals. As she prepared to leave office, Sirleaf unabashedly admitted in January 2017 that she had failed to meet the anti-corruption pledge made at her inauguration.

In 2018, Sirleaf's successor, George Manneh Weah, a former international soccer star with reproachful eyes, ordered investigations of ExxonMobil for allegedly paying bribes to former government officials in 2013 to obtain a license for the Block 13 oil field. The block was originally awarded by the state oil company, NOCAL, in 2005 to the Liberian-Anglo company Broadway Consolidated/Peppercoast, but it later emerged that a former mining minister and a former deputy minister had already allocated the block to a company in which they had interest. So, when ExxonMobil acquired it, according to the *Newsweek* magazine report of March 2018, it knew the deal worth $120 million was stained with corruption since the two officials had obtained it illegally in the first place. "Exxon knew its purchase might enrich these former politicians…. Despite these corruption red flags, Exxon didn't walk away from the deal," *Newsweek* quoted Global Witness.[203] One of the recipients of bribe money was said to be the president's son.

Ironically, the man who was selected to lead the investigation, Frank Musa Dean, was also the head of NOCAL when the bid was floated, raising conflict-of-interest questions.

Missing millions

In a theft that shocked the country, $104 million intended for the Central Bank of Liberia went missing under mysterious circumstances in 2017. The newly printed currency, equivalent to 5 percent of the country's GDP, was on route from printers in Sweden and China when it disappeared after passing through Roberts International Airport and the Freeport of Monrovia, respectively. The containers carrying the money reportedly arrived in 2017 when Sirleaf was still in office, but officials could not find

---

[203] Cristina Maza, "Rex Tillerson's ExxonMobil Involved in Corrupt Oil Deals in Liberia, Investigation Reveals," *Newsweek,* March 29, 2018.

who picked up the consignment.

President George Weah blamed Sirleaf's government, which had placed the order in 2016, and directed that 15 people, including Sirleaf's son Charles, who at the time was the deputy governor of the Central Bank, and his boss Milton Weeks be barred from leaving the country. Weeks denied knowing about the disappearance, and the former president Sirleaf said the investigations were baseless and aimed at soiling her reputation. Nevertheless, Charles Sirleaf was arrested in March 2019 and charged with economic sabotage related to the unlawful printing of money worth millions of dollars. Four other former senior bank officials were charged, but two of them had fled. Weeks had earlier been charged with economic sabotage, misuse of public money, and criminal conspiracy. In August, an additional charge of money laundering was added to the charge sheet.

However, by May 2019, Liberians were already showing signs of frustration with Weah's government over corruption and the misuse of public funds. Thousands of protesters took to the streets to press for a change in government following revelations of graft that people claimed was responsible for escalating food prices.

NIGER

Niger's president, Mahamadou Issoufou, came to power in 2011 determined to erase years of inequality and greed, but when he tried to investigate graft within the armed forces, he became a victim of a foiled assassination attempt. Ten army officers, including a major and a lieutenant, were arrested for plotting to kill him. Corruption has been boiling in Niger since the nation's independence from France in 1960, but it peaked exponentially during the regime of Mamadou Tandja, who took power in 1999 and was overthrown in a military coup in February 2010. During his 11-year rule, $186 million was found missing from the exchequer. Tandja presided over a corrupt government of which he was the leading player. He was expressly sensitive to criticisms of his government on matters of graft and routinely arrested journalists who wrote about corruption and opponents who reproached him. In one instance, eight media owners were arrested after publishing a story that an internationally owned company, Niger Uranium Venture SA, had paid Tandja's son, Hadia Doulaye, and a journalist, Ibrahim Hamidou, a bribe of $5 million to permit the mining of uranium north of Niger.

There is no doubt that France "has a de facto monopoly on Niger's uranium output,"[204] even though investors from other countries like China have also entered the market to explore for uranium, oil, and other materials. In 2008, the China National Petroleum Corporation (CNPC) was allocated a block in Agadem in the far eastern region in a $5 billion deal to produce oil and gas. Beijing paid a signing bonus of $300 million through President Tandja's son Ousmane, who was the commercial attaché at the Nigerien embassy in Hong Kong. It was widely believed the appointment of Ousmane was deliberately geared at currying favor with President

---

[204] Cassandra Vinograd and David Gauthier-Villars, "Soldiers Oust President in Coup in Uranium-Rich Niger," *The Wall Street Journal,* February 19, 2010.

Tandja. In the Agadem deal, a Mobil-Petronas consortium had done most of the preliminary exploration, but it was disqualified without any reasons. CNPC also built the 20,000-barrels-per-day, $5 billion Soraz refinery at Zinder, and a 600-kilometer, $350 million oil pipeline to move oil from the production area in Agadem to Doba Basin in Chad, linking it with the Chad–Cameroon pipeline. Those deals were opaque.

It was alleged Tandja used his son as the go-between in deals with China, thus feeding "suspicions of corruption that contributed to precipitating Tandja's fall in 2010."[205] Then there was the cost of the refinery. Local economists accused CNPC of escalating the price to win the contract. At the signing of the contract between CNPC and Niger's Societe de Raffinage de Zinder (SORAZ), the price tag was $600 million, but upon completion in 2011 the cost had gone up to $980 million. Delays and unexpected costs were blamed for the inflation, but reports said kickbacks to government officials took a big chunk of the money, which was loaned by China's Export-Import Bank. The bill, plus a 3.1 percent interest payable in 10 years, went to Nigerien taxpayers.

The French journal *Liberation* claimed in August 2009 that corruption was behind many of the mining permits in Niger, and it stated that a Hong Kong company close to Ousmane Tandja was a slush fund of the Tandja family and was the intermediary between Tandja's government and the CNPC on the Azelik mine in Agadem. Hong Kong's Trenfield Holdings owned 51 percent in the Canada-owned Govi High Power Exploration Holdings, now GoviEx Uranium Incorporated (GOVIEX), which had uranium permits in Tagaza, Madaoiuela, and Anoiu Melle.[206] The main beneficiary of revenue from those mines was the Tandja family.

---

[205] Faoud Farhaoui, Gulsum Boz, Mehmet Hecan, "The Great Power Struggle for Africa: The Crisis in Mali," International Strategic Research Organization, research report, 37, https://www.jstor.org/stable/resrep02583, 2013.
[206] "Niger's Coup and Uranium: Weakening of China's Sphere of Influence," *Inforguerre*, March 11, 2010.

Upon his ouster for trying to extend his rule beyond the two-term limit, Tandja, who enjoyed unfettered support from Libyan leader Colonel Muammar el-Qaddafi, was arrested for corruption and kept in custody for 14 months until an appeals court dropped all charges against him, ruling that "it was impossible to try a Head of State after leaving office."[207] He left prison on May 11, 2011.

One of his sons, Mamadou Tandja, and four others—including journalist Hamidou; a former mines minister, Mohamed Abdoulayi; and an employee of the ministry, Oumarou Matsalabi—were arrested and charged with money laundering. In another scandal, codenamed "Uraniumgate," finance minister Hassoumi Massaoudou, who had served as Issoufou's chief of staff in 2011, allegedly signed a $320 million uranium transaction, and the money was paid, but for some reason it never reached the Treasury. He was exonerated after a parliamentary investigation.

President Issoufou's declared commitment to fighting graft was a threat to corruption cartels, but he was undeterred. In June 2011, less than three months after taking over, he ordered the sacking of the budget minister and two other top officials after $3.3 million was embezzled. The following month, the president created an anti-corruption body, the High Authority to Combat Corruption and Related Infractions (HALIA), consisting of government officials, private sector executives, and civil society leaders, and set up a hotline to report incidences of misconduct.

But corruption always fights back. In January 2012, unknown people set the Justice Ministry offices on fire, destroying hundreds of files of anti-corruption investigation reports on senior government officials, including judges. At the time of the fire, 20 judges were under scrutiny for corruption and embezzlement of public funds. That incident blew open the vulnerabilities of the government in the fight against graft and the relentlessness of corruption cartels to resist change.

---

[207] "Niger Court Drops Charges against Ex-President Tandja," *BBC,* news, May 10, 2011.

In August and September 2015, $24.7 million in foreign currency and gold bullion were found at Niamey's international airport after reports circulated that senior government officials had instructed customs officers to clear them without the carriers paying taxes. The goods reportedly emanated from Nigeria, but the carrying of such huge amounts of money violated the West African States Monetary Union rules, which limit the physical movement of currency across national boundaries. The discovery, as well as the release order by the government, raised suspicions of corruption and money laundering.

In March 2016, President Issoufou won a second term amid an opposition boycott and vowed to continue the fight against corruption. Early in 2018, the government erected a huge billboard at the entry into Niamey, the capital of Niger, with an inspirational message in French: "Together, let's fight against corruption at the borders." But with the high level of the malfeasance in the country, the billboard was viewed as only a decorative poster.

Corruption has been rampant along the borders with Niger's seven neighbors. While immigration and customs officers are notorious in demanding bribes, the police and the military are the most egregious, especially in the underground trade of human trafficking. Every year, hundreds of Nigeriens die in the Mediterranean while traveling to North Africa and Europe. Corrupt border officials connive with human smugglers to sneak men, women, and children through frontiers into dinghies and squeaky boats for the dangerous sea journey. In June 2014, 20 people, including opposition leader Hama Amadou, were arrested for trafficking. Amadou, who lives in France, was given a one-year jail term in absentia.

The landlocked Republic of Niger, with a population of 15 million people, borders Nigeria, Benin, Burkina Faso, Mali, Algeria, Libya, and Chad, and it has been ranked by the UN as one of the world's poorest countries, with perennial chronic food shortages. It has "undeveloped, weak, and fragmented" financial systems, but thanks to uranium and oil exports, its economic standing has been robust in the last few decades.[208]

Avera, a French state-owned company, has been operating in the country since the early 1970s and is the largest uranium producer in Niger. Its two mines, Arlit and Cominak in northern Niger, contribute to the ranking of Niger as the world's fourth-largest uranium producer after Kazakhstan, Canada, and Australia. However, activists claim the agreement between Niger and the company was exploitative since it "generously exempted" Areva from customs, export, fuel, materials, and revenue taxes.[209] When, in 2014, the Issoufou government attempted to renegotiate the agreement, Avera closed shop for two weeks, ostensibly for maintenance reasons, denying the government revenue. The workers' union, Synamines, called it a negotiating tactic. Although a new deal was reached to give Niger a greater share of the revenue from uranium, activist Ali Idrissa believes the former French colony would never get a satisfactory business arrangement with a company owned by France. "Don't forget Niger isn't just negotiating with a regular company, but with the French State.... Our dependency from France goes hand in hand with crooked business deals."[210] Niger produces half of France's uranium needed for nuclear reactors.

As much as Nigeriens had hopes that under President Issoufou corruption would be a thing of the past, the new leader has turned out to be a big disappointment even to donors who had resumed their economic ties with Niger after suspending them during Tandja's administration. A few low-level public servants have been jailed, but the big culprits, who have been stealing money through bribes and kickbacks, have not been touched. There are those who believe corruption has become even more rampant in Niger today than it was during Tandja's rule. Street demonstrations demanding

---

[208] 2018 Index of Economic Freedom.
[209] Lucas Destrijcker and Mahadi Diouara, "A Forgotten Community: The Little Town in Niger Keeping the Lights on in France," African Arguments, commentary, July 18, 2017.
[210] Ibid.

the overthrow of Issoufou are now common in Niamey, not only because of increased corruption but also because of sustained human rights violations against opposition politicians, journalists, civil society leaders, and street protesters. In July 2014, two journalists and an activist were arrested after accusing Issoufou of corruption and spent almost two weeks in police cells before being released after protests from global journalists' organizations.

Arms deals

In February 1983, Niger entered into a contract with a West German aircraft maintenance company, Dornier Reparaturwerft GmbH, to perform aircraft maintenance. Because the Nigerien government did not have enough money to pay Dornier, Dornier had to find an American contractor as a partner for the country to qualify for financing from the US Foreign Military Sales program (FMS). The program facilitates sales of US arms, defense equipment, defense services, and military training to foreign governments. Through it, foreign governments can access loans to purchase defense items.

As a partner, Dornier chose the Minnesota, United States-based Napco International Incorporated, and the two companies began cooperating in 1983. Between December 1983 and March 1987, Napco entered into four purchase contracts for aircraft parts, maintenance, and other defense items with the Nigerien government. Three of the contracts, worth $3.2 million, were approved by the US Defense Security Cooperation Agency (DSCA), which provides security sector assistance to foreign governments, militaries, and international organizations. Anxious to get the contracts, Napco's vice president in charge of the aerospace division, Richard H. Liebo, bribed two Nigerien officials with $130,000: a diplomat at the Niger Embassy in Washington, DC and a captain in the Niger Air Force.

That information was leaked to the DOJ, and on April 20, 1989, the DOJ charged Napco before the District Court of Minnesota for violating FCPA regulations, specifically the provisions regarding anti-bribery, books and records, and aiding and abetting the filing of false corporate tax returns. The following month, Napco pleaded guilty and was ordered to pay a $785,000 fine, restitution of $140,000 to the DSCA, and restitution to the US Internal Revenue Service amounting to $75,000. Liebo was convicted in 1992 for aiding and abetting the anti-bribery provisions and making false statements to the DSCA. He was sentenced to 18 months in jail. He appealed and, based on new information, a retrial was ordered. The jury again found Liebo guilty, and he was sentenced to three years' probation, two months of home detention, and 400 hours of community service. By that time, he had already served two months in prison, so he was set free. No action is known to have been taken against the two Nigerien officials.

NIGERIA

Nigeria hosts some of the biggest and most profitable multinationals, including the major oil companies Chevron, Shell, Mobil, and Total; high-tech conglomerates like Google, IBM, and GE; and communications, banking, pharmaceuticals, and beverage giants. They bring with them huge capital investments, jobs, and skills and contribute substantially to the country's economic indicators, although they are also blamed for unethical practices.

Aside from the positive attributes, MNCs in Nigeria are also vastly responsible for pollution and its aftermath, including the destruction of farmlands, wildlife, and sea creatures, especially in the Niger Delta, and are blamed for an increase of "anti-social activities such as drug abuses, prostitution, kidnapping, armed robbery and murder"[211] promoted through films and videos. Those activities have contributed not only to the loss of revenue but to the loss of life and the degradation of cultural norms. Other losses to the Nigerian economy emanate from corruption, mismanagement, and mispricing, as well as missing payments related to concessions and production-sharing arrangements.[212]

In most of Africa, multinationals tend to influence policies and certain decisions of the executive and legislative branches of government. They use bribes and other unorthodox methods to entrap government officials and lawmakers into passing legislation and taking actions favorable to their operations, the idea being to make as much money as possible while using "the least costly production of goods."[213] Some call such practices modern-day imperialism. BAT is a good example of how a multinational can

---

[211] Professor J. Eluka, "Multinational Corporations and Their Effects on Nigerian Economy," *European Journal of Business and Management,* 8, no. 9, (2016).

[212] Annie Barbara Chikwanha, "Combating Corruption in the Extractive Industry in Africa," Swiss International Development Cooperation Agency (SIDA), Paper 1, no. 3, October 2016.

[213] Godwin Onyewuchi Osuagwu and Ezie Obumneke, "Multinational Corporations and the Nigerian Economy," *International Journal of Academic Research in Business and Social Sciences* 3, no. 4 (April 2013): 361.

pay millions of dollars in kickbacks to legislators and government officials to sustain its market position.

Nigeria is one of the world's biggest producers of oil and gas, number one in Africa and eighth in the world. Crude petroleum represents 76 percent of total export revenue, followed by petroleum gas at 13.8 percent, contributing 9.6 percent of the country's GDP in 2018. Since the discovery of these natural products in 1956, however, the country's economy has been struggling, despite the fact that 2.5 million barrels of oil are produced daily.

A rights group operating in the Niger Delta, Ijaw People's Development Initiative, chastised the government of Muhammadu Buhari, accusing it of being "a puppet in the hands of multinationals.... It is sad," he said, "that Nigeria is governed by oil companies."[214] He was referring to the government's apparent failure to force oil multinationals to relocate their operational headquarters to the Niger Delta, the source of most of the country's oil, instead of Lagos and Abuja.

MNCs are the biggest polluters of the environment through the uncontrolled spillage of oil. Despite the fact that the spillage damages everything from wildlife to farmlands to humans and wildlife, the Nigerian government appears either helpless to intervene or the regime has been captured by foreign firms. So, when a Nigerian writer and environmentalist, Ken Saro-Wiwa, protested against the environmental degradation of his home area of Ogoniland by oil foreign companies in the 1990s, he was hanged—along with eight of his followers—by military officers on orders from President Sani Abacha. Amnesty International immediately called for an investigation, accusing the Anglo-Dutch Shell company, which operated in Ogoniland, of being complicit in human rights abuses committed by the Nigerian military. Shell, which pulled out of the area in early 1993 for security reasons, agreed to pay a compensation of $15 million to Saro-Wiwa's family

---

[214] "Buhari's Government a Puppet in the Hands of Oil Multinationals, Says Ijaw Group," *Sahara Reporters,* May 14, 2018.

to settle the matter. Jennie Green, a lawyer for the US-based Center for Constitutional Rights, a non-profit legal and educational organization, said after the settlement in mid-2009 that this was one of the first cases against an MNC for violating human rights. It confirms "that multinational corporations can no longer act with the impunity they once enjoyed."[215]

Early in 2019, four widows of Nigerians who were executed along with Saro-Wiwa filed a suit in the Netherlands, backed by Amnesty International, demanding that Shell compensate them for its alleged complicity in their husbands' deaths which, they claimed, had left them traumatized. That case was still pending by mid-2019.

As wealthy as Nigeria is in terms of natural resources, it still suffers from ever-present poverty. Estimates are that 100 million people out of the country's population of 185 million live on less than one dollar a day. The economic iniquity in Nigeria is mind-boggling—a "resource curse," some say, using a term describing "a country with abundant natural resources such as oil, diamonds, or gold, (but) is worse off economically and politically, compared to countries with fewer natural resources."[216]

Crippled by military coups and internal rifts since its independence on October 1, 1960, the country has been unable to shake off its reputation as one of the most corrupt countries in the world. In his book *The Fortunes of Africa: A 5000-Year History of Wealth, Greed and Endeavor,* Martin Meredith says the practice of embezzlement spread from top to bottom, from politicians to tax collectors, customs officers, policemen, postal clerks, and dispensary assistants. Once in office, he claims, Nigerian politicians "loot public funds, amass fortunes large enough to pay for bribes to win the next election ...

[215] Ed Pilkington, "Shell Pays Out $15.5m over Saro-Wiwa Killing," *The Guardian*, June 8, 2009.
[216] "The Resource Curse: Oil Corruption in Nigeria," Development in Action, newsletter, May 12, 2017.

and the wealth the new elite acquired was ostentatiously displayed in grand houses, luxury cars, and lavish lifestyles: 'platinum life' it was called in Abidjan."[217]

Olusegun Obasanjo, Nigeria's first elected president in 1999, was the first leader to seriously commit himself to eradicating corruption in the oil-rich nation. As it turned out, his was only a derailed train with no movement whatsoever. Leaders who followed him also failed to nail in the dragon of graft, and the majority of them even became active participants. President Abacha alone stole an estimated nearly $400 billion between 1960 and 1999, equivalent to 2 percent to 3 percent of the country's GDP for every year he was president.[218] "Officials not only took kickbacks from foreign oil companies, they sometimes stole the oil itself," Peter Truell and Larry Gurwin say in their book, *False Profits: The Inside Story of BCCI, the World's Most Corrupt Financial Empire.* "Nigerian crude would be loaded onto tankers with no bill of lading issued, making it possible to sell the cargo abroad and pocket the entire proceeds."[219]

In Nigeria, oil production is infiltrated by ruthless cartels who use technical sophistication and sophisticated networks of facilitators, elites, militant groups, and oil company workers, with the facilitation of bribe-prone public sector officials.[220] The cartels compete with legitimate businesses to make as much money as possible.

It is not surprising, therefore, that 80 percent of energy revenues in Nigeria benefit only 1 percent of the population.[221] In a country of

---

[217] Martin Meredith, *The Fortunes of Africa: A 5000-Year History of Wealth, and Endeavor* (Public Affairs, 2014), 599.

[218] "Nigeria's Corruption Busters," United Nations Office on Drugs and Crime, statement, November 2019.

[219] Peter Truell and Larry Gurwin, *False Profits: The Inside Story of BCCI, the World's Most Corrupt Financial Empire* (Houghton Mifflin Company, 1992), 161.

[220] "Unmasking Nigeria's Oil Cartel," OilPrice.com, article, June 8, 2017.

[221] "Oil in Nigeria: A Cure or Curse," *The Global Citizen*, article, August 31, 2012.

such potential, one would expect Nigerian people to be free of poverty, but they are not. The Washington-based Brookings Institution estimates that the number of impoverished people in Nigeria grows by six people every minute. The pauperization is evident immediately when one enters the major cities of Lagos and Abuja and is multiplied many times in rural areas.

Each one of the administrations in power has been caught in serious corruption and bribery scandals involving billions of dollars dished out to government officials by willing multinational organizations. During Abacha's reign, the president and his trusted cronies in the military pillaged the national treasury of an estimated $3.5 billion and funneled off the money to offshore accounts in Switzerland, London, and Jersey.[222]

At the same time, an estimated $182 million was paid as bribes and kickbacks to Nigerian officials by a consortium of foreign companies in what came to be known as the Halliburton bribery scandal. The consortium included Japan's JGC Corp, France's Technip SA, and Italy's Snamprogetti S. p. A. In 1999, between the governments of Abdulsalami Abubakar and General Olusegun Obasanjo, $37.5 million in bribe money was paid, and in 2001 and 2002, under Obasanjo, $51 million and $37.5 million were paid, respectively. Those payments continued until the scandal broke open in 2003.

The middleman who helped bank the money in foreign entities was a British lawyer. He is the one who handled kickbacks for $6 billion engineering and construction work at the Bonny Island natural liquefied gas project in Rivers State undertaken by international firms, including a subsidiary of Halliburton.

According to documents, some of the bribes were conveyed in some rather bizarre ways, like when a courier sent by the British lawyer dropped a "travel back stuffed with USD $1 million in $100

---

[222] Nick Kochan, *The Washing Machine: Money, Crime & Terror in the Offshore System* (Gerald Duckworth & Co. Ltd, 2006), 161.

bills in the foyer of a luxury hotel"[223] in Switzerland for officials of the Nigerian National Petroleum Corporation (NNPC) to pick up and transmit to top government and party officials. The lawyer, who owned a Spanish-based company, used at least 12 Swiss bank accounts to pay off the Nigerians. Other bribe monies were conveyed through secret bank accounts and offshore destinations.

The Halliburton deal roped in the former US vice president, Dick Cheney, who was the company's chief executive officer between 1995 and 2000. However, Cheney's lawyer, Terence O'Donnell, said the accusations against his client were "entirely baseless."[224] Nigeria agreed to suspend the charge against Cheney after Halliburton agreed to pay Abuja $35 million in compensation, including $2.5 million in legal fees incurred by the West African government on the matter. Halliburton also agreed to help Nigeria recover up to $130 million said to be stashed in the Swiss accounts of Nigerian officials. In 2009, the oil company pleaded guilty to foreign bribery in a US court and paid a $402 million criminal fine and another $177 million civil complaint settlement arising from the deal.

At least one Halliburton executive was not lucky enough to escape jail. Albert "Jack" Stanley, former chief executive officer of a Halliburton subsidiary, Kellogg, Brown and Root (KBR), was imprisoned for two and half years by a Houston federal court in 2009 for orchestrating the bribe. He is the one who reportedly recruited the two consulting companies, one based in Gibraltar and another in Tokyo, to pass along $132 million and $50 million in bribe money to Nigerian officials to secure the natural gas contracts.

Lawyer Jeffrey Tesler, who, according to prosecutors, was "the bagman" in the scheme, was imprisoned for 21 months, fined $25,000, and ordered to forfeit $149 million. Wojciech J. Chodan,

---

[223] Will Fitzgibbon, "Files Point to $182mn Halliburton Bribery Scandal in Nigeria," *The Indian Express*, February 9, 2015.
[224] "Dick Cheney and Halliburton Avoid Bribery Charges in Nigeria … by Forking Over $250 Million," *Los Angeles Times*, December 24, 2010.

a Polish national and a salesman at KBR, was sentenced to one year in jail and ordered to forfeit $726,000 obtained illegally from the deal. Individual companies were also fined large sums of money. KBR and Halliburton have since split, and the former said it was not involved in the case against the latter.

During a BBC interview in March 2009, Obasanjo denied being involved in the highly sensitive scandal. However, a government-appointed panel led by Inspector General of Police Mike Okiro reported in 2010 that the former president shared $74 million of the bribe money with his vice president, Atiku Abubakar, and others. Although the Halliburton affair continues to haunt the oil-rich nation because of the high-level people it ensnared and the damage it caused to the country's economy, no top Nigerian official was prosecuted.

The clearing and forwarding matter

In 2010, the SEC charged numerous foreign companies on allegations of bribing officials in Nigeria with millions of dollars in exchange for preferential treatment in clearing and freight forwarding services.[225] The companies were GlobalSantaFe Corp, which in 2007 merged with a subsidiary of Transocean Incorporation; the Swiss-linked Noble Corporation; Transocean Incorporated, a Cayman subsidiary of the Switzerland-based Transocean Ltd; Tidewater Incorporated, a subsidiary of the New-Orleans-based Tidewater Incorporated; the Houston-based Pride International Incorporated; SNEPCO, a Nigerian subsidiary of Royal Dutch Shell Plc; and the Swiss-based forwarding firm Panalpina Incorporated. SEC officials told a court in Washington, DC that the payments, which violated the FCPA, involved millions of dollars in kickbacks and were disguised as legitimate transactions. Panalpina alone admitted paying at least $49 million in bribes and kickbacks to government officials in Angola, Nigeria, Azerbaijan,

---

[225] Samuel O. Idowu and Abubakar S. Kasum, *People, Planet and Profit: Social Economic Perspectives of CSR* (Routledge, 2016), 39–41.

Brazil, Kazakhstan, Russia, and Turkmenistan, and was fined $81.5 million. The bribes, paid between 2002 and 2007, allowed Panalpina clients to evade customs taxes and to smuggle contraband medicines and explosives, among other goods. The court levied varying penalties against the six oil companies and Panalpina, totaling $156.5 million in criminal fines and $80 million in civil disgorgement, plus interest fees.

In another case, Siemens, the giant German technology conglomerate, was charged in a German court in 2007 for paying $2.1 billion in bribes to senior Nigerian government officials, among them a Cabinet minister, a senator, and others, in a continuing effort to monopolize the sector. The company and some of its top executives were fined $248 million by a Munich court on 4 October 2007 for paying bribes to Nigerian, Libyan, and Russian officials, and faced similar allegations in Egypt, Cameroon, and Libya, where it allegedly used $100 million to seek favors from officials there. In turn, the Nigerian government of President Umaru Yar'Adua ordered investigations into the bribe claim against five former ministers for receiving $14.6 million in bribes between 2001 and 2004 from a manager of Siemens' telecommunications unit. An SEC official, Linda Thomsen, described the Siemens scandal as "unprecedented in scale and geographic reach."[226] While in Nigeria, Siemens was not punished and instead was rewarded with a multibillion-dollar contract for the construction of three new turbines for the Geregu power plant in Kogi State, in Germany several Siemens top officials were convicted and sentenced to various prison terms. No more was heard about the Nigerian investigation of officials who allegedly received bribes from Siemens. The German firm has dominated the Nigerian telecommunications industry for years, and it has all been about bribes. In 2009, during the reign of Yar'Adua, who ruled between

---

[226] Securities and Exchange Commission, "SEC Charges Siemens ACG for Engaging in Worldwide Bribery," press release, December 15, 2008.

2007 and 2010, the company was banned from conducting business in the country following the scandal, but the restriction was lifted in 2010 because of Siemens' "sober expression of regret."[227]

Marubeni Corporation

A contract to build liquefied natural gas facilities on Bonny Island in Nigeria got several entities in trouble in 2012 after it was revealed that billions of dollars were set aside to bribe Nigerian government officials. Marubeni Corporation, a Japanese trading company based in Tokyo, Japan, and a joint venture called TSKJ made up of Technip, Snamprogetti Netherlands, KBR, and JGC Corporation, operating from Madeira, Portugal, conspired to unlawfully obtain $6 billion in contracts from Nigeria LNG Limited (NLNG), in which the state-owned NNPC was the largest shareholder.

TSKJ hired a British attorney and a Japanese company as agents to arrange and pay bribes to high-level and working-level state officials in the African country for four engineering, procurement, and construction (EPC) contracts between 1995 and 2004. The DOJ said successive holders of a top-level office in the executive branch of the Nigerian government played a part in the scandal by designating a representative with whom TSKJ should negotiate bribes to Nigerian government officials.[228]

Throughout the scheme, Nigerian officials received millions of dollars in bribes, some of which were transferred from the Netherlands by KBR to obtain EPC contracts for TSKJ. Some of the meetings related to the contracts were held in Houston, Texas, where the contracts and fees were discussed, hence the involvement of the US DOJ. Court documents showed that TSKJ paid $132 million to a Gibraltar corporation controlled by the British

---

[227] Tobi Soniyi, "Nigeria: Bribe Scandal -Siemens Fined N7 billion," *This Day*, November 22, 2010.
[228] US Federal Bureau of Investigation, "Marubeni Corporation Resolves Foreign Corrupt Practices Act Investigation and Agrees to Pay a $54.6 Million Criminal Penalty," press release, January 17, 2012.

lawyer and $51 million to Japan's Marubeni Corporation for use in the bribery.

Marubeni was charged with one count of conspiracy to violate the FCPA and one count of aiding and abetting KBR in violating the FCPA and agreed to pay a $54.6 million criminal penalty under a two-year DPA, which mandated that the company continue cooperating with the DOJ on ongoing investigations and improve its compliance and ethics program. In a related criminal case, KBR's successor company, Kellogg Brown & Root LLC, pleaded guilty to violating the FCPA and was ordered in 2009 to pay $402 million. Technip and Snamprogetti were fined $240 million each, and JGC $218.8 million.[229]

Daimler

When SEC officials launched a probe into the German car giant Daimler in 2001 following suspicion of bribery, they were not prepared for what they found. In a five-year investigation, the commission stumbled on a scandal involving millions of dollars and stretching across numerous countries in Africa, the Middle East, Eastern Europe, and Asia amounting to tens of millions of dollars.

The affair in Nigeria, North Korea, China, Vietnam, China, Croatia, Egypt, Greece, Hungary, Indonesia, Iraq, Ivory Coast, Latvia, Russia, Serbia and Montenegro, Thailand, Turkey, Turkmenistan, Uzbekistan, and Vietnam had been going on for a decade as Daimler executives moved from one country to another bribing government officials to get them to buy their vehicles. In some cases, as happened in Turkmenistan, the company gave out an armored S-class Mercedes-Benz worth $343 million to the country's dictator, Saparmurat Niyazov; in others, the reward was cash, as in Indonesia, where $41,000 was dished out to government employees.

[229] "FCPA/Anti-Bribery Alert," Hughes, Hubbard & Reeds LLP, report, summer 2012.

The money was paid either to US bank accounts or to foreign accounts, including via shell companies, and then secretly conveyed to the officials, classified as "commissions," "special discounts," or "useful payments." The SEC jumped into the case precisely because US banks were being used as conduits of illegal transfers. Other mechanisms used to pay the money were through corporate ledger accounts known as "third-party accounts," or TPAs, and corporate "cash desks." In all cases, according to the DOJ, Daimler improperly recorded the corrupt payments in its corporate books and records. "Using offshore bank accounts, third-party agents, and deceptive pricing practices, these companies saw foreign bribery as a way of doing business,"[230] said US Deputy Assistant Attorney General Mythili Raman during the hearing of the bribery case before a district court judge in Washington, DC.

He was referring to Daimler AG's Russian subsidiary, DaimlerChrysler Automotive Russia SAO (SDCAR), now Mercedes-Benz Russia SAO, and its German subsidiary, Export and Trade Finance GmbH (ETF), which pleaded guilty to violating FCPA provisions. The bribes involved more than 200 transactions, including one to Iraqi ministers for the purchase of vehicles for the UN "oil for food" program during President Saddam Hussein's regime.

The Nigerian government opened investigations in 2010 into $15 million allegedly paid as bribes by Daimler to a local company that assembled Mercedes trucks and buses. The Nigerian firm, Anambra Motor Manufacturing Company (Anammco), was a partner in a joint venture with Daimler, the government, and local investors, though Daimler pulled out in 2007. Daimler entered into an agreement to sell vehicles to the president's residence, the Nigerian presidential complex. In the process, it hiked the whole price of the vehicles, parts, and services by 21 percent, or $1.5 million, to be paid as a commission to Nigerian officials who helped

---

[230] "Daimler AG and Three Subsidiaries Resolve FCPA Investigation and Agree to Pay $93.6 Million in Criminal Penalties," Cision PR Newswire, April 1, 2010.

secure the contract. In another sale of vehicles, spare parts, and tools to the state-sponsored Savannah Sugar Company Limited worth $4.6 million, Daimler paid over $600,000 as commissions to officials. Similar questionable deals were entered into with other government entities like the police and the army, and persons including a Nigerian diplomat in Brazil and his wife who were paid $60,000 in kickbacks to facilitate sales of Daimler vehicles to a Nigerian state.

The chief of the SEC's FCPA unit, Cheryl J. Scarboro, said the bribery was so pervasive in Daimler's decentralized corporate structure that it extended outside of the sales organization to the internal audit, legal, and finance departments: "These departments should have caught and stopped the illegal sales practices, but instead they permitted or were directly involved in the company's bribery practices."[231] The court was told Daimler's top executives knew about the illegal payments but did nothing to stop them.

Daimler has been struggling with ethical issues since 1999, when some company executives expressed concern about payments to foreign officials to win contracts. That prompted the board of directors to adopt a code of ethics to comply with a German law which barred tax deductions for foreign bribes. Daimler did not enforce the code due to internal opposition. However, in 2004, a Daimler whistleblower alerted the US Department of Labor after the company sent illegal payments to US bank accounts and the foreign accounts of US shell companies. That immediately brought the company under the jurisdiction of the FCPA. That is when trouble began for the German auto maker.

Who's the most corrupt?

It is difficult to say who among the Nigerian leaders was the most corrupt. Each one had his own way of exploiting the country and amassing wealth. While some worked for kickbacks from

---

[231] Securities and Exchange Commission, "SEC Charges Daimler ACG with Global Bribery," press release, http://www.sec.gov/news/press/2010/2010-51.htm, April 1, 2010.

multinationals, others took to smuggling and embezzlement from the public coffers to fatten their bank accounts. General Ibrahim Badamasi Babangida, who ruled Nigeria between 1985 and 1993, took the latter route. A career soldier who came to be known as IBB or Maradona (after the Argentinian football wizard) for his quick moves in plunder, Babangida consorted with a clique of state criminals and crooked businesspeople to divert public money even though he had promised to end corruption at his installation.

While in Kenya, politicians used politically correct financial institutions like Imperial Bank and Trade Bank to hide and launder money, Babangida and his cronies used the Nigerian branch of the highly controversial and ill-reputed Bank of Credit and Commerce International-Nigeria (BCCI-Nigeria) to barter oil for cash which, instead of being deposited in the exchequer, went into individual pockets.

The Nigerian branch was established in 1979 with Ibrahim Dasuki, one of Babangida's closest allies, as co-founder and chairman. However, the bank itself was owned by a flamboyant Pakistani jet setter, Agha Hasan Abedi. For a decade, the deposit safe at BCCI-Nigeria was filled with money brought in by government bigwigs, drug barons, and oil smugglers. It was the only bank in Nigeria that was seemingly making profits. It was so "successful" that it became the envy of other institutions. Some foreign banks closed down due to poor business, but not the BCCI-Nigeria branch. It was the bank of choice for anyone who wanted to be associated with the elite crowd. Using its political connections and odious schemes, the bank earned huge amounts of money by illegally converting naira, the local currency, into dollars, and then transferring them abroad.[232] The scheme was duplicated by crooked employees who got involved in the illicit transactions.

---

[232] Stephen Ellis, *The Present Darkness: A History of Nigerian Organized Crime* (Oxford University Press, 2016), 188–240.

In the United States, Europe, Asia, Africa, and the Arab world, banker Abedi, the dashing billionaire, mingled with presidents, prime ministers, politicians, and the intelligentsia, gaining in the process a reputation as a financial wizard. Those connections not only enabled BCCI to expand its network but helped it to marshal deposits from central banks in developing countries.[233] BCCI opened new branches everywhere, more than any other bank, and bribed influencers to gain leverage at a breakneck pace.

With its headquarters in Karachi and London and 400 branches in 78 countries, BCCI finally collapsed in July 1991 over worldwide corruption allegations and possible pending criminal charges by US officials, sinking customer deposits worth millions of dollars, some of it from government agencies. One estimate showed that three African countries, Zimbabwe, Cameroon, and Zambia, lost assets worth $190 million deposited at the BCCI-London branch. Kenya alone saw $20 million of its money vanish into thin air.

The director of the US Central Intelligence Agency (CIA), Robert Gates, described the institution as "the bank of crooks and criminals international" (i.e., a play on "BCCI") for its fondness for catering to customers who engaged in arms, drugs, and hot money.[234] It was a criminal enterprise whose client list included warmongers and suspected money launderers like Samuel Doe, Iraq's Saddam Hussein, and Panama's Manuel Noriega.

The collapse of BCCI-Nigeria following the closure of the main office did not, however, discourage Babangida and his cronies from continuing with their wayward ways and using other financial schemes to exploit the oil riches of the Niger Delta. In July 1991, the Nigerian BCCI branch became the African International Bank Limited (AIB), and it was business as usual. Like many other banks

---

[233] Peter Truell and Larry Gurwin, *False Profits: The Inside Story of BCCI, the World's Most Corrupt Financial Empire* (Houghton, 1992), 96.
[234] Steve Lohr, "World Class Fraud: How BCCI Pulled It Off: A Special Report," *The New York Times*, August 12, 1991.

favored by elites, the AIB collapsed in 2013 due to liquidity problems, leading the Central Bank of Nigeria to revoke its license.

In the meantime, in 1994, a court in the UAE convicted 12 senior executives of BCCI for their role in the scandal that led to the collapse of the bank. The founder, 71-year-old wheelchair-bound Abedi, who domiciled in Pakistan, was sentenced to eight years in prison, and the former CEO, Mohammed Swaleh Naqvi, to 14 years in jail, both in absentia. The other 10 were either jailed or set free.

BCCI-Kenya

Although BCCI-Nigeria exhibited an exceptional dynamism in attracting accounts from a diversely bizarre bunch of depositors, the BCCI-Kenya branch too had peculiar characteristics. Formed in 1979 with little fanfare but mired in political correctness, the BCCI-Kenya branch was destined for controversy from the very beginning.

Its founder, Keitan Somaia, a boisterous, heavy-set former co-owner of the looted Trust Bank, together with Ajay Shah, was inherently corrupt. Somaia was involved in everything from dubious arms sales to manipulating Kenyan government contracts. In 1990, he convinced the government to loan him $5 million to buy 500 "London look" black taxicabs, but when they arrived in Nairobi—only 200 of them—they were found to be old jalopies painted black. They never lasted long, and they disappeared from the streets of the city within a few years. The same year, Somaia obtained another $8 million from the government to buy communications equipment for the Kenya Police. He never delivered, but vanished, ignoring four requests to appear before Parliament to explain the non-delivery. He got all those loan authorizations with the support of senior officials in the office of President Daniel arap Moi.

At the Trust Bank, Somaia allowed politicians, politically correct firms, and individuals to borrow huge amounts of money without security and permitted massive withdrawals of funds for purposes of laundering illicitly obtained money. Depositors lost $50 million when Trust Bank collapsed in 1998.

At the time of BCCI's formation, the country was in the midst of a strict foreign exchange regime meant to preserve the little foreign currency Kenya had and to respond to pressure on the balance of payments. But instead of helping the government mop up foreign currency, BCCI-Kenya got itself entangled in a number of dubious activities that violated the country's strict foreign currency regulations. Like elsewhere in the world, BCCI-Kenya operated in a corrupt environment marked by cash bribes, kickbacks to senior Central Bank officials, and special arrangements with the head of state,[235] then Moi.

In 1987, BCCI-Kenya was charged with permitting a coffee exporter to accumulate $34 million worth of foreign exchange currency abroad, money which should have been repatriated to Kenya. Three of its senior executives were arrested. It took the personal intervention of the BCCI owner, Abedi, for them to be released, and the bank agreeing to pay back the money to the government. BCCI also ran into trouble in India, Sudan, Zimbabwe, Nigeria, Pakistan, and Bangladesh, and stayed off the hook only by paying off leaders in those countries.

In Kenya, al-Qaeda operatives who bombed the US embassies in Kenya and Tanzania in 1998 admitted during their trial in a New York district court in 2001 of having bank accounts at BCCI-Kenya. Four of the operatives were convicted and given life sentences for killing 224 people and injuring several thousand others in the two gruesome explosions. BCCI was also linked to the war in Afghanistan, serving as the "de facto central bank" for a multibillion-dollar illegal arms-for-drugs trade between 1979 and 1990.[236]

---

[235] US Senate, "The BCCI Affair," A report to the Committee on Foreign Relations by Senator John Kerry and Senator Hank Brown, 102d Congress, 2d Session, Senate Print 102-40, December 1992.
[236] Bill Engdahl and Jeffrey Steinberg, "The Real Story of the BCCI," *Executive Intelligence Review*, October 13, 1995.

fter the collapse of BCCI in 1991, the Kenyan government—of which some of its top officials were clients—moved quickly to assure Kenyans that BCCI-Kenya branches were financially sound, which was not quite true. Not too long after that, Somaia bought the Kenyan branch and renamed it Delphis Bank. Like BCCI, Delphis too was a conduit for money laundering. In 1993, Delphis Bank was one of four "political" banks—including Exchange Bank, Pan African Bank, and Post Bank Credit—to be investigated by the CBK after the IMF and donor nations complained about the irregular transfer of huge amounts of money. Suspicion was raised when, on April 2, 1993, $3 million was transferred from Delphis Bank to Exchange Bank. A few days later, over $4 million was transferred from Exchange Bank to Delphis. Because of a massive drainage of money through unsecured loans to politicians and officials, Somaia's Delphis Kenya lasted only a few years before it collapsed in June 2001, joining a slew of 50 financial institutions, mostly owned by individuals connected to top government officials, to flop between 1988 and 1998. Two other Delphis banks owned by Somaia in Mauritius and Tanzania also came tumbling down in 2002 and 2003 respectively.

Somaia was the chief executive of the Bermuda-registered offshore company known as Dolphin Holdings whose chairman was a former British Conservative MP, Lord Parkinson. Cunning and extremely crafty, Somaia was a close collaborator of Kamlesh Pattni, another Kenyan businessman who featured prominently in the country's biggest scandal, Goldenberg, involving trade in gold that never existed. The Exchange Bank owned by Pattni featured prominently in the scandal, since some of the fraudulently obtained money from Goldenberg was banked there. No one was convicted in the Goldenberg scandal.

Cas-Global Limited

Another case which raised eyebrows in the United Kingdom involved allegations that a British firm, CAS-Global Limited, bribed a Norwegian official "to forge the export license of seven naval vessels that ended in the hands of a Nigerian warlord."[237] According to reports, the UK-registered company paid $154,000 to a Norwegian government employee to secure the lucrative contract without disclosing that the end user was a Nigerian warlord, Chief Government Ekpemupolo, popularly known as Tompolo.[238]

One of Tompolo's several companies, Global West Vessel Specialist, reportedly entered into a 2014 deal to buy seven former gunships worth $10.4 million from Norway via CAS-Global. The ships, including a 2,530-tonne KNM Horten, were transported via the UK's Ramsgate port in southeast England, after which the Horten was moved to Nigeria.

Tompolo became famous for leading bombing attacks on oil pipelines and the kidnapping of foreign company employees in the oil-producing Niger Delta between 2006 and 2009. He was the leader of a ragtag army of the defunct Movement for the Emancipation of the Niger Delta (MEND).

Four countries—the United Kingdom, the United States, Norway, and Nigeria—launched an investigation of CAS-Global Limited in 2017 following pressure from the watchdog Corruption Watch. Norway charged a Norwegian civil servant, Bjorn Stavrum, for allegedly receiving $154,000 from CAS-Global, deposited directly into his back account in two installments in 2013, as a bribe to secure the sale. Stavrum denied the charge but was nevertheless found guilty and sentenced to five years in jail. Tompolo, on the other hand, was still in hiding at the end of 2018, wanted by the government on charges of money laundering, conspiracy, and theft.

---

[237] "UK Firm Probed for Bribery in Multinational Dollar Defense Deal," Organized Crime and Corruption Reporting Project (OCCRP), May 15, 2017.

[238] Mildred Europa Taylor, "How the UK Approved the Sale of Warships to a former Nigerian Warlord in Deal that Shocked the World," Face-to-Face Africa, online bulletin, October 28, 2018.

Smuggling of oil

Pius Okigbo, one of Nigeria's most respected economists, estimated that $12.4 billion disappeared from the Nigerian Exchequer between September 1988 and June 1994, much of it through bank accounts operated by President Babangida. Much of the money was earned during the Gulf War of 1990/1991, when oil prices had skyrocketed[239] and politicians cashed in on the smuggling and theft of the commodity.

Even after Babangida's departure in 1993, the smuggling of oil continued. In 2004, two oil tankers with their original names painted over, MT Jimoh and MT African Pride, were caught with 11,000 tons of stolen oil on board. However, as investigations continued while in custody, the ships mysteriously disappeared.[240] Corruption was blamed for the disappearance of the vessels, and two Nigerian navy admirals were sacked. In March of the same year, 38 locals and foreigners were arrested aboard two ships carrying 10,000 tons of illegally bunkered crude oil. And a few months later, 15 Russian nationals were caught stealing 11,300 tons of crude oil. Between October 2003 and March 2004, 82 people, among them Russians, Poles, Romanians, Ghanaians, Sri Lankans, Georgians, and Nigerians, were caught stealing Nigerian crude oil in the Niger Delta, in rivers and on the high seas.[241] They were jailed.

While some of the thefts were the "work of lower-level syndicates,"[242] initiated by criminal gangs and politically-inclined movements, others were led by smuggling barons "under the control of the nation's top political 'godfathers' able to influence the executive and security forces."[243] The military, which was expected to protect

[239] E. E. Osaghae, *Crippled Giant: Nigeria Since Independence* (Hurst & Co., 1998), 278–279.
[240] Stephen Ellis, *This Present Darkness: A History of Nigerian Organized Crime* (Oxford University Press, 2016), 148.
[241] Patrick Edobor Igbinovia, *Oil Thefts and Pipeline Vandalization in Nigeria* (Safari Books Ltd., 2014), 68.
[242]Stephen Ellis, *This Present Darkness: A History of Nigerian Organized Crime* (Oxford University Press, 2016), 149.
[243] "Unmasking Nigeria's oil cartel," OilPrice.com, June 8, 2017.

the oil resource, was itself "up to the eyeballs in oil theft."[244] Army officers are the people with resources to pump illegal oil into tankers at export terminals, siphon crude from terminal storage tanks onto trucks,[245] or transfer it between ships[246] in what is called bunkering. Ordinary Nigerians do not have the wherewithal to achieve that.

In January 2014, finance minister Ngozi Okonjo-Iweala, under Goodluck Jonathan's government, surprised the country when he announced that $11 billion earned from crude oil sales between January 2012 and July 2013 had vanished from the federal exchequer. Perhaps because of the involvement of senior officials in the theft, nothing was done to trace the money. Petroleum minister Diezani Alison-Maduke, referred to in some quarters as "Jonathan's ATM,"[247] was herself entangled in a misappropriation case and was charged in court, as will be seen below.

President Atiku Abubakar's woes

The US government has always had an eye on top Nigerian leaders on matters of corruption. A 2010 US Senate subcommittee report investigating suspect funds into the United States discovered that Jennifer Douglas Abubakar, wife of Atiku Abubakar, vice president and later president of Nigeria, had helped her husband bring $40 million into the United States between 2000 and 2008, including "at least $1.7 million in bribe payments from Siemens AG, a German corporation, and over $38 million from three little-known offshore corporations, Let's Go Limited, Incorporated, Guernsey Trust

---

[244] Sarah Chayes, *Thieves of State: Why Corruption Threatens Global Security* (W. W. Norton & Company, 2015), 124.
[245] Christina Katsouris and Aaron Syne, "Nigeria's Criminal Crude: International Options to Combat the Export of Stolen Oil," report, Chatham House, 4, September 1, 2013.
[246] Stephen Ellis, *This Present Darkness: A History of Nigerian Organized Crime* (Oxford University Press, 2016), 152.
[247]Sarah Chayes, *Thieves of State: Why Corruption Threatens Global Security* (W. W. Norton & Company, 2015), 123.

Company Nigeria Limited, and Sima Holdings Limited."[248]

Half of the funds were wire-transferred by the offshore corporations, but Jennifer Douglas—Atiku's fourth wife and a former Nigerian television journalist—insisted the money came from her husband and distanced herself from the corporations. The congressional report showed she used the money to maintain a lavish lifestyle, with part of it going to a non-profit foundation she founded in the United States in 2002, Gede Foundation, and the American University of Nigeria, started by her husband in 2003.

The sub-Committee found evidence showing the transfers of large sums of money from the offshore corporations to a number of entities, including lawyers who oversaw Abubakar's legal transactions. Before becoming vice president in 1999, Abubakar worked for the customs service. While serving at the number two position in the executive branch, Abubakar was named in corruption allegations relating to the mismanagement of the Nigerian Petroleum Technology Department Fund. The fund was established in 1973 to develop local manpower and technology transfer acquisition in the petroleum industry. It was also alleged that between 1999 and 2006, Atiku approved the release of $20 million from the Treasury without appropriation and approval from the Cabinet and had the money allegedly deposited in a commercial bank.

Siemens, for its part, was said to have transferred $2.8 million in "bribe payments to a US bank account belonging to Douglas as part of a scheme to bribe Nigerian officials," in violation of the FCPA.

In December 2008, the DOJ and SEC filed criminal and civil charges alleging Siemens AG had violated FCPA provisions by making illegal payments to several overseas officials in exchange for contracts and had infringed book- and record-keeping

---

[248] US Senate, Permanent Sub-Committee on Investigations, "Keeping Foreign Corruption Out of the United States: Four Case Histories," February 4, 2010.

provisions. Douglas's share of the bribe money was channeled through a bank account in Potomac, Maryland. Siemens pleaded guilty and was ordered to pay penalties totaling $1.6 billion.

Minister and oil scandal

In another scandal, the former Nigerian petroleum minister, Diezani Alison-Madueke, and two others, Kola Aluko and Jide Omokore, were named in a complaint filed as part of a civil matter by the DOJ that they received $144 million in bribes to facilitate oil contracts to the Atlantic Energy Drilling Concepts Nigeria Limited (AEDC) and the Atlantic Energy Brass Development Limited, two shell companies owned by Omokore. The DOJ wanted the money, allegedly laundered in the United Kingdom and the United States, to be forfeited, together with a luxury condominium apartment in New York and an $80 million yacht.

In July 2017, the DOJ issued a statement saying the FBI's International Corruption Squad was handling the matter. "Corrupt foreign officials and business executives should make no mistake: if illicit funds are within the reach of the United States, we will seek to forfeit them and to return them to the victims from whom they were stolen,"[249] the statement affirmed.

The case was also spotlighted in Nigeria. In May 2018, the government said the investigation was ongoing against the three officials for allegedly looting $3 billion from the NNPC.

Also in the spotlight in Nigeria was an investigation launched by the DOJ over bribes to Nigerian officials by the China Petroleum and Chemical Corporation (Sinopec) in 2015. The juicy bribes, estimated at $100 million, were paid in 2015 to help resolve a $4 billion dispute between the Nigerian government and a Chinese company, Addax Petroleum Unit in Geneva, relating to drilling, tax

---

[249] US Department of Justice, "Department of Justice Seeks to Recover Over $100 Million Obtained from Corruption in the Nigerian Oil Industry," press release no. 17-777, July 14, 2017.

breaks, and how royalties were to be divided between Addax and the NNPC on Nigerian construction projects.

According to Bloomberg News, the attorney general allegedly influenced the government to settle the matter out of court in exchange for the government to drop demands that Addax pay $3 billion in previous tax breaks and reimbursements to capital costs. The auditing firm of Deloitte questioned some payments made by Addax to a Nigerian construction firm, Kaztec Engineering Limited, owned by politician Emeka Offor, for what were described as questionable projects. Another $20 million was said to have been paid to four Nigerian lawyers through banks in New York and California, according to the Swiss newspaper Le Temps. In 2018, the non-governmental Human and Environmental Development Agenda Resource Center (HEDA) urged the state Economic and Financial Crimes Commission (EFCC) to follow up on the Deloitte findings and investigate the bribery claims.

The fiasco triggered an investigation by a joint team from the DOJ and SEC to find out whether "an unidentified Nigerian lawyer who is a member of the California bar was used to pay some of the alleged bribes."[250] The outcome of that investigation is unknown.

Sinopec bought Addax in 2009 to entrench its presence in Geneva and expand its oil production capacity in Africa.

The Malabu affair

One of the biggest oil scandals in Nigeria was the Malabu bribery scandal, in which an Italian oil company, Eni, and the Anglo-Dutch peer Royal Dutch Shell paid middlemen bribes totaling $1.1 million to help explore a Nigerian offshore oil field purchased by the company, Malabu Oil and Gas Limited, in 2011 for $1.3 billion. By the time of the deal, the company had not started production due to license controversies.

---

[250] "US Probes Chinese Oil Firm over $100m Bribe Paid to Nigerians," The Cable, August 31, 2017.

The controversy over the award to Malabu spiraled after the death of Abacha in 1998 when, in 2011, President Olusegun Obasanjo revoked the license and gave the contract to Shell. Malabu protested and took the matter to the House of Representatives Committee on Petroleum, which ordered the license to be given back to Malabu. The decision was affirmed by the Nigerian Court of Appeal.

Unsatisfied with the decision, Shell took the matter to the International Center for the Settlement of Investment Disputes in Washington, DC, demanding $2 billion from the Lagos government for breach of contract. The matter was eventually settled by Shell paying the government $1.2 billion and getting Malabu to relinquish its rights. That is when detectives swung into action against former justice minister Mohammed Adoke and the former petroleum minister in Abacha's regime, Dan Etete, for diverting the original amount from the government accounts to other accounts.

Among those charged were Eni CEO Claudio Descalzi and four former Shell managers, including the chairman of the Shell Foundation, Malcolm Brinded. Emeka Obi of Nigeria and Gianluca Di Nardo of Italy, who were the middlemen in the transaction, were each jailed for four years by a Milan court in September 2018. The judge also ordered that $94.4 million be seized from Obi and $21.9 million from Di Nardo.

Shell, the biggest oil investor in Nigeria, denied that the two worked for the company. An Italian prosecutor claimed the money was deposited in a company account belonging to Etete. It was further alleged that $520 million from the deal was paid to Nigerian president Goodluck Jonathan and other government officials.

In a dramatic twist of events, the Nigerian government of Muhammadu Buhari sued the US banking group JP Morgan Chase Bank in a London court in November 2017 for $875 million, claiming the bank failed to block the payments from the Malabu deal. Nigeria said the bank had been "grossly negligent" and did not act "with the reasonable care and skill to be expected of a bank in compliance with the laws of England and Wales"[251] when it authorized the deal. But JP Morgan countered the claims in court documents in April 2018 and blamed the UK Serious Organized Crime Agency (SOCA) for authorizing the payments. It said it repeatedly asked for permission to make the payments, and instead of being told to block the transfers, the bank gave it the green light for two payments in 2011 and 2013. The case was still ongoing by mid-2019. The surprise development came on the heels of a campaign by President Buhari to recover huge amounts of money fleeced by officials in previous governments.

In December 2016, Adoke was charged in absentia in Nigeria, together with others, for aiding and abetting money laundering relating to the $1.1 billion Malabu payoff.

A bribery conspiracy

In 2007, the SEC moved into action following reports that a foreign company dealing in construction engineering in the oil and gas industry, Wilbros Group Incorporated, and its wholly owned subsidiary, Wilbros International Incorporated, had conspired to pay $6.3 million in bribes to Nigerian officials to assist in obtaining and retaining a $387 million contract for the construction of the Eastern Gas Gathering System in violation of the FCPA's provisions. The money was paid to officials of the state-owned oil company, the NNPC; the NNPC subsidiary, the National Petroleum Investment Management Services (NAPIMS); a senior unnamed official in the executive branch of the Nigerian federal government; unidentified officials of a multinational oil company; and a Nigerian political party. The offenses were committed between 2003 and 2005.

---

[251] Oladeinde Olawoyin, "Malabu Scandal: Court Papers Expose Nigerian Offaicials Who Authorized Controversial Payments," *The Premium Times*, April 12, 2018.

The Wilbros Managing Director, Jim Bob Brown, and several executives were criminally charged and ordered to pay various amounts to Nigerian authorities. Brown was sentenced to 12 months in prison by the US district court judge Simeon T. Lake III in Houston, Texas. Another former Wilbros executive, Jason Edward Steph, was given a 15-month prison term. They were also to serve two years and one year, respectively, of supervised release after their release from prison. Both had pleaded guilty to one count of conspiracy to violate the FCPA's provisions.

And in another dubious deal, the US-based ITXC Corporation, a global telecommunications provider, was accused of paying $450,000 as bribe to telecommunications officials in four African countries—Nigeria, Rwanda, Senegal, and Mali—to obtain and retain contracts for the Princeton, New Jersey company. In Nigeria, ITXC agreed to pay a consulting company headed by an official of NITEL, the state-owned Nigerian telecommunications authority, $166,541.31 in exchange for assistance in obtaining agreements with other service providers in the country.[252] ITXC allegedly wired the money to the Nigerian bank account of a foreign official's company between November 2002 and May 2004. A number of company officials, including the executive vice president for global sales, Steven J. Ott, were charged with conspiracy, bribery of foreign officials, and commercial bribery and were sentenced to varying probation periods, as well as being fined.

There are many ways in which foreign companies bribe Nigerian officials. The following incident, which occurred between 2003 and 2004, was not about winning contracts but about getting corrupt Nigerian officials to reduce expatriate employment taxes. A subsidiary of the Houston-based Bristow Group, Pan African Nigeria Ltd (PAAN), which provides helicopter transportation services and deals in oil and gas production facilities operations,

---

[252] United States Securities and Exchange Commission, "Summaries of Foreign Corrupt Practices Act Enforcement Actions by the United States, 1 January 1998 – 30 September 2010, Appendix C, 85.

was caught after paying $423,000 to bribe employees of two Nigerian states to influence them to improperly reduce the amount of pay-as-you-earn (PAYE) taxes payable to the authorities by PAAN.

The company secured a $854,000 tax reduction as a result of the bribe payment. In addition, Bristow was also accused of wrongly reflecting payroll-related expenses, mischaracterizing them as legitimate payroll expenses in its books and records. In September 2007, the SEC ordered Bristow, a New York Stock Exchange–listed company, to desist from committing further violations of the FCPA.

NNPC in more troubles

Between 2003 and 2005, Paradigm B. V., a provider of enterprise software for the global oil and gas exploration and production industry, used intermediaries to pay between $100,000 and $200,000 in bribes to Nigerian politicians to obtain a contract for services for a subsidiary of the NNPC. The names of the politicians were not disclosed. Nigeria is one of several countries, including China, Indonesia, Kazakhstan, Latvia, and Mexico, where Paradigm B. V. reportedly bribed officials to secure various tenders in the oil and gas industry.

The Netherlands-headquartered Paradigm discovered the illegal payments when conducting due diligence for its planned Nasdaq IPO and self-disclosed them to US prosecutors. The company accepted responsibility and agreed to pay a $1 million criminal fine, implement strict controls, and retain an outside compliance counsel. It also agreed to disclose all information with respect to its activities and report any criminal activities by any of its employees.

In Nigeria, as in many African countries, officials use multimillion-dollar projects as a conduit for bribery and corruption. So, when Nigeria first decided to build a $3.6 billion deep-water oil drilling project called the Bonga South/West/Aparo oil and gas project, multinational companies were ready to pounce on the opportunity to squeeze favors from corrupt officials. The 60-square-kilometer offshore project was being carried out by the Shell Nigeria Exploration and Production Company (SNEPCO) on behalf of the NNPC under a production-sharing contract, with Esso, Nigeria Agip, and Elf Petroleum Nigeria Limited as partners holding 20 percent, 12.5 percent, and 12.5 percent shares respectively.

Between 2002 and 2005, a company called Vetco International Limited, a global supplier of products and services for oil drilling production, and its partners allegedly used $2.1 million to bribe Nigerian government officials. The companies made 378 illicit payments through a major international freight, forwarding, and customs clearance company to Nigerian customs officials to shield Vetco from paying customs duties. Vetco Gray Controls Incorporated, Vetco Gray Controls Limited, and Vetco Gray UK Limited pleaded guilty in 2004 to conspiracy to bribe foreign officials and bribery of foreign officials, and they agreed to pay fines of $6 million, $8 million, and $12 million respectively. Another wholly owned subsidiary of Vetco International entered into a DPA on the same charges. In November 2008, Aibel Group, which provided engineering and procurement services for the drilling operations, pleaded guilty and was ordered to pay a $4.2 million criminal fine for violating FCPA provisions and to serve a two-year term of organizational probation, during which time it was to submit periodic reports regarding its progress to implement anti-bribery compliance measures.

Apart from companies, individuals have also faced the wrath of US government agencies for going against FCPA provisions. In June 2007, Congressman William J. Jefferson of New Orleans became the first American public official to be penalized for bribing foreign officials. He committed the offense while serving in the US House of Representatives. Investigators said the congressman was responsible for negotiating, offering, and delivering payments of bribes to a high-ranking official in the executive branch of the Nigerian government to secure approvals for a telecommunications joint venture. At one point, Jefferson allegedly stashed $90,000 in his freezer, intended for the vice president of Nigeria.[253]

In return, the joint venture "agreed to pay Jefferson and his family things of value."[254] Those things of value, according to court records, included hundreds of thousands of dollars of bribes in the form of payments, including monthly fees or retainers, consulting fees, percentage shares of revenues and profits, flat fees for items sold, and stock ownership in the companies seeking his official assistance. On June 4, 2007, he was charged in an Alexandria, Virginia court with bribing a foreign official, money laundering, obstruction of justice, and racketeering to advance various business endeavors in which he and his family had a financial interest. He was convicted in November 2009 on 11 charges that included conspiracy to commit bribery, wire fraud, and violating the FCPA. He was sentenced to 13 years' imprisonment followed by three years' supervised release and ordered to forfeit more than $470,000.

The DOJ said Jefferson led delegations to Africa and used his office to promote businesses and businesspeople, including entering into telecommunications deals in Nigeria and Ghana; oil concessions in Equatorial Guinea; satellite transmission contracts in Botswana, Equatorial Guinea, and the Republic of Congo; and the development of various plants and facilities in Nigeria.[255] US district judge T. S. Ellis III called Jefferson's action "venal." In December 2017, after eight years in jail, Jefferson was let out on time served.

---

[253] Rachel Weiner, "Former Congressman William Jefferson Goes Free, Thanks to Supreme Court Ruling in McDonnel Case," *The Washington Post*, December 1, 2017.

[254] "Government's Sentencing Memorandum," US District Court for Eastern District of Virginia, November 13, 2009.

[255] US Department of Justice, "Former Congressman William J. Jefferson Sentenced to 13 Years in Prison for Bribery and Other Charges," press release no. 09-1231, November 13, 2009.

Oil subsidy scam

Parliaments all over the world work through committees, and those committees often investigate issues of national interest. But when a committee member turns around and uses committee findings for personal enrichment, questions of integrity come into play. That is what happened in Nigeria when an MP and chairman of an ad hoc committee of the House of Representatives, Farouk Lawan, collected $500,000 of a $3 million bribe to remove the names of Zenon Petroleum & Gas and African Petroleum, now known as Forte Oil Plc, from the list of companies named in a fuel subsidy scam. The committee was the one that wrote the report of the scam in 2012, occasioning a loss of $6.8 billion.

Another company mentioned in the parliamentary report was the local subsidiary of ExxonMobil. The rip-off involved fraudulent transactions from which government officials and oil marketers reaped millions of US dollars without delivering any oil. Zenon alone allegedly received $232 million from subsidy claims but provided no petroleum products. In one case, payments of $6.4 million flowed from the state treasury 128 times within 24 hours to "unknown entities."[256] The owner of Zenon, billionaire Femi Otedola, who was a close ally of President Goodluck Jonathan and one of the biggest donors to the ruling People's Democratic Party then, said the transaction was video-recorded and showed Lawan demanding the money. A clerk of the Parliamentary Fuel Subsidy Committee, Emenalo Boniface, was also allegedly given $120,000, according to Otedola. Lawan and Boniface were arrested in 2012, and the following January they pleaded not guilty to seven counts of bribery. Boniface later turned prosecution witness.

---

[256] Monica Mark, "Damning Oil Fraud Offers Hope to Nigerians," *The Mail & Guardian*, July 9, 2012.

The whole drama, which was exposed in a taped conversation between Otedola and Lawan, appeared to feature the latter telling the former to deliver the money to his house, with Otedola retorting that it was a lot of money and needed to be collected. Subsequently, Lawan allegedly agreed to send an emissary to pick up the loot. The committee clerk, Emenalo Boniface, told the Federal Capital Territory High Court in 2016—four years down the line—that he collected $100,000 in $100 bills from Otedola on behalf of Lawan.

In defense, Lawan said he took the money to expose blackmail by Otedola, who was pestering him to remove his company's name from the list, and that he informed the committee and the anti-corruption body, the EFCC, about it. The latter denied receiving any such information. The case, with all its political overtones and high-profile controversy, was moved from judge to judge and eventually returned to the original judge, Justice Angela Otaluka, in January 2018 for resolution.

SIERRA LEONE

This African country on the Atlantic Ocean may be known to the world as a staging point for slaves being forced to cross the seas to the new world in the eighteenth and nineteenth centuries, before it was converted into the "Province of Freedom" and a settlement housing thousands of Africans liberated from slave ships. But those following Sierra Leone's political history since its independence in 1961 know it was also a theater of civil wars and military coups that left thousands of people dead and displaced.

Relative peace came only in 2002 after the UN completed an exercise of disarming tens of thousands of fighters of various factions. That ushered in a new era of democratic elections and allowed war crime courts to begin trials for those suspected to have masterminded the massacres in more than three decades since 1967.

In April 2018, Julius Maada Bio was sworn in as president, taking over from Ernest Bai Koroma, who had completed his constitutionally mandated two terms in office. Bio had a checkered political career. He was formerly an opposition leader and a coup initiator of the 1992 overthrow of President Joseph Saidu Momoh.

One of the first major acts of his government was to cancel a $300 million loan from China toward a new international airport, saying the disbursement was unnecessary and beyond the means of the West African nation. With liabilities of close to $4 billion and interest of $262 million a year from loans, Bio did not want to make further financial commitments that could drain the country's meager resources. Sierra Leone's rare decision surprised many leaders in Africa who had been trooping to China for loans and assistance. Zambia, Djibouti, and Kenya have all fallen into a Chinese debt trap, with loans for mega-infrastructure projects piercing a deep hole in revenues, leaving those countries in extreme debt.

According to Grant T. Harris, who was President Barack Obama's White House Director for Africa, Chinese debt had become "the methamphetamines of infrastructure finance: highly addictive, readily available, and with long-term negative effects that far outweigh any temporary high."[257] Indeed, all three countries named above are under threat of losing their assets should they default on the multibillion-dollar loans advanced by China. At the end of 2017, Kenya was the third-most-indebted nation to China at $9.5 trillion, behind Angola at $42 trillion and Ethiopia at $13 trillion, yet President Kenyatta was still journeying to China for more loans in 2019 despite warnings from economists about the dangers ahead.

Like almost all African countries, mineral-rich Sierra Leone, bordering Guinea and Liberia, has fallen prey to bribery scandals involving multinational companies. Just as the presidential campaigns were heating up in 2017, it was discovered that one of the candidates, wealthy businessman John Bonoh Sisay, a cousin of the then-outgoing President Koroma, was involved in bribe payments to senior government officials to secure mining rights.

His name came up during a post-acquisition secret investigation by an Australian miner, Iluka Resources, upon taking over the London-listed Sierra Rutile Limited, a British Virgin Islands–registered mineral sands company run by Sisay. Iluka bought the company for $294 million in a transaction which brought four mines producing rutile, titanium dioxide, ilmenite, and zircon under its portfolio. Sisay denied bribing Sierra Leone officials.

Iluka said it had evidence that Sisay—who stepped down as chief executive of Sierra Rutile in November 2016 to run for the presidency in 2018, which was won by opposition leader Julius Maada Bio—approved a $86,000 bribe payment, which was routed through a West African logistics company and deposited in a third-party bank account.[258]

Also nabbed in the web was a Sierra Leonean minister for lands,

[257] Dionne Searcey and Jaime Yaya Barry, "One African Nation Put Brakes on Chinese Debt. But Not for Long," *The New York Times*, November 23, 2018.
[258] Sylvia Villa, "Sierra Leone News: ACC Investigates Alleged Iluka Bribery Scandal," *Awoko*, August 24, 2017.

county planning, and environment, Diana Konomanyi, whose international flights worth $39,000 were allegedly paid for by the Perth-based Sierra Rutile. The alleged bribery took place before Iluka took over Sierra Rutile in December 2016.

The money scandal soon fell into the hands of the SFO, which began investigating the matter parallel to a probe by Sierra Leone's own Anti-Corruption Commission. Iluka managing director Tom O'Leary said the misconduct was inconsistent with the company's code of conduct and that the company was "committed to conducting its business in accordance with the highest standards of corporate governance."[259]

After taking over the government, Bio formed a judicial commission of inquiry led by the chief minister, Professor David Francis, to investigate the plunder of resources by the previous regimes. The commission's report presented to Bio in June 2018 found that former president Koroma had facilitated the sale of the state's 30 percent share in Sierra Rutile to former chief executive Sisay for a pittance using a Sierra Leone–registered company and a British Virgin Islands firm to make the purchase. The value of one share in the company was $113, but Koroma sold it for only $12.3, which was in violation of the law stating that government assets must be auctioned. *Africa Confidential* reported in 2015 that it was "widely believed" Koroma had a beneficial interest in the shares.[260]

In addition, because the five major mining companies[261] owned through intermediaries in the tax havens of Bermuda and the British Virgin Islands do not declare profits and hardly pay corporate tax,[262] the amount of money secretly leaving the country could be in the billions of dollars every year.

---

[259] "Media Reporting on Sierra Rutile Regulatory Investigations," Australian Securities Exchange Notice, August 16, 2017.
[260] "Koroma Accused of Grand Corruption," *African Confidential*, December 2, 2018.
[261] African Minerals, Sierra Ruite, Sierra Mineral Holding 1, and Koidu Holdings.
[262] "Not Sharing the Loot," Dan Watch, report, October 2011.

TOGO

Family successions are common in African leaderships. Omar Bongo inked his son Ali to take over from him in Gabon; Faure Gnassingbe succeeded his father, Gnassingbe Eyadema. In Kenya, Jomo Kenyatta was the founding president; two presidents later, his son Uhuru became the fourth leader of the East African nation. The same happened in Botswana, where Ian Khama was elected president 27 years after his father; and in Mauritius, where 13 years after his father's rule, Navin Ramgoolam became the prime minister.

But no one African family has ruled a country continuously for over a half a century as in Togo, a narrow strip of land on the west coast of Africa. The Gnassingbes have been in power since 1967, with a whole generation not knowing anyone else at the helm but them. Gnassingbe Eyadema ruled for 37 years until he died in office in 2005. His son, Faure Gnassingbe, took over and is still the president in 2019. Surrounding President Gnassingbe are close family members and associates who participate in governing the supposedly democratic country as if it were a totalitarian caliphate.

In cases where family dynasties exist, the chosen few at the top loot the country aggressively and rule selfishly, with associates enjoying unprecedented perks. Such scenarios have happened in countries led by totalitarian leaders, such as Zimbabwe during Robert Mugabe's time, Angola when Jose Eduardo dos Santos was president, and Uganda, where Yoweri Museveni has ruled since 1986 surrounded by members of his immediate family. Museveni's wife, Janet, has served in several Cabinet positions; his son, Muhoozi Kaineragaba, has had an unprecedented, meteoric rise in the military, reaching the level of lieutenant general in February 2019. Museveni's sister, Violet Kajubiri Froelich, is a deputy chairperson of the Education Service Commission; siblings and many extended family members have been deployed in public service. This group is the main beneficiary of government wealth. In Zimbabwe, Mugabe's wife Grace was the de facto deputy head of state, and in Angola, the dos Santos family was the key supporting crew.

Apart from massive corruption, Togo, a former French colony, is also a notorious hub for money laundering fueled by the country's huge phosphate deposits. The mineral provides 40 percent of the country's revenue and more than 20 percent of the GDP. However, corruption, mismanagement, and periodically low prices continue to interfere with production levels, thus stagnating the country at number 19 among global phosphate producers.[263] *Africa Intelligence* posited in 2014 that in Togo, phosphate "is managed at the presidency ... [and that] the Mines Minister, who is a loyal servant of the presidency, has no room for maneuver."[264] Broadly, this means that the policies, investments, and day-to-day supervision of the mining sector are in the hands of a small clique of elites in President Gnassingbe's court. The clique sells phosphate to "whomever they want and at whichever price they want."[265]

The potential for a boom in phosphate production has lured foreign multinational companies to the country, giving the elites an opportunity for kickbacks. Elenilto Mineral, an Israeli group led by billionaire Jacob Engel, and its partner Wengfu, a Chinese conglomerate with interests in several other African countries, entered the market in 2015 with an investment of over $1 billion. Elenilto, a global oil, gas, and minerals company, won a multimillion-dollar international tender, beating two bids to develop a two-billion-ton phosphate mining and fertilizer plant 25 kilometers from the country's capital of Lome, enabling it to produce low-cost phosphate concentrates. Negotiations for those bids and the details of the contract are known to only a few.

---

[263] Dirk Kohnert, "Togo: Recent Political and Economic Development," Munic Personal RePec Archive (MPRA), Report, February 2015.

[264] "Togo's Phosphates Fall Under Presidential Spell," Africa Intelligence, report, June 26, 2014.

[265] Abdi Latif Dahir, African Oligarchs: "Africa's Political Elites Have Built the Same Wealth Plundering Structures as the Colonialists," Quartz Africa, article, October 12, 2017.

In the past decade, Togo has been at the center of an international racket. The country does not produce gold, but every year Switzerland imports tons of the metal allegedly from the country. The gold actually comes from Burkina Faso and is smuggled through Togo territory to a refiner in Switzerland with the full approval of Gnassingbe. The bone of contention, in a report entitled "A Golden Racket,"[266] is that most of the Burkina Faso gold is mined by children, which is against international labor norms. A firm known as Valcambi, owned by an Indian jewelry company, Rajesh Exports, is based in Switzerland and is one of the world's largest metal refiners; it is also behind the phosphate exports.

The body responsible for fighting graft, the National Commission for the Fight Against Corruption and Economic Sabotage, is helped by police, gendarmes, and courts, but it has done little to prosecute the big fish in the president's office, who are palm-greased by international companies on mining deals. Those who have been convicted are normally Gnassingbe's opponents.

The most famous case of bribery involved a family with the name Gupta (not to be confused with the Gupta brothers in South Africa), which—in collusion with top Togolese officials—has been buying phosphate at a substantially reduced price of two-thirds the going rate and exporting it to Asia. That arrangement, entered into with the knowledge of the presidency, has exposed the state as a conspirator in an illegal scheme that deprives the country of its wealth. Togo's Guptas of Ashok and his Kalyan Resources firm, a subsidiary of the family-owned Kalyan Group, dealing in dry bulk shipping, commodities and fertilizer trading, real estate, and diamond and mining exploration, as well as investments and funds, have been compared to South Africa's Gupta family which, through connections reaching the presidency of Jacob Zuma, reaped billions of dollars in revenue before the South African leader left office in 2017. Both Zuma and Gnassingbe have been

---

[266] "A Golden Racket: The True Source of Switzerland's 'Togolese' Gold," Public Eye, report, September 8, 2015.

victims of the so-called "state capture" in which private companies "manipulate policy formulation to their ends other than the national interest, or, even shape rules of the game to their own, very substantial advantage."[267]

It came as no surprise, therefore, when in 2016 Gnassingbe subsidized the purchase of the $73 million Radisson Blu 2 Fevrier hotel by Ashok Gupta along the beach at Lome. The 36-floor structure is the tallest hotel building in the country and is owned in partnership with Emaar Hospitality under the brand Address Hotels and Resorts.

Despite frequent street demonstrations calling for an end to the Gnassingbe dynasty, the exclusivity continues unabated.

Bollore magic

Ask anyone in political and business circles in West Africa about Vincent Bollore and the response would be either a subdued, cynical smile or a quick reaction of praise. The French billionaire and his Bollore Group command an interesting mix of disgust and admiration, especially in Africa where his companies have dominated some strategic contracts for more than three decades.

The Bollore Group has deep-seated roots in 46 African countries, where it commands businesses ranging from energy and telecommunications to palm production and port management. It operates 16 container terminals and plantations and holds majority shares in three railway concessions in the continent: in Ivory Coast, Burkina Faso, and Benin.

An African mechanic, talking of Lome port, said, "This port is for Togolese. But it is Bollore who runs everything … the Frenchman is too cozy with African presidents."[268] This statement sums up the stranglehold foreigners have on African resources, a kind of solicited "capture." Bollore is known in France as a shrewd

---

[267] Martin Zhuwakinyu, "Uncanny Similarities," Creamer News, December 1, 2017.
[268] "One of France's Best-Known Tycoons Is Arrested," *The Economist*, April 28, 2018.

businessman and a formidable dealmaker who turned a family business making paper for cigarettes and Bibles into an empire with sales of over $25 billion annually and 81,000 employees worldwide.

However, the meteoric success of the Bolore MNC was in jeopardy in April 2018 when police stormed his posh residence in the Paris suburb of Nanterre and hauled him away for questioning over his business interests in Africa and the methods he used to obtain two port contracts at Lome in Togo and Conakry in Guinea.

Additionally, a whistleblower and former Bollore associate who was jailed for misappropriating company assets, Jacques Dupuydauby, reported to French authorities that Bollore's African communication arm, Havas, had undercharged the president of Togo, Faure Gnassingbe, and the president of Guinea, Alpha Conde, on election campaign work it did for them in exchange for contracts, including port concessions in the two countries.

The billionaire and two of his officials at Havas, group chief executive Gilles Alix and head of the international division Jean-Philippe Dorent, were presented to French judge Serge Tournaire after two days of police interrogation. They were charged and became the first high-flying French business executives to be indicted for offenses committed in Africa. The shocking arrest momentarily collapsed the group's stocks by over eight points and sent shock waves across Europe and the former French colonies.

Havas played a role in the election of Conde in 2010. A few months after taking power, the Guinean leader terminated a contract of Conakry's port operator—a subsidiary of the French shipping company NCT Necotrans—and gave it to Bollore. The businessman denied being favored, and in 2016, Conde said in an interview, "Bollore fulfilled all the conditions of the bids. He's a friend. I favor friends, so what?"[269] Necotrans filed a suit to protest the takeover and was awarded compensation of $2.4 million, but

_____
[269] Angela Charlton, "French Billionaire Detained in Africa Corruption Probe," AP – *The Financial Post*, April 24, 2018.

shortly afterwards, Bollore bought out that same company. It was also alleged that after winning his second term in 2010, Togo's President Gnassingbe gave Bollore a 35-year contract to manage the Lome port.[270]

In May 2019, the flamboyant Bollore stepped down from the board of directors, and for a farewell gift he gave each employee three bottles of wine from his personal vineyard.

[270] "Billionaire French Tycoon Bollore Detained in Africa Corruption Probe," AFP – News 24, April 24, 2018.

PART FIVE

CHAPTER 8

_____

CENTRAL AFRICA

Angola's oil wealth can no longer buy impunity. – Eugen Iladi

ANGOLA

Until Joao Lourenco took over the presidency of Angola in 2017, the Central African country was in a free-fall in terms of bribery and corruption. His predecessor, Jose Eduardo dos Santos, who had ruled the country for 38 years since the first presidential election in 1992, had kept the resource-rich country a preserve of his family, close military associates, and the ruling party, the Popular Movement for the Liberation of Angola (MPLA). As the elites live luxuriously, occasionally jetting first class to world-class destinations in Europe and the UAE, the majority of Angolans subsist in shanties that sit on the outskirts of Luanda—rated as the world's most expensive city for expatriates[271]—like the stretch of savannah in Serengeti.

Close allies in a group called Futungo, named after the old presidential palace Futungo de Belas, held influential positions in the administration and were on the frontline of bribery and corruption. Within Futungo was an inner group called the "Presidential Triumvirate" composed of General Manuel Vicente, vice president from 2012 to 2017; General Manuel Helder Vieira Dias Junior, known simply as "Kopelipa," head the Intelligence Bureau at the presidency; and General Leopoldino Fragoso Nascimento, advisor to the president. The three most powerful officials often appeared in major financial scandals like the one involving an Angolan company called Portmill Investimentos e Telecomunicacoes S. A., in which it allegedly committed fraud during its acquisition of a majority share in the Banco de Espirito Santo-Angola (BESA) in 2009.

According to whistleblowers who provided documents to the anti-corruption body, Maka Angola, it was discovered that Portmill did not use any of its money to pay for the $375 million BESA stock but obtained funds from three companies owned by the "Triumvirate." But more disturbing was the fact that BESA approved millions of

---

[271] "Angolan capital 'most expensive city for expats," *BBC,* news, June 21, 2017.

unsecured loans to top Angolan officials—including a sister of President dos Santos—and kept no records of the transactions. To enhance their plan, the "Triumvirate" formed a company called Grupo Aquattro International, at least three shell companies, and dozens of subsidiaries, among them Portmill, which applied for and got loans from BESA, including the $375 million. To ensure that no paper trail remained, the companies conjured a convoluted method of depositing and withdrawing of money through the network of Grupo Aquattro firms to confuse investigators. The Maka Angola information showed that in December 2009, Portmill deposited the entire $375 million, which was in the account of Portugal's Banco de Espirito Santos (BES), into a Bank of America account in New York. Subsequently, the money was transferred to an account held by BES with the Banque Privee in Switzerland.[272]

In Angola, some of the officials known to engage in corruption were named and shamed during a court case in 1984 in which 124 people were charged with smuggling diamonds. In a trial shown live on television by the state broadcaster, the government of dos Santos was publicly embarrassed when the accused took the microphone and exposed "the involvement of a web of high-ranking figures of the ruling MPLA in illegal trade."[273] A report by the British Economist Intelligence Unit in 2003 named 59 top Angolans who had wealth estimated at $4 billion, mostly obtained from oil trading and diamond smuggling. A number of those corrupt officials were arrested in a sweep in 2018.

Angola's economy relies heavily on oil and diamonds. While the Luanda-based state-owned company Sociedade Nacional de Combustiveis de Angola Empresa publica (Sonangol) is charged with the production and sale of oil, Empresa Nacional de Prospeccao, Exploracao, Lapidacao e Commercializacao de Diamantes de Angola (Endiama), also owned by the government,

[272] Rafael Marques De Morais, "Angola's Path to Justice: Prosecuting the Guilty and Recovering the Stolen Billions," Maka Angola, October 23, analysis, 2018.
[273] Rafael Marques De Morais, Blood Diamonds: Corruption and Torture in Angola, Maka Angola, analysis, (2011), 19–20.

is the exclusive concessionary of mining rights for diamonds, even though its role both as an operator and regulator has been criticized by the WB as imposing constraints to transparency and accountability. Both organizations have seen their share of corruption, smuggling, and theft allegations.

In October 2018, thousands of migrants, mostly from the DRC, left in a hurry or were expelled by Lourenco's government on suspicion of diamond smuggling. The exercise, called "Operation Transparency," was denounced by the DRC and the Human Rights Watch, which accused the state of brutalizing and killing Congolese migrants and refugees.

From 1987 to 1989, over 17,000 large diamonds of more than seven carats each, totaling 134,328,88 carats and worth over $11 million, disappeared into someone's hands in a massive operation that was sophisticated and meticulously planned and executed. Peasants' homes and crops were destroyed to pave the way for mining operations by foreign multinationals. Several high-ranking officials in positions of responsibility at the government diamond mining conglomerate, Sociedade Mineira do Cuango; the state diamond firm, Endiama; and the Department of Industry were involved,[274] claimed a government report. So were some executives of Rosan Selection Trust International Limited (RST), a subsidiary of the Luxembourg-registered holding company ITM International.

Military generals too entered into crooked deals and flaunted their power and influence with the president and the civil service in exchange for their loyalty, obtaining shares in mining concessions and state businesses seemingly as a matter of entitlement.[275] The generals also sent soldiers to raid mining areas to take control of workers. Diggers who refused to hand over finds were brutalized and sometimes killed, as happened in October 2005 when one soldier, "having confiscated a valuable diamond during the gravel

---

[274] Rafael Marques De Morais, 59.
[275] Ibid., 49–51.

washing of dug material, killed all of the diggers."[276]

Theft of mining revenue was also rampant. An IMF report in 2002 showed that $1 billion had vanished from the Treasury that year and over $4 billion could not be accounted for during the previous five years,[277] almost all of it being revenue from oil and diamonds. In 2012, a US Senate subcommittee investigation showed that between May 1999 and December 2002, Aguinaldo Jaime, the governor of the central bank—Banco Nacional de Angola (BNA)—attempted to transfer $50 million from the bank to a private account in the United States. Documents showed the transfer "was part of a fraudulent 'prime bank' investment scheme that likely would have resulted in the funds being lost or stolen."[278] The conveyance was blocked. He tried again to transfer the money to the United States two months later using different accounts, but it was disallowed. By that time, Jaime had left the bank and had been appointed assistant to the prime minister under President dos Santos. The $50 million was seized and returned to the BNA.

This is one illustration of how senior Angolan government officials use their lofty positions to steal from public coffers. The question is: was the returned money used to provide better health care and better education for the people, or did it end up in the pockets of dos Santos and his unquenchable cronies? No one outside Futungo may know the answer to that question. Jaime was not charged and instead was elevated from his post at the prime minister's office to deputy prime minister of Angola, and later to the chairmanship of the Angolan Commission dealing with private investments, Agencia Nacional para o Investimento Privado.

---

[276] Ibid.,

[277] "IMF Report: Angola Staff Report for the 2002 Article 1V Consultation," IMF, March 18, 2002, 9.

[278] US Senate, "Keeping Foreign Corruption Out of the United States: Four Case Histories," Committee on Homeland Security and Governmental Affairs, 1 of 2, February 4, 2010.

What was obvious is that in dos Santos's Angola, nepotism was treasured. Relatives and close party allies enjoyed prominent positions in government. One of the president's daughters, Isabel, once noted by *Forbes* magazine as Africa's richest woman, was the CEO of Sonangol and owned or held shares in hundreds of companies. In March 2018, the Lourenco's government took away all expired diamond exploration licenses issued to Isabel and offered them to investors. The licenses were for the Camafuca-Camazambo, Mulepe, Sangamina, Chiri, and Tchiegi diamond fields located in Lunda Norte and Lunda Sul, in the northeastern part of the country.

Dos Santos's son, Jose Filomeno dos Santos, was the head of the $5 billion Angola's Sovereign Wealth Fund. After coming to power, Lourenco fired both Isabel and Filomeno. In March 2018, Jose Filomeno dos Santos and Valter Philipe, former head of the central bank, were charged with fraud for illegally transferring— allegedly on instructions from President dos Santos— $500 million from the Angolan Central Bank account at the SCB to an HSBC bank account in the United Kingdom. The transfer raised a red flag, and bank officials at HSBC froze the account in April 2018 and reported it to the UK's National Crime Agency (NCA), which seized the money and aborted the fraud.

In September 2018, Filomeno, known by the nickname "Zenu," was arrested alongside his Swiss-Angolan business partner Jean-Claude Bastos on suspicion of money laundering, embezzlement, and fraud involving fraudulent transactions of $1.5 billion. A state prosecutor said there was sufficient evidence to convict the two on various crimes including criminal associations, receipt of undue advantage, corruption, participation in unlawful business, money laundering, embezzlement, and fraud. The army chief general, Geraldo Sachipengo Nunda, and intelligence head, Andre de Oliveira Sango, were fired along with at least 20 other officials.

Sonangol, the state-owned oil company, is everything in Angola. The contracts it signs with MNCs had to be approved by only one man—dos Santos—and the contents of the contracts are not known by anyone else, even Parliament, making it difficult to audit and account for its revenue. During his more than three decades in power, former President dos Santos ruled with an iron fist, restricted civil liberties, and stifled the opposition. He was "on the same level as an emperor,"[279] said a human rights lawyer, Zola Bambi.

But he also entrenched corruption and accumulated billions of dollars derived from graft in offshore accounts. "Until 1986, we … had reasonable control over the oil money," said a former finance minister in an interview. "After that, some of it went directly to Futungo, and bypassed us. That is when the trouble really started."[280] The dos Santos were also big spenders. They bought Christmas trees from Europe and celebrated birthdays with friends jetted in from abroad.

When the country appeared on the brink of financial collapse due to extravagance and theft by the Futungo group, and after the West had turned down requests for a bail-out, dos Santos turned to China in the 1990s. The summit of the Forum on China–Africa Cooperation in Beijing in 2000 gave African leaders from 44 countries an opportunity of improved trade with the Asian giant. The meeting was followed by a high-profile visit to Luanda by China's Vice Premier Zeng Peiyan and a return visit by Angolan officials to Beijing. From that point onward, China and Angola became close business partners; Angola offered oil in exchange for development loans amid allegations of bribery and corruption that implicated Chinese companies and Angolan officials. As all this was going on, dos Santos and his allies in Futungo were milking the country and exporting money to hideouts abroad.

---

[279] Antonio Cascais, "Angola: The Fall of the dos Santos Clan," *Deutsche Welle*, September 30, 2018.
[280] Nicholas Shaxson, *Poisoned Wells: The Dirty Politics of African Oil* (Palgrave, 2007), 51.

During the oil crisis of 2008, however, the country fell into dire need of financial rescue and called on the WB and the IMF to help. But when the IMF examined Angola's books in 2011, it found $32 billion had gone missing, most of it traced to off-the-books spending by Sonangol between 2007 and 2010, and $4.2 billion was completely unaccounted for:[281] "The Futungo 'shadow state' had looted the money."[282] By the time dos Santos left office in September 2017, an estimated $30 billion belonging to him, was believed stashed in overseas accounts.[283]

Angola was perennially listed among the world's most corrupt nations by TI's CPI, and locally, the Portuguese word *gasosa*, meaning a fizzy drink, was the buzz word for corruption. For decades, paying *gasosas* was the key to services as mundane as obtaining electricity or as big as winning multibillion-dollar government tenders.

The Center for Public Integrity, a US independent investigative journalism organization, provided this narrative to illustrate the shady side of MNCs in Angola:

One July 15, the Marathon Oil Company sent USD 13,717,989.31 to an account in Jersey, an island in the English Channel with stringent bank secrecy laws. The owner of the Jersey account was Sonangol, Angola's state oil company. The sum represented one-third of a bonus that the Houston Texas-based company agreed to pay the Angolan government a year earlier for rights to pump the country's offshore oil reserves. That same day, Sonangol transferred an identical sum of money out of Jersey to another Sonangol account in an unknown location. Over the course of that summer, large sums of money traveled from the Jersey account to, among others, a private security company owned by a former

---

[281] Tom Burgis, *The Looting Machine: Warlords, Oligarchs, Corporations, Smugglers, and the Theft of Africa's Wealth* (Public Affairs, 2015), 11–12.
[282] Ibid., 173.
[283] Rebecca Engebretsen, "President Lourenco's Anti-Corruption Drive Changes the Rules in Angola," African Arguments, article, October 10, 2018.

Angolan Minister, a charitable foundation run by the Angolan President, and a private Angolan bank that counts an alleged arms dealer among its shareholders.[284]

Such transfers were common in a country as corrupt as Angola, but they are usually handled in such a secretive way that few get to know about them.

With oil money floating around a small enclave of people, however, Luanda is not the capital for all Angolans. On one side of the city is an expatriate community of Europeans and Americans working for multinational oil companies who live side by side with Angola's political and business elite, drive posh cars, and live in expensive homes; and on the other side are millions of Angolans residing in shanty dwellings with no running water and no electricity, existing on less than two dollars a day.

Big oil and gas companies like BP Amoco, Chevron, ExxonMobil, Total, and others have a strong presence in the country; so do dozens of state-owned Chinese companies. Ninety percent of the country's foreign exchange revenue comes from oil: 1.8 million barrels a day. But fueling the oil industry were acts of corruption involving dos Santos and top government and military officials on one hand, and crooked businesspeople on the other, going all the way back to the early 1990s when MPLA was fighting with US-backed UNITA rebels.

A 486-page report prepared by French prosecutors in 2008 showed how dos Santos received $791 million worth of illegal arms from a Russian and a French operative in exchange for lucrative oil contracts with western multinationals. The deal included 170,000 anti-personnel mines, 420 tanks, 12 helicopters, six warships, and 150 shells. The deal nicknamed "arms for oil" or "Angolagate," was brokered by Jean-Christophe Mitterrand, then a presidential advisor on African affairs in France. For his intervention, Mitterand

---

[284] Phillip Van Niekerk and Laura Peterson, Making a Killing: "Greasing the Skids of Corruption," The Center for Public Integrity, article, November 4, 2002.

allegedly received $2.6 million from the Angolan government. But Mitterrand said the money represented consulting fees for an oil-mortgaging deal between dos Santos' regime and Brenco International, owned by arms broker Pierre Falcone.[285]

According to the report, the Russian-born Israeli billionaire Arkady Gaydamak and Falcone in turn funneled the money to Angolan officials in return for political and commercial favors. It took more than a decade, up to the time when Nicolas Sarkozy was president of France, for the Paris government to take some of its citizens to court on charges of corruption.

In 2000, Franco-Brazilian national Falcone and Gaydamak, who was not in court, were accused of illegal weapons sales, influence trafficking, tax evasion, corrupt practices, and misuse of company funds for facilitating the sale of tanks, landmines, and other armaments from the former USSR to dos Santos' Angola between 1993 and 1998. Both were sentenced to six years in prison.

Jean-Christophe Mitterrand, son of the then-president Francois Mitterrand, who was identified as a point-man between Santos and the businessmen, stood charged with complicity in illegal trade, embezzlement, and receiving a bribe of $1.9 million from Brenco International, a company dealing in arms and owned by Falcone. Forty other people, including politicians connected to the scheme, were also charged in a Paris court in October 2009. Mitterrand was given a two-year suspended sentence and fined $430,000 for the illegal arms sales to Angola. Not a single Angolan was prosecuted anywhere.

There was a political angle of the scandal in the United States as well. Falcone's wife, Sonia, who lived in Arizona in the United States, made numerous contributions to political entities: $2,800 to the Democratic National Committee in 1999, followed by $80,000 to the Republican National Committee (RNC), $1,000 to George W. Bush's presidential exploratory committee, and $2,800

---

[285] Alexandra Brunais, "Mitterrand's Son Posts Bail in Arms Case: Inquiry Sullies Fame of French Ex-Leader," *The Washington Post*, January 13, 2001.

to Arizona Senator John McCain, all in 2000. Reports in Federal Election Commission books showed all the contributions were returned to the giver after the scandal surfaced.

Angola's history of bribery and corruption is one of the most deplorable on the continent. International companies, from Brazil's engineering conglomerate Odebrecht, to Germany's logistics and freight company Bertling, to America's oil firms Halliburton and Oil Services company, among many, were caught in schemes to bribe Angolan officials.

A Swiss NGO, Berne Declaration, found that Claude Dauphin, co-founder of a leading Swiss commodities company called Trafigura, had been running shady business ventures with Angolan companies affiliated with prominent officials, among them General Leopoldino Fragoso do Nascimento, a top presidential advisor. The ventures were in real estate, mining, and cargo shipping. Some blamed the trend prevalent during dos Santos' rule to "lack of checks and balances, insufficient institutional capacity, and a culture of impunity."[286] The NGO report came out a few months after President dos Santos authorized five investment contracts worth $931 million between Puma Energy, a subsidiary of Trafigura, and an Angolan company called Cochan. Trafigura received Angolan crude oil and, in return, delivered all petroleum products for domestic consumption in Angola, with some of it going to the Chinese parastatal Sinopec.[287]

The contract, according to an international magazine *Energy Compass,* was handled by a Singaporean provider of information, analysis, and intelligence on the Singapore private sector, the DP Group, which is in a joint venture with Trafigura and Cochan to which General dos Nascimento is a director. It is not known how much in kickbacks dos Santos got for approving the five contracts, but speculation was that they ran into the millions of dollars.

[286] "Angola Corruption Report," Business Anti-Corruption Portal, article, August 2016.
[287] "Trafigura and the Angolan Presidential Mafia," Maka Angola, article, January 5, 2013.

In March 2017, Odebrecht—one of the largest private-sector employers in Angola—admitted paying $50 million in bribes to secure construction, mining, and Agri-processing contracts in Angola during dos Santos' reign. The admission was part of a guilty plea in a New York court the previous December involving $788 million it paid as bribes to officials in Angola, Mozambique, and nine Latin American countries. The company CEO, Marcelo Odebrecht, was subsequently jailed for 19 years.

Pay-to-play fiasco

Sonangol's reputation is as notorious as the cold breezes of Antarctica. The coming-to-power of President Lourenco has done nothing to impede corruption and bribery by multinational oil companies in Angola using the state-run oil corporation, even though some changes have occurred, especially in dealing with the past corrupt activities of his predecessor, dos Santos. It is like a massive fire that keeps on burning despite the frantic efforts of firefighters to put it out.

In September 2017, a UK-based logistics and freight operations company, F. H Bertling Limited, and six of its former employees pleaded guilty to paying kickbacks to an official of Sonangol to secure a $20 million contract for freight and forwarding services. The offense took place between 2004 and 2006. Francisco Bravo Paulo, the official whose authority was needed to explore an oil block situated off the coast of the country, was a critical individual for the operations of the oil company BP, which had access rights to the block. Bertling, a subsidiary of Bertling Group headquartered in Hamburg, Germany, allegedly paid $100,000 to a middleman, who passed on $80,000 to the Angolan official, who demanded more under threats of cancelling Bertling's contract with BP. Desperate and afraid of the consequences, Bertling's board of directors agreed to pay an additional $350,000 as well as another $250,000, with both payments being channeled through an agent, who passed it on to the Sonangol official. But even with those payments, Bertling's contract with BP was cancelled after officials refused to sign key customs documents to allow the transportation of goods to the block. The companies that replaced BP, Panalpina and DHL, ran into similar problems even after allegedly bribing Sonangol personnel.

Joerg Blumberg, the former chief finance officer (CFO); Dick Juergensen, former managing director of the UK subsidiary F. H. Bertling Limited; and Marc Schweiger, the former manager responsible for the Africa region, were each jailed for 20 months with a two-year suspension and fined $25,000 by a London court in October 2017 for violating the Prevention of Corruption Act 1906, a precursor to the Bribery Act 2010.

Several Bertling executives were involved in another bribery scandal in the United Kingdom. Three were convicted in a London court in January 2019 after admitting to paying $445,000 in bribes and facilitation payments to employees of ConocoPhilips (CP), an American energy corporation, to help in securing a $21 million oil exploration project in the United Kingdom's North Sea, called the Jasmine project. They were also found guilty of paying bribes to get CP employees to approve and pay Bertling's inflated invoices.

The company's former managing director, Colin Bagwell, was sentenced to nine months in prison and fined $6,430, while the former CFO, Stephen Emler, was given 12 months in prison for the North Sea bribery plot and 18 months for the Sonangol scheme, with a fine of $19,300. Two other executives—Giuseppe Morreale, the managing director for London, and Christopher Lane, a former logistics head at CP—were jailed for 15 months and six months respectively. All sentences were suspended for two years. "These senior executives failed to show any integrity, resorting to bribery to secure lucrative contract and hide their illicit activities. It is our mission to bring criminals like these to justice." That was the summation of SFO director Lisa Osofsky after the sentencing of the Bertling executives. The case against F. H. Bertling Limited was adjudicated on June 3, 2019, and the company was fined $1 million for its involvement in bribes in Angola.

As Bertling was engulfed in its own woes, the oil company Halliburton faced its own "pay-to-play" fiasco. The company got into trouble after its vice president, Jeannot Lorenz, directed $13 million to a local company owned by a former Halliburton executive with links to the state-owned Sonangol in order to secure oil field services contracts. Halliburton's questionable contracts yielded the company a profit of $14 million. The American company did not admit or deny wrongdoing but agreed to pay $30 million to the DOJ. It also agreed to surrender $14 million in profits plus interest of $1.2 million. Similarly, Lorenz was ordered to pay a fine of $75,000 for falsifying books and circumventing internal controls.

The lure of lucrative contracts

Sonangol Angola was in trouble again in November 2017. Two executives of a Dutch oil services company, SBM Offshore, N. V., Anthony Mace and Robert Zubiate, were fined in a Houston, Texas court for conspiring to violate the FCPA by bribing officials of three state-owned companies in exchange for lucrative contracts. The companies were Sonangol Angola, Brazil's Petroleo Brasileiro S. A. (Petrobras), and Equatorial Guinea's Petroleos de Guinea Ecuatorial (GEPetrol).

The Amsterdam-headquartered SBM Offshore, N. V. (SBM), through its SBM Offshore US subsidiary, did bag the contracts and made an estimated $2.8 billion between 1996 and 2012. The company owns a fleet of floating oil storage vessels, "ships that gather oil and gas, process it, and offload it onto tankers or into pipelines."[288] On September 28, 2018, Mace was sentenced to three years in federal prison and fined $150,000, while Zubiate was jailed for 30 months and fined $50,000. Mace, formerly the company's CEO, admitted authorizing the payments but said he didn't know they were meant for bribes. Apart from Angola, Guinea,

---

[288] Cameron Langford, "Dutch Oil Firm to Pay $238M to Settle US Bribery Charge," Courthouse News Service, November 30, 2017.

and Brazil, SBM Offshore was also caught in scandals in Kazakhstan and Iraq, and in total paid middlemen an estimated $180 million as bribes to secure contracts.

Malfeasance in mining fields also includes violence on innocent peasants. In the diamond mines of northeastern Angola, acts of brutality by soldiers and private security guards against local miners are regular. Reports of beatings and even killings by armed personnel attempting to drive peasants away to take control of diamond fields have been reported. The atrocity is similar to what has happened in the Zimbabwean mineral pits. And like in Zimbabwe, such heinous activities are ordered by influential people in government and the military.

In his book, *Blood Diamonds: Corruption and Torture in Angola*, Rafael Marques de Morais, a celebrated journalist who has exposed corruption and human rights abuses in Angola, explains how military generals organized troops to enter diamond fields to torture innocent people trying to eke out a living. He mentions the mass grave of 45 diggers he discovered in the village of Cavuba, on the border between Luremo commune, 30 kilometers north of Cafunfo, and Xa-Muteba municipality. Soldiers arrived at the diamond field with crowbars, tore out the props supporting the entrance to the pit, and caused it to cave in. A total of 45 miners perished.[289] In 2015, de Morais was given a six-month suspended jail term for allegedly defaming army generals in comments he made in the book.

Cobalt International Energy

In one of the biggest corporate wrangles involving a multinational company in Africa, US-based Cobalt International Energy (CIE) went toe-to-toe with Angola's government in 2012 over the secret involvement of three of the country's most powerful individuals in companies linked to Cobalt. Dos Santo's "Triumvirate" members—

---

[289] Rafael Marques De Morais, Blood Diamonds: Corruption and Torture in Angola, Maka Angola, March 2015.

Vice President Manuel Vicente, General Manuel Helder Vieira Dias Junior, alias "General Kopelipa", and General Fragoso do Nascimento—were identified as individuals who owned concealed shares in Nazaki Oil and Gaz, a junior partner in Cobalt's oil operations.

Cobalt, an oil exploration and production company, was a major player in the Angolan oil industry. Early in 2014, it discovered significant quantities of oil offshore, believed to be the biggest find up to that time. A few months after the announcement of the discovery, the SEC said it was pursuing investigations on the activities of the Texas-based firm on allegations that through the three influential officials, the company was awarded a substantial oil exploration concession by Sonangol. However, Cobalt said it did not know that the Angolan officials owned Nazaki Oil and Gaz.

Relations between Cobalt and Sonangol dipped in mid-2017 after the latter cancelled an agreement in which it was to buy a 40 percent share worth $500 million, which it owned in two oil blocks that were to yield Cobalt $1.75 billion. CIE complained that the cancellation made it difficult to find a new buyer and went ahead and sued the state-owned company. The matter was arbitrated, and the two reached an "amicable deal" in December 2017, with Sonangol agreeing to pay the Houston-based Cobalt $500 million instead of the $2 billion Cobalt had demanded.

The revelations came on the heels of pressure from the anti-corruption watchdog Global Witness that oil companies Statoil, BP, and Cobalt had paid more than $350 million to Sonangol to fund a new research center, which did not appear to exist. The money was suspected to have been "eaten." In December 2017, Cobalt filed for bankruptcy after falling $3 billion in debt and was delisted from the New York Stock Exchange the following month. The SEC suspended any action against the company.

The Mysterious Queensway Group

The group's website opens with a catchy, welcoming phrase —

"Sincere hospitality. It's just our way"—and goes on to boast about the company's methods of investments. The group is the Hong Kong–based Queensway conglomerate, which has expansive connections in Africa and massive investments in Angolan oil and Zimbabwean diamonds, as well as in projects worth billions of dollars around the world.

Behind this behemoth is a small-framed Chinese national by the name of Sam Pa. This unassuming individual has trotted the continent to endear himself to African leaders. "He has garnered power and wealth by making himself a middleman in China's courtship of Africa," said one report, and "has helped to build from scratch a sprawling network of companies linked by common owners, directors, and a registered address at 88 Queensway in Hong Kong."[290] American researcher J. R. Mailey calls the Queensway Group the prototypical predator investor, which pounces on resource-rich, fragile, and crisis-ridden African countries with high levels of official corruption and underdeveloped government oversight and accountability mechanisms, such as Zimbabwe, South Sudan, the Central African Republic, Niger, and Guinea.[291]

Pa's entry into Africa was in 2004 through Angolan president Jose Eduardo dos Santos. There he convinced dos Santos to channel Angolan oil to China through a joint venture called Sonangol and used Luanda as a springboard to visit state houses in eastern, western, central, and southern Africa, cutting deals and luring continental leaders in Zimbabwe, Tanzania, and Guinea to Chinese loans and investments.

To endear himself to corrupt African leaders, Queensway provided millions of dollars to cash-strapped nations, as it did to Guinea in 2009, where it offered $45 million in emergency budgetary

---

[290] Tom Burgis, "China in Africa: How Sam Pa Became the Middleman," *The Financial Times*, August 8, 2014.
[291] J. R. Mailey, "The Anatomy of the Resource Curse: Predatory Investment in Africa's Extractive Industries," *ACSS Special Report* (May 2015): 81.

support. The same year, in Zimbabwe, it donated 200 Nissan pickup trucks; and in Madagascar in 2014, the Queensway Group gave out 350 Nissan and Hyundai 4x4s to President Hery Rajaonarimampianina. That year, Pa also travelled to West Africa and met Mahmoud Thiam, the minister for mines and geology, who helped him get oil mining contracts in that country. Thiam was later jailed for receiving bribe money from both Sonangol and China International, two companies Pa promoted in Africa. But Pa is as mysterious as the African night runner. He has six other names apart from Sam Pa: Tsui King Wah, Xu Songhua, Sa Muxu, Sam King, Antonio Famtosonghiu, Sampo Menezes, and Ghjiu Ka Leung. However, to many around the world, he is known only as Sam Pa.

His maverick business model did not please the Chinese leadership, which was keen to find fault for any criminal infraction. Finally, on October 8, 2015, Beijing found a reason to arrest Pa—a former arms dealer—and connected him to a corruption investigation involving the state-owned Sinopec. He was accused of earning huge amounts of commissions as an intermediary, helping Sinopec to secure access to Angola's oil fields.

Fresenius Medical

Manipulation of health workers, especially in government hospitals and centers by multinational companies to get physicians to prescribe a specific medicine made by a specific company, continues to be a worrying phenomenon the world over, but more so in developing countries in Asia and Africa. Competing companies are prepared to offer anything from cash to all-expense-paid vacations, household equipment like air conditioners and washing machines, and even luxury cars. In Pakistan, for example, a doctor writing 200 prescriptions of a company's high-priced drug is rewarded with the down payment for a new car.[292]

---

[292] Sarah Boseley, "Drug Firms Try to Bribe Doctors with Cars," *The Guardian,* October 30, 2007.

In recent years, anti-corruption legislation such as the FCPA in the United States and the Bribery Act in the United Kingdom have focused particular attention on the health sector, and those who have been caught bribing doctors have been fined or jailed. A German-based provider of medical products and services, Fresenius Medical Care AG & Co. KGA, for example, was nabbed offering kickbacks to health workers in 17 countries: Angola, Benin, Bosnia, Burkina Faso, Cameroon, Chad, China, Gabon, Ivory Coast, Mexico, Morocco, Niger, Saudi Arabia, Senegal, Serbia, Spain, and Turkey. The Hamburg, Germany-based firm admitted to manipulating public health care workers and other government workers in those countries to obtain business advantages between 2007 and 2016 that yielded it a profit of millions of dollars.

In Angola, Fresenius bribed a senior military officer at the medical services division of the Angolan armed forces and prominent government nephrologists by giving them shares of 15 percent each in a Fresenius joint venture called NefroAngola. Further, the company entered into an agreement with sons of the military officer for a warehousing space, which it never used, and into "consultancy agreements" with government doctors for which no services were ever provided, all intended to retain its business in Angola.

In Morocco, a Fresenius "corporate agent" and a sales manager in Germany paid a commission to chief nephrologists between 2006 and 2010 in exchange for contracts to develop kidney dialysis centers in two of the country's military hospitals. The payment was channeled through a bona fide employee of the company elsewhere in Africa, who then passed it on to the officials. In the other countries, Fresenius paid tens of thousands of dollars in cash and shares for bogus "consulting" services which were not covered in any contracting agreement. "Bribery, in all forms, is corrosive and illegal"[293]—that is what a US assistant attorney, Andrew E.

---

[293] US Department of Justice, "Fresenius Medical Care Agrees to Pay $231 Million in Criminal Penalties and Disgorgement to Resolve FCPA Charges," press release no. 19-290, March, 29 2019.

Lelling, said after the company agreed to pay approximately $231 million in penalties, pre-judgment interests, and disgorgement for using an estimated $30 million to bribe government doctors and other health workers.

The SEC said Fresenius senior executives personally engaged in corruption schemes and directed employees to destroy records of company misconduct for fear of being found; "[l]ower-level employees were berated if they didn't destroy their laptops or delete emails."[294] As part of the settlement with the DOJ, the company was required to retain an independent compliance monitor for two years and self-report for an additional one year. Fresenius is one of the world's biggest providers of dialysis equipment and operates more than 3,700 dialysis clinics worldwide, with 37 production sites.

---

294   Richard L. Cassin, "At Fresenius, Management Owned the Graft," *The FCPA Blog*, April 4, 2019.

THE DEMOCRATIC REPUBLIC OF CONGO (DRC)

With its vast mineral resources, the DRC was from day one an attractive haven for exploitation by foreign companies. Since independence, each one of its presidents, from Joseph Kasavubu to Joseph Desire Mobutu to Laurent Desire Kabila to Joseph Kabila, has been linked to bribery and corruption in some ways, creating an elite of super-rich individuals owning high-end properties in Paris, Belgium, and other trendy world capitals. But it was during Mobutu's 32-year rule from 1965 to 1997 that bribery and corruption shot up to a particularly astronomical level. In his book, *Big Men, Little People: The Leaders who Defined Africa,* Alec Russell says: "Mobutu's technique was childishly simple: Zaire was his personal bank account to be debited at will."[295] Throughout much of the 1980s, says George B. N. Ayittey, author of *Africa Betrayed,* an estimated $1.32 billion worth of diamonds were illegally taken out of Zaire and the proceeds deposited in a Swiss bank account.[296]

Surprisingly, dictator Mobutu, a former military officer, had unflinching support from the WB, the IMF, and the United States, which kept on pouring aid money into the country like the thundering waters of Zambia's Mosi-oa-Tunya (Victoria Falls) even as Mobutu continued to gobble it. Most of disbursements were unaccounted for and ended up in Mobutu's personal accounts and useless projects of his choice. "It was one big freebie," one American diplomat said.[297] During his visits overseas, including trips to Addis Ababa, Ethiopia, as chairman of the OAU between September 1967 and September 1968, Mobutu was accompanied by a plane-load of family members and allies whose assignments were undetermined.

---

[295] Alec Russell, *Big Men, Little People: The Leaders who Defined Africa* (MacMillan, 1999), 19.
[296] George B. N. Ayittey, *Africa Betrayed* (St. Martin's Press, 1992), 256.
[297] Russell, 23.

Mobutu took bribes from some of the biggest mining players in the world dealing in diamonds, gold, copper, coltan, and other precious minerals. To obtain concessions, multinational companies had to routinely pay millions of dollars in commissions to Mobutu and his officials. And whenever mining assets were sold, Mobutu was part of the deal. One report by the NGO Global Witness said public assets were "sold in secret, initially transferred at knockdown prices to a series of offshore companies, which then made sales to the major multinational companies."[298] In other words, MNCs colluded with Mobutu to ransack the country.

When things to steal ran out, he put some of his foreign properties—some of which had already been mortgaged to raise cash for relatives—on sale. And as his prostate cancer worsened in the 1990s, he used a personal jet—a fabulously furnished supersonic Concorde—he leased from Air France to fly him to Europe for his cancer treatment.[299] At least Mobutu was generous in spreading the mineral wealth among his family and close associates.

By the time of his death in exile in Morocco in September 1997, Mobutu had amassed a personal fortune of $3.2 billion,[300] much of it schemed off multinational firms. Among his possessions were opulent estates in Portugal, Switzerland, Spain, and France, and a marble palace at Gbadolite, which was left to rot in the bushes after his departure. John Perkins says in his book, *The Secret History of the American Empire: Economic Hit Men, Jackals, and the Truth About Global Corruption*, that "Mobutu's long rule was ruthless, as well as corrupt, and deeply disturbing to neighboring countries."[301] The only relic remaining as an enduring memorial to Mobutu is a marble tomb in the European cemetery in Rabat marked with a cross at the top and his initials at the entrance—

[298] "Congo's Secret Sales," Global Witness, report, May 13, 2014.
[299] Alec Russell, *Big Men, Little People: The Leaders Who Defined Africa* (MacMillan, 1999), 29.
[300] Mike Pflanz, "Corruption Runs Deep in Gold Mines in Congo," *The Telegraph*, March 14, 2007.
[301] John Perkins, *The Secret History of the American Empire: Economic Hit Men, Jackals, and the Truth About Global Corruption* (Dutton, 2005), 256.

MSS (Mobutu Sese Seko)—to identify the resting place of one of the most brutal dictators on the African continent.

In comparing Mobutu with his successor Joseph Kabila, one writer said, "Mobutu used to steal with a fork – at least some crumbs would fall between the cracks, enough to trickle down to the rest of us. But Kabila, he steals with a spoon. He scoops the plate clean."[302]

After Mobutu's exit, Laurent Desire Kabila took over the government and allowed his son Joseph Kabila to befriend an Israeli billionaire, Dan Gertler, known as the "gatekeeper" to Congo's mining sector. The looting continued. The Global Witness report claimed some of Gertler's companies paid under 5 percent of the market value for mines which were then sold many times over to multinationals such as Eurasian Natural Resources Corporation. Gertler arrived in the DRC in 1997 during the civil war as a diamond merchant and, over time, became one of the most influential foreigners in the country, with unlimited access to president Kabila. Gertler, The South Africa–based *Mail and Guardian* newspaper said, was synonymous with "grabbing and flipping,"[303] and through his nefarious dealings made the DRC lose billions of dollars in revenue. In one transaction, Glencore, the British/Swiss commodity trading and mining company, paid over $75 million to Gertler for mining assets, money which should have gone to the state mining company Gécamines, which handles research, exploration, and production of mineral deposits. "Gertler is a well-known corruption risk in Congo's mining sector and Gécamines is famously opaque," says Pete Jones of Global Witness. Gécamines is "hemorrhaging money in suspect transactions."[304]

---

[302] Jason K. Stearns, *Dancing in the Glory of Monsters: The Collapse of the Congo and the Great War of Africa* (Public Affairs, 2011), 322–231.

[303] Stefaans Brummer, Craig McKune, and James Wood, "Tokyo Sexwale and the DRC's grab," *Mail & Guardian*, August 17, 2012.

[304] "Glencore Redirected Over $75 Million Mining Payments to Scandal-Hit Friend of Congolese President, Global Witness Reveals," Global Witness, report, March 3, 2017.

The plunder of the DRC's resources was confirmed in a UN Security Council report in 2002 in which big companies like De Beers, Anglo-American, and Barclays Bank were singled out as facilitators. The report said 85 multinationals based in the United States, Europe, and South Africa were among those that violated the OECD's ethical guidelines by making it easy for elite networks to pillage the country of gold, diamonds, cobalt, and copper, among other resources. The networks consisted of government officials, military officials, and entrepreneurs from the DRC, Zimbabwe, Uganda, and Rwanda who colluded to transfer $4.1 billion worth of assets from state-owned mining corporations to private companies over a period of three years.

The Spanish newspaper *El Pais,* in October 2002, surprisingly named Zimbabwe's Speaker of the National Assembly among those facilitating the smuggling of DRC diamonds through Harare International Airport. Top Rwandan and Ugandan army officials were also identified. The looting that was previously conducted by the army was replaced by organized systems of embezzlement, tax fraud, extortion, the use of stock options as kickbacks, and diversion of state funds, said the UN report. Emmerson Mnangagwa, who later succeeded Mugabe, denied being a member of such networks when his name was mentioned.

The UN report was written by members from Belgium, the United States, Canada, Egypt, and Senegal, and had Swiss and British technical advisors. Mugabe ignored the report, and leaders of Rwanda and Uganda, countries that took over control of a large swath of eastern Congo, denied the allegations. As a show of embarrassment, Kabila fired three of his ministers suspected of involvement in the scandal. In June 2000, forces of Rwanda and Uganda clashed and fought for six days over the control of coltan, whose price on the world market had skyrocketed. Once refined into tantalum, coltan becomes a key component in the making of computer chips, VCRs, and laptop computers.[305]

---

[305] Robert B. Edgerton, *The Troubled Heart of Africa: A History of the Congo* (St. Martin's Press, 2002), 230.

The Brussels, Belgium-based non-profit International Crisis Group (ICG) asked the shamed multinationals to accept responsibility for the plunder: "Even providing a bank account to those who are exploiting the resources is a substantive role .... They [multinationals] benefit more from this dirty business than those doing the digging and mining."[306]

In 2009, Gertler reportedly received a $45 million loan from Glencore Plc to secure mining rights in the DRC, according to the Paradise Papers—a partner of the US-based non-profit ICIJ—released in 2017. Part of the money was used to bribe Congolese officials, which was a violation of anti-corruption rules in Switzerland. However, Glencore, the world's biggest miner of cobalt and a leading copper producer, said the loan was made on commercial terms and "negotiated at arm's length."[307]

In one deal involving Switzerland-based Katanga Mining Limited, in which both Gertler and Glencore had interest, the commodities and mining giant paid the DRC-owned mine operator, Generale des Carrieres et des Moines (Gécamines SA), only $5 million for rights that could typically have cost $240 million. Katanga Mining is now 87 percent owned by Glencore after the company paid Gertler $534 million to buy his stake. The Paradise Papers examined mining contracts in the DRC totaling $440 million in 2008 and indicated Gertler may have had a role in obtaining the larger discounts.[308] But Glencore said the price was right.

In 2013, the Africa Progress Panel—a group of distinguished individuals from both the private and public sectors advocating for equitable and sustainable development—estimated that five deals connected to Gertler were undervalued, occasioning a loss to the

---

[306] Rory Carroll, "Multinationals in Scramble for Congo's Wealth," *The Guardian,* October 21, 2002.

[307] Tom Wilson, "Glencore's Role in Paradise Papers: What You Need to Know," Bloomberg, November 5, 2017.

[308] "Paradise Papers Research Raises Questions Over Glencore's $440m Congo Discount," International Consortium of Investigative Journalists, report, December 14, 2017.

country of at least $1.36 billion. Conversely, when in 2007 China entered into a joint venture with Gécamines to improve the mining sector and build roads in exchange for ore, 32 percent of the joint venture shares went to the country and 68 percent went to China. David Van Reybrouck in his book, *Congo: The Epic History of a People*, says: "It was indeed, an impressive agreement [though] … the West began screaming bloody murder."[309]

A 2017 report said $750 million in mining revenues had been diverted from the DRC public coffers—in the form of royalties, taxes, and dividends—to corrupt state-owned companies and national tax agencies over the past three years. Gécamines reportedly receives $100 million every year from shares in two dozen mining projects, but only a "tiny percentage" reaches the Treasury, partly because "the majority of the mining exports are not declared and … the badly equipped tax authorities are not capable of tracking the transactions," said journalist Eric Mwamba, adding that massive underbilling, smuggling, and fraudulent contracts and book-keeping[310] were some of the other problems stifling government revenue.

Underhand dealings spiced with intrigues, political overtones, and personality clashes over mineral rights and bribery commissions have created volatile and sometimes unpleasant corporate showdowns in the DRC. In 2016, a Canadian company, Africo Resources Ltd., which owned a copper mine in the DRC, was a victim of intrigue and sabotage by highly placed government officials who conspired with the Israeli mining guru Gertler to take over its operations. To clear the way, the Israeli, using his political connections, allegedly paid a bribe of $500,000 to Congolese officials, including judges, to ensure the Canadians lost the mine. According to US documents presented to a US court in Brooklyn,

---

[309] David Van Reybrouck, *Congo: The Epic History of a People* (Harper Collins Publishers, 2010), 529.
[310] Eric Mwamba, "Getting Rich in Poverty-Stricken Congo," *Mondiaal Nieuws*, February 1, 2013.

New York in October 2016, Africo was ejected from the site soon after the bribe was paid, and the Israeli won majority control and assets. A week later, the transfer was approved by Africo shareholders. US government documents show Gertler gained 60 percent of Africo shares in June 2008, days after the money exchanged hands.

In a related development, the American hedge fund Och-Ziff Capital Management Limited was found to have colluded with the Israeli businessman to pay a bribe estimated at $100 million to DRC officials in exchange for mining concessions. Kabila was said to have received $10.7 million between December 2010 and February 2011. The SEC said Och-Ziff was directly involved in the acquisition of Africo, including paying "legal expenses." In 2016, the company pleaded guilty before a US court to bribing Congolese officials as well as officials in Guinea, Libya, Niger, and Chad, in violation of the FCPA. The DOJ ordered Och-Ziff to pay $412 million to settle the matter. Gertler, who denied wrongdoing, was not charged anywhere. The only action taken by the US government against him for bribing Congolese officials was to impose sanctions, including shutting him out of the dollar market—the dollar is the main currency in the Congo—and banning American companies from dealing with him.

In a surprise announcement in 2016, Glencore said it paid $15 million to Gécamines as "settlement of historical commercial disputes."[311] No details were given about the payment, but speculation was that the company wanted to get back into the good books of the state organizations to preserve its vast interests in the country. And in December 2018, Katanga Mining paid $22 million to the Ontario Securities Commission to resolve allegations of inadequate historical disclosure of its finances and activities in

---

[311] "Katanga Mining Announces Settlement of DRC Legal Dispute with Gecamines and Agreement for the Resolution of KCC's Capital Deficiency," statement, June 12, 2018.

the DRC. The company was accused of providing misleading information about compensation to some of its executives and failing to provide accurate information about its internal controls in the DRC between 2014 and 2017. Glencore promised to improve reporting of its affiliate's operations going forward.

THE REPUBLIC OF CONGO

This Central African country is among the top 20 most corrupt countries in the world, according to TI. Rich in oil—it is sub-Saharan Africa's fourth-biggest oil producer—the Republic of Congo, also known as Congo-Brazzaville, has seen a good share of bribery and corruption in its oil industry. President Denis Sassou Nguesso, members of his family, and top government and military officials have all been accused of taking bribes from foreign companies wanting to get a piece of the country's oil reserves.

In 2017, Pascal Collard, a former oil trader of the Geneva, Switzerland-based Gunvor Group, found himself in serious trouble, leading to his appearance before a Swiss federal court on charges of bribing public officials in Congo and Ivory Coast seven years earlier. Among the beneficiaries of the bribe amounting to millions of dollars, according to court papers, was a son of Congo's president, Denis Christel Sassou Nguesso, who was a director at the state-owned oil company, Societe Nationale des Petroles du Congo (SNPC), at the time the bribe was exchanged. The trader, a Belgian citizen, was charged with allegedly bribing the officials to secure two untendered contracts to export 22 tankerloads of crude oil valued at $2.2 billion. According to a report entitled "Gunvor in Congo: Oil, Cash Payments and Embezzlement: The Adventures of a Swiss Trader in Brazzaville,"[312] Private Eye, an NGO, said Gunvor signed a total of six pre-financing agreements with SNPC, each worth an estimated $149 million, between September 2010 and June 2012. Gunvor also dished $31.9 million to intermediaries who funneled the money to the Brazzaville officials.

Public Eye obtained video footage that showed a man claiming close association with the president's son, Denis, complaining to a Gunvor official that the young Nguesso was not receiving enough money in proportion to his influence. In response, a Gunvor executive was shown in the video as saying that the company was

---

[312] "Gunvor in Congo," Public Eye, report, July 2012.

ready to pay commissions via a Russian company, "which will be a discreet way of avoiding any 'trouble.'"[313] Gunvor co-founder Gennady Timchenko was known to have close ties with the Russian president, Vladimir Putin. Collard, who worked for Gunvor—one of the world's biggest commodity and energy traders—was charged with fraud, embezzlement, and money laundering with respect to the Congo contract. He entered into a plea bargain with prosecutors in August 2018 and was given an 18-month suspended sentence by a Swiss court on the condition he does not commit any offense within a three-year period. He was also fined $34,000 after pleading guilty to bribing the Congolese and Ivory Coast officials between 2009 and 2012.

A Public Eye investigation[314] estimated Collard received up to $43 million in commissions. It said a special advisor to the president of Congo received $10.5 million in commissions through a Geneva-based private bank, Clariden Leu, while Maxime Gandzion, a Congolese public official who was the intermediary between Collard and the president, received $15 million. Part of the bribe money amounting to $2.4 million went to President Nguesso and his wife Antoinette in exchange for oil contracts, according to Swiss court documents. The bribe was channeled through a presidential aide and a company in Belgium.

Collard also admitted to bribing officers close to the presidency in Ivory Coast in exchange for contracts. Approximately $7.6 million allegedly passed through the Belgium company for transmission to close associates of President Laurent Gbagbo in 2010 and 2011. Another five payments went through a bank in Switzerland and another in Belgium, intended for a presidential economic advisor, a head of the country's refinery, and a chief executive of the state-owned petroleum company Petroci. A statement from the Swiss attorney general said Collard "worked in an atmosphere in which

---

[313] Charles Bouessel du Bourg, "Republic of Congo: Gunvor, the Kremlin, Oil and Corruption," *The Africa Report*, November 20, 2017.
[314] "Corruption in Congo and Ivory Coast: Gunvor in the Spotlight," Public Eye, report, August 28, 2018.

corruption appeared to be an accepted way of doing business."[315]

In August 2018, the trading company Gunvor said in a statement that it "wholly rejects the possibility of a conscious and desired involvement of any other employee or executive"[316] in the act. Ivory Coast and Congo officials also denied bribes were paid, and Denis Christel Nguesso, the possible heir apparent to his father, called the allegations of his involvement "a fable." "If anyone has proof, let the person produce it,"[317] he said in his defense.

In 2018, Gunvor announced it was suspending all activities in the Congo and Ivory Coast.

---

[315] Ibid.

[316] Hugo Miller and Andy Hoffman, "Ex-Gunvor Oil Trader Found Guilty of Bribing African Officials," Bloomberg, August 28, 2018.

[317] Elie Smith, "Congo Leader's Son Denies Payments from Ex-Gunvor Trader Bribes," Bloomberg, September 4, 2018.

PART SIX

CHAPTER 9

_____

SOUTHERN AFRICA

Corruption is a cancer, a cancer that eats away at a citizen's faith in democracy, diminishes the instinct for innovation and creativity.
– Joe Biden

LESOTHO

More than four decades ago, a big scandal hit the landlocked highland kingdom of Lesotho, a relatively small nation completely surrounded by South Africa. Formerly known as Basutoland during the colonial rule, Lesotho became independent in 1966. Ruled throughout the eighteenth century by King Moshoeshoe II until he was dethroned in 1990 by King Letsie III, Lesotho had a devastatingly unstable history characterized by military coups. It was not until 1993 that a democratically elected government, led by the Basotho Congress Party, was elected. More military coups followed, people died, and by 1999 the capital of Maseru was left wobbling like a jelly ready to tumble.

Today, the country is still ruled by a king, Letsie III, but it has a prime minister, Tom Thabane, as head of government.

The big scandal of the Lesotho Highlands Water Project (LHWP) implicated the powerful and highly influential Masupha Sole, the chief executive of the Lesotho Highlands Development Authority, in the late 1980s. He is the one who oversaw the process of the multimillion-dollar dam construction project smudged in corruption. The Lesotho dams were to supply South Africa's industrial center of Gauteng province with water and Lesotho with electricity. In Lesotho, water is a major natural resource that is often referred to by the locals as "white gold."

Conceived during the apartheid era when South Africa was under international sanctions, the LHWP used intermediaries and a London-based trust fund to launder money for the project, seemingly with the full knowledge of the WB, which was the main funder providing $150 million toward the dams. That act of circumvention was illegal, since it went against UN agreements meant to counter white rule in South Africa. The other financiers were the European Investment Bank, commercial banks, UK companies, and British, French, and German aid agencies, among others.

The enormous project was to be constructed by Spie Batignolles,

Sogreah, and Dumez International of France; Lahmeyer Consulting Engineers, ED Zublin, and Diwi Consulting of Germany; LHPC Chantiers (an international consortium); and the Swiss/Swedish ABB, Acres International of Canada, Salini Impregilo of Italy, the Highlands Water Venture, and the Lesotho Highlands Project Contractors.[318] Incidentally, both Spie Batignolles and Songreah had been involved in the construction in the late 1980s of the graft-ridden Turkwel Gorge hydropower dam in northwest Kenya, a project that sucked former President Daniel arap Moi and his most trusted Cabinet minister, Nicholas Biwott, into a multimillion-shilling corruption payoff. There was no competitive bidding in the Turkwel project, and the project cost of $198 million was highly inflated.

In the Lesotho project, due diligence was not done on Salini Impregilo, Dumez, and Lahmeyer, companies that built the controversial Yacyreta dam in Argentina, described by Argentina's president, Carlos Menem, as "a monument to corruption."[319] In addition, Lahmeyer (which was bought by the Brussells-based Tractebel in 2014 and now operates as Tractebel Engineering GmbH) and Salini Impregilo were also the builders of Guatemala's Chixoy dam, to which between $350 million to $500 million was reportedly lost to corruption. Similarly, Swiss/Swedish ABB and Dumez were at the center of corruption allegations involving the Itaipu dam on the Brazil/Paraguay border, where the original construction cost of $3.4 billion skyrocketed to $20 billion.[320] Patrick McCully of International Rivers, a global organization advocating the protection of rivers and the communities that live around them, said the list of companies in the Lesotho project read "like a who's who of the dam-building industry."[321] But it could also have been a

[318] *Business Day* (South Africa), July 29, 1999.
[319] Shirley Christian, "Buenos Aires Journal: Billions Flow to Dam (and Billions Down Drain?)," *The New York Times*, May 4, 1990.
[320] "Lesotho Highlands Water Project: What Went Wrong?" International Rivers, report, October 31, 2005.
[321] "Bribery Taints World Bank-Funded Lesotho Water Project," International Rivers, report, August 1, 1999.

who's-who in dam construction graft.

The multinationals working on the LHWP were accused of allegedly paying Sole bribes ranging between $2,500 and $733,000 in French francs, US and Canadian dollars, German marks, and British sterling pounds between February 1988 and December 1998, totaling more than $6 million even before the contracts were finalized. The money was allegedly remitted to the accused's six accounts in Switzerland and France and to the bank accounts of third parties. And even after Sole was fired in 1995, bribe monies continued to pour into his accounts up to 1998. In the years that followed, all of the construction companies involved in the project were charged with bribery in Lesotho and were heavily fined.

Sole was convicted by a Maseru court of 13 counts of bribery in 2002 and sentenced to 18 years in prison. The 64-year-old member of the Basotho National Party, then a junior partner in a coalition government, served nine of those years, and on release claimed his conviction was politically motivated. The involved firms were ordered to pay varying fines for their participation in the scandal, and the WB debarred them from bidding on its funded projects for a number of years.

It was rare for an African country to take powerful private-sector companies head-on over corruption. Lesotho's determination to stamp out the supply side of graft was laudable. "We are taking the big companies by the horns," said the country's attorney general, Fine Maema. "You can see from this case that it is not only Africa that is corrupt."[322]

---

[322] Chris McGreal, "Taking Multinationals to Task," The World Press Review online, *The Guardian Weekly*, July 4, 2001.

MOZAMBIQUE

After years of negotiations, five MNCs and the national oil and gas company, the National Hydrocarbons Company (ENH), were finally given contracts by the Mozambique government in August 2018 to explore for oil. Italy's Eni, ExxonMobil, Delonex Energy, Norwegian Statoil, and South Africa's Sasol were granted exclusive rights in the Northern Zambezi basin. It took four years to negotiate the contracts, indicating a transparent exercise in a country ingrained with corruption and bribery. The licenses came on the heels of natural gas discoveries in Cabo Delgado province and the Mozambique Basin that could either transform the lives of the 24 million Mozambican people or result in a "resource curse," as evidenced in other oi-producing African countries such as Nigeria, the DRC, and Angola.

However, Mozambique has not always been transparent. In 2016, the IMF terminated funding to the country after $2 billion in "secret" loans could not be explained. The "secret" loans were advanced by European banks on the urging of a mysterious group of investors, supposedly to help the country rebuild following years of civil war. It happened that a group of individuals, including a former finance minister, were involved in the deal. Some of them were arrested in the United States and charged before a New York court for creating dubious maritime and coastal protection projects as fronts, raising money to enrich themselves, and intentionally diverting parts of the loan proceeds to pay at least $200 million in bribes and kickbacks to themselves, Mozambican officials, and others. In fact, the entire amount was plundered.

In January 2019, three former Credit Suisse Group AG bankers—Andrew Pearse, Surjan Singh, and Detelina Subeva—were arrested in London, and former finance minister Manuel Chang was nabbed in South Africa. The bank accused the three of hiding information from the bank. Chang, on the other hand, was cited for allegedly signing guarantee documents on behalf of Mozambique in case the loans were not paid. The authenticity of those documents was, however, questioned since the government was not aware of the transaction. A 47-page indictment, dated December 19, 2018, named the three former bank employees who are citizens of New Zealand, the United Kingdom, and Bulgaria respectively, as well as other entities and individuals. It narrated how they planned the fake project and how they shared the bribe money, each receiving between $2 million and $15 million. They were charged with defrauding investors and obtaining money by false pretenses, making false statements, bank fraud, and money laundering.

The tuna bonds scandal

In 2016, the IMF stopped lending to Mozambique after discovering part of the $2 billion it loaned to the country for the so-called "tuna bonds" scandal was squandered through bribes and never benefited the Mozambican people as intended. At least $200 million was allegedly skimmed off by bankers, businessmen, and a former finance minister from the money meant to fund a state tuna fishery project in Mozambique. Another $500 million could not be accounted for.

It was said the schemers arranged the loan for the tuna project and then created maritime projects as fronts to hide part of the money from the IMF. On January 4, 2019, three former bankers of Credit Suisse—Andrew Pearse, a New Zealander; Surjam Singh, a British citizen; and Detelina Subeva, a Bulgarian—who were arrested in London the same week were charged in a federal court in Brooklyn, New York with bribery and fraud related to the scandal. The DOJ claimed the three hid the loans from Credit Suisse and concealed information from the bank's compliance group about corruption-related risks. They were charged with four counts of conspiracy to violate FCPA anti-bribery and internal controls provisions, wire fraud, securities fraud, and money laundering.

Also indicted was former Mozambican finance minister Manuel Chang, who was arrested in South Africa. Chang, as well as Jean Boustani—an executive of Privinvest, an Abu Dhabi–based marine projects company, who was picked up at JFK airport in New York a few days earlier—were charged with three counts of conspiracy. Court documents showed Privinvest promoted the project and allegedly arranged for the people to receive bribes from the loans.

In 2018, the British Financial Conduct Authority dropped investigations into Credit Suisse's role in the Mozambique loan drama,[323] saying it had no power under the anti-bribery act to proceed with the prosecution. The same year, the IMF scaled up its campaign to investigate rich countries known to give bribes and financial institutions suspected to be laundering dirty money. The campaign was directed at the Group of Seven (G7) industrial nations including the United States, Britain, Japan, Italy, France, Canada, and Germany, along with Austria and the Czech Republic. "The flip side of every bribe taken is a bribe given," said the IMF's managing director, Christine Lagarde, in a post on the IMF website. "And funds received through corruption are funds concealed outside the country, often in the financial capitals of major capitals."[324] The IMF campaign was an extension of a crackdown on poor countries to find out how transnational bribery networks worked in rich countries. The campaign was part of an anti-corruption push initiated by the IMF back in 1997 in which the G7 countries agreed to be assessed on the preparedness of their financial systems in preventing and criminalizing money laundering, which was closely linked to bribery.

Another multilateral organization that has demonstrated a penchant for combating corruption is the Organization of American States (OAS), which in 1997 adopted the Inter-American Convention against Corruption. Today, OAS, whose main objective is to promote justice, peace, and solidarity, has 35 member states. However, TI, which was formed in 1993 and which is supported by major European development agencies, foundations, and private

---

[323] Richard L. Cassin, "Ex-Credit Suisse Bankers Charged with FVPA Violations," *The FCPA Blog*, January 4, 2019.
[324] Andrew Mayeda and David Biller, "IMF to Probe Role of Advanced Economies in Feeding Corruption," *The Globe and Mail*, April 22, 2018.

companies, "is the only international organization devoted entirely to the elimination of corruption."[325] Its periodic corruption and perception indexes are well-regarded by most of the developed and developing nations and remain the most credible measurement of graft in individual countries.

No bribe, no contract

In October 2016, the government launched an investigation to find out who among officials at the national airline LAM had received a bribe of $800,000 from the Brazilian aircraft manufacturer Embraer to secure an agreement for the purchase of two aircraft for LAM at a cost of $65 million. The official was said to be an intermediary designated by a high-level official at LAM, but neither the LAM official nor the so-called high-level official were publicly named in what was suspected to be a "false agency agreement."

The allegations of bribery were made in a DOJ statement, prompting the Mozambique Central Office for the Fight Against Corruption (GCCC) to open investigations of its own. In December 2017, the former Mozambican transport minister, Paulo Zucula; the former LAM chief executive, Jose Viegas; and the former head in Mozambique of the South African Petrochemical Company (Sasol), Mateus Zimba, were arrested in connection with the scandal and charged with money laundering and illicit participation in business. It was alleged that Viegas was the one who pushed for LAM to purchase the Embraer E-190 aircraft,[326] insisting "no bribe, no contract." The officials allegedly rejected Embraer's original offer of an $80,000 bribe, calling it an insult, and instead demanded $1 million. Eventually, a compromise of $80,000 was reached.[327]

---

[325] Transparency International Mission Statement.
[326] "Mozambique: Former Transport Minister, Two Executives Arrested for Graft," APA News, December 7, 2017.
[327] "Mozambique: Embraer Bribe Case Sent to Maputo City Court," AllAfrica.com, news, January 10, 2018.

Zimba then allegedly opened a shell company called Xihevele in the island nation of Sao Tome and Principe, off the coast of Africa, to which the bribe money was channeled. Although Zimba did not offer any services to Embraer, the Brazilian company accepted from Xihevele two invoices of $400,000, each referred to as "sales commissions." Zucula, Viegas, and Zimba were ordered to pay the state approximately $1 million in compensation for the embarrassment they caused to the country.

In the meantime, following its own investigations, the DOJ filed charges against Embraer, and in October 2016 the company agreed to enter into a resolution to resolve criminal charges, allowing it to pay $205 million in a global resolution to resolve the matter, which also included charges of bribing government officials in the Dominican Republic and Saudi Arabia and of falsifying payment records in India through a sham agency agreement.

In the case of Saudi Arabia, the state oil company Saudi Aramco awarded Embraer a $93 million contract to supply three new aircraft. Colin Stevens, a UK citizen living in Dubai and a vice president of sales and marketing in Embraer's executive jets division, arranged a $1.5 million bribe to a Saudi official to help with the sale and took $130,000 from the bribe, disguised as "commission," to a South African company owned by Stevens' personal friend. The money was then transferred to an intermediary, and part of it to Stevens. It was Stevens himself who reported the kickback to Embraer in 2013, triggering a massive internal investigation and Embraer's disclosure of the illicit deal to the DOJ. Saying that crime does not pay, Assistant Attorney General Leslie R. Caldwell remarked: "Embraer tried to bribe their way into several profitable aircraft contracts around the world, [but] instead of reaping a nice profit, their criminal conduct earned the Brazilian aircraft manufacturer a substantial penalty that more than wiped out their gains from these contracts."[328] Stevens pleaded guilty in a New York court

[328] Department of Justice, "Embraer Agrees to Pay More Than $107 Million to Resolve Foreign Corrupt Practices Act Charges," press release no. 16-1240, October 24, 2016.

in December 2017 to three counts of violating the FCPA, wire fraud, and money laundering; three counts of conspiracy; and one count of making false statement. In December 2018, he was fined $25,000 for paying a bribe to Saudi Aramco and agreed to forfeit $174,000 to the DOJ.

Another shady deal was the one that got Vitol, one of the biggest oil traders in the world, in trouble. The Swiss oil trading firm had difficulty explaining accusations that between 2014 and 2015, it exploited the people of Mozambique into losing at least $80 million through highly complicated pricing methods. The Vitol scandal was highlighted by the media, causing the government to demand a refund of the money which the state-owned monopoly, Importadora Mocambicana de Petroleos Limitada (IMOPETRO), paid to Vitol.

Cases of multinational companies overcharging for oil have been reported numerous times by the Centro de Integridade Publica (CIP), a Mozambican anti-corruption NGO, which also suggested the money almost always found its way to government officials and politicians. Vitol strongly denied engaging in corruption.

Military collusion

There were also reports that military generals of the ruling Mozambique Frelimo Party corruptly colluded with a British company to displace locals from farms to pave the way for the mining of rubies and other minerals. In return, the military men received a percentage of every ruby sold. All Mozambican oil fields are infected by the scam. In some cases, as it is with Montepiuez Ruby Mining (MRM), a subsidiary of the London-based Gemfields, army men own shares, giving them the clout to enforce the illegal displacement of people. A senior member of Frelimo, for example, owned 25 percent of shares in the company, which has been accused of human rights abuses. In April 2018, 100 Mozambicans filed a suit in London through the law firm of Leigh Day seeking compensation for acts of serious violence and abuses including sexual molestation, unlawful detention, and personal harm committed by the expatriate security personnel contracted by the company on and around the Montepuez Ruby Mine in Northern Mozambique. MRM has held mining rights on a 36,000-hectare piece of land in the country since 2011.

Tobacco menace

Tobacco multinationals have also suffered heavy fines from US and UK officials for bribing government officials in Africa over the years. The Brazilian subsidiary of Universal Corporation, Universal Leaf Tabacos Ltda. (Universal Brazil), for example, was caught in a bribery scandal in Mozambique, where it paid more than $165,000 to gain exclusive rights to purchase tobacco from regional growers and procure legislation beneficial to the company's business. The money was paid between 2004 and 2007 through subsidiaries in Belgium and Africa. The Richmond, Virginia-based Universal was also accused of spending $850,000 to grease the palms of two high-ranking government officials and a politician in Malawi between 2002 and 2003 in violation of the FCPA. Both payments were not recorded in Universal's books.

In August 2010, the SEC charged Universal before a US court with those violations, as well as another one involving a bribe of $800,000 to officials of the government-owned Thailand Tobacco Monopoly (TTM), in exchange for securing $11.5 million worth of tobacco contracts for its subsidiaries in Brazil and Europe. In August 2010, Universal pleaded guilty and was sentenced to three years of organizational probation and a fine of $4.4 million. In addition, it was ordered to pay a disgorgement of $4.5 million and to retain an independent compliance monitor for three years.

Also charged with corruption with Universal were two of its competitors, Dimon Incorporated and Standard Commercial Corporation, which merged to become Alliance One International Inc. It was accused of bribing TTM officials with $1.2 million to obtain sales contracts in Thailand. Alliance One agreed to pay a criminal fine of $9.5 million.

Tobacco companies in Malawi operate like a cartel, exercising influence on the country's economic and trade sectors. They even place their own representatives in government policy-making committees that advise the government on tobacco-related trade policy: "The corporate representative's presence prevents other committee members from taking positions against the tobacco industry and ensures government policy that advances industry interests to obtain low-cost tobacco."[329] The tendency to trying to monopolize the tobacco trade led the Malawian president at the time, Bingu Mutharika, to warn companies in 2016 to either end their non-competitive practices or leave the country. Malawi exports 98 percent of its leaf to 68 countries, with the EU nations topping the list.

Tobacco lobby in Kenya

And talking of tobacco, one of the biggest tobacco lobbies ever seen in Kenya hinged around the tobacco control legislation tabled in Parliament in 2004. Apart from passing out cash to leaders of the relevant committees of the House, the tobacco industry and growers, with the backing of a leading MNC, took 40 MPs on an all-expenses-paid luxury holiday to the coast in an attempt to get them to water down the Tobacco Products Control Bill. One report said the tobacco industry spent $87,000[330] to pamper the lawmakers on a piece of legislation they did not favor. Many considered the perks as a bribe to get the legislators to side with the industry.

Kenya is among several African countries named in a stash of secret papers from a British whistleblower implicating BAT in illegal payments to politicians and public officials in order to undermine anti-smoking legislation. The BBC acquired the documents from Paul Hopkins, a former employee who had worked with BAT in Africa for 13 years, which showed $300,000 was paid as bribes to Africans over several years.

---

[329] Marty G. Otanex, Hadii Mamudu, and Stanton A. Glantz, "Global Leaf Companies Control the Tobacco Market in Malawi," *Tobacco Control* 16, no. 4, (2007): 261-269.
[330] Issah Ali and Musah Labram, "Tobacco Industry: Interference in Tobacco Control & Public Health Policies in Ghana," report, undated.

Among the recipients of the illegal payments was a senior Burundian Health Ministry official who allegedly pocketed $3,000 to help the company draft a tobacco law. A Rwandese representative of the World Health Organization Framework Convention on Tobacco Control (WHO-FCTC) received $20,000, and a public officer from the Comoro islands, also an FCTC delegate, got $3,000 to get them to undercut the WHO-backed tobacco control laws. Also bribed was a Ugandan MP, who was paid $25,000, and a former trade minister in Kenya, who received a business-class return trip to London for his wife.

The proposer of the bill in the Ugandan Parliament reportedly received "thousands of dollars to infiltrate, influence, and spy" on tobacco control activists and accommodate BAT views in the tobacco control bill.[331] Some of the payoffs were approved by a BAT regional executive, the BBC report claimed. However, BAT's director for East and Central Africa, Gary Fagan, denied giving permission for the payments. Ironically, Dr. Sheila Ndyanabangi, the principal medical officer and an anti-tobacco activist in Kampala, described the BBC report as "hugely biased."[332] All the named officials denied being bribed, but the head of WHO-FCTC, Dr. Vera da Coast e Silva, accused BAT of "using bribery to profit at the cost of people's lives."[333]

AT is a global organization but holds shares in the US company Reynolds American Incorporated, which produces Newport and Camel cigarettes and which distributes leading British brands, such as Lucky Strikes, in the United States. BAT controls the world market alongside Philip Morris, Japan Tobacco, and China National Tobacco Corporation. In Africa, where it sells 70 percent

---

[331] "The Secret Bribes of Big Tobacco," African Tobacco Control Alliance (ATCA), report, undated.
[332] "Experts Speak Out on Tobacco Industry Bribery Claims," *The New Vision,* January 7, 2016.
[333] Jonathan Owen, "British American Tobacco Accused of Bribing Senior Politicians in Order to Sabotage Anti-Smoking Laws," *The Independent,* November 30, 2015.

of its cigarettes, BAT is the biggest tobacco company.

The BBC report was so explosive that members of the US Congress asked the DOJ to investigate BAT, Britain's fifth-largest tobacco producer. In August 2017, the SFO opened its own investigations to confirm "suspicions of corruption in the conduct of businesses by BAT Plc, its subsidiaries and associated persons."[334] The focus was on allegations of bribery to officials in East Africa to get them to block regulations BAT believed harmed its business in Africa. BAT allegedly sent letters of intimidation to governments in Ethiopia, Burkina Faso, DRC, Uganda, Namibia, Gabon, and Togo, warning of unspecified dangers should they enact anti-smoking regulations, including banning cigarette advertising.

For years, the WHO has warned of the dangers of cigarette smoking, which reportedly causes over six million deaths yearly from tobacco-related diseases. That figure is expected to rise to over eight million deaths by 2030.[335]

The Kenya Tobacco Control Bill, which bans tobacco sales of single cigarette sticks, advertising, promotion, and sponsorship, was finally passed in August 2007 against fierce opposition from the industry. It was signed into law by President Mwai Kibaki, giving the country a head start in Africa's fight against smoking. In the meantime, in 2018, BAT fiercely opposed the Nairobi County tobacco bill providing a six-month jail term and a fine of $500 for anyone caught smoking or holding a lighted cigarette product in public places in the city. During a hearing early in 2019 in Nairobi, BAT argued the ban would have negative "unintended consequences."[336]

---

[334] "British American Tobacco Investigated by Serious Fraud Office," *BBC, news*, August 1, 2017.
[335] C. D. Mathews and D. Loncar, "Projections of Global Mortality and Burden of Disease from 2002 to 2030," PLoS Medicine, 2011–2030, November 3, 2006.
[336] "BAT Fights Nairobi Bid to Enforce Law on Public Smoking," *The Business Daily*, March 4, 2019.

NAMIBIA

Four months after an independent study identified bribery and kickbacks as the most common types of corruption in Namibia's private sector, two Chinese nationals, Xu Siyong and Yang Huaifen, began serving a jail sentence of two years each after pleading guilty to a count of trying to bribe a police officer in Windhoek. The two employees of the Chinese construction company, New Era Investment, admitted offering $275 to a police inspector on September 5, 2018 to get him to stop a money laundering investigation against Yang involving $69,000.

Magistrate Vanessa Stanley described the actions of the two as "morally repugnant," adding that "by offering a bribe to the police officer in a bid to have an investigation stopped, the two accused showed that, to them, money was a tool to buy corruption.[337] The harsh sentence illustrated the determination of Namibian authorities in tackling graft. But it also lent credence to the study of the Institute for Public Policy and Research that incidences of bribery were rampant in the country abutting South Africa. The study, *The Role of the Private Sector in Tackling Corruption*, showed that supply-side corruption existed hand in hand with the demand side. In the above case, the police officer reported the bribery attempt, a rare show of ethical humility.

But when it comes to private-sector corporations, greed is the driving force. Almost two decades earlier, in 2009, Namibia became the first African country to indict a Chinese company for corruption. The multinational Nuctech, which was headed by Hu Haifeng, son of the Chinese president Hu Jintao, was accused of paying illegal kickbacks to a private consulting firm called Teko Trading. The payment was related to an award of a $56 million contract to the Chinese company to supply high-tech X-ray scanners for use at Namibia's airports and harbors. The deal was for the Chinese Export-Import Bank to contribute $43 million and Namibia $13

---

[337] Werner Menges, "Bribery Lands Chinese Citizens in Prison," *The Namibian,* September 17, 2018.

million for the scanners.

The Chinese portion was allegedly paid to accounts controlled by Lameck and Mokoxwa. Thereafter, Lameck went on a spending spree, buying luxury cars, a farm, and clearing a house mortgage. When the allegations became public, the Namibian Anti-Corruption Committee opened investigations, and on July 9, 2009, the powerful public service commissioner, Teckla Lameck, a co-owner of the consultancy with Jerobeam Kongo Mokaxwa, and Nuctech's Africa representative Yang Fan were arrested in connection with the scandal after a local bank reported huge suspicious transactions between Nuctech and Teko Trading. It was alleged that Teko received $13.2 million from Nuctech to facilitate the deal, which the receivers allegedly split among themselves. Mokaxwa was an accountant with Namibia Contract Haulage (NCH), a subsidiary of Kalahari Holdings, a wholly owned outfit of the ruling party, the South West African Peoples' Organization (SWAPO).

Facing 18 charges of fraud, corruption, and money laundering, the accused, who pleaded not guilty, spent six weeks in detention and their assets were frozen. The young Hu was not directly implicated in the illicit deal, but his involvement "fueled assumptions of 'friends in high places' on both sides."[338] Nuctech denied wrongdoing. In January 2019, the prosecution case ran into trouble when a High Court judge, Christie Liebenberg, ruled that the summons used by the government to collect evidence were invalid since the Anti-Corruption Committee did not have authorization in writing, as required by law, to access the bank accounts of the accused.

The Chinese Communist Party (CCP) and Namibia's SWAPO have maintained close relations since the 1960s, when the latter was fighting for independence from South Africa. After independence, President Hu Jintao became a close friend of President Sam

---

[338] Clever Mapaure, "Chinese Investments in Zimbabwe and Namibia," Center for Chinese Studies, report, September 2014, 36.

Nujoma, and the two met in Beijing and Windhoek to discuss Chinese loans to the southern African nation. In one of the delegations to China, Lameck accompanied the president.

"Shalli Shafted"

In an unrelated case in 2009, President Nujoma fired the chief of defense forces, Lieutenant General Martin Shalli, after reports emerged that he colluded with his Chinese counterpart in corrupt deals involving a mining exploration license. As newspapers reacted with succinct headlines, the news of Shalli's suspension sent jitters running through the usually divided armed forces. The no-nonsense top officer was accused of receiving $250,000, and other senior officers who accompanied him $100,000 each, from arms dealers during a visit to China a few weeks earlier. Shalli denied the allegation, but there were reports that up to $500,000, suspected to be the proceeds of corruption, was hidden at a British-owned bank in Zambia.

In September 2011, the Namibian prosecutor general sought a High Court preservation order for two deposits into Shalli's account, amounting to $499,950 in October 2008 and $249,975 in February 2009. At the time of the deposits, a Chinese company, Poly Technologies Incorporated, had bagged a $126.4 million contract to supply arms to Namibia. The Windhoek government ordered the money frozen.[339]

Crooked mine sale

Two senior executives of the French energy giant Areva were charged in a French court in 2018 with corruption in relation to the overvalued purchase in 2007 of Canada's UraMin Trekkopje uranium mine in Namibia for a staggering $2.5 billion at a time when world uranium prices were low. The sale included its mining rights in South Africa, Namibia, and the Central African Republic.

---

[339] "Ex-Namibian Army Commander Keeping Corruption Money in Standard Chartered Zambia," Zambia Watchdog, report, February 24, 2012.

It was hoped that Areva would produce an additional 7,000 metric tons of uranium a year from the new mine beginning in 2010, but the controversy that followed did not allow it, resulting in a loss of $2.7 billion to Areva.

Sebastien de Montessus, head of the mining division, and Daniel Wouters, head of development, as well as Haddis Tilahun, the co-owner of a private Namibian company, United Africa Group (UAG), were charged in March 2018 with bribery of foreign officials, embezzlement, and breach of trust. All denied the accusations. Two years earlier, in 2016, the company's former CEO, Anne Lauvergeon, was charged with publishing Areva's false accounts for 2010 and 2011 and spreading false information about the sale of the UraMin mine. The problem for the company came when it was revealed that the sale of the Trekkopje mine by Areva, now known as Orano SA, was overvalued. The plant, located in the Erongo region, 30 kilometers north of Swakopmund, was estimated at only $211 million because of its poor performance. The Paris-based Areva said it relied on information by a company paid by UraMin to determine the value and did not seek an expert opinion.[340]

An inquiry was also been launched in France into two contracts of about $6.9 million allegedly disbursed to UAG in 2009/2010 to facilitate the sale of UraMin and into an alleged monthly consultation fee of $10,000 to a Namibian government minister between 2008 and 2009. President Geingob made it clear in 2018 that he would cooperate with the French judges probing the matter and would not testify in France.

Hage Geingob, who later became the president of Namibia but at the time of the transactions was the minister of commerce and industry, reportedly admitted to the *Namibian* newspaper in June 2015 that he helped UraMin renew its license and that he "received

---

[340] Marie Maitre, "Areva Uranium Deal Eyed Amid Fraud Allegations," Reuters, January 13, 2012.

payment," [341] but paid part of it to two unidentified South Africans who allegedly represented him in the transaction. Quoting French officials, the news agency AFP described the payments as "illicit monthly transfers."[342]

It was also alleged that Geingob approved the Trekkopje uranium mine to enjoy export processing zone status, thus allowing it to escape paying taxes for five years, a privilege other mining companies did not have. Geingob strongly denied wrongdoing. A Swiss private detective agency, ALP Services, which investigated the deal, claimed Geingob—who admitted offering consultancy services in the deal through his HG Consultancy—was paid through an offshore account in the British Virgin Islands. The long-time Namibian politician was the prime minister of Namibia from 1990 to 2002 and again from 2012 to 2015 before becoming president in 2015.

---

[341] "Avera Corruption Saga Implicates Namibia," *The Namibian*, August 4, 2018.
[342] "Namibia: 'Illicit' French Payments Haunt Geingob," *AllAfrica.com*, news, April 10, 2018.

BOTSWANA

There are only a few African governments that have done more than just fatten the pockets of the elite. At independence in 1966, Botswana had only seven kilometers of tarred road and a capital that amounted to little more than a railway station.[343] A year later, after diamond was discovered, the country suddenly leaped from one of the poorest countries in the world into "one of the continent's most celebrated 'success stories.'"[344] That, however, does not mean Botswana escaped all the problems facing other African countries, even though corruption and bribery are much more subdued in Botswana than in the neighboring South Africa or in countries like Nigeria and Kenya, among Africa's leading economies.

As the diamond exports brought growth of 9.2 percent in the first twenty years, so did elite corruption bring misery to people of the Southern African nation. The country has had to deal with egregious corruption problems stretching from deals involving fighter aircraft, armored vehicles, and tanks to fraud and money laundering, all linked to President Seretse Khama, members of his family, allies, and top members of the armed forces. The Khamas became so rich they were referred to as Botswana's "military millionaires."[345]

Three separate presidential commissions were appointed in the 1990s to investigate cases of graft. One of them, in 1991, found profound irregularities in a land deal worth millions of dollars that was linked to a vice president, ministers, and senior government officials. Established procedures were not followed in acquiring the land at Mogodisthane for community use, and bribery and kickbacks were suspected. This and other cases of public-sector

[343] E. Cropley, "At 50, Botswana Discovers Diamonds Are Not Forever," Reuters World News, September 26, 2016.
[344] Monageng Mogalakwe and Francis Nyamnjoh, "Botswana at 50: Democratic Deficit, Elite Corruption, and Poverty in the Midst of Plenty," *Journal of Contemporary African Studies* 35, no. 1 (2017): 1-14.
[345] T. Motlogelwa and M. Civilini, "The Khamas – The Making of Military Millionaires," *The Business Weekly and Review*, November 14, 2015.

corruption and abuse of office led the Botswanan Parliament to pass the Corruption and Economic Act in 1994 establishing a directorate to investigate corruption and economic crimes, which provides prison terms of up to 10 years and a fine of $50,000, or both.

In the early 1990s, the Botswana Democratic Party (BDP), which has ruled the country since 1965, faced particularly challenging times with corruption. Senior government officials, including President Masire himself, had taken huge loans from private banks and then refused to pay. Festus Mogae, who was then minister of finance and development planning, asked the BDP government to put pressure on defaulters. When they resisted, their names were leaked to the media, resulting in a rush to pay.

One of the first major corruption cases in Botswana involved a Lebanese multinational company called Zakhem Construction, which is active in most parts of Africa. A director in the Department of Roads was charged with receiving a bribe of approximately $9,000 from an executive of the company to influence him into awarding Zakhem Construction Botswana a multimillion dollar road project linking Monametsana and Rasesa. A senior engineer was also charged with receiving a bribe of $25,000. While the engineer went scot-free, the director was sentenced to four years in prison. That was one of several cases of corruption implicating Zakhem both in Botswana and in other countries. In Kenya, the company built a 450-kilometer pipeline from Mombasa to Nairobi, but there was a price variation of $440 million, which Zakhem claimed was caused by delays—yet pundits suspected bribery and kickbacks to be the cause.

Conflict of interest and nepotism are other elements confronting Botswana. Officials are not barred from owning companies, and those businesses tender for government contracts. At one time, the defense minister was President Khama's cousin, and both were relatives of the director of the Directorate of Corruption and Economic Crime, Rose Seretse. In 2018, a commission of inquiry faulted Seretse, who is now the CEO of the Botswana Energy Regulatory Authority (BERA), for engaging a Tanzanian consultant for BERA projects under questionable circumstances. The commission, which was specifically appointed to look into the matter, ruled that Seretse acted in complete negligence of duty by engaging the Tanzanian without consulting the board of directors and without clearing the process with the Ministerial Tender Committee. The authority's chief operations officer, Duncan Morotsi, fell victim to the crisis and was suspended in June 2018. BERA was established in 2017 with the responsibility of providing an efficient energy regulatory framework for electricity, gas, coal, petroleum products, solar, and other forms of renewable energy.

The presence of European and American multinationals in Botswana is also responsible for fueling corruption in that country. Competition for contracts among major players in the oil and gas industry, as well as in other minerals sectors, has ratcheted up bribery within government and deepened the poverty and marginalization of certain communities. Yet when the country celebrated its 50th anniversary in September 2016, the official mantra was "Botswana 50: United and Proud." It is doubtful the peasant population in a country dubbed "Africa's success story" is united and proud, given the ruthlessness and exclusivity of the regime.

For example, when the government offered a $4.9 billion concession to Anglo-American PLC to explore diamonds around the Central Kalahari Game Reserve in the 2014, the bushmen community was evicted from the area without being provided with an alternate place to live. That move was condemned by Botswanan human rights groups, which wondered why a government would mistreat its own people in favor of a foreign company. Anglo-American PLC, the majority shareholder of the giant diamond multinational De Beers, has developed a suspiciously chummy relationship with Gaborone and the ruling party BDP to the point of influencing economic and political events. De Beers and its subsidiary, De Beers Botswana, are blamed for hampering the diversification of diamond mining activities by opposing the processing of diamonds in-country and expanding into manufacturing. Diamond contributes 80 percent of the country's foreign exchange earnings and is a major employer.

Moreover, the diamond mining agreement between Botswana and De Beers, which has never been divulged, may not after all be beneficial to the country. For years, everything, including information on the sale of diamonds by the company, was shrouded in secrecy, causing reports to suggest De Beers could be robbing Botswana of millions of dollars through profit-shifting. Figures showed all adjustments of Botswana's diamond export price ended in De Beers' account outside the country. That fleecing could be seen in the 2018 accounts that showed Botswana received only $1.25 billion from diamonds while DeBeers got a staggering $6.1 billion, a 23 percent difference.[346]

---
[346] "Inside Botswana/DeBeers' Secret Agreement," *The Sunday Standard* (Botswana), March 18, 2019.

SOUTH AFRICA

This southern African country is one of the most prosperous on the continent, with the second-largest economy in Africa after Nigeria. In May 1994, after decades of white rule, the African leadership of Nelson Mandela took over a nation bestowed with a superbly developed infrastructure that featured multiple-lane roadways, a buoyant financial sector, an advanced telecommunications system, a vibrant civil service, a war-ready military apparatus, and an educated class of both whites and blacks. Mandela had spent the past 27 years in prison on treason charges for fighting for the country's independence.

But South Africa also suffered from corruption and bribery throughout its white-dominated rule and the years that followed independence. The country's isolation from most of the world, starting with the UN arms embargo of 1963, helped mask the country's ills to the extent that internal corruption became a taboo subject. There were dozens of cases involving corruption between 1976 and 1994 involving billions of SA rand, but those were either inadequately investigated or were swept under the carpet.

It was not until 2015 that things started unraveling, as the secrets behind the apartheid regime began to peel. A thick dossier of unresolved corruption cases was compiled by the South African ISS and presented to a corruption committee chaired by the minister for public service and administration, Geraldine Fraser-Moleketi. The dossier included allegations against former presidents P. W. Botha and F. W. de Klerk, the Afrikaner Broederbond (a secret male-only brotherhood organization advocating for Afrikaner interests), and the SA Reserve Bank. Also named was the powerful former minister Pik Botha and two previous Reserve Bank governors, Dr. Gerhard de Kock and Dr. Chris Stais.

Corruption scandals during the apartheid related to questionable arms purchases and defense financing, graft within the executive branch of the "white state," illegalities in foreign exchange, and illicit oil purchases by the government to the violation of sanctions against the apartheid South Africa by a section of the international community. There were also multimillion-dollar scandals involving big foreign companies that ensnared Cabinet ministers, MPs, and civil servants. Because of the large South African bureaucracy consisting of the "white state," "homelands," racial parliaments, and local authorities, the inner workings of apartheid were fertile ground for corruption.[347]

Funds secretly hidden by top government officials were estimated at more than $23 billion during the almost two decades preceding independence. The corruption committee wanted investigations done to establish the source of the money and the individuals behind it. In one case, in 1980, $1.6 million was found in a Swiss bank account belonging to the then-finance minister, Nico Diedrichs. It was suspected that the money came from a deal in which the minister was paid 10 US cents for every ounce of South African gold sold in exchange for agreeing to move the base of South African gold sales from London to Zurich in the 1970s. Diedrichs was evidently corrupt, having been involved in several other scandals, including illegal land sales, involving huge amounts of money.

Unfortunately, most the documents that could shed light were maliciously destroyed. As Terry Bell and Dumisa Ntsebeza explain in their book, Unfinished Business, "Tons of files, microfilm, audio and computer tapes and disks" were shredded, wiped, and incinerated. "In a little more than six months in 1993 … some 44 metric tons of records from the headquarters of the National Intelligence Service alone were destroyed…. There was so much material that the state incinerators could not cope,"[348] and the

---

[347] Hennie Van Vuuren, "Apartheid Grand Corruption: Assessing the Scale of Crimes of Profit from 1976 to 1944," a report prepared by civil society for presentation to the National Anti-Corruption Forum, May 2006, 40–41.
[348] T. Bell, D. B. Ntsebeza, et al. *Unfinished Business: South Africa, Apartheid and Truth*, Verso, 2003, 14.

government had to hire the services of private companies to carry out the enormous task of destroying the information before the winds of change were felt in South Africa. In the meantime, the entire bourgeoisie establishment, including the government bureaucracy, the police, and the defense force—knowing they had only a few years left—went on a plundering spree and enriched themselves shamelessly.[349] They bought lavish homes and sent their children to private schools.

There was also the so-called information scandal, in which huge amounts of public funds were used to publish propaganda books against the ANC. On investigation, it was found the costs had been inflated. And then there was a campaign to manipulate and buy politicians and the critical media. While the government-run South African Broadcasting Corporation (SABC) was obliged to support apartheid policies, the Afrikaans-language media and a large proportion of the English publications were a fanatic appendage of the racist government. Graft was so rampant among white politicians and bureaucrats that a new term was born: "taking a brown paper bag to Pretoria," illustrating how senior civil servants or ministers were bribed with money stuffed in brown envelopes.[350]

Hennie van Vuuren, who wrote books and articles about corruption in the apartheid era, talks of the loss of hundreds of millions of SA rand in secret overseas deals in the mid-1980s: a nuclear energy deal that went awry, occasioning a loss of approximately $4.6 million to the state-owned electricity supply commission; massive fraud cases in infrastructure and communications sectors involving government officials; and private-sector players. In his book, *Apartheid Guns and Money,* for example, van Vuuren reveals how heads of state, journalists, bankers, and lobbyists made huge profits from economic crimes.

---

[349] Dan O'Meara, *Forty Lost Years: The Apartheid State and the Politics of the National Party, 1948-1994* (Ravan Press, 1996), 352.
[350] Brian Bunting, *The Rise of the South African Reich* (Penguin Africa Library, 1965), 39.

Of South Africa's many scandals, however, none was as dramatic and costly as the 1984 "tanker scam" described by the *Guinness Book of Records* as "the biggest shipping fraud in the 20th Century."[351] The scam was manufactured as part of the apartheid government's subterfuge to evade an international arms embargo. The South African government was duped by international tricksters into buying $50 million worth of stolen oil from Kuwait and was persuaded to acquire a Liberian-registered supertanker, the *Salem*, to transport the oil to Durban via Europe.

En route to Europe, the tanker was secretly diverted to Durban, where it off-loaded its crude—about 180,00 tons, with a value of $56 million. After the tricksters were paid, the 92,228-ton *Salem*, now renamed *Lema*, was filled up with sea water in order to create the impression it was still laden with oil. Off the coast of Senegal in West Africa on January 16, 1980, the ship was scuttled, and the crew, who were preparing for evacuation—suitcases in hand— were conveniently "rescued" and taken to Dakar, and subsequently to Greece.[352] It was learned during investigations by Scotland Yard that the ship was sunk by its own crew to conceal its cargo of water. Crewmen walking out in dry clothes carrying personal effects was evidence enough that the whole episode was a ploy.

An insurance probe recommended that Pretoria pay $52.5 million as compensation to Shell Oil company, which had bought the oil from a Swiss company, Pontoil, only days before it was loaded on the *Salem*. Frederick Soudan, a Lebanese-American president of the Texas-based Oxford Shipping, which owned the vessel, was convicted by a Houston, Texas court in April 1985 of wire fraud, perjury, conspiracy to defraud the US government, conspiracy to obstruct justice, and making a false statement to the Internal Revenue Service. But while in prison in Fort Worth, Texas, he escaped and was never captured. That same year, a Greek court

[351] "Book Brings Ship-Sinking Fraud to Surface," *JOC.com*, April 5, 1988.
[352] Hennie van Vuuren, "Apartheid Grand Corruption: Assessing the Scale of Crimes of Profit from 1976 to 1994," a report prepared by civil society for the National Anti-Corruption Forum, May 2006, 64.

sentenced a shipping agent, Nicholas Mittakis, to 11 years, and four seamen to four years in jail, for their role in scuttling the tanker and stealing oil from Shell. South Africa was the biggest loser for spending $30.5 million in litigation.

As all this was happening, South Africa's economy was in bad shape. Anti-apartheid campaigns were escalating worldwide, and banks like Citibank and Chase Manhattan had stopped loaning money to the country, insisting pending loans had to first be paid. In the years that followed, President de Klerk began releasing political prisoners, including Nelson Mandela in February 1990. From there, things started to move quickly toward independence.

In the post-apartheid years that followed, corruption assumed a new face in South Africa as Africans in power went all-out to amass wealth for themselves. The ruling African National Congress (ANC) privatized government enterprises, and through them benefited itself and officials running them, while falsely touting a commitment to end corruption. The ANC adopted a strong anti-corruption party manifesto and passed legislation criminalizing corruption and bribery but failed to follow through. By doing so, the government sent a mixed message which civil servants, the military, and ordinary South Africans interpreted as a *carte blanche* to engage in the malfeasance.

A few months after the African government came to power, an "arms deal" was hatched in South Africa concerning a $5 billion strategic arms procurement package involving helicopters, four frigates, three submarines, and Gripen fighter aircraft for the South African Defense Force (SADF). The deal was controversial from the very beginning, with politicians bashing each other over the huge expenditure for the arms at a time when there was no external threat and as millions of its citizens were starving and unemployed. The deal was also shrouded in the suspicion of corruption.

In return for signing on the dotted line, the German builders of the warships, a consortium of three European firms—UK's BAE

Systems, Sweden's Saab, and the Italian helicopter builder Agusta, a unit of Finmeccanica—offered the South African government $18 billion in "offset" benefits to help stimulate the economy and to create 65,000 jobs. "Offsets" are side deals or "sweeteners" offered to a government by a company and may include promises of jobs or wealth for the economy. Experts say "offsets" "are a pivotal feature of international arms trade – a scam perpetrated by arms companies with collusion of corrupt politicians to fleece the taxpayers of both recipient and supplier countries."[353]

That is how South Africa found itself in that deal: as a country with vast natural resources, but one that was mismanaged by bureaucrats and exploited by complicit multinationals. In the deal, the so-called benefits never materialized. Instead, politicians and government officials collected nearly $300 million in bribes from the seller companies. German state prosecutors who investigated the deal claimed they had found documents showing the South African arms contract was ridden with kickbacks.

The whole idea of the arms purchase came from Defense Minister Joe Modise with the backing of the ruling party, ANC. Things appeared calm until a whistleblower, Patricia de Lille, of Partnership Africa Canada (PAC), revealed in Parliament that some senior ANC members were bribed by the bidders. The matter blew out of proportion, with a crescendo of criticisms coming from ANC opponents.

To assuage the growing cries for action, President Thabo Mbeki ordered an audit. When the powerful Standing Committee on Public Accounts (SCOPA) was shown the audit, it recommended investigations under the chairmanship of Judge Willem Health, who was bestowed with powers to reverse the deal if he found it to be corrupt. That recommendation was denied by Mbeki. Instead, in 2000, a joint investigation comprising the public protector, the auditor general, and the national prosecutor was launched. When

---

[353] "South Africa's Arms Deal Saga," War Registers' International, article, undated.

the trio presented their report, the ANC went ballistic, terming its contents a "litany of lies," and said there was no corruption involved.

In attempting to distance himself from the sour transaction, Mbeki— president between June 1999 and September 2008—tried to cover it up. In June 2005, he dismissed his deputy, Jacob Zuma, over corruption allegations which took Zuma's financial advisor Schabir Shaik to court, where he was convicted and sentenced to 15 years in jail for soliciting a bribe from Thint, the local subsidiary of the French arms firm Thomson-CSF, now Thales, on behalf of Zuma. It was alleged the money was to secure the company's interests in a multibillion-dollar arms contract with the government. Shaik was also accused of writing off Zuma's debts, amounting to $154,000. Also implicated in the arms deal, but not prosecuted, was Defense Minister Modise, who died in 2001, and Tony Yengeni, a top ANC official and chairman of the South African Parliament's Joint-Standing Committee on Defense, who was sentenced to four years in jail in 2003 for fraudulently receiving a 4x4 Mercedes-Benz from a bidder in the lucrative deal. A commission of inquiry appointed by President Zuma in October 2011, under Judge Willie Seriti, to investigate corruption in the deal filibustered the process and then concluded "there was no evidence of corruption."[354] It also exonerated prominent politicians, including former president Mbeki, of corruption in the severely controversial arms deal.

Nelson Mandela, the founding father of the independent South Africa, had this to say after the scandal blew up in September 1999 when he was out of office: "We came to government with the zeal of a group of people who were going to eliminate corruption in government. It was such a disappointment to note that our own people who are there to wipe out corruption became corrupt."[355] According to Anthony Sampson in his book, *Mandela: The*

---

[354] "Corruption-Blind Seriti Commission is Our Zero," Corruption Watch, article, April 29, 2016.
[355] Anthony Sampson, *Mandela: The Authorized Biography* (Knopf Doubleday Publishing Group, 2012), 563.

Authorized Biography, Mandela explained that:

When a leader in a provincial legislature siphons off resources meant to fund service by legislators to the people; when employees of a government institution, set up to help empower those who were excluded by apartheid, defraud it for their own enrichment, then we must admit that we are a sick society.[356]

The white Nationalist Party (NP) government had plundered the country to an extent that some critics were already talking of a failed state. Yet what he experienced as leader of the newly independent African nation was even more painful. He found corruption under the ANC to be more "crass [than of the NP], more ostentatious, more concerned with the trappings of wealth, the mansions, the limousines, the convoys, the outriders, the bodyguards, (and) the baubles."[357]

More than 20 other entities, officials of the ruling ANC, and charitable organizations, including the Nelson Mandela Children's Fund and the Mozambique Community Development Foundation associated with Mandela's wife, Graca Machel, were listed as beneficiaries of the bribes. Zuma was reportedly paid an equivalent of $273,000 through his advisor, Schabir Shaik. In the meantime, the United Kingdom investigated the scandal and found BAE had paid bribes amounting to $145 million to secure the business. The investigation was terminated in 2010, however, and BAE agreed to settle with the SFO for $38 million. Cases involving President Zuma's part in the bribery scandal and other corruption cases were still ongoing by the end of December 2018, when the court ordered him to refund $2.2 million paid by the government in legal fees.

In the wake of the arms deal and other corruption-related cases, it became apparent that the South African government was not

---

[356] Nelson Mandela, a Speech in Parliament, South African History Online, February 5, 1999.
[357] Alex Boraine, *What's Gone Wrong? South Africa on the Brink of Failed Statehood* (New York University Press, 2014), 95.

inclined to fight foreign bribery. A September 2018 TI report named the African country as one of 11 nations having limited enforcement on bribery overseas. If South Africa had a definite policy on curbing bribery, says Leanne Govindsamy, head of Legal and Investigation at Corruption Watch, grand corruption, money laundering, and other offenses involving foreign actors would be eliminated.

South African arms industry

The UN imposed an arms embargo and restrictions on the sale of oil to South Africa in 1977 as a response to the country's continued apartheid rule. Shut out of access to arms in a country that was embroiled in internal and external insurgency, the white South African regime had to find other ways of arming itself. It established a domestic arms industry, embarked on a nuclear research and enrichment program, and sought brokers willing to secure weapons from dealers overseas. That was an expensive undertaking, taking away meager resources from the people and directing them to defense and security. At the center of this innovation was the Armaments Corporation of South Africa (ARMSCOR), established in 1968 to spearhead efforts to evade the international sanctions.

Several foreign companies were involved either in secretly supplying arms to Pretoria or in helping build missile systems and providing technical support for the apartheid regime. From the 1960s to the 1990s, the SADF was engaged in war on several fronts: it was fighting SWAPO and ANC elements in Angola while protecting its own borders from invasion. While in Namibia and Angola, SADF personnel were involved in massive poaching operations and the logging of hardwood that turned some areas into "green lifeless deserts."[358] The poaching activities took place between mid-1977 and late 1979 and were spearheaded by

---

[358] Hennie van Vuuren, "Apartheid Grand Corruption: Assessing the Scale of Crimes of Profit from 1976 to 1994," a report prepared by the civil society for the National Anti-Corruption Forum, May 2006, interview with Christon Thirion, November 9, 2005.

senior South African military officers, who directed soldiers to kill elephants and rhinos. The animal trophies were temporarily stored in Namibia before being sold to dealers. The money collected from the ivory sales was used to recoup the costs of funding Jonas Savimbi's opposition group, the National Union for the Total Independence of Angola (UNITA), in its war against the Angola government.

The defense sector was not the only one cited for corruption, though. The sale of oil and gold was also steeped in graft as the country tried to evade sanctions. Because of its pariah state, anything it bought from abroad was inflated in price, and anything it sold commanded a lower price. Corrupt government officials took advantage of that to add commissions, and brokers increased prices to accommodate their percentage.

Shady agents

On the issue of arms purchases by South Africa, the Swedish defense firm Saab—one of the largest security companies in the world—confessed in 2011 that millions of dollars were paid to "shady agents" to clinch a contract for the 26 Jas-39 Gripen aircraft and the British Hawk aircraft. However, Hakan Buskhe, the company CEO, claimed it was BAE Systems that paid the money which was subsequently handed over to a South African consultant. Saab claimed it did not know about the payment of $3.5 million paid by BAE in salaries and bonuses between 2003 and 2005, and the amount was not reflected in account books.

After its own investigation, however, Saab admitted the money was paid to Sanip Pty Limited, a subsidiary of Saab and British BAE Systems, following the signing of a contract between Sanip and Fana Hlongwane of Hlongwane Consulting Limited, an advisor to the South African defense minister then, in exchange for the sale of Gripen jet fighters. That admission got opposition parties to request investigations by the Directorate of Priority Crimes, known as the Hawks. BAE subsequently sold its stake in Saab for approximately $198 million.

According to a Swedish newspaper, *The Expressen*, over $10 million was paid to a Saab consultant and advisor to the late defense minister Modise. About $136,000 of that money was reportedly deposited into the minister's account in Switzerland. On investigations, it was found that Modise had four Swiss bank accounts with $12,000 believed to emanate from the arms deal.

Since President Zuma took office as the fourth president of South Africa in 2009, he faced serious graft allegations ranging from receiving questionable payments to money laundering and racketeering, many of them connected to arms deals. Two months after he was forced out of office by his party, the ANC, on February 14, 2018, he was arraigned in a Durban court to face 16 charges of corruption. He was accused of receiving a bribe in an arms deal, among other payments, when he was deputy president. The matter was also reported to the SFO for investigation because some of the companies had a British connection.

Companies, including the accounting firm KPMG, the German software company SAP, and the US global consultancy firm McKinsey and Company, viewed internationally as the godfather of management consulting, were also cited for corruption. KPMG South Africa was the accounts auditor of Linkway Trading, which was blamed for the diversion of huge sums of money that had been meant for a public dairy project to a Gupta family member's wedding. For its part, SAP admitted paying $7 million in 2017 to firms associated with the billionaire Gupta family of Atul, Ajay, and Rajesh to secure contracts with Transnet and Eskom worth $46.6 million.

Using Gupta connections, McKinsey, together with Trillian Capital Partners Pty Limited, signed illegal contracts with Eskom Holdings SOC Limited, a state-owned utility company, and allegedly benefited to the tune of $74 million between 2015 and 2016 through overcharging. The $120 million contract with Eskom, which provides 90 percent of the nation's electricity, was one of the biggest in South African history. Trillian Capital was controlled by the three Gupta brothers at a time when the family was accused of using its friendship with President Zuma to influence government tenders.

The controversy generated by the scandal forced McKinsey to apologize to South Africans and pay back the $74 million received from Eskom, even though the two firms denied engaging in corruption. Zuma and the Guptas denied wrongdoing. The consequences of its illicit action, which McKinsey said indicated "the violations of our professional standards,"[359] was that it lost most of its clients in South Africa, including two premier banks, Barclays Africa and Standard Bank Limited. At the end of 2017, McKinsey announced it was suspending all its work with state-owned companies in the country.

Following those allegations, KPMG's chief executive, Trevor Hoole, its chairman Ahmed Jaffer, and numerous other top executives resigned. The chairman of KPMG International, John Veihmeyer, admitted the firm made "serious mistakes"[360] by working for the Guptas, who were among the richest individuals in South Africa. KPMG had produced a troubling report for the South African Revenue Service (SARS) which named some top SARS officials as the perpetrators of serious corrupt activities. The scandal led to the resignations of senior officials and the firing of the then-finance minister Pravin Gordhan in 2017. The report was, however, criticized by some as a "political conspiracy"[361] to get some SARS officials sacked.

In October 2017, the German company SAP voluntarily disclosed to the SEC and DOJ $6.8 million in commissions it paid to the Guptas' family-owned companies. It admitted the contracts with

---

[359] "McKinsey Finds 'Violations of Professional Standards' but No Bribery at SA Arm," WorldECR, analysis, October 2017.
[360] Eugene Costello, "KPMG South Africa CEO Sorry for Gupta Mistakes," *International Investment*, October 5, 2017.
[361] Naashon Zalk, "Investigating South Africa's Mire of Gupta-Linked Corruption," Al Jazeera, March 27, 2018.

Transnet and Eskom were concluded with the help of the Guptas, singled out three of its South African managers for misconduct, and sent them on administrative leave. However, its own investigation did not reveal evidence of any payment to a South African government official, including Transnet and Eskom employees. Nevertheless, SAP placed the managers on administrative leave. SAP also eliminated sales commissions in all African countries except Botswana, Rwanda, Mauritius, Cape Verde, and Namibia.

That was not the first time Transnet—a government-owned logistics and transport company with annual revenue of over $4 billion—was named in a corruption scandal. In 2013, it was linked to a scam in which the Gupta family was paid about $355 million in kickbacks by the China South Rail to help purchase 1,064 new trains worth $44.4 billion.

In July 2017, a South African investigative journalism group, AmaBhungane (meaning "dung beetle" in isiZulu), named seven foreign companies it said made kickbacks to shell companies associated with the Gupta family in order to secure contracts with Transnet. AmaBhungane accused SAP, Germany's T-Systems, China South Rail, Shanghai Zhenhua, Switzerland's Liebherr International AG, McKinsey, and Neotel of paying varying amounts of bribes to secure business contracts in South Africa. Several of those companies denied the charge.

One report estimated that the Gupta brothers may have siphoned $7 billion in illegal payments from the Pretoria regime[362] before they fled the country after Zuma's ouster.

Weighed down by widespread corruption allegations, Transnet declared bankruptcy in February 2019.

---

[362] Karan Mahajan, "State Capture: How the Gupta Brothers Hijacked South Africa Using Bribes Instead of Bullets," *Vanity Fair*, March 2019.

ZAMBIA

For many years, Zambia's prosperity has been tied to how much copper it exports to the world market. Small mines strewn along the Copperbelt between northern Zambia and the southern DRC have been the driving force, but as more mines were discovered in other areas, production increased, bringing new prospects for the landlocked nation in south-central Africa. Both raw and refined copper earns the country more than $7 billion yearly, but cobalt, petroleum, tobacco, and other products also make Zambia the 83rd largest export economy in the world.

Copper was first discovered in Zambia in 1929, and for years, until independence in 1964, the country's economy was relatively strong. In 1974, however, the government of Kenneth Kaunda nationalized the mines, reverting all ownership and mining rights to the state, precipitating a collapse of the price of copper and an outcry from Western donors to have the mines privatized. That was done. But while the value of the commodity showed promise, that promise dissipated in 2008—after almost five years of a copper boom—when the government imposed a windfall tax. Once again, the price of copper tumbled, and the country was again in a financial crisis until Lusaka was forced to remove the tax. The general thinking among Zambians then was that the two main Western multinationals mining the commodity were working as a cartel in a conspiracy of sabotage.

The two companies, Nchanga Consolidated Copper Mines and Roan Consolidated Mines, coalesced in 1981 and formed one big organization, Zambia Consolidated Copper Mines (ZCCM). However, there were big financial and management problems within ZCCM, resulting in the company's inability to access essential tools for copper production and a lack of capital flow. With the country's economy on a downward spiral due to falling production, a decline in copper prices, and international competition, there was a need for the IMF to intervene. It did so by introducing sweeping structural adjustment programs (SAPs), opening the doors for substantial international aid.

After Kaunda retired in early 1991, Fred Chiluba took over the administration, and under pressure from the WB, ZCCM was privatized starting in 1997 until the last copper mine was sold in 2000. According to Professor Mpanda, "ZCCM was split into seven units and cumulatively sold for just $627 million accompanied by bribes."[363] The buy-out and entry of new players in the copper industry temporarily disorganized the industry, but at the end there was hope as new towns around mines came alive and employment soared.

In the meantime, China was expanding its economic zone to encourage Chinese investments in the African country by establishing the Non-Ferrous Company Africa Mining Plc, a subsidiary of the state-owned China Nonferrous Metal Mining Group Company (CNMC). The company broke the ice for China in Zambia by purchasing the Chambishi copper mine for $20 million in 2010. The broader plan was to develop a multi-facility economic zone that would include a metallurgy industrial complex producing cables and wires for export.[364] The economic zone was the first in Africa, and it permitted Chinese investors to operate without paying taxes to the government in Lusaka.

But first Chambishi had to be rehabilitated, so China poured in another $130 million. The investment was strategic, giving the Asian nation a head start in a lucrative industry that was the mainstay of Zambia's economy. It also fortified relations between the two countries that started with the building of the Tanzania/Zambia Railway in 1970 that stretched from the copper mines in Zambia to the Tanzania port, and the signing of the Zambia-China Economic and Trade Cooperation Zone (ZCCZ) agreement in February 2007, intended to build copper processing plants and

---

[363] Khadija Sharife, "Copper in Zambia: Charity for Multinationals," Pambazuka News, June 2, 2011.
[364] Deborah Brautigam, *The Dragon's Gift: The Real Story on China in Africa* (Oxford University Press, 2009), 101.

create jobs for locals. The purchase by China of Chambishi Mine paved the way for China to acquire other mines. CNMC opened three other mining industries: a copper processing plant, Sino Metals Leach Zambia; a smelting plant, the Chambishi Copper Smelter; and an underground open-cast mining operation, the China Luanshya Mine.

In January 2002, Levy Mwanawasa won the elections and immediately reinstated the windfall tax to boost mining revenue, to the annoyance of overseas donors and mine owners. But the heat was on to have it removed. It was during Michael Sata's reign that the tax was scrapped in 2009.

All of this shows how much multinationals are determined to manipulate the government of Zambia to do virtually all they want to make money from the country's natural resources. Apart from depriving the country of tax revenue, some multinationals also engaged in unethical activities detrimental to the interests of the country, such as underpaying workers and violating environmental rules. In one instance in April 2005, 46 Zambian workers were killed in an explosion at Chambishi. The tragedy led to an intense condemnation of Chinese labor standards, with some even demanding they be ejected from the country. "We have to be very careful, because if we leave them unchecked, we will regret it," then-opposition leader Michael Sata said. "China is sucking from us. We are becoming poorer because they are getting our wealth."[365] He warned that China was taking over Zambia. When, the following day, workers protested outside the mine, one was shot dead by security guards and five were injured by Chinese fire. At the Collum coal mine in Sinazongwe province in 2010, Chinese managers shot 11 Zambian miners who were protesting poor wages and conditions of work at the mine, leaving some with broken limbs and others in critical condition.

---

[365] Isabel Chimangeni, "Zambia: Is China Sneaking in Deals through the Back Door?" Inter Press Service, March 27, 2007.

One situation in particular bolstered Sata's theory of a potential Chinese takeover of some aspects of the country. At the end of 2017, $6.4 billion out of a national debt of $8.7 billion in Zambia was owed to Chinese creditors, sparking rumors that China was poised to take over the Kenneth Kaunda International Airport because the country had defaulted on its debts. That was considered possible, given that China had already reportedly seized Sri Lanka's Hambantota Port for similar reasons.

The vanishing copper

Much of the copper that Zambia exported in 2008—half of which was destined for Switzerland—did not arrive at its destination. It reportedly disappeared into thin air, occasioning—together with transfer mispricing—a loss of $11.4 billion to the Zambian Treasury. That shortfall was huge, given the fact that Zambia's entire GDP for 2008 was $14.3 billion.

The Extractive Industry Transparency Initiative noted in a report that while multinational mining companies in Zambia paid $463 million in taxes to the government in 2011, there were $66 million of "unresolved discrepancies" between actual payments and companies' tax liabilities in the same year.[366] That raised questions not only about the bad intentions of mining companies but also about the government's lack of oversight. Zambian media reports that multinationals were "robbing Zambia of an estimated $3 billion annually through tax evasion and illicit financial flows" have circulated widely over the years. However, they have been disputed by Global Financial Integrity, a non-profit body that works to curtail illicit financial flows, which insisted the reports were "not strictly true."[367] In 2013, Parliament passed a piece of legislation mandating investors to deposit export revenues locally, but that

---

[366] Khadija Sharife, "Transparency Hides Zambia's Lost Billions," Al Jazeera, June 18, 2011.
[367] Maya Forstater, "Stop Spreading the Myth: Zambia is Not Losing $3 Billion to Tax Avoidance," Center for Global Development, analysis, October 23, 2017.

directive was not followed to the letter, and money from multinational companies still slips through the cracks into accounts overseas.

Theorists also blame multinationals for contributing to the creation of a managerial bourgeoisie class. This class is generally "capitalist in its orientation"[368] and controls political power. The bourgeoisie class in Zambia, says Gilbert N. Mudenda, is divided into three sections: the imperial/comprador bourgeoisie, the bureaucratic/managerial bourgeoisie, and the petty bourgeoisie.[369] Our interest here is the second layer, which consists of "[t]op level party and government functionaries; top level executives in the state-owned corporations and the top-ranking officers in the defense and security forces."[370] It is in this class that major corruption scandals are found. This class goes for big tenders in collaboration with public officials in the procurement sector. A TI report said that in most institutions in Zambia, corruption increased from 8.5 percent in 2014 to 10 percent in 2017, despite the fact that the country ratified the Southern African Development Community's protocol against corruption in 2003 and the UN Convention Against Corruption in 2007.

Zambia too has been captured by foreign interests. In 2012, two subsidiaries of a major French engineering company, Alstom Corporation: Alstom Network Schweiz AG (Switzerland) and Alstom Hydro France, were blacklisted by the WB for three years after admitting to bribing a senior Zambian government official to help in a bid for the rehabilitation of the bank-funded hydropower systems in Victoria Falls. After the tender was issued in 1999, Alstom signed a $45 million contract with the Zambia Electricity Supply Corporation (ZESCO), but in July 2008, when the work was finalized, the WB received a bill of $51 million. The inflation of

---

[368] H. Jeffrey Leonard, "Review: Multinational Corporations and Politics in Developing Countries," *World Politics* 32, no. 3 (April 1980): 473.
[369] P. Mufune, "The Formation of Dominant Classes in Zambia: Critical Notes," *Africa Today,* Indiana University Press, 35, no. 2, (2nd Quarter, 1988): 5–19.
[370] Ibid.

cost raised the suspicion of corruption. An illicit payment of $124,000 was reportedly paid to the unnamed senior official in 2002, two years after France outlawed the bribing of foreign officials. Alstom has had a turbulent history of corruption. More than 30 countries have collaborated with the SFO to investigate the company. In December 2018, its global sales director, Nicholas Reynolds, was jailed for four years and six months by the Blackfriars Crown Court in London for his role in a conspiracy to win contracts worth $274 million in Lithuania. Alstom companies reportedly paid $5.7 million in bribes to officials and politicians to secure contracts at the Elektrenai power station in Lithuania.[371]

There were other cases implicating Zambian top officials in foreign corruption. In 2015, mines minister Christopher Yaluma and Copperbelt minister Mwenya Musenge were implicated in a $2 million mining scandal. It was alleged they received the money to facilitate an illegal takeover by the China Copper Mine Company of a prospecting area allocated to another company, Donald Investments. According to *Zambia Reports*, the two Cabinet officials instructed the local authority in the area to hand over the lot to the Chinese.[372] The Chinese company insisted it was the legitimate owner of the mines, though it could not produce any documents to back up its claim. The two officials denied receiving bribes.

The same year, Zambia's former mines minister Maxwell Mwale, who served under President Rupia Banda between 2008 and 2011, was jailed for one year with hard labor for using his office to illegally award a license to a Chinese mining company, Zhonghui International Mining Group, in 2009. In return, the Chinese company bought 5,000 bicycles worth $126,000 for Mwale's company. The minister, who was arrested during a crackdown on corruption ordered by President Michael Sata, allegedly ensured

---

[371] Harry Cassin, "Former Alstom UK Director Jailed for 'Sophisticated' Corruption," *FCPA Blog*, December 21, 2018.
[372] Charles Sakala, "Zambian Officials Linked to $2m Mining Scandal," *Zambia Reports*, September 2, 2015.

the company was issued the license within three days, when such a process normally took months. Chinese officials arrested with Mwale were acquitted, and the bicycles were returned to the former official. Magistrate Lameck Mwale said corruption in Zambia had become rampant and needed to be stopped.

The Chinese have stoked controversies in Zambia as they have in most of Africa. In May 2019, another Chinese company, Nantong-based Jiangsu Zhongtian Technology Company Limited (ZTT), was debarred by the WB for 20 months after submitting falsified documents when bidding for the Lusaka Transmission and Distribution Rehabilitation Project. The $210 million project, under the supervision of the state-owned ZESCO, was intended to increase the capacity and improve the reliability of the electricity transmission and distribution system in Lusaka, one of the fastest-growing cities in Africa. Demand for electricity in the city has been growing at the rate of 6 percent per year for the past decade. As a condition to resume bidding for WB-funded projects, ZTT committed itself to developing an integrity compliance program in line with the WB Group Integrity Compliance Guidelines.[373] The Chinese company engages in the manufacture and sales of communication products and has footprints in Europe, the Americas, the Middle East, Africa, and Asia Pacific.

[373] Harry Cassin, "World Bank Debars Chinese Fiber Optic Cable Company," *FCPA Blog*, May 22, 2019.

ZIMBABWE

If there is one leader in Africa who espoused hope for his people but delivered doom, that leader is Robert Mugabe of Zimbabwe. Coming in with a spectacular liberation curriculum vitae to become prime minister in 1980, after the end of British rule, and president on December 31, 1987, Mugabe was everything a newly independent government needed. He was known for his nationalism and the extravagance of his rhetoric, and he was a breath of fresh air for a population that had suffered decades of minority colonial rule.

Landlocked in southern Africa, with a mesmerizing landscape, colorful people, and an enduring tradition of stone sculpture, Zimbabwe has an abundance of natural resources: gold, copper, nickel, iron ore, platinum, coal, and oil. In all aspects, the country—which sits between two celebrated rivers, the Zimbabwe and the Limpopo—is, or should be, a rich country. Unfortunately, however, it is not—a fact that can be attributed to the selfish policies of Mugabe and his inner circle, including his high-rolling and avaricious second wife, Grace, and their devastatingly boorish children. During his long reign from December 1987 until November 2017, Mugabe was Zimbabwe and Zimbabwe was Mugabe; in essence, the former freedom fighter, his family, and his allies owned the beautiful country.

The late Edgar Tekere, Mugabe's long-time companion during the freedom struggle, expressed frustrations in 1989 about colleagues who were stealing money and banking it in Switzerland: "We all came from Mozambique [liberation camps] with nothing, not even a teaspoon. But today, in less than two years, you hear that so-and-so owns so many farms, a chain of hotels, and his father owns a fleet of buses. Where did all that money come from in such a short period? Isn't it from the very public funds they are entrusted to administer?"[374] For expressing those sentiments, Tekere was expelled from the ruling ZANU party.

---

[374] G. Ayittey, *Africa Unchained: The Blueprint for Africa's Future,* Springer, 2016, 103.

In the meantime, Mugabe signed an agreement with Agha Hasan Abedi in November 1980 making BCCI the only foreign financial institution allowed to trade in Zimbabwe. The deal was suspect, since BCCI had already been named by investigators in the United States and Europe as one of the world's most corrupt banks. For Mugabe, however, BCCI was the bank he was to use to siphon public money out of the country.

The nationalization of farms in Zimbabwe, beginning in the 1980s and intended to tamp down incessant complaints from indigenous Africans, was one of the biggest blunders made by Mugabe and saw hordes of white farmers leaving the country in dismay and anger. The whites' departure put an estimated 110,000 square kilometers of arable land in the hands of inexperienced members of Mugabe's party and military. Within a few years, agricultural production had significantly dropped, and the hope of prosperity had virtually been trashed. Foreign direct investment dropped from $435 million in 1998 to almost zero in 2001, and exports plummeted from $2.1 billion to $1.3 billion during the same period.[375] In 2001, the United States announced restrictions on US support for multilateral finance to the country and followed that with financial and travel sanctions against a section of the elite in the government and the military. It also banned transfers of defense items and services and suspended non-humanitarian government-to-government assistance to encourage good governance and end human rights abuses.

Ten years after independence, Mugabe took another controversial step. He partially nationalized the mining sector on the premise that foreign companies were plundering the country's resources, leaving little for Zimbabweans. Money was rippling out of the country like the gushing waters of the Zambezi River. It was discovered in 2005 that five mining companies had smuggled minerals worth $100 million that year alone. Mugabe's reasoning

---

[375] John Mutenyo and Brandon Routman, "Nationalization of the Zimbabwe Mining Sector: Another Blunder by the Mugabe Regime?" Brookings Institution, commentary, March 21, 2011.

was good, but the tactic was wrong. The government could have sat down with the mining companies and renegotiated fresh terms for the operational contracts. That way everyone would have been happy. But he didn't, deciding instead to take the more radical option.

But even that option would perhaps not have saved the drain of resources, as happened in Equatorial Guinea in 1998, when the government there demanded a renegotiation of a bad oil contract with ExxonMobil. President Obiang had made a similar complaint as Zimbabwe, saying the country had been duped into signing a document that favored the oil company. But even after the new deal was signed, giving Equatorial Guinea a few more billion dollars per year in revenue, and even after Mobil happily passed it as satisfactory, the contract still came out skewed in favor of the company. Obiang had refused outside technical support to fine-tune the agreement and instead relied on close allies who had inadequate qualifications to negotiate with a seasoned multinational like Mobil.

Consequently, in Zimbabwe, mining companies were left to their own whims, without proper government oversight of their activities. In one scandal involving the state-owned Zimbabwe Mining Development Corporation (ZMDC), the government was duped into believing that Canadile Miners, a joint venture partnership between ZMDC and South African Core Mining and Minerals (SACMM), had the capacity to fund mining operations at the controversial Marange gem fields. It turned out the joint venture had no money and had to borrow $1.5 billion to start operations. In the process, the government lost $2 billion. The joint venture was eventually disbanded. Like SACMM, Canadile Miners was owned by South Africans.

The 60,000-hectare Marange fields, "the richest diamond fields ever seen by several orders of magnitude,"[376] were for years

---

[376] "Fabulous Wealth in Marange Diamonds," *The Sunday Times* (South Africa), August 8, 2010.

surrounded by controversy over mining rights and abuses by the military officers, who forced locals to mine gems for them under threats of beatings. The military also used women and children to smuggle diamonds out of the mines, reports said. Those atrocious activities are not too far from what the archbishop of Canterbury, Rowan Williams, said during a sermon in Zimbabwe in 2011:

We have begun to see how this mineral wealth can become a curse – as it is so often has been in Africa, as people are killed and communities destroyed in the fight for diamonds that will forever be marked with the blood of the innocent.[377]

PAC, the Ottawa-based NGO—now known as IMPACT—surmised in a 2012 report that the scale of "illegality" at the Marange fields, situated four hours' drive from Harare, was "mind-blowing" and that the fields had enriched top government officials, military personnel, and international gem dealers. That report supported what Global Witness had found that same year, specifically blaming the security sector for being actively involved in the extraction of diamonds to fund overt missions, projects, and operations meant to keep the ZANU PF government in power.[378]

By 2013, Zimbabwe was in chaos. The national currency had collapsed to the extent of introducing a 100 trillion bank note, inflation was upwards of 100 percent, and the national treasury was bankrupt.[379] Things got worse as bribery, corruption, and impunity took over the day-to-day of activities in a country of 16 million people. The same year, TI ranked the country 157th out of 177 countries in the CPI. Corruption was both systemic and systematic, and many inside and outside the country saw that as part of Zimbabwe's "DNA."[380]

[377] "Archbishop of Canterbury on 'Healing' Zimbabwe Trip," BBC, news, October 9, 2011.
[378] Tawanda Majoni, "Why Marange Diamonds Corruption is Too Hot for Zacc," *The Standard*, November 27, 2016.
[379] Max Fisher, "How Bad is Robert Mugabe? The Answer, in Three Scathing Paragraphs," *The Washington Post*, August 1, 2013.
[380] Knox Chitiyo and Steve Kibble, "Zimbabwe's International Re-engagement: The Long Haul to Recovery," Chatham House, report, April 2014.

In another shocker, Mugabe announced in 2015 that $15 billion had been spirited out of Marange, a revelation which subsequently got the Parliamentary Energy Portfolio Committee on Mines to summon Vice President Kembo Mohadi, Finance Minister Patrick Chinamasa, former police chief Augustine Chihuri, and other senior officials in April 2018 to explain the disappearance. That probe did not go anywhere, and no one was prosecuted.

There is no doubt that if it were to be used properly, Zimbabwe's wealth would immensely improve the standard of living for its people, but figures show only 10 percent of the $800 million in revenues from exports of gold between 2010 and 2012 reached the national treasury;[381] the rest was squandered by the elites. The same story could be told of revenue from other profitable sectors of the economy, given than an estimated $1 billion yearly is lost to corruption in Zimbabwe.

Sakunda and the Dema Diesel Power Plant

When, in 2016, Zimbabwe faced acute power shortage due to massively reduced water levels at its principal Kariba Dam, it commissioned the first phase of the $250 million Dema Diesel Power Plant, located 40 kilometers from the capital of Harare, to provide temporary respite as the country waited for the expansion of the Kariba hydro-peaking station plant and the Hwange thermal project. The problem with the deal was the dubious manner in which the contract was concluded. It was awarded to President Mugabe's family under "unclear and controversial circumstances."[382] Moreover, the project, which was to be managed by the Zimbabwe Electricity Supply Authority, was not subjected to a mandatory environmental impact assessment and did not go through tendering.

---

[381] According to a statement made by the finance minister, Tendai Binti, during her budget presentation in 2013.

[382] Tatenda Dewa, "4 Big Reasons Why Dema Power Plant Is Bad for Zimbabwe – PDP," Nehanda Radio, September 28, 2016.

In an explosive exposé, independent journalist Elias Mambo alleged that a fuel procurement and distribution company called Sakunda Holdings was awarded the tender on December 24, 2015, even though it did not bid. The winner was actually an American company.

Sakunda won the tender because it was owned by Kuda Tagwurei, who had strong connections to the ruling ZANU PF. And his partner in Dema Diesel Power Plant, according to the report published in the *Independent* newspaper, was Derrick Chikore, brother of Simba Chikore, husband to President Mugabe's daughter Bona. The tender required the winning bidder to demonstrate experience in power generation, but "Sakunda Holdings never participated and, in any event, did not have this required experience."[383] Consequently, Sakunda hired a Glasgow-based business concern called Aggreko International Power Projects Ltd.—which was one of the bidders who lost—to provide expertise and equipment in an arrangement described as irregular and unlawful. In April, Aggreko announced it had signed a three-year contract with the government to provide 200 megawatts of diesel-fueled power per hour to the national grid. Sakunda was initially exempted from paying duty on the fuel imported for the project, but that privilege was suspended due to misuse of the facility. "What has happened is a classic case of rent-seeking: a local company with no capacity gets a contract irregularly, simply because it is local and its beneficiaries are politically connected, and then enters into a partnership deal with a foreign company with the capacity they lack."[384] No one was ever prosecuted.

The entry of President Emmerson Mnangagwa, after Mugabe left, did not end bribery and corruption scandals in Zimbabwe's high places. In July 2018, former energy and power development minister, Samuel Undenge, was found guilty and jailed for four years by a Harare court for issuing a contract worth $12,650

[383] Alex Magaisa, "Multinationals, Corruption, and Poverty in Zimbabwe: The Murky Case of the Dema Diesel Plant," analysis, August 2, 2016.
[384] Ibid.

without tendering. One-and-a-half years of that sentence was suspended for good conduct. Two years earlier, Undenge had hand-picked a PR company, Fruitful Communications, owned by Zanu PF lawmaker Psychology Maziwisa and a former news anchor at Zimbabwe Broadcasting Corporation, Oscar Pambuka, to do some work for the Zimbabwe Power Company without resorting to tender. The company was paid $12,000 for the work. Undenge was the first Mugabe-era Cabinet official to be convicted for corruption and jailed.

Mugabe died in September 2019 at the age of 95 while receiving treatment in Singapore.

PART SEVEN

CHAPTER 10

CHINA IN AFRICA

Beijing wants Africans to believe that it has their best interest at heart, but the frequent use of corruption by some of its state-owned or government-linked firms to gain unfair advantage demonstrate otherwise. – Joshua Meservey, Heritage Foundation

China's investments have increased exponentially in all sectors of African economies since the historic Forum for China–Africa Cooperation (FOCAC) in 2000. Today, China's presence on the continent is felt in all the major fields of development: infrastructure, telecommunications, energy, construction, oil, gas, and defense. Since the turn of the millennium, China's trade relationship with the continent has been growing at approximately 20 percent per year.[385]

While African countries see increased Chinese investment as a foundation for growth, some experts believe China is not investing in Africa for the sake of the African people; "China is in Africa for China,"[386] a belief which rubbishes Chinese leaders' perennial claim that their assistance to Africa is totally selfless and altruistic.[387] China disagrees.

A 2018 McKinsey & Company report says the reason why Chinese corporations are in Africa is simple: to exploit the people and take their resources. "It's the same thing European colonialists did during mercantile times, except worse. The Chinese corporations are trying to turn Africa into another Chinese continent. They are squeezing Africa for everything it is worth."[388] China did not care about the lives of the people of Darfur when it exchanged oil for arms in Sudan, though they knew the arms were to be used to murder people. What China cared was how many arms it could sell to Sudan. It provided arms and support to the "Janjaweed" militias who went from village to village burning families alive, brutalizing women and taking them for sex slavery.[389]

[385] Kartik Jayaram, Omid Kassiri, and Irene Yuan Sun, "The Closest Look Yet at Chinese Economic Engagement in Africa," McKinsey & Company, article, June 2017.

[386] Natalia Isaeva, "WikiLeaks Reveals China's Impure Intentions for Africa," The Borgen Project, November 12, 2013.

[387] "China's Aid to Africa: Monster or Messiah?" Brookings Institution, commentary, February 7, 2014.

[388] Panos Mourdoukoutas, "What is China Doing in Africa?" *Forbes,* article, August 4, 2018.

[389] Deborah Brautigam, *The Dragon's Gift: The Real Story of China in Africa* (Oxford University Press, 2009), 281.

Economists in governments and the private sector have produced tons of material on the China/Africa economic relationship, but none is as comprehensive as "Dance of the Lions and Dragons: How are Africa and China Engaging, and How Will the Partnership Evolve?" This report contains interviews with African businessmen and government leaders, as well as the owners and managers of more than 1,000 Chinese firms spread across eight African nations: Angola, Kenya, Nigeria, Ethiopia, Tanzania, South Africa, Côte d'Ivoire, and Zambia.[390]

The report narrates stories of both big and small companies in rural and urban Africa, such as the ceramic tile-making factory, Twyford—a joint venture between two Chinese firms, the SunDa Group and Keda Clean Energy Company—which sits unassumingly in the dusty little town of Kajiado outside Kenya's capital of Nairobi, to mega-projects in agriculture, banking, housing, roads, transport and logistics, and information communications technology, among others. Twyford provides 1,500 jobs to the traditionally nomadic Maasai people and others and stands out as an example of how lives in remote areas of the country can be transformed with an injection of moderate investment. But they also warned Chinese and African actors to address issues of corruption. While it is agreed that Chinese investments in Africa have spurred development, they have also introduced dishonest practices and perpetuated a system of corruption in Africa that harms ordinary Africans.[391]

A senior manager of Exim Bank, which finances most of the projects in Africa, says that by 2025, China would have channeled a trillion dollars to Africa in investments and loans.[392] That is far more than what the West is expected to deliver to African countries. For the

---

[390] Kartik Jayaram, Omid Kassiri, and Irene Yuan Sun, "The Closest Look Yet at Chinese Economic Engagement in Africa," McKinsey & Company, June 2017.

[391] Joshua Meservey, "Chinese Corruption in Africa Undermines Beijing's Rhetoric about Friendship with the Continent," The Heritage Foundation, analysis, August 8, 2018.

[392] Tom Burgis, *The Looting Machine: Warlords, Oligarchs, Corporations, Smugglers, and the Theft of Africa's Wealth* (Public Affairs, 2015), 137.

relationship between China and Africa to prosper, issues of graft, safety, and cultural barriers have to be addressed.

Unlike many Western nations that are hindered by tough regulations from engaging in bribery and corruption overseas, China sees nothing wrong in dancing with the lions. It disregards its own laws and is quite comfortable with the idea of bribing overseas officials. In fact, "the more the West enforces anti-bribery laws, the greater the incentive for China not to enforce,"[393] says US anti-corruption specialist Andrew Spalding of the University of Richmond. To Chinese companies, bribery overseas is the *modus operandi* of doing business. They pay "tips," "baksheesh," "chai," "hongo," "gasosa," "laalush," "dash," or whichever colloquial phrase one may want to use to describe bribes, in order to secure contracts.

The Chinese anti-bribery law completely ignores corrupt Chinese nationals abroad, partly because of lack of political will in fighting corruption that doesn't have a domestic impact at home.[394] China also operates within the so-called "Beijing Consensus," a concept that stresses non-interference in the affairs of sovereign states. This is in contrast with the United States' FCPA and United Kingdom's Bribery Act, which have been very active since they were established in 1977 and 2010 respectively. Companies registered in the United States and United Kingdom and nationals from those countries risk being heavily fined and jailed if found violating the FCPA and Bribery Act provisions. Through bribery, Chinese companies avoid rudimentary requirements such as feasibility studies or due diligence, unlike their counterparts in the West, and go to Africa without any strategic plans.[395] In addition, Chinese investors are generally secretive about their financial information, and some maintain two sets of books to deceive authorities and avoid taxes.

[393] Jeffrey Young, "Corruption Concerns Taint Burgeoning China-Africa Trade," *VOA,* news, September 1, 2014.
[394] John Tso, "The Global Anti-Corruption Blog," commentary, May 14, 2018.
[395] Mark Kapchanga, "China Corruption in Africa," *The Caribbean Current*, November 5, 2013.

There are plenty of examples of China's malpractice on the continent. In the DRC, a Chinese company paid a staggering $350 million to grease government officials in order to win a multibillion-dollar mining deal called Sicomines in 2007. The $9 billion deal, described as one of the largest agreements of its kind on record, eventually collapsed after China had disbursed $3 billion, and the project stayed moribund for years until China's Exim Bank issued new money to revive it.

In Cameroon, Chinese companies bribe government officials to export timber illegally. Greenpeace Africa, a non-government environmental organization, says the country's rain forests are vanishing rapidly from illegal logging, threatening the ecosystem of thousands of plants and hundreds of mammal species as well as the livelihood of four million Bantu and Pygmy people. The Chinese do the same in the DRC, where they are decimating forests for "red wood," known in China as *hongmu* and in the DRC as *mukula*, which is used to make Chinese furniture. Tons of *mukula* wood leaves the DRC every month for the biggest processing plant in Zhang Jiagang in eastern China. Chinese businesspeople also use locals to chop down trees illegally in Mozambique and Angola and bribe officials to look the other way as they transport the timber to ports destined for China.

Cases of Chinese bribery, which are too many to list, have been reported across Africa from east to west, south to north. To obtain quicker results, Chinese companies go for the top honchos, such as the wives, sons, or daughters of the highest individual in the land. In Equatorial Guinea, the state-owned CCCC went for the influential son of President Obiang and allegedly gave him $19 million to get a roads contract in the 2000s.

China and Equatorial Guinea have had cordial relations since the regime of Nguema. Although those ties were temporarily discontinued after Nguema's departure, they came to life under Obiang, who had visited China at least half a dozen times before taking over the presidency. Since then, Chinese companies continue to dominate Equatorial Guinea's economy through multinationals such as Huawei, China Dalian International, Senohydro, China Roads and Bridges Corporation, the Heilongjiang East Co., and Zhongxin, among others, and for survival they use cash and other benefits to buy influence.

In Equatorial Guinea, China has built roads, improved the water supply in cities and towns, and built a number of office structures, including an office of the president, a stadium, and other projects, in exchange for access to the country's oil and timber resources. Two Chinese timber manufacturing companies, Sijifo Industrial and Sinosa, were given concessions of 50,000 hectares each, while the Hong Kong–based timber company Vicwood had two concessions of 80,000 hectares.[396] All those contracts had consideration of "commissions" to members of the ruling elite. That same year, China extended a $2 billion loan to the Malabo government, to be repaid in oil and to be used mainly on Chinese products and projects contracted to Chinese companies. Was it a win-win situation? One writer was rather cynical: "Thanks to this deal, Beijing gets the oil, Chinese companies and workers get the money, and Equatorial Guinea gets some facilities and fancy buildings."[397]

Through collusion with local officials, Chinese companies have also been cited for shoddy work and flooding the continent with poor-quality goods. In Zambia, a major road linking the capital Lusaka and Chirundu and leading to South Africa, Mozambique, and Swaziland washed away during heavy rains in 2009, while a $12 million bridge embarrassingly collapsed in Kenya in 2017 two weeks after President Uhuru Kenyatta inaugurated it. Some of those poorly constructed infrastructure projects have caused

---

[396] Nigel Sizer and Dominiek Plouvier, "Increased Investment and Trade by Transnational Logging Companies in ACP-Countries: Implications for Sustainable Forest Management and Conservation," WWF-International, report, 2000, 54.

[397] Mario Esteban, "The Chinese Amigo: Implications for the Development of Equatorial Guinea," *The China Quarterly*, no. 199 (September 2009), 667–685.

deaths.

In Angola, the Chinese-built $8 million Luanda General Hospital, built by China Overseas Engineering Group Company, had to close down in 2010, barely four years after construction, after deep cracks emerged in the walls of the pediatrics and gynecology wings.[398] And in 2018, Zimbabwe returned thousands of condoms supplied by a Chinese company, Beijing Daxiang and His Friends Technology Company, saying they were too small to accommodate the typical Zimbabwean man.[399]

There have also been complaints throughout Africa about China's work practices. They bring in too many Chinese workers to the disadvantage of local labor, pay African workers poorly, subject them to physical abuse, disregard their safety, evade taxes, and above all, violate national anti-corruption regulations. Several examples have been given above about their atrocities in the mining sites of Angola, Zimbabwe, and Zambia. In Kenya, a video showing a Chinese manager insulting the Kenyan president caused consternation on social media.[400] The manager was deported.

In many countries, Chinese nationals are gradually replacing Africans in the informal sector. They hawk cheap products on the streets and participate in retail business to the detriment of Africans. Such activities anger locals, who fear losing their sovereignty to foreigners from the East.

African leaders' greed

Many of the travels to China by African leaders are funded by the Chinese, even as the leaders draw huge allowances from their own exchequers. When the Zambian minister of information and broadcasting, Fackson Shamenda, took a delegation to visit the

---

[398] "Chinese-Built Hospital Risks Collapse in Angola: State Radio," *Terra Daily,* July 6, 2010.

[399] Laura Zhou, "Chinese-Made Condoms Too Small, Zimbabwe's Health Minister Complains," *The South China Morning Post,* March 1, 2018.

[400] "Chinese Businessman Arrested After Describing Kenyans, Including the President, as "Monkey People," Agence France-Presse, September 6, 2018.

Huawei and ZET plants in May 2012, they were lavishly treated to free services, even though they had collected allowances for lodging, food, per diem, and local transport from the Zambian Treasury.[401]

The same happens when African leaders troop to the regularly held China–Africa Summit in Beijing. Apart from the air travel expenses, everything else, including five-star hotel accommodation and local transport, were met by the Beijing authorities, allowing them to save huge amounts of allowances they had carried with them from their home countries. They were also showered with expensive gifts from their host on top of multimillion-dollar, no-strings-attached commitments from China.

Those who chose not to fly commercial hired private jets at great cost. Zimbabwean President Emmerson Mnangagwa leased a luxury jet from a Switzerland-based aviation company at a cost of $2.3 million when he travelled to China in April 2018 instead of using the national airline. He returned home with a trolley of goods, including loans for mega-projects in his country and personal gifts from President Xi Jinping.

Kenya's president, Uhuru Kenyatta, went to China for the first time in August 2013, less than three months after being denied a "photo opportunity" with British prime minister David Cameron during a conference on Somalia in London and two months after being ignored by US president Barack Obama who, during a visit to Africa that June, chose to overfly Kenya and land in Tanzania instead. Presumably the Americans did not want to be seen with a man then facing criminal charges at the International Criminal Court at the Hague following the post-election violence of 2007. His visit to China and Russia was therefore seen as thumbing his nose at those Western governments. But in essence, at least for China, it was also a follow-up to a relationship built by his predecessor, Mwai Kibaki, who had travelled to Beijing in 2005

[401] "Chinese Companies Engaged by PF for Digital Migration Banned in Algeria, investigated in Uganda, Nigeria," Zambian Watchdog, article, June 11, 2012.

and signed numerous agreements of cooperation.

In 2018, a few months after attending the FOCAC in Beijing in September, Uhuru was back in China with a delegation of farmers to negotiate agricultural and trade pacts, in particular for the export of Kenyan cashew nuts, avocadoes, and mangoes to the Asian country. Some Kenyans commenting on social media about the visit felt Kenyatta was giving China too much priority and costing his government too much in expenses and expensive loans. Kenyatta was back again in China in April 2019 to ask for more Chinese loans, even after being reminded by pundits that Kenya's debt was close to $6 billion. He expected to bag $3.8 billion for the extension of the SGR line from Naivasha in the Rift Valley to Kisumu, on Lake Victoria, but China turned him down, arguing that the line would be unsustainable. Instead, China loaned Kenya $6.7 billion for two other projects.

China knows how to soften the souls and minds of African leaders. In 2012, China spent $200 million to build the AU headquarters in Addis Ababa and gave a $31.6 million interest-free grant to the Economic Community of West African States to build its head office in Nigeria.

By 2016, China had expended $140 billion in debt financing in Africa. But when it comes to bilateral financial arrangements, China's loan money is not always spent prudently as agreed. For example, only half of the loan of $144 million advanced to Zimbabwe for a water and sewerage project was disbursed. An audit showed some of the money was used to pay kickbacks to officials to get the project implemented. Data also shows that African leaders use Chinese loans to benefit their home villages. A study by the US associate professor Paul Raschky at Monash University and his team on 1,650 projects in 49 countries showed $83.3 billion disbursed for development between 2000 and 2012 went to the birth regions of those in leadership.[402]

Some claim Chinese aid to Africa is all about the bounty of riches in

---

[402] "The (Mis)use of Chinese Aid in Africa," Research Story, research, June 14, 2016.

the continent: oil and gas, timber, gold, diamond, copper, and other products; and that China wants "to establish a firm control of Africa's natural resources"[403] to eventually usurp them. Others feel China is in Africa to spy, and allege the building housing the computer network it donated to the AU headquarters in Addis Ababa in 2012 had a back door to facilitate the daily transfer of data to servers in Shanghai,[404] and that the telecommunications equipment Beijing gave the Kenya National Security and Intelligence Service in 2018 was being used to infiltrate the African spy agency. The AU discovered the bug in 2017 and replaced all the servers donated by the Chinese and installed its own. The African organization condemned China for the hacking, but Chinese officials called the allegations "absurd." In the meantime, individual African countries remain mum for fear of antagonizing Beijing.

The narration about spying could be true. In 2014, 77 Chinese nationals were arrested in a house in Nairobi with an assortment of sophisticated hacking and telecommunications equipment capable of infiltrating banks, mobile money systems, and ATMs. The illegal cyber-center was described as the biggest of its kind in Africa, capable of causing irreparable damage to the financial sector. They were charged and pleaded not guilty. Twenty more Chinese were arrested in April 2016, and another five in October 2018, on similar charges. Their fate remains a mystery.

In 2010, WikiLeaks, quoting American documents, reported that China could also be providing military and intelligence support to Kenya with the help of a corrupt official. A memo from the American embassy in Nairobi in February 2010 did not divulge the name of the official nor give any evidence to support its allegations, but the

---

[403] "Africa at Risk or Rising? The Role of Europe, North America, and China on the Continent," Conference organized by the Stanley Foundation and the Aspen Atlantic Group. A Stanley Foundation Policy Dialogue Brief, May 4–6, 2007, 8.

[404] "Addis-Abeba, le siege de l'Union africaine espionne par Pekin," *Le Monde*, January 26, 2018.

documents were emphatic that China was providing weapons to Kenya "in support of its Somali policies"[405] and increasing their involvement with the country's intelligence agency. The only hint on how far the two countries were cooperating came in 2017, when President Kenyatta assured China that Kenya was ready to deepen its cooperation with China in the areas of defense and security.

The American embassy in Nairobi claimed China was also supplying ammunition, as well as textiles for making military and police uniforms, through the Chinese Military Import-Export Corporation (CATIC), a state-owned defense company. Kenya denied the allegations, but immediately after President Kenyatta returned from the China–Africa Summit in Beijing in September 2018, Kenyan police were outfitted with blue colors, resembling China's police, a development that was greeted with both criticisms and cynicism from Kenyans. "Must we copy Chinese in these uniforms?"[406] asked Kenya citizen Mary Muchai on social media.

In June 2018, Major General Hu Changming, director of the Office for International Military Cooperation, told a meeting of the China–Africa defense and security forum in Beijing that China was ready to help African countries tackle complex security issues ranging from piracy to epidemics, a clear indication that the Asian country was expanding its sphere of influence on the continent from building infrastructure to broad military assistance.

ZTE and graft

Another major Chinese firm that has stoked controversies around the world is the technology conglomerate ZTE Corporation, formed by the China Ministry of Aerospace. It was accused of corruption in 19 countries—Algeria, the DRC, India, Ethiopia, Pakistan, Papua New Guinea, Tajikistan, Thailand, Mongolia, Malaysia, Kyrgyzstan,

---

[405] "Chinese Engagement in Kenya," US Embassy cable leaked by Wikileaks, February 17, 2010.
[406] Michael Musyoka, "Kenyans React to New Police Uniforms," Kenyans. co.ke, article, September 13, 2018.

Kazakhstan, Zambia, the Philippines, Myanmar, Nigeria, Kenya, Liberia, and Benin—and flagged by the United States for allegedly training and sending scientists and businessmen abroad under diplomatic cover to spy for Beijing.

In 2010, ZTE was contracted to install a security communications monitoring network for Abuja and Lagos in the wake of attacks by the terror group Boko Haram. By 2016, the $470 million project had become a white elephant with "exploding batteries and cameras that see nothing."[407] The citizenry raised issues of corruption and slipshod work by ZTE. A joint committee of police, public procurement, debt management, and IT officials was formed to find out if due process was followed in awarding the tender to the company. A report of that investigation was not made public, but it was suspected the deal was done "with clandestine connivance of top Nigerian officials."[408]

Also terminating a contract with ZTE was Zambia. In 2013, the country cancelled a $210 million contract for closed circuit television cameras with the Chinese company on allegations of corruption. The contract was entered into by a senior government official in the Ministry of Home Affairs without an open tender procedure. "It smelt of corruption," Cornelius Mweetwa, Chairman of the African Parliamentarian Network Against Corruption, said.[409] If the tender, intended to assist in crime prevention, had not been cancelled, Zambia would have lost $100 million.

The graft-tainted ZTE project did not stop Zambia from contracting another Chinese company to deliver the country's digital television migration program that same year. However, it wasn't long before the authorities realized that the $270 million project with the Star

---

[407] David Z. Morris, "China's ZTE Under Investigation in Nigerian Security Network Failure," *Fortune*, February 16, 2016.
[408] Adewole Martins, "How Chinese Firm, ZTE, Scammed Nigeria of $470 Million in Security Contract," *The Eagle,* online, December 15, 2015.
[409] Michael Malakata, "Zambia Terminates $210m Contract over Corruption Allegations," IDG News Service, September 11, 2013.

Software Technologies company was infested with malfeasance. The government quickly cancelled the contract, only to give it back to the same company in 2014. "We see something rotten here because this contract is not clean," said Amos Kalunga, a telecommunications analyst at the Computer Society of Zambia.[410] The leadership of Zambia has been blamed on several occasions for entering into shady contractual arrangements with foreign companies without conducting due diligence or following proper tender procedures.

ZTE was investigated in 10 other countries. In Algeria in 2012, two ZTE executives and one from Chinese telecommunications company Huawei were found guilty, jailed for 10 years, and fined $65,000 for bribing officials of Algerie Telecom in exchange for contracts. ZTE's Dong Tao and Chen Zhibo, and Huawei's Xiao Chunfa, were sentenced in absentia for giving an employee of Algeria Telecom, Chami Medjdoub, a sum of $10 million in bribe money between 2003 and 2006. Medjdoub was sentenced to 18 years in prison and fined $65,000. ZTE and Huawei were also banned by the Algerian government from tendering for telecommunications contracts for two years. They denied involvement, saying they were victims of fraud by the employees.

In 2013, Kenya awarded ZTE a $17 million contract to deliver communication equipment to the Kenya Police. However, the civil service boss, Francis Kimemia, cancelled the deal, claiming the contract was heavily overpriced and should have cost no more than $12 million. He alleged some Internal Ministry officials had received kickbacks to influence the awarding of the contract. ZTE appealed the decision to the Kenya Public Procurement Administrative Review Board, but the appeal was denied, and the decision was reaffirmed by the High Court in 2014.

In 2015, numerous people admitted paying bribes on behalf of ZTE to officials in Kenya, Zambia, Nigeria, and Liberia, among other countries. A June 2015 report of the Norway-based Council of

[410] Ibid.

Ethics, which traces corporate ethical standards, assumed that the large number of allegations in many different countries indicated ZTE was making systematic use of corruption in its business.

In June 2018, ZTE was reported to have undermined an American telecoms company, Universal Telephone Exchange, to win a contract in Liberia and in other West African nations through bribing government officials. In 2003, Universal entered into negotiations with Liberian officials for an upgrade of the country's telecommunications system. ZTE's American subsidiary knew about the deal when Universal asked it to provide switching equipment for the project. However, the Liberian Telecommunications Corp. (LTC) offered the contract to Universal. That is when the Chinese-owned company approached Liberian officials to cancel the contract in favor of ZTE.

Alfred D. Bargor, the deputy managing director of LTC, admitted being offered a lifetime commission of 5 percent of ZTE's revenue from sales to LTC, in addition to a $30,000 cash kickback, which Bargor received from ZTE representative Liu Ruipeng. The same offer was given to Amara M. Kromah, the LTC's managing director, in addition to a $30,000 cash payment and an all-expenses-paid holiday to China.

Also bribed, according to documents filed by the American company in a Dallas court, was the then-chairman of the transitional government of Liberian president Gyude Bryant, government officials, and some judges. ZTE denied all charges of bribery, saying it adhered to "a high standard of ethics and integrity in its business activities throughout the world."[411]

---

[411] Annie Wu, "Court Records Reveal ZTE's Corruption Scheme in Liberia," *The Epoch Times*, June 3, 2018.

CHAPTER 11

OF CHINA: A KENYA CASE STUDY

"The only innovation China has brought to Kenya is the envelope full of cash." – The Clean Boardroom

Kenya and China have maintained business relations since before independence in 1963, when the former enjoyed an advantage in exports of raw cotton, pyrethrum, and sisal fiber, while the latter sold tea, base metals, and sundry manufactured goods to Kenya. There was no whiff of corruption then. However, after independence, as China diversified its exports to Kenya and changed its investment policies abroad, bribery and corruption became a bane of the Chinese presence in the country.

And although there followed years of tense moments between the pro-West President Jomo Kenyatta and his pro-East nemesis Oginga Odinga, relations between Kenya and China improved greatly in the 1970s with the coming to power of President Daniel arap Moi in 1978. The two countries signed a number of bilateral economic agreements which resulted in the construction of the first huge Chinese project in Kenya in 1987: the Moi International Sports Center at Kasarani outside Nairobi, to which Kenya contributed 48 percent of the total cost of $52 million. Today, dozens of private Chinese companies and state-owned corporations are engaged in projects in the country, mainly of an infrastructural nature.

In the meantime, Xi Jinping came to power in 2013 and declared a renewed commitment to fight corruption in his country. Since then, thousands of state officials have been convicted in China, and dozens of them have been executed. Multinationals and individuals have also been punished in China—as well as in their own jurisdictions at home—for bribing Chinese government officials. When three former employees of the Norwegian firm Norconsult were found to have paid $146,500 to Tanzanian officials of the Dar es Salaam Water and Sanitation (DAWASA) WB project in 2011, they were deported, and when they got back to Norway, they were convicted and one of them jailed. However, China's story overseas is different. Chinese people freely bribe foreign officials overseas but face no consequences at home.

When, in 2015, two senior officials of a state-owned Chinese construction firm were caught attempting to bribe Kenyan officials, the incident was treated like any other case of petty corruption in the East African nation, and in China it was seemingly ignored. Liuy Yabin and Tang Ju of the China Road and Bridge Corporation were arrested for offering bribes of $285 and $1,000 respectively to avoid being charged for overloading company trucks. The bribes were relatively small considering the size of the project, but they were in line with the local mantra of *kitu kidogo,* "something small," that Kenyan officials often ask in return for favors. The Chinese executives were convicted and fined, but no further action was taken against them by either the company or the Kenyan government.

In another incident, three Chinese officials of the China-built SGR were nabbed in November 2018 for trying to bribe Kenyan officials with $5,000 to influence the outcome of fraud investigations which were being carried out in the railway operations. Investigators found $10,000 was being stolen daily through ticket fraud. Li Gen, head of transport; Li Xiaowu, security manager; and Sun Xin, a staff member, who were employed by the state-owned CRBC, were charged in court.

This is how they executed the scam: employees created a number of refunds for tickets already issued to passengers and then diverted the refunds elsewhere. The high number of refunds triggered suspicion within the Kenya Railways Corporation (KRC), which launched an investigation. When the Chinese employees learned of the probe, they attempted to bribe the director of criminal investigations (DCI), who immediately arrested them. They denied the allegations. As of May 2019, the fate of the accused was unknown.

Another case of Chinese bribery emerged in August 2019 when the anti-corruption authority EACC reported that a Chinese-owned company had bribed officials of the state-run parastatal, Lake Basin Development Authority (LBDA), to secure a $2.5 million contract for the construction of a shopping mall in Kisumu on the shores of Lake Victoria. The company reportedly inflated the cost of the project to compensate for the kickbacks which were reportedly paid out in the form of cash, apartments and shops. The managing director of the Chinese-owned Erdermann Properties Ltd., Zeyun Yang, and several former and serving officials of LBDA were arrested and charged with corruption-related offences.

The above incidents reinforce the notion advanced by many Western governments that China uses its state-owned companies to fuel corruption abroad in violation of its own 2011 law that criminalizes the bribery of foreign public officials. The Criminal Law of the People's Republic of China, which was adopted by the Second Meeting of the Fifth Session of the National People's Congress on July 1, 1979, and which came into effect in January 1980, bars Chinese officials from giving "property to any foreign public official or official of an international public organization for the purpose of seeking illegitimate commercial benefit."[412] That provision is in line with the obligations of the United Nations Convention Against Corruption (UNCAC) and the OECD, of which China is a member.

The two cases of Chinese bribery in Kenya were only the tip of an iceberg—a small part of dozens of scandals that have dogged Chinese-built projects in Kenya. The $4 billion SGR project links the coastal town of Mombasa and the capital of Nairobi over a stretch of 400 kilometers. The railway contract to the CCCC, the parent company of the CRBC, was issued without competitive bidding and "was apparently made possible by a unilateral decision by the Kenyan President [Uhuru Kenyatta]."[413] The Washington-based China Africa Research Initiative (CARI) also talked of the "widespread perception that established that Kenyan political elites

---

[412] "Bribery and Corruption 2019: China," Global Legal Insights, website, 2019.
[413] Uwe Wissenbach and Yuan Wang, "African Politics Meets Chinese Engineers: The Chinese-Built Standard Gauge Railway Project in Kenya and East Africa," (working paper, no. 13, China Africa Research Initiative, June 2017).

pocketed large sums as kickbacks from the SGR."[414] That explains why the executive branch of government took a personal interest in the initiation, construction, and operations of the SGR. The railway is part of the "Belt and Road Initiative" funded by Chinese banks and Chinese multilateral financial institutions to open East and Central Africa to international trade and investment. Like in all major corruption scandals involving senior Kenyan government officials, it is difficult to know precisely who among the elites benefited from the kickbacks and facilitation payments from the project, whose cost was allegedly grossly inflated.

Kenyans were outraged not only by what they saw as the excessive cost of the project compared to similar but more modern projects elsewhere, but by the government's inability to explain how the huge Chinese loans would be repaid given the country's other pressing domestic needs.

In December 2018, Kenya's auditor general, Edward Ouko, warned that the nation could lose its strategic port of Mombasa if it defaulted on a $2.3 billion loan advanced by the Chinese bank. The payment agreement "substantively" specifies that should KRC not be able to meet its obligations, the revenue of the KPA, which was offered as a security for the loan, would be used to clear the debt,[415] even though Chinese officials have denied any plan to take over the port. The bad news is that the repayment could take years, since the KPA's annual revenue as of June 2018 was only $4.2 billion. Statistics early in 2019 showed the SGR was losing money on both the passenger and cargo services. In the first year of its operation, the train service made a loss of Sh 10 billion (approximately $100 million), according to the Kenya ministry of transport.

---

[414] Ibid.
[415] "Report: Kenya Risks Losing Port of Mombasa to China," *The Maritime Executive*, December 20, 2018.

But what was even more disturbing was that, though favored by Kenya, the CCCC—a publicly-traded, multinational engineering and construction company—had been debarred by the WB for eight years in 2009 for carrying out fraudulent practices during the building of a bank-funded Philippines national roads improvement and management project. Although the ban had expired at the time of the SGR tendering, the bloat of misconduct was still hanging from its neck like an albatross.

Two Kenyan parliamentary committees, Transport and Public Investment, together with the EACC, investigated allegations of corruption in the project and questioned top treasury and railway officials over the actual cost of the project, but found nothing wrong—even though the original cost of $2.1 billion had risen systematically to $3.2 billion and then to $4.5 billion.

TI said in a 2018 report that Chinese, along with Israeli, firms were among international contractors who regularly bribed Kenyan officials to win lucrative tenders in multibillion-dollar public infrastructure contracts.[416] A classic example was the contract to install security cameras along Nairobi's major streets in 2012 by the Ministry of Nairobi Metropolitan Development. The deal with China's Nanjing Les Information Technology Limited was so nebulous that it raised eyebrows. The $4.3 million arrangement was for the installation, testing, and commissioning of 42 CCTV cameras. Either Kenyan officials did not read or understand the fine print on the agreement or they were bribed to ignore its contents. Moreover, Kenyan authorities left everything to the Chinese and did nothing to seek guarantees of the efficacy of long-term use of the cameras before the Chinese technicians left. Within a few years, most of the cameras had stopped working. When Kenyan officials went back to Nanjing to ask for maintenance work to be done, they were told that repairs were not included in the contract and were asked to pay an additional $720,000 to mend 26 faulty

---

[416] "How Israel, China Firms Bribe Kenyan Officials," *The Business Daily,* September 25, 2018.

gadgets. But since the company was yet to officially hand over the project to Kenya, the latter could not undertake the repairs on its own. Kenya's Auditor General, Edward Ouko, said the whole project "was failure costing taxpayers millions of shillings."[417] The central government, which should have investigated how the deal was consummated, remained mum, a traditionally clear sign of a corruption cover-up.

Concerns that Chinese companies were manipulating Kenyan government officials have often been expressed by foreign countries friendly to Kenya. A US Congressional subcommittee on Africa and global human rights, held in Washington in March 2018, was presented with a paper claiming some of the contracts between China and Kenya were "shady, greased with bribes and other antecedents, such as all-expenses paid shopping trips to China and scholarships to Kenyan elite." It added that "China plays a big part in corrupting leaders to gain business advantages through corruption within Africa, especially in Kenya."[418]

Power wrangles

The much-maligned Chinese conglomerate ZTE has also been involved in shenanigans in Kenya. In 2016, its subsidiary, ZTE Kenya Limited, was named for not paying corporation and withholding taxes amounting to $14 million since 2011. It was also engulfed in a dispute over the installation of electricity meters to Kenya Power, the state-run electricity company. The power tiff became public after a competing Chinese company, Shenzhen Star Instrument Company Limited, filed a complaint with the Public Procurement Administrative Review Board (PPARB) in 2016, seeking the cancellation of a $2 million tender to ZTE involving

---

[417] John Mutua, "City Hall Contractors Blamed for Sh437 million CTTV Glitch," *The Business Daily*, February 28, 2019.
[418] US House of Representatives, "China in Africa: The New Colonialism? Hearing Before the Sub-Committee on Africa, Global Health, Global Human Rights, and International Organizations of the Committee on Foreign Affairs," 115th Congress. 2nd session, serial no. 115-117, March 7, 2018.

the procurement, designing, supplying, and installation of an advanced metering infrastructure system.

After studying the complaint, the PPARB read mischief in the way the tender was awarded, and the contract was eventually suspended and re-advertised. Kenya Power, previously known as the East African Power and Lighting (EAP&L) and later as Kenya Power and Lighting (KP&L), is one of several energy sector parastatals named in a number of tendering and financial scandals. An internal audit in 2018 revealed cases in which Kenya Power employees colluded with private companies and individuals to win tenders and even steal transformers. Parastatal employees received bribes and kickbacks, which they shared. In addition, some of the hundreds of companies pre-qualified for parastatal tenders were found not to be registered, while others were owned or associated with personnel in the power company. That contravened the Public Procurement and Disposal Act, which calls for transparency and accountability in the awarding of public tenders.

In July 2018, several Kenya Power executives and directors of private companies were charged in court for irregularly issuing tenders and fraudulently receiving thousands of dollars for a labor and transport services tender. They included Ken Tarus, the managing director and CEO; his predecessor, Ben Chumo; the general manager for corporate affairs, Beatrice Meso; and the general manager for regional coordination, Peter Mwicigi, as well as seven other top managers. They pleaded not guilty to conspiring to commit an economic crime between 2012 and 2018. Two companies, one Kenyan and another Indian, allegedly conspired with officials at Kenya Power to purchase thousands of defective transformers worth $4 million, which were unusable. Dozens of employees of the power firm were sacked. But in October, it was discovered a crucial file relevant to the case had mysteriously disappeared from Kenya Power thus occasioning a delay in court proceedings. Three company workers were charged with conspiracy to defeat justice.

The huge amounts of money involved in energy projects and the ease with which contractors are willing to pay kickbacks to get their way are enough incentives to create turfs not only among civil servants but also among lawmakers in Parliament. A good example is the administrative and political infighting that surrounded the Thwake multi-purpose dam in Makueni, east of Nairobi. At the center of the kerfuffle was China's Gezhouba Group, a company blacklisted by the AfDB, which provided 65 percent of the financing, and the WB. The initial decision by a principal secretary of the ministry of water and irrigation —against the advice of the AfDB and the Kenya Attorney General—was to give the tender to Sinohydro Tianjin Engineering Limited, which quoted $391 million, but a minister objected and wanted it to go to Gezhouba, which had quoted $365 million. Boardroom fights continued for months, with each side rooting for their favored side until President Kenyatta stepped in and removed the permanent secretary from the ministry, allowing the minister to have his way. Suspicion was rife that personal interests took the higher ground during the processing stage.

That was not the only example of wrangles in government over contracts. In one instance, similar wrangles caused the Hong Kong Offshore Oil Services Limited (HOOSL) to quietly walk away with a cool $14 million from a deal involving the drilling of 15 to 20 geothermal wells in Kenya's Rift Valley region in 2016. The $14 million was an advance representing a portion of the $590 million energy project, which was commissioned by the state-run Geothermal Development Company. The money was to come from the Frankfurt-based German development bank Kreditanstalt für Wiederaufbau (KfW). Called the Baringo-Silali Block, the project was to be undertaken in three phases, to produce 100 megawatts of power each. An exposé published by the Standard in Nairobi in April 2019 showed how the deal, intended to power the country's manufacturing sector, was bungled by Kenyan officials. Although Kenyan officials did not want to admit it, indications were clear that money had changed hands with the foreign company. By February

2019, the work had not started, though the agreement called for the commencement of drilling within three months of the advance payment, and HOOSL could not be traced in China.

CHAPTER 12

_____

AFRICA THE DUMP!

Africa has become a dumping ground for the world's unwanted goods. – Darren Olivier

Toxic waste

Every day, seven days a week, Martin treks to the massive Dandora landfill on the fringes of Kenya's capital from his shack perched in some nearby bushes. Together with dozens of other grimy-looking young boys, men, women, and stray dogs, the 16-year-old primary school drop-out digs into mountains of medical, industrial, and household waste to scavenge for anything to sell—copper wire, recyclable pieces of old electronic equipment, toys, and even food scraps. In a normal day, he could earn up to $2, which he uses to buy food.

The 30-acre landfill is the largest in Nairobi—and the final destination of most of the city's mammoth amount of waste. Every few hours, rickety contractor-owned trucks bursting with trash drive in for deliveries amid smoldering toxic smoke from the waste, which shoots up into the sky like a volcano disposing ash plume. Since the dump is unrestricted, city authorities have no clue whether all the waste dumped there is from local establishments or part of a global conspiracy to dispose of dangerous material in Africa. What has been established is that some of material found at Dandora, including lead, mercury, cadmium, and PCBs, are dangerous to human life and are likely to imperil Martin's health and the health of many others.

Ironically, the Dandora landfill, established in 1975 with WB funds, sits only a few kilometers from the Gigiri headquarters of the UN Environmental Program (UNEP)—the global environmental watchdog. The UNEP is fully aware of the dangers posed by the dump but has found little inspiration from the government to do anything to mitigate the situation.

Of most concern is that dozens of African countries, among them Ghana, Nigeria, Somalia, Ivory Coast, Guinea, Zimbabwe, Guinea-Bissau, South Africa, and Kenya, are dumping grounds for toxic waste that includes obsolete electronic gadgets and hazardous medical junk from abroad. Sometimes it is all about money. In

1988, *The New York Times* reported that Guinea-Bissau had entered into a five-year contract to bury 15 million tons of waste from European tanneries and pharmaceutical companies in return for a yearly payment of $120 million. In Congo, the government agreed to store a million tons of chemical waste from a European enterprise for $84 million. The arrangements were so controversial within and outside the countries that they had to be abandoned.[419] Waste dumping is now a multibillion-dollar business that enriches some and kills others.

Yearly, Kenya alone receives 15 tons of unwanted electronics from overseas, including old refrigerators, unserviceable television sets, mobile phones, digital cameras, computers, and printers, say UNEP officials. All this waste is harmful to human beings and animals, as it seeps into the ground and contaminates the land, water, and air.[420]

Thus, on the periphery of most African capitals, toxic smoke billows from the smoldering remains of irreparable electronic goods. In Accra, Ghana, the 20-acre Agbogbloshie landfill is a standing example of how Africa is used by industrial countries as a dumping ground for dangerous waste. Tens of thousands of old, broken pieces of electronic equipment litter the vast e-waste dump. Within the perimeter of the dump are small stalls where electronic goods coming from overseas are dismantled and prepared for sale by people oblivious to the risks. While the UNEP says 85 percent of the waste dumped in Ghana and other West African nations is local, the other 15 percent is suspected to consist of imports deemed hazardous. Several West African countries, among them Ivory Coast, Liberia, Togo, and Gambia, have enacted legislation providing heavy fines and jail time for anyone convicted of importing toxic waste.

---

[419] James Brooke, "Waste Dumpers Turning to West Africa," *The New York Times*, July 17, 1988.
[420] John Vidal, "Toxic E-Waste Dumped in Poor Nations, Says United Nations," Our World, U.N University, article, December 16, 2013.

In Nigeria, a site outside Lagos, known as the Ikeja computer village, is constantly busy with vendors scavenging through piles of old equipment looking for anything they could sell. Most of the junk is loaded with highly toxic materials like plastics which, when burned, emit carcinogenic dioxins and polyaromatic hydrocarbons that are not safe for the environment.

It was in Nigeria that the most shocking dumping incident occurred in 1998. Two Italian firms paid $100 to a villager to use his land in the Koko fishing village to store 18,000 drums of toxic waste disguised as building materials. By the time the matter reached higher authorities, the drums were already leaking and emitting an offensive odor, and people were getting sick. Nigeria forced Italy to remove the drums, and the villagers of Koko were eventually compensated.[421] Since then, a number of cases have been reported of multinationals dumping industrial waste in Nigerian villages, including Koko.

In 2006, a Dutch multinational, Trafigura, was found guilty by a Dutch court for transporting high-risk waste from Amsterdam to Ivory Coast, where it imperiled the lives of thousands of people. Dozens of people died, and many others contracted diseases.[422] The waste was unloaded at dozens of sites in Abidjan in contravention of the Basel Convention, which bars the exportation of hazardous waste from developed to developing countries for final disposal, recovery, or recycling,[423] as well as the 1998 Bamako Convention, ratified by 25 African countries, which prohibits importation into Africa of toxic goods. Trafigura denied breaking the laws. The company was fined $1.25 million by a Dutch court for using its Panama-registered ship *Probo Koala* to transit through Amsterdam and declaring its cargo as "harmless." The court gave $200 million

---

[421] Stephanie Buck, "In the 1980s, Italy Paid a Nigerian Town $100 a Month to Store Toxic Waste – and It's Happening Again," The Medium App, article, May 26, 2017.

[422] Rob Evans, "Trafigura Fined 1m Euros for Exporting Toxic Waste to Africa," *The Guardian*, July 23, 2010.

[423] The Basel Convention was passed by the UN Environment Program (UNEP) in 1989.

of the money to Ivory Coast to clean up the waste and $50 million to victims and families.

Writing in the *Columbia Journal of Environmental Law*, Professor Rebecca Bratspies blamed international laws that allowed northern trading partners to profit enormously from unlawful conduct in southern states, adding that the Ivory Coast incident revealed an implicit form of corruption embedded in a global trading system structured to allow plausible denials of involvement in illegal or corrupt transactions.[424]

In Somalia, European and Asian MNCs took advantage of the on-and-off turmoil following the overthrow of Mohamed Siad Barre in 1991 to discharge tons upon tons of perilous waste. When a tsunami hit the Somali coast in 2004, it washed onto the shores containers and disposable barrels leaking hazardous waste. An undetermined number of people in the surrounding areas died as a result. Radioactive materials and hydrogen peroxide toxic wastes were also found in southern and central Somalia.[425]

Despite African and international efforts to stop the dumping of chemicals and other wastes on the continent, multinational companies continue to use Africa as a dumping ground, sometimes with permission from corrupt leaders. In the late 1980s, during the presidency of Daniel arap Moi, Kenya was searching for a suitable and permanent site for the dumping of foreign toxics in exchange for cash, even though senior government officials had previously pushed back on requests from global contractors. A report quoting officials said in 1989 that Kenya was working with the Atomic Energy Agency to import radioactive materials for disposal. There was suspicion that the materials were already entering the country through the coastal town of Malindi. No evidence is available to suggest any such dumping took place.

---

[424] Rebecca Bratspies, "Corrupt at Its Core: How Law Failed the Victims of Waste Dumping in Côte d'Ivoire," *Columbia Journal of Environmental Law,* 43, no. 2 (2018): 1-46.

[425] Report of the non-governmental organization Common Community Care, 2006.

A German businessman stationed in Nairobi, Joachim Petry, an agent of German companies who was keen on disposing of industrial waste in Africa, had demanded $225,000 from the companies to bribe officials across Africa, including Kenya, to accept the waste. In 1990, a Cyprus-registered freighter, *Bruna Americana,* arrived at the port of Mombasa with 20,000 tons of leaking toxic waste loaded in the Netherlands. It was denied entry and escorted to the high seas. Nevertheless, one report in 1999 identified 38 different locations in Kenya where obsolete pesticides were stored.[426] In a dramatic turn of events, Petry was shot dead on a Nairobi street in September 1990. It could not be determined if the attack had any connection with his bizarre business.

Many African countries are also the final terminus of used clothing from the United States and Europe, popularly known as *mitumba* (throw-away) in East Africa and *obroni wawu* (dead white men's clothes) in Ghana, consisting of everything from underwear to socks, bras, swimming gear, suits, and wedding dresses. It's big business for foreign firms, NGOs, and even churches—and it has virtually destroyed local manufacturing industries. More importantly, few countries have dared to look into the potential health risks used merchandise poses to the wearers. Some doctors have warned that such clothes present the risk of spreading skin diseases. In April 2019, Tanzania intercepted and destroyed four tons of imported used underwear, and the government warned importers that they stood to be penalized heavily.

In African secondhand clothes stores around Africa, items such as baby pacifiers known to cause choking deaths and fire-retardant baby pajamas containing the chemical Tris (2,3-dibromoproptiyl), which causes kidney cancer in children, are sold by unsuspecting traders. The US-manufactured pajamas, meant to protect children from fire, were banned by the US Consumer Product Safety Commission after deaths were reported overseas.

---

[426] Andreas Bernstorff and Kevin Stairs, "POPs in Africa: Hazardous Waste Trade 1980–2000, Obsolete Pesticide Stockpiles," Greenpeace International, article, 2000.

Was a Kenyan leader a victim?

In 1979, when one of Kenya's most promising leaders, Tom Mboya, was felled by an assassin's bullet one afternoon on a street in Nairobi, medics rushed forward and plugged into his body what was believed to be the latest US-manufactured resuscitative gadget, Res-Q-Aire. What the medics didn't know, according to Mother Jones, a non-profit organization, was that the product, which was meant to improve blood flow to the heart and the brain, was ineffective and had been recalled from the US market by the government.

For decades, countries in the developing world, especially those in Africa, have been used to dump useless drugs and equipment no longer wanted in the developed world. By using unethical methods, including bribery and corruption, such companies have been colluding with avaricious African leaders to dump such items as contaminated foods, expired or banned drugs, toxic pesticides, and other life-threatening products.

One of the biggest drug dumps in the developing world was that of thalidomide, the drug administered to pregnant women for morning sickness. In the 1950s and 1960s, the drug's German manufacturer, Chemie Grünenthal, flooded dozens of countries with the medicine, which turned out to be outrageously harmful to developing fetuses. The so-called "thalidomide babies" came out with missing or abnormal limbs, cleft lips or palates, and absent or abnormal external eyes, according to the WHO, which also reported cases of heart, kidney, and genital abnormalities.

Promoted as "completely nonpoisonous … safe … astonishingly safe … nontoxic … and fully harmless,"[427] thalidomide was "worthless"[428] and caused more than 10,000 birth defects in more than 46 countries, according to the WHO. One of the victims was a

---

[427] John Braithwaite, *Corporate Crime in the Pharmaceutical Industry* (Routledge & Kegan Paul, 1984), 68.
[428] Russell Mokhiber, *Corporate Crime and Violence: Big Business Power and the Abuse of the Public Trust* (Sierra Club Books, 1988), 410.

Kenyan baby named Freddy whose mother had taken thalidomide. Freddy was born in 2004 with no arms or legs. Thinking he had been bewitched, the family abandoned him in a panic. He was rescued by a British nurse, Knott-M'Tile, who mobilized for his medical care in the United Kingdom. Freddy was among an unknown number of babies born with severe disabilities in Africa thanks to thalidomide.

Marketed by a German company, Chemie Grünenthal, under different names, thalidomide was sold in Angola, Ghana, Guinea, Sudan, Mozambique, South Africa, Eritrea, Ethiopia, Egypt, and Nigeria. By 1962, according to one report, African women in those countries started giving birth to deformed children.. Thalidomide was not licensed in the United States because it was considered harmful there, but it was sold in Africa with devastating results.[429] And that was not the only such drug.

Aminopyrine and dipyrone, which were promoted as a panacea for headaches, were banned by the United States and most Western European countries after they were found to cause a blood disease called agranulocytosis, which hinders the body's ability to produce white blood cells. Aminopyrine and dipyrone drugs were, nevertheless, shipped to developing countries, including those in Africa, resulting in immense trauma for patients there.

In the 1970s, birth control products Depo-Provera and Dalkon Shield, manufactured by Upjohn and A. H. Robins respectively, which were not approved for use in the United States, found their way into the African market with false promises of preventing conception. Depo-Provera was approved by the United States Food and Drug Administration (FDA) only for use in the treatment of endometrial and kidney cancer and not as a contraceptive.

The continued controversy generated by those drugs got the US Intergovernmental Relations Committee of the House of Representatives to summon executives of the two pharmaceutical companies for a hearing. What came out was that hundreds of

[429] Dr. Opiyo Oloya, "How Much Has Monsanto Paid Uganda Scientists for the GMO Experiments?" *The New Vision*, February 1, 2011.

previously undisclosed "unfavorable" reports about the Dalkon Shield had been filed with A. H. Robins from physicians and patients complaining of pelvic inflammatory diseases, perforation of the uterus, and blood poisoning. By 1974, 17 deaths had occurred, and thousands of uterine infections were reported from the use of the Shield. Zimbabwe banned Depo-Provera in 1981 out of safety concerns.

What made the matter even more bizarre was that professional organizations, including the American Medical Association (AMA) and the Office of Population of USAID, supported the approval of the injectable drug, and USAID even agreed to its exportation to developing countries. *Mother Jones* magazine reported that USAID's Office of Population spent $125 million of its contraceptive budget on Dalkon Shields after the manufacturer offered it a 48 percent discount for bulk purchase. By the time USAID recalled the Shield from developing countries in 1975 following continued warnings about its dangers, tens of thousands of African women were already using it, and the device was already "lying in the drawers of countless private practitioners and tiny rural family planning clinics."[430]

Depo-Provera was found to cause "irregular bleeding disturbances," described as "menstrual chaos." It could cause birth defects and, in the case of female fetuses, masculinization and enlargement of the clitoris.[431]

A Kenya Medical Research Institute study in 2015 also showed Depo-Provera contained chemicals that made women 40 percent more prone to HIV infection than those who weren't using the contraceptive. For some reason, Kenya continues to allow the importation of the drug, which is the most commonly used injectable. The report put the 39 percent of Kenyan women who use it in a state of panic. The findings supported those announced

---

[430] Mark Dowie, Barbara Ehrenreich, and Stephen Minkin, "The Charge: Gynocide," *Mother Jones*, December 1979.
[431] Ibid.

in 2011 which said Depo-Provera "may double a woman's risk of contracting and transmitting HIV."[432] Other tests have also shown the drug causes cancer.[433] Why Kenyan authorities have continued to allow the use of the drug calls for an explanation from Nairobi authorities. Anyone can buy the product off the shelves in pharmacies in the country.

When the Swiss company MNC Ciba-Geigy introduced clioquinol in the United States for the treatment of amoebic dysentery and diarrhea in the 1960s, it was found to cause a disease known as SMON (subacute myelo-optic neuropathy), which damages the spinal cord, body, and optic nerves. In Japan, where the drug was widely dispensed in the 1960s and 1970s, doctors discovered that the tongues of some SMON victims had turned greenish, and that other users were excreting greenish urine.[434] By that time, it had been withdrawn in the United States, although it continued to sell in Africa and the rest of the world under different names until 1985, when Ciba-Geigy pulled it out of the world market altogether.

Companies often use tricks to get their medical products sold on the markets of developing nations even when they are banned elsewhere: they may change the name when a drug gets bad publicity after withdrawal from the US market; label the product "for export only," so the manufacturer need not inform the importing country of the ban in the United States; close the company altogether and begin manufacturing close to a good market; change a formula slightly by adding or subtracting an inert ingredient; or take advantage of loopholes in the importing country to sneak in the banned product.[435] By taking those steps, a foreign

---

[432] Keegan Hamilton, "Depo Danger: AIDS, Africa, and the UW Researchers Who Rocked the Medical World," C-FAR, University of Washington/Fred Hutch Center for AIDS research, article, December 2011.
[433] "Banned in America, Peddled in Africa," *The Christian Science Monitor*, December 5, 1980.
[434] Olle Hansson, "Is Entero-Vioform a Killer Drug? *The New Scientist,* 80, no. 1130, Reed Business Information, November 23, 1978: 1-80.
[435] John Braithwaite, *Corporate Crime in the Pharmaceutical Industry* (Routledge & Kegan Paul, 1984), 257–77.

company could avoid detection.

In addition, drugs and faulty equipment continue to flood emerging markets. The WHO estimates that 90 percent of all medical equipment donated to developing countries is not in perfect condition. Also, because it is either secondhand or reconditioned, it is susceptible to malfunction and frequent breakdowns. In 2018, for example, 700 microscopes delivered through a partnership between the Kenya Treasury and the Global Fund for use in the diagnosis of malaria were found to be defective. That exposed 34 million Kenyans to the risk of contracting the disease.

More recently in 2019, WHO warned Kenya about the circulation in the country of fake Augmentin – a powerful first line antibiotic - saying it could be fatal if used over a long period of time. The UN agency said the drug did not meet its standards.

The Kenya Medical Supplies Authority (KEMSA), which is in charge of the procurement, storage, and distribution of quality drugs for use in hospital and pharmacies, is one of the most corrupt state-run corporations in the country. Concerned about the overpricing of drugs on the market, anti-corruption authorities investigated KEMSA in 2008 and found the agency was demanding bribes to process orders from private hospitals and pharmacies, which then increase prices. The CEO of the organization was sacked following audits.

There is a common talk in Africa that Africans are gullible people who view anything foreign as good for their well-being. Take the case of an American pastor who introduced what he called a "miracle mineral solution" to Ugandans, claiming it cured everything from HIV to malaria. The solution, which was condemned by the US Food and Drug Administration (FDA), turned out to be nothing but a concoction of industrial bleach, sodium chlorite, and citric dioxide, a potentially dangerous mix which caused diarrhea, low blood pressure, and nausea. The intentions of Pastor Robert Baldwin were unknown, but the fact that he was allowed to distribute the fake mixture after church services, with the full knowledge of

Ugandan authorities, was further proof of the exploitation of Africa by foreign elements.

Feeding on contaminated foods

For many years, international companies have been unpacking in Africa contaminated food products such as unwanted American chicken in South Africa, adulterated baby formula in Tanzania, and radioactivity-contaminated meats in West Africa, where, in the late 1980s, a number of countries there turned away EU cargo ships carrying polluted meats. According to one report, Ghana, Sierra Leone, Liberia, Togo, and Benin are some of the African countries that fought off pressure from European and Asian exporters to have their cargo ships of contaminated foods dock at the West African ports. Most of the ships that arrived with unwanted cargo were promptly escorted out of the territorial waters by naval patrol boats. In other cases, the tainted cargo was confiscated by authorities and destroyed. It was widely believed that the contamination of agricultural products in some European countries resulted from the Chernobyl nuclear explosion in Kiev, Ukraine, in 1986.[436] The foods grown in those countries became unfit for human consumption in Europe but were, nevertheless, transported to Africa for sale.

One case of food contamination that caused a storm involved milk powder tainted with melamine, which was sold in East Africa by a Chinese company. Widespread melamine poisoning had occurred in China in 2008, resulting in more than 50,000 children developing kidney problems and urinary tract stones, triggering an international outcry. Melamine is an industrial chemical used primarily as a plastics stabilizer and fire retardant and is a major component in coatings, glues, dishes, and kitchenware.[437]

In 2018, the UN banned the baby food formula made with melamine-contaminated milk powder. Subsequently, the formula

---

[436] Dirk Bannink, "Contaminated Foodstuffs Dumped on the World Market," *The Nuclear Monitor*, no. 349–350 (April 5, 1991).
[437] Dagmar Schoder, "Melamine Milk Powder and Infant Formula Sold in East Africa," *Journal of Food Protection* 73, no. 9 (2010): 1709-1714.

was proscribed in 24 countries, including Tanzania, Burundi, and Gabon. Half a dozen Asian countries, among them Singapore, Taiwan, Japan, Indonesia, and Malaysia, also banned Chinese milk products.

In Tanzania, a total of 49 milk powder batches were collected in Dar es Salaam, some of them unlabeled and believed to come from the black market. Many were found to contain melamine, a potentially dangerous ingredient for babies, according to Dagmar Schoder of the University of Vienna.

In 2016, after 17 years of trying to penetrate the South African market in the wake of the anti-dumping duty imposed by Pretoria on US chicken bone-in portions, US firms were finally allowed to export chicken thighs and drumsticks, beef, and pork tariff-free to South Africa and sell them at "dumping" prices. Since Americans prefer chicken breasts and wings, the disposal of thighs and legs to a developing country was considered particularly profitable to US farmers. The agreement between the United States and South Africa was part of the negotiations of the US African Growth and Opportunity Act (AGOA), a piece of legislation enacted in 2000 meant to enhance market access to the United States for qualifying sub-Saharan countries.

In the meantime, what was described by *The Telegraph* newspaper as "the worst outbreak of food-borne disease in recorded global history" killed 200 South Africans, including 80 babies, early in 2018 after they consumed contaminated cold meat produced by Tiger Brands, the country's largest food company. They died of listeriosis caused by the listeria bacteria suspected to have been festering in a batch of ready-to-eat "Polony" sausage meat—a type of cold meat made from pork, chicken, and turkey—popular among poor South Africans. The South African government ordered the destruction of all cold meats and declared the situation to be under control.[438] Close to 1,000 cases of listeriosis were discovered in

---

[438] Adrian Blomfield, "Listeria Contaminated Food Kills 200 in South Africa, Including 80 Babies," *The Telegraph*, May 18, 2018.

the country, forcing the neighboring countries of Mozambique, Zambia, and Swaziland, among others, to recall the South African meat brand.

If that is not enough, in the 2000s, South Africa was also the victim of contaminated honey from China said to contain a poisonous antibiotic called chloramphenicol, believed to cause liver cancer and other blood disorders. The antibiotic is used to cure severe cases of typhoid fever in humans and diarrhea diseases that afflict honeybees. Several European countries, as well as the United States and Canada, banned the importation of the honey. An attempt to sell the rejected honey to Latin American countries was thwarted as a safety precaution.

In Kenya, cases of contaminated sugar are linked to greedy and corrupt cartels that have not only destroyed the sugar industry in the country but have caused a great deal of anxiety among the population. Every so often, batches of contaminated imported sugar are discovered at either the port of entry or in shops. The government has seized thousands of bags of illegally imported sugar containing high levels of mercury and copper. In a few cases, ships arriving at the Kenyan port from Brazil have been turned away or their cargo dumped at sea to save the people from potentially dangerous substances. The Kenya Bureau of Standards (KBS), which regulates food safety, has been flagged for corruption and some of its officials prosecuted for passing on to consumers adulterated foodstuffs such as maize, and other consumables. In one case in 1995, 100 tons of powdered milk imported from Ukraine was found to contain radioactive material and was declared unfit for human consumption and returned. Since then, more contaminated food imports have been discovered. In 2018, 1,000 bags of mercury- and copper-laden sugar were seized in stores in Kenya. The KBS chief executive, Charles Ongwae, was arrested and charged with allowing the tainted foods to enter the country. The case was still ongoing by mid-2019.

In 2018, Tanzania seized 140 tons of expired imported foodstuffs, including rice, maize, sugar, and cooking oil, meant for consumption during the holy month of Ramadan. Similarly, African-manufactured foods entering EU nations have also been flagged for impurities. Nigerian nuts and seeds, for example, were in 2017 found to contain high levels of microbes such as salmonella, aflatoxins, and mold, and were rejected by the receiving countries. Dozens of other imports were turned back for other reasons as well, such as not having health certificates or correct labels or for having poor packaging.

"African quality" fuels

Apart from food contamination, foreign companies have also been blamed for dumping in Africa adulterated diesel and gasoline which have substances that cause health risks. A 2016 report by the Switzerland-based watchdog Public Eye singled out Swiss commodity trading companies for taking advantage of weak fuel standards on the continent to dump poor-quality fuel that cannot be sold in Europe. The report said the companies mix cheap but toxic intermediate petroleum products containing high levels of sulfur, benzene, and aromatics to make what the industry calls "African quality" fuels. "By selling such fuels at the pump in Africa," Public Eye claims, "the traders increase outdoor air pollution, causing respiratory disease and premature death."[439] In West Africa, there were reports of people suffering from bronchitis and asthma, resulting in premature deaths, because of breathing dirty fuel from Europe and the United States. The bad oil also causes damage to cars. Numerous countries, including Kenya and Zambia, have established fuel-marking programs that conduct tests of fuels at petrol stations and bulk storage facilities to check the quality of petroleum products. There are no reports to show that such action has discouraged crooked overseas companies from selling contaminated products to African countries.

---

[439] "Dirty Diesel: How Swiss Traders Flood Africa with Toxic Fuels," Public Eye, article, September 2016.

Underground cartels

Global Fund, which was established in 2002 by the G-8 leaders and the UN as a clearinghouse for drugs from wealthy nations, has faced many criticisms over the years for the way it has handled the donation and distribution of drugs. A large number of medicines, which were supposed to be given free of charge, often disappeared only to land in the hands of underground cartels that sell them at exorbitant prices.

In Togo in 2005, most of the drugs to treat malaria, valued at $10 million, were channeled through Global Fund (GF) to a local agency, Essential and Generic Medicine Procurement Agency (CAMEG), and were stolen. Corruption is also at the center of the failure to fight AIDS and tuberculosis in Africa. Antiretroviral drugs are misdirected from the needy to crooks who sell them to underground sources who, in turn, hawk them for profit.

In Uganda, a disbursement of $45.3 million by the GF revealed acts of misconduct by public officials, government ministers, and community health workers.[440] The money, which was meant to fight AIDS, malaria, and tuberculosis, was squandered, and antiretroviral drugs for use by HIV patients were stolen and sold to commercial enterprises. As a result, HIV treatment was temporarily disrupted, resulting in adverse consequences for the recipients.[441]

In 2005, a Ugandan government official whose company, Uganda Center for Accountability (UCA), was contracted to monitor recipients of money from the GF, was jailed for ten years for stealing $56,000. "The company was a sham," said Justice J. B. Katutsi of the anti-corruption court of the UCA. He added that the accused person, Teddy Ssezi, "intended to feather his own nest with ill-gotten money."[442] Ssezi, who in the 1990s ran a newsletter

---

[440] J. Cohen, "HIV/AIDS: Uganda Confronts Corruption, Slowly," *Science*, 321, issue 5888, 2008: 522-525.
[441] Ibid.
[442] Bernard Rivers, "Uganda Government Official Jailed for Ten Years for Stealing Global Fund Money," Aidspan, News, issue 103, April 17, 2009.

called *Uganda Confidential* which specialized in exposing financial scandals in government, was dismissed by witnesses as a fraud who never did any monitoring work for the GF. He established the UCA while working as a director of the Internal Security Organization, the state spy agency. A year after his release in March 2017, he was killed by a speeding motorbike as he crossed a road in Kampala.

According to a report by independent auditors, the HIV and tuberculosis program in Uganda was hit by misappropriation, forgeries, nepotism, and a lack of accountability. In Zimbabwe, President Mugabe's government stole $7.3 million donated by the GF in 2008 to fund treatment for AIDS, tuberculosis, and malaria and deposited it in the country's Reserve Bank. The state refused to refund it upon request, citing a lack of currency. It was reported in 2011 that $34 million of GF money was misused in Djibouti, Mali, and Mauritania. In Zambia, the fund lost $3.5 million, and one accountant walked away with $104,130. In February 2012, Germany, Ireland, and Sweden, three key donors, temporarily suspended support to the GF.[443]

In some other cases, corruption in public hospitals in Africa has led to an over-purchase of drugs, rendering such drugs unusable once they reach their expiry date. In 1981, *Cultural Survival Quarterly Magazine* reported that, in Tanzania, a British doctor found a 45-year supply of an antibiotics from the international drug manufacturer Hoechst. The shelf life of the antibiotics is two years under ideal conditions and only six months in the tropics, so the drugs were unsuitable for use. It was not known whether the expired medicine was still being prescribed to patients at the time it was discovered, but the fact that it was still in storage raised questions of accountability and how expired drugs could be disposed of without causing damage to the environment.

And in Kenya, expired drugs worth $3.2 million were found in the stores of the state-run KEMSA in 2018. Police also found a

---

[443] J. Cohen, 2008: 522-525.

consignment of expired surgical gloves, X-ray protective gowns, drugs, surgical syringes, and sutures in a private house in Nairobi. Early in 2019, another batch of expired drugs worth $1.2 million and belonging to KEMSA were found. The presence of large quantities of expired drugs in health facilities in Africa points to corruption in the procurement process. Officials tend to order in bulk to maximize their commissions, even when there is a limited need for the drugs.

Counterfeits

Then there is the billion-dollar counterfeit industry, which is responsible for smuggling into Africa illegal and dangerous substances under the guise of genuine drugs. At least 100,000 deaths in Africa, according to the WHO, are linked to counterfeit drugs. "Counterfeiting is more than a criminal act," said Professor Pierre Ambroise-Thomas, the WHO expert on malaria and tropical parasitic diseases. Writing in the *Mediterranean Journal of Haematology and Infectious Diseases,* Thomas added, "Manslaughter is perfectly justified to describe such an act although some prefer calling it simply murder."[444]

Fake drugs are usually packaged and labeled in such a way that an unsuspecting buyer is unable to tell the difference between the genuine and the counterfeit version. Moreover, the medicines are sold cheaply on the streets so as to attract those who cannot afford the real or generic brands. Some of the fakes even add active ingredients that pass quality test controls but don't provide any benefit to the user, says a study published in *The Lancet,* a peer-reviewed medical journal.[445]

---

444 Jocelyne Sambira, "Counterfeit Drugs Raise Africa's Temperature," *Africa Renewal,* analysis, May 2013.
[445] Ibid.

Europe is not the only country that dumps fake or substandard goods in Africa. China, which is known for selling fake goods of all kinds to sub-Saharan Africa, makes useless copies of Western medicines and manufactures them under unhygienic conditions in dingy factories. Since China does not have consumer protection laws, some of these medicines could have cancer-causing agents.

CHAPTER 13

A CASE OF COLONIAL SUBJUGATION

The real aim of colonialism was to control the people's wealth, what they produced, how they produced it – Ngugi wa Thiong'o.

France carries a heavy burden of blame for corruption and bribery in its former colonies in Africa. Its dilly-dallying approach with corrupt African leaders and its lackluster support for human rights have attracted immense criticisms from global human rights and anti-corruption organizations. It was only after the conviction in France of Equatorial Guinea's vice president Teodoro (Teodorin) Obiang on charges of corruption in 2017 that Paris's reputation was somehow redeemed. Human rights activists lauded President Teodoro Obiang Nguema's favorite son's three-year suspended sentence for corruption as the end of "a culture of impunity"[446] in France. And TI's lawyer, William Bourdon, called the verdict "historic."[447]

Francophone Africa has remained France's biggest trading partner since before Burkina Faso, the first French-speaking country, received independence from France in August 1960. The region exports large quantities of commodities to the European country, including cocoa, oil, and gas. In return, France pours in billions of dollars in development aid and loans while maintaining thousands of troops there through agreements signed in the 1960s, ostensibly as a precaution against terrorism.

However, the elephant in the room is the so-called "colonial debt," which its former colonies are forced to pay as compensation for the infrastructure France built before independence. Multiple reports estimate that the French African countries pay their colonial master more than $500 billion each year in fulfillment of the debt. Failure to remit the money could attract the seizure of national monetary reserves, which each country had to deposit with France's central bank. To most of the countries, that amounts to between 20 percent and 40 percent of their national budget. The payments appear to be in perpetuity and constitute a form of neo-colonialism, ensuring

---

[446] "French Court: African Leader's Son Embezzled Millions in Public Money," AP and Reuters, October 27, 2017.
[447] David Chazan, "France Convicts Equatorial Guinea's Vice President of Corruption in Landmark Trial," *The Telegraph,* October 27, 2017.

the continued hegemony of the African nations by France. It also reaffirms former president Charles de Gaulle's perception "that French world power and French power in Africa were inextricably linked and mutually confirming."[448]

But there have also been emerging views that African leaders in former colonies have also been corrupting European leaders to perpetuate their continued stay in power. Philippe Bernard, a onetime Africa-based journalist with the French newspaper *Le Monde,* in 2011 accused the former president Jacques Chirac and Prime Minister Dominique de Villepin of receiving enormous bribes in the form of suitcases stuffed with cash from the leaders of Congo, Burkina Faso, Senegal, Ivory Coast, and Gabon, intended toward Chirac's election campaign. "I saw Chirac and Villepin count the money in front of me," alleged Robert Bourgi, an unofficial former advisor to French president Nicolas Sarkozy, who admitted running the "wire" transfer system for 25 years. In total, Bourgi claimed, Blaise Campaore of Burkina Faso, Laurent Gbagbo of Ivory Coast, Denis Sassou Nguesso of Congo, Omar Bongo of Gabon, and Obiang Nguema of Equatorial Guinea contributed more than $8 million to Chirac's 2002 presidential campaign.[449]

Before that, the former dictator of the Central African Republic, Jean Bedel-Bokassa, gave President Valery Giscard d'Estaing 30 carats of diamonds worth $250,000 when the latter was foreign minister in the 1970s. Under pressure from the media, d'Estaing claimed France sold the jewels and that the proceeds were given to charities in the Central African Republic. Ironically, Bokassa was overthrown in 1979 in a French-backed coup d'etat.

---

[448] Bruno Charbonneau, "Dreams of Empire: France, Europe, and the New Interventionism in Africa," *Journal of Modern and Contemporary France* 16, no. 3 (2008): 281.
[449] Michael Schmidt, "How African Dictators Corrupt European Politics," *Pambazuka News,* April 19, 2012.

"Mr. Africa"

The French oil giant Elf Aquitaine was created in 1967 from two agencies established in the 1930s and 1940s to ensure France's self-sufficiency in natural gas and crude oil, but it gradually became a tool for funding political parties and financing presidential candidates. An estimated $455 million was found to have been siphoned off from the company's safe and used to bankroll election campaigns, bribe foreign politicians, and enrich a few managers.[450] That revelation led to a trial in 2003 of 37 people in what The Guardian newspaper dubbed the biggest political and corporate sleaze scandal to hit a Western democracy since the Second World War.[451] It involved the payment of "royalties" to African leaders in oil-producing states and kickbacks and illegal commissions to French foreign businessmen and top French officials belonging to networks formed to fleece the organization.

In 2003, the chief executive of France's Elf Aquitaine, Loik Le Floch-Prigent, was sentenced to five years in prison for using company money to bribe officials in France and abroad. His former wife, Fatima Belaid, was also convicted of receiving $5.2 million from Elf to cover up the illicit deals. She was sentenced to three years in prison, with two years suspended, and fined $1.1 million.

Andre Tarallo, who was the company's "Mr. Africa"—because of his intense interest in the continent—was jailed for four years and fined $2.2 million. Thirty-five other executives also received varying jail terms for stealing $347 million from Elf Aquitaine, paid as "royalties" to secure business contracts in Nigeria, Gabon, Togo, the Republic of Congo, Russia, Spain, Germany, and South America. In one transaction, $190 million was paid to President Sani Abacha to secure drilling rights in Nigeria in 1995, according to French prosecutors.

---

[450] Robert Graham, "French Trial Paints a Picture of Graft on a Grandiose Scale," The Financial Times, April 22, 2003.
[451] Jon Henley, "Gigantic Sleaze Scandal Winds Up as Former Elf Oil Chiefs Are Jailed," The Guardian, November 12, 2003.

In France, the money was channeled to political parties, especially the center-right RPR party founded by President Jacques Chirac. Later, at the urging of President Francois Mitterrand, the money was split to include other parties. Judges who investigated Elf concluded that the company was bilked of as much as $400 million over a period of four years, beginning in 1993.[452]

Elf, which changed its name to TotalFinaElf and later Total in 2003, had a long-standing relationship with Africa, especially the French-speaking part of the continent. It had a strong presence in Gabon, Cameroon, Nigeria, Angola, and Congo-Brazzaville, later the Republic of Congo, since the 1960s, during General Charles de Gaulle's administration. It oiled its presence by bribing African officials with cash estimated at millions of dollars, which the French government—a shareholder—was aware of. Part of Elf's illicit money was used to prop up authoritarian African leaders in the French sphere of influence, paid as bribes to advance French diplomatic and corporate interests,[453] as well as ensuring the African leaders' alignment with France.[454]

The secrecy in which Elf maintained its accounts made it difficult for authorities to nail it earlier. It took a seven-year investigation by Judges Eva Joy and Renaud Van Ruymbeke to unearth the malfeasance. A Global Witness director, Simon Taylor, said the dirty deals would have been discovered much earlier if companies had been required to openly and accountably declare their payments to governments.[455] Moreover, Elf's deals with African governments were tilted to benefit the company and not the countries. In the Republic of Congo, for example, the company signed contracts which gave the government only 13 percent of oil profit revenues

---

[452] Pierre-Antoine Souchard, "Judges Implicate 43 in French Oil Scandal," *The Washington Post,* February 5, 2002.

[453] Leif Wenar, *Blood Oil: Tyrants, Violence, and the Rules that Run the World* (Oxford University Press, 2016), 127.

[454] "France – Corruption Scandals," GlobalSecurity.org, analysis, October 2017.

[455] "Elf Trial Throws Spotlight on Oil and Corruption," Global Witness, press release, March 17, 2003.

while it kept 51 percent to itself.

Alstom Corporation

The Paris-based power and transportation company French Alstom Corporation has been at the center of bribery scandals around the world for decades. In 2011, it was fined $35 million by Swiss authorities for failing to stop some of its employees from accepting bribes. The following year, two of its subsidiaries, Alstom Network Schweiz AG (Switzerland) and Alstom Hydro France, were ordered to pay a restitution settlement penalty of $9.5 million to the WB for bribery in relation to a bank-funded hydropower project in Zambia.

The bribe to the Zambian official was in relation to the rehabilitation work of hydropower systems at Victoria Falls, whose tender was issued in 1999, and a $45 million contract signed with ZESCO. By the time the project was completed in 2008, it had gobbled $51 million. The WB did not name the receiver of the bribe, saying such a disclosure could "jeopardize the security of witnesses," but it did give the name of the culprit to the Zambian government.

In 2015, the French company that manufactures rail, power, and electricity transmission sectors met the wrath of the DOJ and was ordered to pay $772 million in a restitution settlement after pleading guilty to two criminal charges involving $4 billion projects in Egypt, Indonesia, Saudi Arabia, the Bahamas, and Taiwan. Deputy Attorney General James M. Cole said Alstom paid more than $75 million in bribes, disguised as "consultancy services" to secure projects in those countries, in a scheme he described as "astounding in its breadth, its brazenness and its worldwide consequences."[456]

Leonard McCarthy, the vice president of the WB Integrity Unit whose responsibility it is to prevent and investigate fraud, collusion, and corruption in WB projects, said the penalty was a wake-up call

---

[456] US Department of Justice, "Alstom Pleads Guilty and Agrees to Pay $772 Million Criminal Penalty to Resolve Foreign Bribery Charges," press release no. 14-1448, December 22, 2014.

to global companies involved in development projects that they must ensure their operations with the WB are clean. In mitigation before a federal court in Connecticut in the United States, the company said it was committed to the highest levels of integrity and that it would continue to develop compliance programs to fight bribery and corruption.

There were other cases of Alstom employees facing charges of giving bribes to secure transport contracts in Tunis, New Delhi, Warsaw, and Jakarta. In 2014, SFO officials filed charges against a former managing director of Alstom Transport India, Robert Hallett, and other company officials in connection with a bribery investigation. Prosecutors believed the company paid up to $8.5 million as bribes to officials in the three countries to secure contracts between 2000 and 2006.

Alcatel

Among multinationals with the highest incidences of foreign bribery, the French telecommunication company Alcatel occupies one of the top positions. It has been linked to irregularities in Uganda, Kenya, Nigeria, Angola, Ivory Coast, Mali, Ecuador, Bangladesh, and French Polynesia. The company, which merged with the US-based Lucent Technologies Incorporated in 2006 to become Alcatel-Lucent, S.A., made $48.1 million in profits between 2001 and 2006 and ticked off payments to foreign officials amounting to $8 million. In Kenya, the French-based company reportedly paid bribes to a consultant in 2000 with respect to an $82 million supply contract to lay undersea fiber-optic cables—the first telecommunications link between Kenya and the rest of the world. The contract was issued to Alcatel-Lucent in 2006—after edging out four competitors—for the East African Marine Systems (Teams) fiber-optic cables from Fujairah in the UAE to Mombasa, Kenya. The money to the unnamed consultant was believed to be a bribe to assist in getting the tender. The DOJ filed a criminal complaint in a Florida court, charging Alcatel-Lucent with one count of violating the internal control provisions of the FCPA and one count of violating its books and records provisions. Alcatel-Lucent and three of its subsidiaries, Alcatel-Lucent France S. A., Alcatel-Lucent Trade International A. G., and Alcatel Centroamerica S. A., agreed to pay $82 million to settle the criminal and civil charges on bribes it paid to Kenya and the other countries. No action was taken by the Kenyan government against the mysterious consultant.

Divestiture woes in Africa

In numerous cases involving the divestiture of telecommunication entities, money derived from privatizations was sometimes directed to third parties, with "the mostly likely recipients being very senior political figures."[457] That happened in Kenya when the government there wanted to sell its shares in Safaricom to a strategic investor. According to Ewan Sutherland, who has written extensively on telecommunication matters, the stake for the Vodafone Group Plc was raised from 30 percent to 40 percent to cover the transfer of shares to a company in Guernsey reportedly owned by firms in Anguilla and Antigua. Consequently, the anonymous companies continued to receive dividends from Safaricom for several years, until their shares were bought by Vodafone.

The case of Telecom Kenya, the country's third-biggest operator, is another. In 1999, President Daniel arap Moi allowed Telekom Kenya to sell a 40 percent stake to Vodafone Kenya for $42 million. But it turned out that Vodafone had been guided on securing the shares by Mobitelea, a Guernsey-registered company. Mobitelea was allowed in 2001 to buy shares in Safaricom, which yielded Mobitelea a profit of $51 million by 2009. The existence of Mobitelea remained a secret until 2007, when President Mwai Kibaki announced plans to sell 60 percent of Telekom Kenya shares to a strategic investor to fund a major restructuring of the state parastatal. But still no one knew who was behind Mobitelea,

---

[457] Ewan Sutherland, "Bribery and Corruption in Telecommunications: Best Practice in Prevention and Remedies," TPRC: 40th Research Conference on Communication, Information, and Internet Policy, September 21-23, 2012, 10–11.

although it was widely assumed Moi and close friends may have had a stake.[458]

The mystery got the SFO to intervene and find out the true owner of the company. But Vodafone said it could not publicly divulge the owner "for reasons of commercial confidentiality."[459]

Sutherland, who is a professor at the University of the Witwatersrand in South Africa, investigated four of the biggest mobile operators in Kenya to find their participation in corruption. One manufacturer, he says, channeled $20 million in bribes to an unnamed middleman in Mauritius on behalf of an operator. Another operator had the then-president and minister (in charge of telecommunications) as an "investor." A third had a mysterious investor from the UAE, and the fourth took half a decade to begin operations due to unknown reasons. This may suggest that the Kenyan telecommunications industry is fraught with corruption and bribery and that the recipients were top government officials.

In Zambia, the 2010 privatization of ZAMTEL was tainted with corruption after the minister of communications and transport, Dora Siliya, signed a contract, deemed illegal, with a company in Cayman Islands regarding the sale of the state-owned company. The contract was revoked by President Michael Sata, who took over from Rupiah Banda following a damaging report by Justice Minister Sebastian Zulu that showed Siliya did not follow proper procedures in signing the contract. Critics said the controversial deal was marred with illegality, procedural irregularities, and corruption, and was against the public interest, forcing Minister Siliya to resign. The 75 percent stake was granted to Libya's LAP Green at a much-reduced price. Siliya was cleared by the Supreme Court of any charges relating to the transaction.

---

[458] Ewan Sutherland, "Bribery and Corruption in Telecommunications: The Case of Kenya," info, Emerald Group Publishing Ltd., 17, no. 3, 38–57, May 11, 2015.

[459] George Turner, Nick Mathiason, and Jamie Doward, "Revealed: How Vodafone Allowed Elites to Reap Profits of Africa's Mobile Boom," *The Observer*, November 11, 2017.

However, in 2012, the government compulsorily acquired the $257 million contract from LAP Green, froze ZAMTEL bank accounts, and launched a money-laundering investigation against the parastatal and LAP Green. President Sata urged that the shares be sold to Zambians: "Selling the shares to foreigners is tantamount to stealing the life-long "sweat" of Zambians."[460] The opposition United Party for National Development (UPND) accused President Banda, his children, and Minister Siliya of benefiting from what he called a "dirty" transaction.

LAP Green defended itself and said the acquisition was transparent and the process was competitive. In 2017, Zambia offered to pay LAP Green $382 million in compensation for the forceful retrieval of shares worth 75 percent sold to the company.

---

[460] "Sata Wants Zamtel Shares Sold to Zambians," Zambian Watchdog, article, July 25, 2009.

THE LAST WORD

Much of the world's costliest forms of corruption could not happen without institutions in wealthy nations; the private sector firms that give large bribes, the financial institutions that accept corrupt proceeds, and the lawyers and accountants who facilitate corrupt transactions – World Bank.

GLOSSARY

Acronyms

AfDB – African Development Bank

AU – African Union

BEIC – British East India Company

BCCI – Bank of Credit and Commerce International

CBK – Central Bank of Kenya

CNLCEI – Commission to Combat Illicit Enrichment

CPP – Convention People's Party

CREEP – Committee to Re-elect the President

DCI – Directorate of Criminal Investigation

DEA – Drug Enforcement Administration

DFID – Department for International Development

DGSM – Directorate of Geological Survey and Mines

DSCA – Defense Security Cooperation Agency

EACC – Ethics and Anti-Corruption Commission

ECGD – Export Credit Guarantee Department

EFCC – Economic and Financial Crimes Commission

IEBC – Independent Electoral and Boundaries Commission

FBI – Federal Bureau of Investigations

FCPA – Foreign Corrupt Practices Act

FCTC – Framework Convention on Tobacco Control

GMO – Genetically Modified Organism

HALIA – High Authority to Combat Corruption and Related Infractions

HEDA- Human and Environmental Development Agenda Resources Center

ICC – International Chamber of Commerce

ICIJ – Consortium of Investigative Journalists

IFC – International Finance Corporation

IMF – International Monetary Fund

KPA – Kenya Airports Authority

KEPSA – Kenya Private Sector Alliance

KRA – Kenya Revenue Authority

KVDA – Kerio Valley Development Authority

NAPIMS – National Petroleum Investment Management Services

NARC – National Rainbow Coalition

NDC – National Democratic Congress

NNPC – Nigerian National Petroleum Corporation

NPTDF – Nigerian Petroleum Technology Department Fund

OECD – Convention of the Organization for Economic Development

OACU – Overseas Anti-Corruption Unit

OAU – Organization of African Unity

PCCB – Prevention and Combating of Corruption Bureau

POCAMLA – Proceeds of Crime and Anti-Money Laundering Act

SOCA – Serious Organized Crime Agency

TJN-A -Tax Justice Network - Africa

UNCAC – United Nations Convention Against Corruption

UNECA – United Nations Economic Commission on Africa

URA – Uganda Revenue Authority

USAID – United States Agency for International Development

SELECTED BIBLIOGRAPHY

BOOKS

Adamafio, Tawia. *By Nkrumah's Side* (Westcoast Publishing House, 1982).

Ayittey, George B. N. *Africa Betrayed* (St. Martin's Press, 1992).

Ayitttey, George B. N. *Africa unchained: The blueprint for Africa's future,* (Springer, 2016).

Boraine, Alex. *What's Gone Wrong? South Africa on the Brink of Failed Statehood*, (New York University Press, 2014).

Bartos, Judeen. *Corporate Corruption* (Green Haven Press, 2012).

Braithwaite, John. *Corporate Crime in the Pharmaceutical Industry* (Routledge & Kegan Paul, 1984).

Brautigam, Deborah. *The Dragon's Gift: The Real Story on China in Africa,* (Oxford University Press, 2009).

Bunting, Brian. *The Rise of the South African Reich,* (Penguin Africa Library, 1965).

Burgis, Tom. *The Looting Machine: Warlords, Oligarchs, Corporations, Smugglers, and the Theft of Africa's Wealth* (Public Affairs, 2015).

Chayes, Sarah. *Thieves of State. Why Corruption Threatens Global Security* (W. W. Norton & Company, 2015).

De Morais, Rafael Marques. *Blood Diamonds: Corruption and Torture in Angola,* (Maka Angola, 2011).

Edgerton, Robert B. *The Troubled Heart of Africa: A History of the Congo*, (St. Martin's Press, 2002).

Ellis, Stephen. *The Present Darkness: A History of Nigerian Organized Crime,* (Oxford University Press, 2016).

Idowu, Samuel O. and Kasum, Abubakar S. *People, Planet and Profit: Social Economic Perspectives of CSR* (Routledge, 2016).

Igbinovia, Patrick Edobor. *Oil Thefts and Pipeline Vandalization in Nigeria* (Safari Books Limited, 2014).

Kaydor Jr., Thomas. *Liberian Democracy: A Critique of the Principle of Checks and Balances* (Author House, 2014).

Kochan, Nick. *The Washing Machine: Money, Crime & Terror in the Offshore System* (Gerald Duckworth & Co. Limited, 2006.

Manning, Patrick. *Slavery and African life* (Cambridge University Press, 1990).

Meredith, Martin. *The Fortunes of Africa: A 5000-year History of Wealth, Greed, and Endeavor* (Public Affairs, 2014).

Mokhiber, Russell. *Corporate Crime and Violence: Big Business, Power, and the Abuse of the Public Trust*, (Sierra Club Books, 1988).

Montero David. *Kickback: Exposing the Global Corporate Bribery Network* (Viking, 2018).

Neild, Robert. *Public Corruption: The Dark Side of Social Evolution* (Anthem Press, 2002).

Obermayer, Bastian and Obermaier, Frederik. *The Panama Papers: Breaking the Story of How the Rich and Powerful Hide Their Money* (One World Book, 2016).

O'Meara, Dan. *Forty Lost Years: The Apartheid State and the Politics of the National Party, 1948-1994,* (Ravan Press, 1996).

Osaghae, E. E. *Crippled Giant: Nigeria Since Independence* (Hurst & Company, 1998).

Perkins, John. *The Secret History of the American Empire: Economic Hit men, Jackals, and the Truth About Global Corruption* (Penguin Group, 2007).

Pontell, Henry N. and Geis, Gilbert. *International Handbook of White-Collar Corporate Crime* (Springer, 2007).

Roberts, Adam. *The Wonga Coup: Guns, Thugs, and a Ruthless Determination to Create Mayhem in an Oil-Rich Corner of Africa*, (Public Affairs, 2006).

Robin, Marie-Monique. *The World According to Monsanto: Pollution, Corruption, and the Control of Our Food Supply, an Investigation into the World's Most Controversial Company* (The New Press, 2010).

Russell, Alec. *Big Men, Little People: The Leaders Who Defined Africa,* (New York University Press, 1999).

Sampson, Anthony. *Mandela: The Authorized Biography*, (Knopf Doubleday Publishing Group, 2012).

Shaxson, Nicholas. *Treasure Islands: Tax Havens and the Men Who Stole the World* (Vintage, 2012).

Shaxson, Nicholas. *Poisoned Wells: The Dirty Politics of African Oil* (Palgrave, 2007).

Silverstein, Ken. *The Secret World of Oil* (Verso, 2014).

Stearns, Jason K. *Dancing in the Glory of Monsters: The Collapse of the Congo and the Great War of Africa,* (Public Affairs, 2011).

Truell, Peter and Gurwin, Larry. *False Profits: The Inside Story of BCCI, the World's Most Corrupt Financial Empire* (Houghton Mifflin Company, 1992).

Van Reybrouck, David. *Congo: The Epic History of a People,* (HarperCollins Publishers, 2010).

Wenar, Leif. *Blood Oil: Tyrants Violence, and the Rules That Run the World* (Oxford University Press, 2016).

Whyte, David. *How Corrupt is Britain*? (Pluto Press, 2015).

Wrong, Michela. *It's Our Turn to Eat: The Story of a Kenyan Whistle-Blower*, (HarperCollins, 2009).

RESEARCH JOURNALS AND ARTICLES

Appel, Hannah C. Walls and White Elephants: Oil extraction, responsibility, and infrastructural violence in Equatorial Guinea, *Ethnography*, (December 2012).

Bratspies, Rebecca. Corrupt at its core: How law failed the victims of waste dumping in Cote d'Ivoire, *Columbia Journal of Environmental Law,* (2018).

Campos, Jose Edgardo and Pradhan, Sanjay. The Many faces of corruption: Tracking vulnerabilities at the sector Level, *World Bank*, (2007).

Charbonneau, Bruno. Dreams of empire: France, Europe, and the new interventionism in Africa, *Journal of Modern and Contemporary France,* (2008).

Cooksey, Brian. IPTL, Richmond and "Escrow": The price of private power procurement in Tanzania," *Africa Research Institute*, Briefing Note 1702, (November 2017).

Eluka, Prof. J. Multinational corporations and their effects on Nigerian economy, *European*

Journal of Business and Management, (2016).

Engdahl, Bill and Steinberg, Jeffrey. The real story of the BCCI," *Executive Intelligence Review,* (October 13, 1995).

Esteban, Mario. The Chinese amigo: Implications for the development of Equatorial Guinea, *The China Quarterly,* (September 2009).

Farhaoui, Faoud. The great power struggle for Africa: The crisis in Mali, *International Strategic Research Organization,* (2013).

Forstater, Maya. Stop spreading the myth: Zambia is not losing USD 3 billion to tax avoidance, *Center for Global Development,* (October 23, 2017).

Hamilton, Keegan. Depo danger: AIDS, Africa, and the UW researchers who rocked, *University of Washington/Fred Hutch Center for AIDS research,* (December 2011).

Human Rights Quarterly, (John Hopkins University Press (2011).

Kaikati, Jack G. and Label, Wayne A. American Bribery Legislation: An Obstacle to International Marketing, *Journal of Marketing,* (Autumn 1980).

Lallemand, Alain. The Field Marshal, *US Center for Public Integrity,* (November 15, 2002).

Lawson, L. The Politics of Anti-Corruption Reform in Africa, *Journal of Modern African Studies,* (2009).

Leibold, Annalisa M. Aligning Incentives for Development, The World Bank and the Chad-Cameroon Oil Pipeline, *Yale Journal of International Law,* (2011).

Leonard, H. Jeffrey. Review: Multinational corporations and politics in developing countries, *World Politics,* (April 1980).

Magaisa, Alex. Multinationals, corruption, and poverty in Zimbabwe: The murky case of the Dema Diesel Plant. *Trust Africa, Corruption, Criminal Law, Economy, Politics,* (August 2, 2016).

Mapaure, Clever. Chinese investments in Zimbabwe and Namibia, *Center for Chinese Studies,* (September 2014).

Marwane, Ahmed. Fighting corruption in Algeria: Turning words into action, *Washington Institute,* (December 12, 2018).

Meservey, Joshua. Chinese corruption in Africa undermines Beijing's rhetoric about friendship with the continent, *The Heritage Foundation,* (August 8, 2018).

Mogalakwe, Monageng and Nyamjoh, Francis. Botswana at 50: Democratic deficit, elite corruption, and poverty in the midst of plenty, *Journal of Contemporary African Studies,* (2017).

Mountain, Thomas C. Destroying Africa with Western "Democracy," *Foreign Policy Journal,* (May 1, 2012).

Mufune, P. The formation of dominant classes in Zambia: Critical notes, *Africa Today,* (2nd Quarter 1988).

Mukerjee, Dilip. An Asian role in Africa, *Far Eastern Economic Review,* (July 18, 1980).

Ndikumana, Leonce. The issue of private sector corruption in Africa, *Third World*

Resurgence, (May 2016).

Osuagwu, Godwin Onyewuchi and Obumneke, Ezie. Multinational corporations and the Nigerian economy, *International Journal of Academic Research in Business and Social Sciences*, (April 2013).

Otanex, Marty G. and Mamudu, Hadii, et al. Global leaf companies control the tobacco market in Malawi, *Tobacco Control*, (2007).

Page, Melvin Eugene and Sonnenberg, Penny M. Colonialism, *An International, Social, Cultural, and Political Encyclopedia*, (2003).

Saprong, David and Sajdakova, Jana et al. The Mabey and Johnson bribery scandal: A case of executive hubris, *Thunderbird International Business Review,* (May 22, 2018).

Schoder, Dagmar. Melamine milk powder and infant formula sold in East Africa, *Journal of Food Protection,* (2010).

Shah, Naman K. Corporate philanthropy and conflicts of interest in public health: ExxonMobil, Equatorial Guinea, and Malaria. *Journal of Public Health Policy*, (January 2013).

Silverstein, Ken. Teodoro's world, *Foreign Policy*, (February 21, 2011).

The (mis)use of Chinese aid in Africa, *Research Story,* (June 14, 2016).

Togo's phosphates fall under presidential spell, *Africa Intelligence,* (June 26, 2014).

Van Niekerk, Phillip. Greasing the Skids of Corruption, *Center for Public Integrity*, (November 4, 2002).

Warf, Barney. Geographies of African corruption, *PSU Research Review*, (2017).

Weber, James and Getz, Kathleen. Buy bribes or bye-bye bribes: The future status of bribery in international commerce, *Business Ethics Quarterly,* (October 2004).

Werlin, Herbert H. The Roots of Corruption – The Ghanaian enquiry, *The Journal of Modern African Studies*, (July 1972).

Wissenbach, Uwe and Wang, Yuan. African politics meets Chinese engineers: The Chinese-built Standard Gauge Railway (SGR) project in Kenya and East Africa, *China African Research Initiative*, (June 2017).

Yorbana, Seign-goura. Representations of oil in Chad: A blessing or a curse? In: African Spectrum, (2017).

REPORTS AND OTHER SOURCES

Abu Mubaik. Joyce Dzidor Mensah mocks Akufo-Addo's National Cathedral: Sarcastically begs foreigners for donations (February 17, 2019)

A Golden Racket: The true source of Switzerland's "Togolese gold", Public Eye, (September 8, 2015).

A Legal Memorandum, Sherpa and Transparency International, French Court of Appeals, (June 2009).

Africa at risk or rising? The role of Europe, North America, and China on the continent: A Stanley Foundation Brief, (May 4-6, 2007).

Ahmed Marwane. Fighting corruption in Algeria: Turning words into action (December 12, 2018).

Ali, Issah and Musah Labram. Tobacco Industry. Interference in tobacco control and public health policies in Ghana, (undated).

Anin, Patrick Dankwa. Final Report of the Commission of Inquiry on Bribery and Corruption, Republic of Ghana, (1975).

Angola Corruption Report, Business Anti-Corruption Portal, (August 2016).

Bell, T. and Ntsebeza, D. B. Unfinished business: South Africa, apartheid and truth, Observatory, (2001).

Bernstorff, Andreas and Stairs, Kevin. POPs in Africa: Hazardous waste trade 1980-2000, obsolete pesticide stockpiles, (2000).

Book brings ship-sinking fraud to surface, JOC.com., (April 5, 1988).

Bosely, Darah. Revealed: How British American Tobacco exploited war zones to sell cigarettes, (August 18, 2017).

Bribery and corruption 2019: China, Global Legal Insights, (2019).

Bribery taints World Bank-funded Lesotho water project, International Rivers, (August 1, 1999).

Buck, Stephanie. In the 1980s, Italy paid a Nigerian town USD 100 a month to store toxic waste – and it's happening again, The Medium App, (May 26, 2017).

Case Information, Stanford School of Law, Foreign Corrupt Practices Act Clearing House, (March 2018).

Cassin, Harry. Former Alstom UK director jailed for "sophisticated" corruption, The FCPA Blog, (December 21, 2018).

Cassin, Harry. World Bank debars Chinese fiber optic cable company, The FCPA Blog, (May 22, 2019).

Cassin, Richard L. Ex-Credit Suisse bankers charged with FCPA violations, The FPA Blog, (January 4, 2019).

Cassin, Richard L. Bribery Abroad: Lessons from the Foreign Corrupt Practices Act, (2008).

Cassin, Richard L. At Fresenius, management owned the graft, The FCPA Blog, (April 4, 2019).

Chan, Lok Yiu. Corporate social responsibility of multinational corporations, University of Washington Tacoma, (Spring 2014).

Chikwanha, Annie Barbara. Combating corruption in the extractive industry in Africa, Swiss International Development Cooperation Agency, (October 2016).

China's aid to Africa: Monster or messiah? Brookings Institution, (February 7, 2014).

Chinese companies engaged by PF for digital migration banned in Algeria, investigated in Uganda, Nigeria, Zambian Watchdog, (11 June 2012).

Chinese engagement in Kenya, US Embassy cable leaked by Wikileaks, (February 17, 2010).

Chitiyo, Knox and Kibble, Steve. Zimbabwe's international re-engagement: The long haul to recovery, Chatham House Report, (April 2014).

Congo's secret sales, Global Witness, (May 13, 2014).

Conley, Heather A. Judy asks: Is the EU too lax on corruption? Carnegie Europe, (October 11, 2018).

Corruption-blind Seriti Commission is our zero, Corruption Watch, (26 April 2016).

Corruption in Congo and Ivory Coast: Gunvor in the spotlight, Public Eye, (August 28, 2018).

Corruption is a Fracture Which Will Disintegrate Tanzania – Nyerere, Jamii Forums, (November 20, 2011).

Costello, Eugene. KPMG South Africa CEO sorry for Gupta mistakes, International Investment, (October 5, 2017).

Dahir, Abdi Latif. Africa's elites have built the same wealth plundering structures as the colonialists, Quartz Africa, (October 12, 2017).

Daimler AG and three subsidiaries resolve FCPA investigation and agree to pay USD 93.6 million in criminal penalties, Cision PR Newswire, (April 1, 2010).

De Morais, Rafael Marques. Angola's path to justice: Prosecuting the guilty and recovering stolen billions, Maka Angola, (October 23, 2018).

Destrijcker, Lucas and Diouara, Mahadi. A Forgotten Community: The little town in Nigeria keeping the lights on in France," African Arguments, (July 18, 2017).

Dieckmann, Sarah. Not sharing the loot, (October 2011).

Dirty diesel: How Swiss traders flood Africa with toxic fuels, Public Eye, (2016).

Dowie, Mark and Ehrenreich, Barbara, et all. "The charge: genocide," Mother Jones, (December 1979).

Drake, St. Clair. Nkrumah the real tragedy, Central Intelligence Agency, (June 5, 1972).

Dreher, Axel, et al. Aid on demand: African leaders and the geography of China's foreign assistance, CESIFO (July 2015).

Elf trial throws spotlight on oil and corruption, Global Witness, (March 17, 2003).

Embraer agrees to pay more than USD 107 million to resolve Foreign Corrupt Practices Act charges, (October 24, 2016).

Engebretsen, Rebecca. President Lourenco's anti-corruption drive changes the rules in Angola, African Arguments, (October 10, 2018).

Equatorial Guinea corruption, GlobalSecurity.org, (undated).

Euphemia Godspower-Akpomiemie and Kalu Ojah. Money laundering, tax havens, transparency and board of directors of banks (March 27, 2018).

Ex-Namibian army commander keeping corruption money in Standard Chartered Zambia, Zambia Watchdog, (February 24, 2012).

Farand, Chloe. Black gold: Mapping London's African oil hub, Desmog UK, (May 14, 2018).

FCPA/Anti-Bribery Alert, Hughes, Hubbard & Reeds LLP, (Summer 2012).

Farhaoui, Faoud. The great power struggle for Africa: The crisis in Mali, International Strategic Research Organization, (2013).

Favas, Mathieu. Sudan's big business is lobbying he Trump administration to help attract foreign dollars, Quartz Africa, (March 19, 2018).

Final report of the commission of enquiry on bribery and corruption (1975)

Foreign Corrupt Practices Act, Department of Justice, (1977)

France – corruption scandals, GlobalSecurity.org, (undated).

Gabonese national pleads guilty to foreign bribery scheme, US Department of Justice, (December 9, 2016).

Glencore redirected over USD 75 million mining payments to scandal-hit friend of Congolese president, Global Witness reveals, Global Witness, (March 3, 2017).

Government's sentencing memorandum, US District Court for Eastern District of Virginia, (November 13, 2009).

Grace Afua Somuah-Annan. Video: American shames Nigerian woman begging on the streets of Canada, (February 2, 2019).

Gunvor in Congo, Public Eye, (July 2012).

Helping Countries Combat Corruption: The role of the World Bank - Corruption and Economic Management, The World Bank Group, (September 1997).

Hilary, John. Extracting minerals, extracting wealth, war on want, (undated).

How Equatorial Guinea turned corruption into an art form, Human Rights Watch, (June 15, 2017).

How the world profits from Africa's wealth, Honest Accounts, (2017).

Ibrahim, M., Wolfowitz P., et al. Who else is to blame? Forbes Policy, (2010).

IMF Report: Angola Staff Report for the 2011 Article 1V Consultation, IMF, (March 18, 2002).

Isaeva, Natalia. Wikileaks reveals China's impure intentions for Africa, The Borgen Project, (November 12, 2013).

Jayaram, Kartik and Kassiri, Omid., et al. The closest look yet at Chinese economic engagement in Africa, McKinsey & Company (June 2017).

Julius Nyerere. Unity for new order, (February 12, 1979)

Katanga Mining announces settlement of DRC legal dispute with Gecamines and an agreement for the resolution of KCC's capital deficiency, Glencore, Switzerland, (June 12, 2018).

Katsouris, Christina and Aaron Syne. Nigeria's Criminal Crude: International options to combat the export of stolen oil, Chatham House, (2013).

Kazeem, Yomi. Tanzania has hit a British mining company with a fine worth two centuries of revenue, Quartz Africa, (July 25, 2017).

Khanna, Parag. These 25 Companies are more powerful than many countries, The Foreign Policy Group, (March/April 2016).

Kohnert, Dick. Togo: Recent political and economic development, Munich Personal RePec Archive (MPRA), (February 2015).

Letting the Big Fish Swim: Failures to prosecute high level corruption in Uganda, Human Rights Watch, (October 2013).

Lesotho Highlands Water Project: What went wrong? International Rivers, (October 31, 2005).

Mahesh Sahantaram. Warren Hastins: Impeachment and estimate, History Discussion, (undated)

Mailey, J. R. The anatomy of the resource curse: Predatory investment in Africa's extractive industries, ACSS Special Report, (May 2015).

Mathers, C. D. and Loncar, D. Projections of global mortality and burden of disease from 2002 to 2030, PLoS Medicine, (2006).

McGovern, Jim. Bipartisan group of 57 lawmakers call on Trump to hold Sudan accountable for corruption, human rights abuses, Press Release, (March 28, 2018).

McKinsey finds violations of professional standards but no bribery at SA ARM, WorldECR, (October 2017).

Measuring corruption in Africa: The international dimension matters, African Governance Report 1V, The UN Economic Commission on Africa, (2016).

Media Reporting on Sierra Rutile regulatory investigations, Australian Securities Exchange Notice, (August 16, 2017).

Melvin Eugene Page and Penny M. Sonnenberg. Colonialism: An international, social, cultural, and political encyclopedia, (ABC-CLIO, 2003).

Montero, David. The second half of Watergate was bigger, worse, and forgotten by the public, Longreads, (November 2018).

Mubarik, Abu. Joyce Dzidzor Mensah mocks Akufo-Addo's National Cathedral;

sarcastically begs foreigners for donations, Pulse News, (February 17, 2019).

Multinational companies cheat Africa out of billions of dollars, Oxfam (June 2, 2015).

Mutenyo, John and Routman, Brandon. Nationalization of the Zimbabwe mining sector: Another blunder by the Mugabe regime, Brookings Institution, (March 21, 2011).

New evidence ties BSGR to company behind Guinea mine bribery, Global Witness, (August 15, 2013).

Niger's coup and uranium: Weakening of China's sphere of influence, Infoguerre, (March 11, 2010).

Nigeria's corruption busters, United Nations Office on Drugs and Crime, (November 2019).

Ngugi, Fredrick. Western multinational corporations are profiting from poor Africans, Face Africa, (February 14, 2017).

Nyambura, Medrine. KEPSA offers solutions to corruption in Kenya, Hapa Kenya, (May 19, 2016).

Oil in Nigeria: A cure or curse," Global Citizen, (31 August 2012).

Okhumale, Irumire David. Africa fighting corruption on its own turf, Corporate Compliance Insights, (June 21, 2017).

Paradise Papers research raises questions over Glencore's USD 440 million Congo discount, International Consortium of Investigative Journalists, (December 14, 2017).

Public corruption, Federal Bureau of Investigations, (undated).

Remarks with Equatorial Guinean President Teodoro Obiang Nguema Mbasogo before the meeting, US Department of State, (January 20, 2001).

Report of the non-governmental organization Common Community Care, (2006).

Report on Richmond Scandal, Tanzanian Affairs, (May 1, 2008)

Rivers, Bernard. Uganda government official jailed for ten years for stealing Global Fund money, Aidspan, (April 17, 2009).

Saadoun, Sarah. Ill-gotten goods: Equatorial Guinea is a case study in self-dealing, Human Rights Watch, (July 20, 2017).

Sata wants Zamtel shares sold to Zambians, Zambian Watchdog, (July 25, 2009).

Securities and Exchange Commission, SEC charges Daimler ACG with global bribery, Securities and Exchange Commission, Press Release, (April 1, 2010).

Securities Exchange Commission. SEC charges Siemens ACG for engaging in worldwide bribery, Securities and Exchange Commission, Press Release, (December 15, 2008).

Sizer, Nigel and Plouvier, Dominiek. Increased investment and trade by transnational logging companies in ACP-countries: Implications for sustainable forest management and conservation, WWF-International, (2000).

Somuah-Annan, Grace. Video: American shames Nigerian woman for begging on the streets of Canada, Pulse News, (February 2, 2019).

South Africa's arms deal saga, War Registers International, (undated).

South Sudan's leadership uses state-owned oil company Nilepet to funnel millions into brutal security services and ethnic militia, Global Witness, (March 6, 2018).

Sudan's deep state: How insiders violently privatized Sudan's wealth, and how to respond, The Enough Project, (April 2017).

Summaries of Foreign Corrupt Practices Act enforcement actions by the United States, (January 1, 1998 – September 30, 2010).

Sutherland, Ewan. Bribery and corruption in telecommunications: Best practice in prevention and remedies, (September 21-23, 2012).

Tanzania: World Bank defends award of Sh. 14 billion tender, Expo Group, (August 18, 2016).

Taylor, Mildred Europa, How the UK approved the sale of warships to a former Nigerian warlord in deal that shocked the world, Face-to-Face, (October 28, 2018).

The BCCI Affair: A report to the Committee on Foreign Relations, US Senate, by Senator John Kerry and Senator Hank Brown, (December 1992).

The cost of corruption across the EU, Greens/EPA, (December 7, 2018).

The effects of bribery and corruption on multinational corporations, seminar in multicultural management, Walden University, (October 2013).

The fall of Nkrumah and the corruption he supervised, Ghana Web, (November 10. 2010).

The first travel and entertainment enforcement action, FCPA, (June 16, 2014).

The national oil and gas policy for Uganda, Ministry of Energy and Mineral Development, (February 2008).

The New Colonialism: Britain's scramble for Africa's energy and mineral Resources, War on Want, (July 2016).

The politics of mining and trading in gold in Sudan: Challenges of corruption and lack of transparency, Sudan Transparency Initiative, Sudan Democracy Group, (undated).

The resource curse: Oil production in Nigeria, (May 12, 2017).

The Rolls-Royce case lands UK's Serious Fraud Office in the anti-corruption big leagues, (February 24, 2017).

The secret bribes of big tobacco, African Tobacco Control Alliance (ATA), (undated).

Trafigura and the Angolan presidential mafia, Maka Angola, (January 5, 2013).

Transparency International, People and corruption: Africa survey 2015 – Global Corruption Barometer, (December 2015).

Transparency International, Persistent corruption in low-income countries requires global action, (September 25, 2007).

Tso, John. The global anti-corruption blog, (May 14, 2018).

Uganda: Free pass on high-level corruption: Large-scale graft deprives Ugandans of basic rights, Human Rights Watch, (October 21, 2013).

Uganda: Undermined, Global Witness, (5 June 2017).

UK firm probed for bribery in multinational dollar defense deal, Organized Crime and Corruption Reporting Project (OCCRP), (May 15, 2017).

Understanding the UK Bribery Bill, McGuireWoods, (undated).

UN Economic Commission on Africa. "African Governance Report 1V, Measuring corruption in Africa. The international dimension matters, (April 1, 2016).

Unmasking Nigeria's oil cartel, OilPrice.com, (June 8, 2017).

US Department of Justice. Alliance One International Incorporated and Universal Corporation Resolve Related FCPA Matters involving bribes paid to foreign government officials, press release, (August 6, 2010).

US Department of Justice. Former Guinean Minister of Mines sentenced to seven years in prison for receiving and laundering USD 8.5 million in bribes from China International Fund and China Sonangol, press release, (August 25, 2017).

US Department of Justice. Marubeni Corporation resolves Foreign Corrupt Practices Act investigation and agrees to pay a USD 54.6 million criminal penalty, press release, (January 17, 2012).

US Department of Justice. Department of Justice seeks to recover over USD 100 million obtained from corruption in the Nigerian oil industry, press statement, (July 14, 2017).

US Department of Justice. Former Congressman William J. Jefferson sentenced to 13 Years in prison for bribery and other charges, press release, (November 13, 2009).

US Department of Justice. Fresenius Medical Care agrees to pay USD 231 million in criminal penalties and disgorgement to resolve PCPA charges, press release, (March 29, 2019).

US Department of Justice. Alstom pleads guilty and agrees to pay USD 772 million criminal penalty to resolve foreign bribery charges, press release, (December 22, 2014).

Vandana Shiva. The seeds of suicide: How Monsanto destroys farming, (October 21, 2018).

Van Niekerk, Philip and Peterson, Laura. Making a killing: Greasing the skids of corruption, (November 4, 2002).

Van Vuuren, Hennie. Apartheid grand corruption: Assessing the scale of crimes of profit from 1976 to 1944. A report prepared by civil society for presentation to the National Anti-Corruption Forum, (May 2006).

Vanderford, Richard. Alleged bribe was a loan, ex-Guinea mines minister tells FBI in interview played for jury, M-Lex Market Insight, (April 27, 2017).

Vidal, John. Toxic e-waste dumped in poor nations, says United Nations, Our World, (December 16, 2013).

Vinson, Robert. Marcus Garvey's Africa: Africa is a country, (undated).

Waliggo, John Mary. Corruption and bribery – An African problem? Africa Files, (March 1, 2007).

Who is more powerful – states or corporations? (July 10, 2018).

World Bank statement on Chad-Cameroon pipeline," press release, (September 9, 2008).

PARLIAMENARY REPORTS

McKinney, Cynthia. Covert Action in Africa: A Smoking Gun in Washington DC, US House Committee on International Relations (April 16, 2001).

The BCCI Affair. A Report to the Committee on Foreign Relations, US Senate, by Senator John Kerry and Senator Hank Brown (December 1992).

UK House of Commons. Tackling corruption overseas, (October 11, 2016).

US Department of Justice. "Foreign Corrupt Practices Act." Tackling Corruption Overseas, International Development Committee, House of Commons, Fourth Report of Session 2016-17 (October 11, 2016).

US Congress Joint Economic Committee. Cost of Corruption to the American Economy, (May 2017).

US House of Representatives. "China in Africa: The New Colonialism? Hearing Before the Sub-Committee on Africa, Global Health, Global Human Rights, and International Organizations of the Committee on Foreign Affairs, 115th Cong, 2nd Session, Serial No. 115-117, U. S. Government Publishing Office, (March 7, 2018).

US SEC. Case Information: In the Matter of Kinross Gold Corporation, (March 2018).

US Senate. "The BCCI Affair:" A Report to the Committee on Foreign Relations, (December 1992)

US Senate. Committee on Homelands Security and Governmental Affairs, Keeping Foreign Corruption out of the United States: Four Case Histories, (February 4, 2010).

US Senate. Permanent Sub-Committee on Investigations, Money Laundering and Foreign Corruption: Enforcement and Effectiveness of the Patriotic Act: Case Study Involving Riggs Bank, (July 15, 2004).

US Senate. Permanent Sub-Committee on Investigations, Private Banking and Money Laundering: A Case Study of Opportunities and Vulnerabilities. Report on President Omar Bongo, (November 9, 1999).

MEDIA

Addis-Abeba, le siege de l'Union Africaine espionne par Pekin, *Le Monde*, January 26, 2018.

Aglionby, John and Sanderson, Henry. Acacia mining accused of operating illegally in Tanzania, *The Financial Times*, June 12, 2017.

An inside job: Kenya's struggles to stop ethanol smuggling, *The East Africa Monitor*, April 29, 2019.

Angolan capital most expensive for expats, *BBC,* June 21, 2017.

Archbishop of Canterbury on "healing" Zimbabwe trip, *BBC*, October 9, 2011.

Athuman Mtulya. Tanzania: World Bank defends award of Sh.14 billion tender, *The Citizen,* August 18, 2016.

Avera corruption saga implicates Namibia, *The Namibian,* August 4, 2018.

Baker, Neal. Meet the world's most terrifying man, *The Sun*, September 10, 2016.

Banned in America, peddled in Africa, *The Christian Science Monitor*, December 5, 1980.

Bannink, Dirk. Contaminated foodstuffs dumped on the world market, *The Nuclear Monitor*, April 5, 1991.

Barrick Gold accused of money deals, *The Citizen*, June 21, 2014.

Barrick-owned miner slapped with USD 190,000 billion tax bill that would take centuries to pay, *The Financial Post*, July 25, 2017.

Barrington, Nicholas. London, the money-laundering capital, *The World Today*, April & May 2018.

BAT fights Nairobi bid to enforce law on public smoking, *The Business Daily*, March 4, 2019.

Bennion, Jackie. BAE will pay USD 450 million to settle long running bribery case, *Front Line World, PBS*, February 5, 2010.

Billionaire French tycoon Bollore detained in Africa corruption probe, *AFP-News24,* April 24, 2018.

Bilton, Richard. The secret bribes of big tobacco," *BBC*, November 30, 2015.

Birrell, Ian. The strange and evil world of Equatorial Guinea, *The Observer*, October 22, 2011.

Blomfield, Adrian. Listeria contaminated food kills 200 in South Africa, including 80 babies, *The Telegraph*, May 18, 2018.

Boseley, Sarah. Revealed: how British American Tobacco exploited war zones to sell cigarettes, *The Guardian,* August 18, 2017.

Boseley, Sarah. Drug firms try to bribe doctors with cars, *The Guardian*, October 30, 2007.

Bouessel du Bourg, Charles. Republic of Congo: Gunvor, the Kremlin, oil and corruption, *The Africa Report,* November 2017.

British American Tobacco investigated by Serious Fraud Office, *BBC*, August 1, 2017.

Brooke, James. Waste dumpers turning to West Africa, *The New York Times,* July 17, 1988.

Brummer, Stefaans and McKune, Craig., et al. Tokyo Sexwale and the DRC's grab, *The Mail & Guardian*, August 17, 2012.

Brunais, Alexandra. Mitterrand's son posts bail in arms case: Inquiry sullies fame of French ex-leader, *The Washington Post,* January 13, 2001.

Buhari's government a puppet in the hands of oil multinationals, says Ijaw Group, *Sahara Reporters,* May 14, 2018.

Burgis, Tom. China in Africa: How Sam Pa became the middleman, *The Financial Times*, August 8, 2014.

Butty, James. New report alleges corruption involving Liberian officials," *VOA,* May 16, 2016.

Carroll, Rory. Multinationals in scramble for Congo's wealth, *The Guardian,* October 21, 2002.

Cascais, Antonio. Angola: The fall of the dos Santos clan, *The Deutsche Welle*, September 30, 2018.

Charlton, Angela. French billionaire detained in Africa corruption probe, *AP- Financial*

Post, April 24, 2018.

Chazan, David. France convicts Equatorial Guinea's vice president of corruption in land-mark trial, *The Telegraph,* October 27, 2017.

Chimangeni, Isabel. Zambia: Is China sneaking in deals through the back door? *Inter Press Service,* March 27, 2007.

Chinese man caught on tape insulting Kenyans and President Uhuru arrested, *Daily Nation,* September 6, 2018.

Chinese-built hospital risks collapse in Angola, *Terra Daily,* July 6, 2010.

Chinese businessman arrested after describing Kenyans, including the president as "monkey people," *Agence France-Presse,* September 6, 2018.

Christian, Shirley. Buenos Aires Journal: Billions flow to dam (and billions down drain?), *The New York Times,* May 4, 1990.

Cohen, J. HIV/AIDS: Uganda confronts corruption, slowly, *Science,* 2008.

Corruption Commission, *Ghanaian Times,* June 29, 1970.

Cropley, E. At 50, Botswana discovers diamonds are not forever, *Reuters,* September 26, 2016.

Dalrymple, William. The East India Company: The original corporate raiders, *The Guardian,* March 4, 2015.

Dennys, Harriet. Tullow oil apologies to Uganda government over bribery allegations, *The Telegraph,* March 22, 2013.

Dewa, Tatenda. 4 big reasons why Dema Power Plant is bad for Zimbabwe – PDP, *Nehanda Radio,* September 28, 2016.

Dick Cheney and Halliburton avoid bribery charges in Nigeria… by forking over USD 250 million, *The Los Angeles Times,* December 24, 2010.

Edwards, Jocelyn. Tullow refutes bribery accusations in Uganda, *Reuters,* April 12, 2012.

Ellen Johnson Sirleaf: Towards African leadership, *Globalist,* October 10, 2011.

Equatorial Guinea's "God", *BBC,* July 26, 2003.

Equatorial Guinea's leaders accused of pilfering oil revenues, *VOA,* October 30, 2009.

Evans, Rob. Trafigura fined 1m euros for exporting toxic waste to Africa, *The Guardian,* July 23, 2010.

Experts speak out on tobacco industry bribery claims, *The New Vision,* January 7, 2016.

Fabulous wealth in Marange diamonds, *The Sunday Times,* August 8, 2010.

Files point to USD 182 million Halliburton bribery scandal in Nigeria, *The Indian Express,* February 9, 2015.

Fisher, Max. How bad is Robert Mugabe? The answer, in three scathing paragraphs, *The Washington Post,* August 1, 2013.

Ford, Tamasin. Ellen Johnson Sirleaf: The legacy of Africa's first female President, *BBC,* January 22, 2018.

French court: African leader's son embezzled millions in public money, *AP/Reuters,* October 27, 2017.

Graham, Robert. French trial paints a picture of graft on a grandiose scale, *The Financial Times,* April 22, 2003.

Gramer, Robbie. Remember South Sudan? Washington would prefer not to, *FP News,* University of Denver, October 4, 2018.

Gwirtzman, Milton S. Is bribery defensible, *The New York Times,* October 5, 1975.

Hairsine, Kate. Panama Papers: Africa's elite are plundering their countries, *Deutsch Welle,* October 18, 2017.

Henley, Jon. Gigantic sleaze scandal winds up as former Elf oil chiefs are jailed, *The Guardian*, November 12, 2003.

Honey, Martha and Ottaway, David B. Idi Amin squandered the wealth of Uganda, *The Washington Post*, May 29, 1979.

How Israel, China firms bribe Kenyan officials, *Business Daily*, September 5, 2018.

Hume, Neil. Rio Tinto CEAO: Decision to tell regulators about USD 10.5 million payment not taken lightly, *The Financial Times*, November 14, 2016.

Inside Botswana/DeBeers' secret agreement, *The Sunday Standar*d, March 18, 2019.

Irujo, Jose Maria. The high price of doing business in Equatorial Guinea, *El Pais*, April 3, 2013.

Liberia; Tripple trouble, *All-Africa.com*, August 15, 2016.

London, the money-laundering capital, *The World Today*, April & May 2018.

Kaaya, Sadab Kitatta. MPs claim they were bribed over GMO bill, *The Observer*, July 5, 2017.

Kapchanga, Mark. China corruption in Africa, *The Caribbean Current*, November 5, 2013.

Kenyans wire back Sh.1 trillion in offshore bank accounts, *The Business Daily*, May 21, 2019.

Kgomoeswana, Victor. Africa still losing billions through illicit financial flows by multinational corporations despite increasing awareness of the problem, *The Sunday Independent*, May 21, 2018.

Koroma accused of grand corruption, *African Confidential*, December 2, 2018.

Langford, Cameron. Dutch oil firm to pay USD 238 million to settle US bribery charge, *Courthouse News Service*, November 30, 2017.

Leigh, David and Evans, Rob. British firm Mabey and Johnson convicted of bribing foreign politicians, *The Guardian*, September 25, 2009.

Mahajan, Karan. State capture: How the Gupta brothers hijacked South Africa using bribes instead of bullets, *Vanity Fair,* March 2019.

Maitre, Marie. Areva uranium deal eyed amid fraud allegations, *Reuters,* January 13, 2012.

McGreal, Chris. Taking multinationals to task, *The World Press Review Online*, *The Guardian Weekly*, July 4, 2001.

Majoni, Tawanda. Why Marange diamonds corruption is too hot for ZACC, *The Standard*, November 27, 2016.

Malakata, Michael. Zambia terminates USD 210 million contract over corruption allegations, *IDG News Service*, September 11, 2013.

Mark, Monica. Damning oil fraud offers hope to Nigerians, *The Mail & Guardian*, July 9, 2012.

Martins, Adewole. How Chinese firm, ZTE scammed Nigeria of USD 470 million in security contract, *The Eagle Online*, December 15, 2015.

Mayeda, Andrew and Biller, David. IMF to probe role of advanced economies in feeding corruption *The Globe and Mail,* April 22, 2018.

Mayoux, Stephane. Equatorial Guinea warning after bank probe, *BBC,* July 21, 2004.

Maza, Cristina. Rex Tillerson's Exxon Mobil involved in corrupt oil deals in Liberia, investigation reveals, *Newsweek*, March 29, 2018.

Mednick, Sam. Oil-rich South Sudan to resume production in war-hit region *AP News*, August 30, 2018.

Menges, Werner. Bribery lands Chinese citizens in prison, *The Namibian,* September 17, 2018.

Mfonobong Nsehe. "Corruption and 'tenderpreneurs' bring Kenya's economy to its knees," (December 1, 2015).

Miller, Hugo and Hoffman, Andy. Ex-Gunvor oil trader found guilty of bribing African officials, *Bloomberg,* August 28, 2018.

Morris, David Z. China's ZTE under investigation in Nigerian security network failure, *Fortune*, February 16, 2016.

Morse, David. How oil drives the genocide in Darfur, *The Sudan Tribune*, August 18, 2005.

Motlogelwa, T & Civilini, M. The Khamas – The making of military millionaires, *The Business Weekly and Review*, November 14, 2015.

Mouawad, Jad. Oil corruption in Equatorial Guinea, *The New York Times*, July 9, 2009.

Mourdoukoutas, Panos. What is China doing in Africa, *Forbes,* August 4, 2018.

Mozambique: Embraer bribe case sent to Maputo city court, *AllAfrica*, January 10, 2018.

Mozambique: Former transport minister, two executives arrested for graft, *APA News,* December 7, 2017.

Museveni 'USD 50 million bribe': The inside story, *The Observer*, March 17, 2013.

Musisi, Frederic. Government officials renew fight over Sh. 8 trillion railway deal, *The Daily Monitor*, June 18, 2018.

Musyoka, Michael. Kenyans react to new police uniforms, *Kenyans.co.ke,* September 13, 2018.

Mutoko, Caroline. Private sector corruption is dangerous, *The Star*, November 16, 2015.

Mutua, John. City Hall contractors blamed for Sh. 437 million CCTV glitch, *Business Daily*, February 28, 2019.

Mwamba, Eric. Getting rich in poverty-stricken Congo, *Mondiaal Niews*, February 1, 2013.

Namibia: 'Illicit' French payments haunt Geingob, *AllAfrica.com*, April 10, 2018.

Niger's coup and uranium: Weakening of China's sphere of influence, *Inforguerre,* March 11, 2010.

Niger Court drops charges against ex-President Tandja, *BBC*, May 10, 2011.

Nsehe, Mfonobong. Corruption and 'tenderpreneurs' bring Kenya's economy to its knees, *Forbes*, December 1, 2015.

Nyassy, Daniel Tsuma. Donor takes back Sh. 30 million equipment after refusing to give out kickbacks, *The Daily Nation*, July 9, 2016.

Olawoyin, Oladeinde. Malabu scandal: Court papers expose Nigerian officials who authorized controversial payments, *Premium Times*, April 12, 2018.

Oloya, Dr. Opiyo. How much has Monsanto paid Uganda scientists for the GMO experiments? *The New Vision,* (Uganda), February 1, 2011.

Omar Bongo, *The Telegraph*, June 8, 2009.

One of France's best-known tycoons is arrested, *The Economist*, April 28, 2018.

O'Shaughnessy, Hugh and Lashmar, Paul. HSBC and Santander slammed in Senate money-laundering report, *The Independent*, September 5, 2004.

Our new best friend – Who needs Saudi Arabia when you've got Sao Tome, *The New Yorker*, October 7, 2002.

Owen, Jonathan. British American Tobacco accused of bribing senior politicians in order to sabotage anti-smoking laws, *The Independent,* November 30, 2015.

Pagnamenta, Robin. Steinmetz bribery contracts not forged, expert says, *The Times*, April 17, 2018.

Peel, Michael. The big African oil grab, The *New Statesman*, April 10, 2008.

Peltz, James. F. Lockheed agrees to pay record fine, *The Los Angeles Times,* January 28, 1995.

Perry, Alex. Gabon faces Bongo's disastrous legacy, *TIME*, June 10, 2009.

Pflanz, Mike. Corruption runs deep in gold mines in Congo, *The Telegraph*, March 14, 2017.

Pilkington, Ed. Shell pays out USD 15.5 million over Saro-Wiwa killing, *The Guardian*, June 8, 2009.

Pressly, Linda. The largest foreign bribery case in history, *BBC*, April 22, 2018.

The secret bribes of big tobacco paper trail, *BBC*, November 30, 2015.

Robin, Marie-Monique. The world according to Monsanto: pollution, corruption, and the control of our food supply, *The New Press*, 2010.

Rogan, Tom. Celebrate Brazil's ambush of a corrupt delegation from Equatorial Guinea, *The Washington Examiner*, September 17, 2018.

Rolls Royce apologies after USD 671 million BP bribery settlement, *BBC,* January 18, 2017.

S. Sudan does not keep oil revenues in Central Bank, *The Sudan Tribune,* August 31, 2017.

Sable's rich seam of bribes, *Africa Confidential,* October 31, 2018.

Sadeh, Shuki. Bribery scandal at Israeli construction giant blows cover off its business practices in Africa, *Haaretz*, March 9, 2018.

Sakala, Charles. Zambian officials linked to USD 2 million mining scandal, *Zambia Reports*, September 2, 2015.

Sambira, Jocelyne. Counterfeit drugs raise Africa's temperature, *African Renewal*, May 2013.

Schmidt, Michael. How African dictators corrupt European politics, *Pambazuka News*, April 19, 2012.

Searcey, Dionne and Barry, Jaime Yaya. One African nation put brakes on Chinese debt. But not for long, *The New York Times*, November 23, 2018.

Serious Fraud Office probe into tobacco giant BAT on 'bribery,' *NewPosts*, September 5, 2017.

Sharife, Khadija. Copper in Zambia: Charity for multinationals, *Pambazuka News,* June 2, 2011.

Shirbon, Estelle. British court approves landmark plea deal over Standard Bank bribery, Reuters, November 30, 2015.

Siakor, Silas Kpanan'ayoung and Knight, Rachael S. A. Nobel Laureate's problem at home, *The New York Times*, January 20, 2012.

Silverstein, Ken. "Teodoro's world," *Foreign Policy*, February 21, 2011.

Smith, Elie. Congo leader's son denies payments from ex-Gunvor trader bribes, *Bloomberg,* September 4, 2018.

Soniyi, Tobi. Nigeria: Bribe scandal – Siemens fined N7 billion, *This Day*, November 22, 2010.

Souchard, Pierre-Antoine. Judges implicate 43 in French oil scandal, *The Washington Post*, February 5, 2002.

Sunday, Frankline. Private sector corruption on the rise, endangers long term investment, *The Standard Digital News*, January 28, 2015.

Takudzwa Hillary Chiwanza. France has assassinated 22 African presidents since 1963, (June 29, 2019).

Talirenyika, Masimba. Illicit financial flows from Africa: track it, stop it, get it, *African Renewal*, December 2013.

Tanzania: Chenge – "I am proved innocent," *The Citizen*, February 13, 2001.

Tanzania PM to resign over graft, BBC February 7, 2008.

Tanzania tax tribunal orders Acacia to pay USD 41.3 million, *Reuters*, April 6, 2016.

Thamm, Marianne. SARS Wars: Massive data leak alleges British American Tobacco SA's role in bribery and corruption, *Daily Maverick,* August 16, 2016.

Tovey, Alan. Bribery a way of life for companies operating in emerging markets, *The Telegraph*, October 26, 2016.

Turner, George & Mathiason, Nick., et al. Revealed: How Vodafone allowed elites to reap profits of Africa's mobile boom, *The Observer,* November 11, 2017.

US government urged to reject BAT-Reynolds merger over bribes to Kenyan officials, *Money Markets*, February 7, 2017.

US probes Chinese oil firm over USD 100 million bribe paid to Nigerians, *The Cable*, August 31, 2017.

Villa, Sylvia. ACC investigates alleged Iluka bribery scandal, *Awoko,* August 24, 2017.

Vinograd, Cassandra and Gauthier-Villars, David. Soldiers oust president in coup in uranium-rich Niger, *The Wall Street Journal,* February 19, 2010.

Wanjama, Paul. Aliko Dangote reveals why he aborted plans of investing in Kenya, *Kenyans.co.ke,* August 21, 2018.

Weiner, Rachel. Former Congressman William Jefferson goes free, thanks to Supreme Court ruling in McDonnel case, *The Washington Post*, December 1, 2017.

Wilson, Tom. Glencore's role in Paradise Papers: What you need to know, *Bloomberg*, November 5, 2017.

What is Alliance One International's fundamental value? *Forbes*, March 23, 2018.

What is Alliance One International's fundamental value? Forbes, (March 23, 2018).

When ExxonMobil came to Chad, *Slate* magazine, (April 5, 2007).

White, Garry. African Barrick mine-raid leaves seven intruders dead, *The Telegraph*, May 17, 2011.

World class fraud: How BCCI pulled it off: A special report, *The New York Times*, August 12, 1991.

Wu, Annie. Court records reveal ZTE's corruption scheme in Liberia, *The Epoch Times,* June 3, 2018.

Young, Jeffrey. Corruption concerns taint burgeoning China-Africa trade, *VOA,* September 1, 2014.

Zalk, Naashon. Investigating South Africa's mire of Gupta-linked corruption, *Al Jazeera*, March 27, 2018.

Zhou, Laura. Chinese-made condoms too small, Zimbabwe's health minister complains, *South China Morning Post*, March 1, 2018.

Zhuwakinyu, Martin. Uncanny similarities, *Creamer News*, December 1, 2017.

INDEX

Utuama, Amos, 43,

V

Valcambi, 217

Veihmeyer, John, 288

Vetco International Limited, 208

Vetco Gray Controls Limited, 208

Vetco Gray UK Limited, 208

Vicente, Manuel, 223

Viegas, Jose, 261, 262

VIP Engineering and Marketing Company (VIP), 77, 78

Visa International, 10, 55

Vithlani, Sailesh, 81

Vitol Oil, 263

Vodafone Group Plc, 355, 356

Vuuren, Hennie van, 279

W

Wah, Tsui King, 239

Wako, Amos, 65

Walmart, 23

Walsh, Sam, 165

Warioba, Joseph, 75

Warf, Barney, 33

Wartsila Nederland BV, 78

Weah, George Manneh, 172, 173

Weeks, Milton, 173

Wengfu, 216

Wierzycka, Magda, 17

Wilbros Group Incorporated, 205, 206

Williams, Rowan, 300

Windward Trading Limited, 57,

Wolfowitz, Paul, 133

Wood, Geoffrey, 130

World Bank (WB), 16, 18, 29, 61, 66, 70, 71, 81, 82, 83, 133, 139, 147, 165, 229, 242, 255, 257, 296, 327

World Health Organization (WHO), 49, 151, 266, 267, 346

World Health Organization Framework Convention on Tobacco Control (WHO/FCTC), 266

Wouters, Daniel, 271

Wurzel, Thomas, 103

Printed in Great Britain
by Amazon

38374934R10233